Lost To Desire

This book covers the work of psychoanalysts in post WWII France with patients beset by somatic problems with little manifest fantasy life, and how their concept of *opératoire* continues to inform the theory and practice of working with patients in crisis.

The author explores what the new concept has elicited in a community of practitioners – close to the *École Psychosomatique de Paris* – over a period of some sixty years. As a 'skin for thought' it facilitated change while preserving coherence, gradually beginning to attract further considerations. Important themes have included: the early groundwork necessary for the configuration of fantasy, the importance of a shared imaginary, the role of denial and obliterated memories as a bond between people, emergency measures of a Me cut off from revitalisation, the effects of the rhythms and atmosphere at the workplace on family life, and the consequences of a crisis suppressed for lack of a holding frame. As psychoanalytic discourse adapted to the challenges, the original perspective changed aspect, moving from a systematic evaluation of what the patients did not produce to what the analyst had to fill in to make sense of the situation. Clashing with the terrain, French psychoanalysts raised important problems about psychic anaemia that are stimulating and deserve cross-cultural discussion.

This book will appeal to psychoanalysts in practice and training who wish to learn more about this ground-breaking work on memory and trauma, and how to apply it to their own practice.

Wolfgang Lassmann is a psychoanalyst in private practice, Vienna, and a member of the Vienna Psychoanalytic Association.

THE NEW LIBRARY OF PSYCHOANALYSIS
General Editor: Alessandra Lemma

The New Library of Psychoanalysis was launched in 1987 in association with the Institute of Psychoanalysis, London. It took over from the International Psychoanalytical Library which published many of the early translations of the works of Freud and the writings of most of the leading British and Continental psychoanalysts.

The purpose of the New Library of Psychoanalysis is to facilitate a greater and more widespread appreciation of psychoanalysis and to provide a forum for increasing mutual understanding between psychoanalysts and those working in other disciplines such as the social sciences, medicine, philosophy, history, linguistics, literature and the arts. It aims to represent different trends both in British psychoanalysis and in psychoanalysis generally. The New Library of Psychoanalysis is well placed to make available to the English-speaking world psychoanalytic writings from other European countries and to increase the interchange of ideas between British and American psychoanalysts. Through the *Teaching Series*, the New Library of Psychoanalysis now also publishes books that provide comprehensive, yet accessible, overviews of selected subject areas aimed at those studying psychoanalysis and related fields such as the social sciences, philosophy, literature and the arts.

The Institute, together with the British Psychoanalytical Society, runs a low-fee psychoanalytic clinic, organizes lectures and scientific events concerned with psychoanalysis and publishes the *International Journal of Psychoanalysis*. It runs a training course in psychoanalysis which leads to membership of the International Psychoanalytical Association – the body which preserves internationally agreed standards of training, of professional entry, and of professional ethics and practice for psychoanalysis as initiated and developed by Sigmund Freud. Distinguished members of the Institute have included Michael Balint, Wilfred Bion, Ronald Fairbairn, Anna Freud, Ernest Jones, Melanie Klein, John Rickman and Donald Winnicott.

Previous general editors have included David Tuckett, who played a very active role in the establishment of the New Library. He was followed as general editor by Elizabeth Bott Spillius, who was in turn followed by Susan Budd and then by Dana Birksted-Breen. Current members of the Advisory Board include Giovanna Di Ceglie, Liz Allison, Anne Patterson, Josh Cohen and Daniel Pick.

Previous members of the Advisory Board include Christopher Bollas, Ronald Britton, Catalina Bronstein, Donald Campbell, Rosemary Davies, Sara Flanders, Stephen Grosz, John Keene, Eglé Laufer, Alessandra Lemma, Juliet Mitchell, Michael Parsons, Rosine Jozef Perelberg, Richard Rusbridger, Mary Target and David Taylor.

A full list of all the titles in the New Library of Psychoanalysis main series is available at https://www.routledge.com/The-New-Library-of-Psychoanalysis/book-series/SE0239

For titles in the New Library of Psychoanalysis 'Teaching' and 'Beyond the Couch' subseries, please visit the Routledge website.

Lost To Desire

The *École Psychosomatique de Paris* and its Encounter with Patients Who Do Not Thrive

Wolfgang Lassmann

LONDON AND NEW YORK

First published 2022
by Routledge
4 Park Square, Milton Park, Abingdon, Oxon OX14 4RN

and by Routledge
605 Third Avenue, New York, NY 10158

Routledge is an imprint of the Taylor & Francis Group, an informa business

© 2022 Wolfgang Lassmann

The right of Wolfgang Lassmann to be identified as author of this work has been asserted by him in accordance with sections 77 and 78 of the Copyright, Designs and Patents Act 1988.

All rights reserved. No part of this book may be reprinted or reproduced or utilised in any form or by any electronic, mechanical, or other means, now known or hereafter invented, including photocopying and recording, or in any information storage or retrieval system, without permission in writing from the publishers.

Trademark notice: Product or corporate names may be trademarks or registered trademarks, and are used only for identification and explanation without intent to infringe.

British Library Cataloguing-in-Publication Data
A catalogue record for this book is available from the British Library

Library of Congress Cataloging-in-Publication Data
Names: Lassmann, Wolfgang (Psychologist) author.
Title: Lost to desire : the École Psychosomatique de Paris and its encounter with patients who do not thrive / Wolfgang Lassmann.
Description: New York, NY : Routledge, 2022. |
Series: New library of psychoanalysis |
Includes bibliographical references and index. |
Identifiers: LCCN 2021026092 (print) | LCCN 2021026093 (ebook) |
ISBN 9781032132617 (hardback) | ISBN 9781032132600 (paperback) |
ISBN 9781003228363 (ebook)
Subjects: LCSH: Psychoanalysis–France–History–20th century. |
Memory. | Psychic trauma.
Classification: LCC BF175 .L357 2022 (print) |
LCC BF175 (ebook) | DDC 616.89/17094409045–dc23
LC record available at https://lccn.loc.gov/2021026092
LC ebook record available at https://lccn.loc.gov/2021026093

ISBN: 978-1-032-13261-7 (hbk)
ISBN: 978-1-032-13260-0 (pbk)
ISBN: 978-1-003-22836-3 (ebk)

DOI: 10.4324/978.003228363

Typeset in Bembo
by Newgen Publishing UK

To the memory of Jean-François Bion (born Dijon,
24th June 1668)

absconded from his job
betrayed his king
gained a world

and to the memory of Joseph Priestley (1733–1804)

native son of Yorkshire
student of French, German and Aramaic
caused a riot
was persuaded to turn migrant

Contents

Acknowledgements		xi
Introduction		1
1	Fragments of a debate	14
2	Background	28
3	Foundations 1: Pierre Marty	42
4	Foundations 2: Michel Fain with Denise Braunschweig	68
5	Basic mechanisms 1: Nicos Nicolaïdis	94
6	Basic mechanisms 2: Gérard Szwec	111
7	Configurations 1: Anna Potamianou	132
8	Configurations 2: Jean Benjamin Stora	153
9	Inquiries: The work of César and Sára Botella	166
10	Second thoughts: Claude Smadja	191
11	Entanglements: The forgotten pre-history of the *opératoire*	216

12	Indispensable extensions: Christophe Dejours	234
13	Bridges: Jacques Press	262
	Conclusion	287
	Index	309

Acknowledgements

Over the years, I hugely profited from a long exchange of ideas with Dr Harald Leupold-Löwenthal, Dr Johannes Ranefeld and Dr. Sylvia Zwettler-Otte, who in their various ways have kept my interest alive in stimulating debates. My association, the *Wiener Arbeitskreis für Psychoanalyse* [Vienna Psychoanalytic Association], has over the years rendered me sensitive to the observation that concepts in use serve multiple functions that keep evolving. If I had not had the privilege to follow and participate in the WAP's development since the 1980s, I might have considered French matters unduly complicated.

Writing about clinical repercussions of what should have happened in its own good time in people's lives, but apparently did not, is always fraught with hazards. The abyss one stares into, it has famously been argued, inevitably stares back. I owe it to my wife, Dagmar, for having made me understand new levels of meaning in Yehuda Amichai's 'Six Songs for Tamar': presence, day by day, scrapes off bits and pieces from the certainty of doom.

This study is the result of a PhD project undertaken between 2011 and 2018 at the University of Essex. I am grateful to the Department of Psychosocial and Psychoanalytic Studies for having provided a stable framework, and in particular to Karl Figlio, willing to supervise a thesis that was clearly going to take a road less travelled by. Discussing the unfolding project with him gave me new ideas on how to present the tangled web of thoughts emerging from the sources. Being able to exchange thoughts with him was a constant stimulus to view things from yet another angle. It confirms my suspicion that things gain shape in constant oscillation between form and formlessness, in a process in which what meets the eye of others plays an important part.

INTRODUCTION

In every voice in every ban
The mind forgd manacles I hear

William Blake, London

In the 1960s, news began to emerge from France that psychoanalysts in place were encountering patients presenting features of mental life quite contrary to expectations. The unfolding debate on how to come to terms with this gained a wider audience at the 23rd *Congrès des Psychanalystes de langues romanes* (Barcelona, June 8–11, 1962). It was there that Pierre Marty and Michel de M'Uzan read a paper on *pensée opératoire*, a mode of thinking geared towards keeping the subject functioning although being strikingly devoid of discernible fantasy.

The term given to it, *opératoire*, frequently found in work-related contexts, suggests worlds in which the task to be performed is perpetually in focus and fantasy finds no soil to thrive. Lines written around the time still reflect the shock of the encounter:

> It was impossible that a human being might really be as two dimensional [*plat*] and lacking in resources [*démuni*] as … [this patient] … tended to make us believe.
> (Marty, de M'Uzan and David 2003/1963, p. 262)

For the most part the patients concerned did not express any wish to enter psychoanalysis. It was others in the health services who had had the sense that their somatic complaint must have been related to something going on in their psyche.

Introduction

This posed new challenges to French psychoanalysis, which had recovered from post-war difficulties, had weathered a major split and was on the verge of seeing two more splits against a backdrop of a hitherto unseen spectacular expansion.

If psychoanalysis was to be regarded as a clinical force to be reckoned with, this new phenomenon called for a response. It was being articulated in a climate of intense competition between rival organisations. As Alain de Mijolla has pointed out, the French splits were the first in the history of psychoanalysis to which doctrine was not central.

This meant that a senior practitioner of the *SPP*, the organisation from which the first split took place, might strive, during its years of consolidation and expansion, to show how existing ways of thinking could be rendered more supple by integrating further perspectives that added new dimensions to previous understanding. Clinical material might be presented to make theory work in a more finely honed way and used to extend new threads and nodal points to a net in constant development, rather than to present a completely new container.

As becomes apparent in the major discussions of the time, reasoned divergence that dug into the ramifications of concepts was highly valued and played an important role in a contest between different strategies of implementation that had already splintered psychoanalytic unity beyond repair. Outside its French context, this intense debate may sometimes have seemed pointless. It was not. Although unrelated to any religious preoccupations, it followed in its own ways, under the pressure of the times, a logic Sergey Dolgopolski (2009), drawing inspiration from the Talmud's discursive structures, aptly termed 'The art of disagreement': what constituted good practice was more germane to it than what constituted sound theory; what was rightful transmission of teaching, in which framework, more a bone of contention than quarrels on proper codification.

In engaging in such a debate, psychoanalysis in France, beset as it was by bitter rifts, paradoxically flourished as never before, establishing a cultural pattern that went beyond allegiance to a particular school. Lacan had laid claim to a return to Freud. Freud, a dead authority superior to that of Lacan, was conveniently open source and in an inspiring way full of fruitful contradictions. It turned out that many young psychoanalysts were eager to accept the challenge and put their mind to tinkering around a shared kernel of practice, happy to

Introduction

dispense with the office of Chief Interpreter altogether. Engaging in debate among themselves, the new generation, viscerally opposed to various parochialisms they had experienced, and encouraged by their progressive discovery of a multi-layered Freud, whose complexity they found a new use for, established a space within which disagreement worked as a fertiliser for their critical imagination. Problems they encountered were increasingly tackled with fine distinctions and made to yield novel solutions.

The whirlwind of thought produced was cast into forms that stand in marked contrast to what Anglophone readers of psychoanalytic literature have been accustomed to. While British authors often want to *show* representative examples of their clinical work, French contributions rather seek to *construct* a frame of understanding. This is typically supported by forms of argumentation that in the English-speaking world might be advanced in legal matters involving a consideration of precedent. Although work produced in France frequently contains an abundance of clinical reflections, it more often than not refrains from giving pride of place to a representative clinical vignette, quietly sceptical of casting into a story what must go beyond it.

Bewilderingly for spectators, French psychoanalysis offers a richly furnished repository of considerations that keep generating new angles to the evaluation of clinical problems. In its non-Lacanian version, it usually does not aspire to an overarching global theory, but suggests ways of reflecting on one's practice in a perspective in which a tentative assessment is reached at some distance from the pressures of the moment. The resulting discussion is very much receptive to interventions along the lines of 'What if, on the other hand, we also have to take into consideration the following, so far underrepresented, aspect'.

Attractive as it might be, a French debate spanning some sixty years cannot be condensed into a string of representative vignettes. If it were possible, it probably would have been done by now and published to great acclaim. Informed by a culture of well-articulated divergence, each case has to be viewed in the light of differences that may yet emerge as we reflect on it and which, if and when they do, will have to matter.

This is even more important in the case of patients who are low on energy, short on fantasy and at a loss to tell their story in any deeper sense. Created as an umbrella term to pinpoint a certain type of recurrent clinical experience at the farther reaches of psychoanalysis's remit, the *opératoire* construct has been useful to spark a number of debates that morphed the question 'What is wrong with that patient?' into 'What is it we do not fully get in this case?'

As a conceptual container for difficulties encountered by practitioners the term *opératoire* changed as it was being put to use. To follow its historical changes in usage and meaning, a static dictionary definition, if attempted, would not be of much help because it would miss something vital, an aspect which Sandler, Dare and Holder address on a more general level:

> We find a situation within psychoanalysis in which the meaning of a concept is only fully discernible from an examination of the context in which it is used.
> (Sandler, Dare and Holder 1992/1973, p. 2)

As Ian Hacking (2004) convincingly shows, the adoption of a concept shapes the perceptions and range of interactions of those who work with it. My book looks at the impact of the introduction of *opératoire* as a concept on a network of practitioners in France over some sixty years. Once they have adopted the new concept, what does it do to them as they work with it? What do they do with it as they appropriate it and connect it with other tools at their disposal within a given repertoire of ways and means?

Those who participated in the development of the notion of *opératoire* were part of a segment of French psychoanalysis facing outwards towards the new, but at the same time heirs to the older European practice of ambitious general practitioners as enlightened investigators. In taking their conceptual stance, they also anchored their discipline in public discourse and the professional mind.

In the case of the baffling patients mentioned earlier, the psychoanalysts whom I present took a radical step that changed all further debate: it was not what was in their psyche that made some patients sick, they contended, but on the contrary, the absence of processes therein that constrained their inner leeway and exposed them to somatic illness.

My book follows the unfolding strands of interconnected discussions by focusing on a number of psychoanalysts who contributed mutually complementary elements to the debate in a shared ecology of concepts. In presenting their thinking, I heed as much as possible

Introduction

Freud's reflection that stones like the onyx guide and restrain by the nature of their substance any skilful use to which they may be put. As Simpson (2018) understood well, things get complicated by the fact that each psychoanalyst presented has been taking part in a living exchange, embedded in the context of previous debates, which is implicitly present but not necessarily spelled out. Though space is restricted, I try to hear practitioners out: concerns expressed by one analyst may reappear with another to give an idea of how these concerns function in different contexts.

Glaring by omission in my discussion of thinkers are two members of the initial circle, Michel de M'Uzan and Christian David, who cooperated in the presentation of key papers in Barcelona, but later did not form part of the core group of *IPSO*, the institutional groundwork for the *EPP*, the *École Psychosomatique de Paris*, following paths of their own. Their work would merit studies of their own.

Secondary literature on the phenomenon I present is scattered and not abundant. As I show in Chapter 1, threads of previous discussions are there but need to be revisited in the light of newer developments.

To make the French debates which were kick-started by Pierre Marty and his colleagues more comprehensible it is important to set them in some of their original context. Chapter 2 will therefore look briefly at the main lines of development within French psychoanalysis from the 1940s to provide the reader with a feeling for the terrain, the main protagonists and some of the major conflicts fought out on it.

If not for Pierre Marty, the group would not have come into existence. Chapter 3 traces the development of the main lines of his early inquiries and follows Marty's attempt to arrive at a systematic presentation of his thought. His explanation of mental structure is rooted in a Vitalist appreciation of the articulations of life that encompass body and mind. He assigns a pivotal role to the preconscious in keeping the psyche adequately hydrated, as it were. Although he has not been followed by most of his colleagues in the theoretical underpinnings of his later systematisation, his acute sensibility to the silent crumbling behind well-maintained facades, and to the importance of ledges for clinging to above a threatening abyss, has remained of lasting interest.

At the time when Pierre Marty was trying to lay the groundwork for a new comprehensive approach to deal with decomposition of structure and loss of vital function, his close colleague and brother-in-law, Michel Fain, both alone and in collaboration with Denise

Braunschweig, was showing a marked interest in the rhythms of presence and absence in early childhood, initiated by the mutual erotic re-investments of the mother and her lover. Chapter 4 is taking a closer look at some of their main contributions, among them Fain's idea of a social link built on a shared, distorted perception of reality which, though seriously incapacitating, at the same time also offers a mainstay to identity. Inasmuch as Fain makes use of the *pulsion/instinct de mort*, he considers it as something that emanates from the mother, reducing the boisterous life of her child to obedient calm.

In Chapter 5, we are following Nicos Nicolaïdis as he takes a look at perception as a substitute for symbolisation. Nicolaïdis makes the point that it does matter to what the individual can regress, and what mental infrastructure is available to process inner stirrings. Transmitted by the mother's culture the elements provided are important in weaning the child off the earlier dyad.

In Chapter 6, a prime focus is on how, in Gérard Swecz's work, perception may or may not connect to self-throttling measures, in which calm is artificially induced and self-exhaustion is made to replace regression. Swecz dedicated a monograph to patients who were hell-bent on transforming themselves into voluntary galley slaves to deal with the otherwise unmanageable burden of self-regulation. He links this to early disturbance of balances between the mother and the child, sometimes leading to digestive problems and gastrointestinal disorders that burden further development.

Chapter 7 looks at how Anna Potamianou has, on various occasions, studied the preservative/obliterative impact of repetition, the effects of identification with a powerful caregiver of unsound mind, and the mixed blessings of hope safeguarded in a bubble of timelessness out of touch with reality. In the inner worlds of which she serves as a cartographer, the Me, possibly by bonding into a community of forgetfulness, has sacrificed large swathes of inner space. Restricted in the territory it can access, the Me has turned into a rather securitarian establishment (Tsoukala 2005) that must defend its borders with tooth and claw.

Chapter 8 turns to Jean Benjamin Stora, who pays attention to shocks that upset the balances necessary for the individual to thrive, and who has a particular sensibility to the necessity of a shared familiarity with the patient's imaginary worlds of reference for psychoanalytic treatment to succeed. His contributions show a marked

Introduction

awareness of material culture from an ethnopsychoanalytic perspective. Illusion, we may gather from Stora, can be conducive to the inception of form. The situation of the psychosomatician at the hospital, at times an outsider on the inside, deserves, as we can learn from him, particular attention.

Chapter 9 looks at César and Sára Botella, who, though not part of the core group, have been in sustained dialogue with *IPSO/EPP* over the years. Their work includes reflections on the plight of a person who finds him/herself left without any adequate mental image for his inner states. There is an omnipresent primal trace of very ancient lack, which has left a dent but not a properly constituted memory, and remains in quest of form. Meaning that is *en souffrance* – capable of gaining shape but not as yet present even in a repressed state – needs the contribution of the psychoanalyst, working as a double for the patient, to emerge from the sessions.

Chapter 10 follows Claude Smadja as he looks back, tracing the development of the *EPP*, and seeks to integrate an appreciation of Freud's Second Topography into Marty's thought. As a measure of the Me against narcissistic depletion, the *opératoire* is context-sensitive. There are instances when the patient's environment is drenched in a culture inimical to personal thriving. Low levels of aversion to being thrown into the unwholesome can lead to 'low subjective density': there is so much the subject does not seem to mind that he/she almost disappears into the background. What remains of his/her narcissism is invested in codes of behaviour mandated by a group. In times of increased difficulty, this may turn the individual into a collective unto him/herself, not well and on the point of breaking. In dealing with this, the analyst is faced with the autonomous logic of both the body and the environment.

Chapter 11 will look at developments in French psychiatry of the workplace up to the early 1960s, when it was being sidelined by *la sectorisation*, the growing psychoanalytic movement and changes in the cultural climate. The ground it covered in its experience with the challenges and rhythms of the workplace, as well as alienating identification, had to be rediscovered, when French psychoanalysts, 'dreaming different dreams [...] but walking in the same footsteps' – as Bernard Fall is reported to have said in a different context (Cohen 1984, p. 161) – returned to the matter of the workplace at a later stage, left unattended for some time because smacking too much of the 'real'.

Introduction

Chapter 12 considers the new directions that reflections on the *opératoire* have taken in the work of Christophe Dejours. Straddling the fields of psychosomatics and the psychodynamics at the work place, this author has studied and documented cases in which self-deafening becomes a mandatory procedure to fit in at the job. If desire is not initiated by a sufficiently tantalising enigma encountered in the parents' world, the dead weight of things will increasingly wear down the individual. Dejours, like few other psychoanalysts, has given thought to the central role of work in the life of the subject and included an interest in inter-generational effects of self-numbing, the vicissitudes of aggression if interdicted from pathways of expression and the storage of split-off zones of personality in an amental sector.

Chapter 13 describes the ways Jacques Press has given thought to what happens when a holding framework shatters, memory is obliterated, and a crisis cannot find external and inner space to be processed. In such a case, traumatic nuclei of (early) experience will leave a negative trace in form of *lacunae*, rather than a positive, if repressed, trace. Weaving contributions of Ethnology into his reflections, he suggests in doing so that the encounter between the psychoanalyst and the patient may not only entail a confusion of tongues, as Ferenczi pointed out, but also a clash of cultures.

In the Conclusion, I try as much as I can to pull threads together and argue that the discussions on the *opératoire* that I have portrayed throughout my book have a wider relevance beyond France.

Due to constraints of the format, the book does not come with a full complement of detailed references. To counterbalance this, I provide a section of Sources for every section of the book that lists essential primary and secondary literature I draw upon in the respective chapter. Readers interested in more detailed references and additional layers of documentation and discussion may want to consult the original PhD (http://repository.essex.ac.uk/24036/).

Once coined as a term, *opératoire* has proved surprisingly resilient to address concerns that had not been present when it was injected into the discussion. What it bundles into one morpheme might well be tackled under a variety of headings in nosologies that owe nothing to the French debates. Naturally, cultural preferences will inform choices: there are zones of the *opératoire* which are very close to 'Keep Calm and Carry On' in the face of exhaustion when the thread of life frays and all feeling becomes threadbare.

But the big courage is the cold-blooded kind, the kind that never lets go even when you're feeling empty inside, and your blood's thin and there's no kind of fun or profit to be had, and the trouble's not over in an hour or two but lasts for months and years.... I reckon fortitude's the biggest thing a man can have — just to go on enduring when there's no guts or heart left in you.

(Buchan 1919, p. 139)

There is certainly something to be gained from such fortitude, but there will also be inevitable loss: transformation and an expansive zest for life has to be put on hold for the sake of preservation in an environment, present or past, that does not permit thriving for the moment and does not provide space for reflections as to why this might be so. In other, more severe cases whole ranges of vital experience will have been violently rendered *desaparecido*, in possibly unwitting complicity of the person concerned, who is left with oppressive results he/she then has to defend against.

As a Central European I am interested in disappearances that have left too scant memories behind, but can by no stretch of the imagination be said to have been self-inflicted by those turned victims of collective selective memory. As I write and think about this in English, I cannot help but notice that I am an uninvited guest to a debate that has in many ways yet to materialise. Despite contacts between British and French psychoanalysis on various levels, and a ground-breaking, amply introduced and richly annotated anthology (Birksted-Breen, Gibeault and Flanders 2010), it is still easier to find a book about the transformation of disease concepts in China than it is to lay hands on a scholarly monograph on non-Lacanian French psychoanalysis produced this side of the millennium.

In the absence of a more comprehensive study, we must fill in some of the background to French clinical thinking as best as we can. Paradoxically, *opératoire* as a concept could only rise to prominence in a cultural climate in which Freud's earlier theories, and in particular his *Interpretation of Dreams*, had shaped clinical expectations. The new concept drew attention because it pointed to something that ran counter to expectations, offering disconcerting evidence of a disturbance that was not on the accepted maps of the clinical terrain. Once the debate broadened, analysts began to make more and more connections. Some of them dug into the history of psychoanalysis. As Michel Fain (1982) caustically remarked, the purity of Freud's

First Topography – his first sketch of the workings of the psyche that gave pride of place to repressed desire – had been among the casualties of the Great War, sending shock waves through the entire psychoanalytic movement.

Worse was still to come. As the century unfolded, psychoanalysts were confronted with trauma on a scale unprecedented in their previous experience. Bad as it was, there was at least some form of collective memory that provided a context to events an individual might be too wounded to talk about.

When Marty and his colleagues presented papers about the patients they had seen, thoughtful observers pointed out that this looked like phenomena encountered elsewhere. As Marion M. Oliner noted,

> Being acquainted with studies of the pathology encountered in former concentration camp victims, I find a striking correspondence between descriptions of some survivor syndromes and the lack of structurization favoring psychosomatic reactions to stress.
> (Oliner 1988, p. 234)

Even if we cannot fully grasp it, we have at least some notion of what concentration camp victims were exposed to. But what exactly was it that *opératoire* patients had been through?

Since they did not know the answer, Pierre Marty and his colleagues used their new conceptual construct as a probe to explore spaces they were not familiar with. Their concept was launched into gravity fields of the undesired and undesirable, places, where a lingering lack of well-being did not adequately register in feelings and thoughts. Whatever the *opératoire* was, it apparently lacked both memory and desire – on the side of the patient, not the analyst – but did not fall short on sometimes diffuse discomfort.

It has been emphasised that Lacan had an enormous impact on French psychoanalysis. This is undoubtedly true. It has more often been overlooked, though, that this, at times, had some curious consequences. Because there had been a parting of ways with Lacan, it was easier for Marty and his colleagues – whose psychoanalytic association was in the process of repositioning itself – to investigate phenomena Lacan was not interested in at the time. Doing so they used an approach that favoured zones beyond words and language. For Marty, steeped in Vitalism, this meant paying attention to patients low on energy and without a story to tell. What he termed *dépression essentielle* was a deep exhaustion, which lacked in mental drama, and which was likely to lead to a quiet withering away. Against this, the *opératoire* evidently worked as a measure of last resort, pulling the subject together when everything else failed.

When the original papers were written, France, and Europe, were still recovering from the devastations of war and genocide. As our own century is witnessing new upheavals, changed circumstances are likely to produce new varieties of mental disappearances. As Virginia de Micco has found in her work with migrants, for children exposed to a loss of stable cultural frameworks in migration, there is nothing that provides links to what goes beyond 'the actual', leading to a two-dimensional image of themselves (de Micco 2016).

This leads to situations in which even to be able to access one's own pain there has to be its reflection in another person's eye,

> Maybe only when one is able to start seeing one's own wound in the wounded gaze of another – another who has been left wounded in his humanity by the inhumane – maybe only then can the mind that has crossed the desert of the inhumane begin to be populated, crowded with nightmares.
>
> (de Micco 2018, p. 123)

For this is what the French concept of the *opératoire* also speaks about: interfaces to a transformative potential gone missing to the subject left to its own devices, leaving only white noise behind.

Reading French psychoanalytic literature has been with me for some time and I have found it to be quite a rewarding experience, especially if one goes to the original that often vibrates with echoes to which a translation cannot do justice.

If I tend towards using words like *pulsion* in the original it is because of the impression that its meaning in the French debates is obscured if translated as drive. Like many words, it is best understood in the context in which it occurs. Readers will also notice that I tend to use the term Me instead of the more usual ego to render the French term *Moi*: it is the object of inner perception, something one might discern in a mirror, although the image discerned might quite conceivably offend one's ego.

I also tend to avoid using 'they' as a singular construct. Writing about 'The real, gendered child, at their birth' does not ring true in the context of the debates to which I refer.

Readers unfamiliar with French psychoanalysis may want to consult Birksted-Breen, Gibeault and Flanders (2010) for additional information. It would make little sense to reduplicate their efforts.

In giving an account of the discussion on the *opératoire* I have to condense things and for this purpose use whatever expedient means I can find, including means of presentation that are not used in the original texts. In general, the translation of texts is mine, unless indicated otherwise.

An eminent Chinese emperor of the Liang dynasty, 6th century CE, is said to have asked a visiting Indian teacher what benefit might be derived from following his way: the legendary reply is famous for cutting both ways – nothingness and spaciousness. Whether we find space where there seems to be nothingness is a constant challenge in clinical work. Not to take into account more than sixty years of reflections emerging from French psychoanalysts on the matter may be a luxury we can ill afford.

Sources

Alvarez, J. (1994), 'Disappeared does not take a helping verb in English', *Syracuse University Magazine* 10(4), Article 9, available at: https://surface.syr.edu/sumagazine/vol10/iss4/9

Bion, W. R. (1967), 'Notes on memory and desire', *The Psychoanalytic Forum* 2(3), pp. 271–280.

Birksted-Breen, D., Gibeault, A. and Flanders, S. eds (2010), *Reading French psychoanalysis*, London: Routledge.

Buchan, J. (1919), *Mr Standfast*, new edition 1998, London: Wordsworth Editions.

Cohen, S. (1984), *Vietnam. Anthology and guide to a television history*, New York: McGraw-Hill.

De Micco, V. (2016), 'La pelle che abito, il nome che porto: Fratture culturali e legami transgenerazionali nei bambini migranti', *Rivista di Psicoanalisi* 62(1), pp. 231–240.

De Micco, V. (2018), 'Migration: Surviving the inhumane', *The Italian Psychoanalytic Annual* 12, pp. 117–125.

de Mijolla, A. (1995), 'Les scissions dans le mouvement psychanalytique français de 1953 à 1964', *Topique* 57, pp. 271–290.

de Mijolla, A. (2012b), *La France et Freud*, volume 2: *1954–1964. D'une scission à l'autre*, Paris: Presses Universitaires de France.

Dolgopolski, S. (2009), *What is Talmud? The art of disagreement*, New York: Fordham University Press.

Fain, M. (1982), *Le désir de l'interprète*, Paris: Éditions Aubier Montaigne.

Hacking, I. (2004), 'Between Michel Foucault and Erving Goffman: between discourse in the abstract and face-to-face interaction', *Economy and Society* 33(3), pp. 277–302.

Marty, P., de M'Uzan, M. and David C. (2003/1963), *L'investigation psychosomatique. Sept observations cliniques*, 2nd edition, Paris: Presses Universitaires de France.

Oliner, M.M. (1988), *Cultivating Freud's garden in France*, Northvale, New Jersey: Jason Aronson.

Sandler, J., Dare, C. and Holder, A. (1992/1973), *The patient and the analyst. The basis of the psychoanalytic process*, London: Karnac Books.

Simpson, R. (2018), 'On being consoled: Engaging with Michel Fain's paper 'Mentalization and passivity', *International Journal of Psychoanalysis* 99(2), pp. 487–494.

Tsoukala, A. (2005), 'Looking at migrants as enemies', in Bigo, D. and Guild, E. eds, *Controlling Frontiers: Free movement into and within Europe*, Abingdon-on-Thames: Taylor & Francis, pp. 161–192.

Vargas, J. H. (2017), *Forms of dictatorship: Power, narrative and authoritarianism in the Latina/o novel*, New York: Oxford University Press.

Widlöcher, D. ed. (2008), *Les psychanalystes savent-ils débattre?* Paris: Odile Jacob.

1

FRAGMENTS OF A DEBATE

In contrast to the abundance of primary literature, a look at the secondary literature shows that we have to come to terms with significant absences: studies which, given the importance of the topic, should – but apparently have not – been written. The sparse, existing literature is dispersed and often fragmentary or summary in nature. In other instances, books were published decades ago but have not been brought up to date and are thus in no position to take into consideration important new developments that have occurred since.

Given the relative lack of comprehensive accounts about the intellectual life within French psychoanalysis beyond Lacanianism, it has mainly fallen to anthologies to attempt to offset and remedy, as best they can, the resulting vacuum: among which, in particular, as older examples, we find Lebovici and Widlöcher (1980) and Chiland (1981). As already mentioned, the hefty volume by Birksted-Breen, Gibeault and Flanders (2010) offered impressive evidence of renewed British interest in French psychoanalysis. This has recently been followed up by Sara Flanders (2018) in her very useful and concise contribution on non-Lacanian strands of psychoanalysis published in a work on the evolution of theory and practice over the decades within the Lacan tradition.

The history of psychosomatics is served competently by the all too slim booklet by Kamieniecki (1994), only a chapter of which – with more attention than usual accorded to Michel Fain and a useful extension on Christophe Dejours – focuses on the *EPP*. There is a short view from Quebec on the *EPP* provided by Fortier (1988), who within the scope of fifteen pages presents a succinct thumbnail sketch of relevant developments, and a view from America in an article by Dodds (undated), who extends the portrayal of positions of the founding generation to a consideration of the second generation, cross-links with neuro-psychoanalysis and an assessment of the divergent positions held by Joyce McDougall. On a slightly more minor scale in terms of length is the manual entry by Chabert (1994), who dedicates five densely argued pages to the *EPP*. In the English language, a choice of papers has been made available in Aisenstein and de Aisemberg (2010). A useful survey of questions involved in psychosomatics with an emphasis on French contributions has recently been presented by Boucherat-Hue, Hulin and Machado (2018). In a short paper, Marilia Aisenstein (2020) has given a succinct overview of the development of psychosomatic thinking in Pierre Marty's school.

If one wants to find out more about the inner cohesion of thought proposed by the founding generation of the *EPP*, the slender volumes within the series *Psychanalystes d'aujourd'hui* are a good starting point. With some variation in structure depending on the choices of the individual authors, they provide some basic biographical information, a concise survey of the *oeuvre*, a basic bibliography and, to conclude with, an anthology of representative extracts from the work of the author discussed. Titles, where they exist, are listed with the literature provided for each chapter. Marilia Aisenstein (2018) has recently presented a very valuable introduction to Michel Fain's thought in English, in which she also includes useful biographical information previously not easily accessible. There is an older, slightly longer, study on Sacha Nacht (Saadja 1972). Regrettably, I have not been able to find any comparable study on Maurice Bouvet. Escaping the categories so far discussed, Chagnon (2012) has published a series of concise commentaries on classical psychoanalytic texts about psychopathology, among which Pierre Marty and Michel Fain are represented. Parisa Dashtipour, from Middlesex University, in cooperation with Bénédicte Vidaillet, from the Université Paris Est, have shown that there is a lot to be discovered in Christophe Dejours that deserves our attention.

It is not easy to find longer works on the development of French psychoanalytic thought outside the Lacanian tradition. The little there is often comes from non-French authors who have noticed a wealth of relevant ideas and are stimulated rather than being repelled by what, from the outside, appears an opaque world operating on an unwonted level of intensity. Although by now inevitably dated, Marion M. Oliner's *Cultivating Freud's garden in France* (1988) remains an outstanding example of this garnering sortie beyond the confines of one's own psychoanalytic culture. Oliner (2010), who states she was drawn to the French by their engagingly multi-faceted approach to psycho-sexual development, draws a broad picture of different non-Lacanian strands of French psychoanalytic life, including several sections useful for an appreciation of Marty's, Braunschweig's and Fain's thoughts. Occasionally, interspersed observations of hers offer rich potential connections, underexplored in the discussion she reports. Thus, for instance, she remarks that the description of the *pensée opératoire* and *dépression essentielle* reminds her of a similar functioning in concentration camp survivors, a connection also made and addressed by Krystal (1985).

This, clearly, has considerable implications: if this mode of functioning can be acquired under duress, it would be reasonable to consider it a last-ditch defence in well-nigh hopeless circumstances rather than inevitably presenting a developmental flaw in the constitution of a character. Robert M. Young (1993, p. 135) stated that 'Juliet Mitchell once said of Grosskurth that her biography of Melanie Klein read as if its author didn't like anyone'. If this is so – and Young has his doubts about the justice of the sentiment he quotes – Oliner would be an example of the converse approach: the attractions of writing about something one finds rewarding. As a pioneer work from abroad, it still makes for indispensable reading. If consulted for the topic of my book, the problem, apart from the publication date, is one of focus: since she aims to give a broad picture, there is only so much available space which she can devote to any given topic. Published one year after Oliner's study, Edith Kurzweil's *The Freudians. A comparative perspective* (1989), includes intriguing glimpses on French Freudianism, and the qualities that set it apart from both Anna Freudians and Kleinians. Oliner has continued taking close interest in the French discussions, showing that a well-informed view from outside may be vital to drawing out latent connections.

As André Green (2010) observed, the mental functioning observed in patients diagnosed with *pensée opératoire* may not be limited to the sole group of psychosomatic patients. With Green's admonition in mind, it is possible to make judicious use of Pirlot (2010), who aims to present the theoretical corpus, comprising different *doxa*, as he says, and clinical hypotheses in the area of psychoanalytic psychosomatic thought (and does so in a work of around 230 pages). As a psychiatrist, psychoanalyst and professor of clinical psychology, he is concerned with the delineation of consolidated positions in this field so as to facilitate transmission to students. Among other strands of thought it presents, it places Marty's work not only within psychoanalytic thinking but also in continuation of psychiatric interrogations voiced by Henri Ey, the great mentor of French psychoanalysts in psychiatry. Useful as the book is, it has to serve, by its very purpose, the function of a reference work for students and has thus limited possibilities to delve more amply into the genesis and development of a strand of thinking of which it provides a thoughtful and sympathetic sketch. By far much further down the road of digestible and memorisable brevity, Pirlot (2013) – which supplements the study aid offered by Pirlot and Cupa (2012a) – summarises in six pages what can be said about some of Pierre Marty's firmly articulated positions. (A similarly condensed survey is presented in Doucet (2000). Broad in compass and interest, Gérard Pirlot indicates to what extent elements of the *EPP's* concerns have become part of accepted standard curricula – a far cry, understandably, from Braunschweig and Fain's provocative statement,

> it would displease us if anyone thought we were striving to explain things clearly and simply. Every clear and simple explanation of mental phenomena is an injury perpetrated to the human being.
> (Braunschweig and Fain 1971, p. 115)

There is, compared to Pirlot (2010), a nuanced shift of focus in Dumet (2002), who, since she covers less, has time to do more in the areas to which she directs her attention. Pirlot has already remarked on the position of the *pensée opératoire* at the very opposite pole of hysteria: Nathalie Dumet reflects that while hysteria was originally discussed in close connection with bodily conversion symptoms to which it often gave rise, it is today thought to exist independently from these symptoms, which can, on the other hand, be found within the framework of different personality structures. If one applied a similar uncoupling operation to the *pensée opératoire,* one has to conclude that it would not necessarily have to occur in conjunction with somatising tendencies and could be studied separately from the domain of psychosomatics, to which, however, it would conserve meaningful potential links. Dumet (2002), more than other authors, traces the development of different positions (including Dejours') over time – from the conjecture of a specific 'psychosomatic' personality structure to mechanisms which can be deployed by any personality type in certain moments of their lives – and recognises the anti-traumatic strategy operated in the frantic grip on the merely factual. There seems to be meaningful agency in the outwardly meaningless stance of robotic thinking and a history, albeit buried in oblivion, therein to be discovered that goes much beyond the mere constatation of a deficiency, presenting a lamentable chink in the armour of *mentalisation* having fallen short of its evolutionary target.

This is not always apparent in the most dominant strata of the alexithymia debate, which in some, but not all of its ramifications, coincides with concerns raised by the *EPP*. Alexithymia, as a concept, was developed on separate lines from Marty's and his colleagues' positions, and was put on different methodological foundations, which placed more emphasis on neuro-physiology and with different clinical recommendations that would, in many cases, favour cognitive behavioural therapy, as pointed out, among others, by Taylor (1990). The latter author also stresses that the hypothesis of a specific link between alexithymia and psychosomatic diseases should be considered premature. In Britain, it is less the alexithymia discussion than the 'mentalization' concept, as proposed by Peter Fonagy (2000) and his colleagues, which one has to consult for a rough equivalent to something of which the *opératoire* construct offers the negative: mental indications of a potential for thriving significantly lacking in the *opératoire*. Holmes (2005) surveys the development and discusses possible objections. On French ground, Corcos and Pirlot (2011) trace essential French psychoanalytic elements towards a contribution to the alexithymia debate in their book, which raises the question not only of the nature of the mechanism but also the inner space (or lack thereof) from which it emerges as a remedial measure within a given inner and outer context. This would resonate with Jacquy Chemouni's reflection (2010) that we should think less of a given disease or patient structure when we study psychosomatics than, rather, of a particular *situation psychosomatique* – a psychosomatic situation, or more loosely translated, an (inner and outer) field. There is a very useful contribution by Claude de Tychey (2010), in which he juxtaposes the alexithymia to the *opératoire* and highlights the difficulties involved in this.

Bronstein (2011) subsumes both Marty and Fonagy under a deficit model perspective, while Fischbein (2011) mentions Marty, whom he briefly summarises before moving on to McDougall. There is an apparently widespread tendency to treat Marty as if he stood for the whole of the *EPP's* past and present thinking on the matter and which may, to some extent, explain the almost exclusive attention accorded to him over his colleagues and successors in two contributions in Spanish (Ulnik 2000; Fernández 2002, who, both, however, pay some attention to Dejours' positions). As often, this lack of more detailed critical study is somewhat mitigated by the existence of a carefully compiled anthology with a wider compass in de Calatroni (1998).

Cultural tendencies and social factors are paid attention to in Pirlot (2009). In this connection, with regard to a wider cultural canvas, however, it is vital to bear in mind the early warning of Zepf and Gattig (1981) – who are themselves highly critical of the *EPP* – against what they see as a oversimplifying tendency in Cremerius (1977), who pointed out against Marty and colleagues that the *mode opératoire* could be a marker of socio-cultural (and class) difference in emotional register rather than a specific personality structure as suggested by the *EPP* at that time. Granted that socio-cultural difference cannot explain everything, we yet have to take care to understand intercultural factors which may impinge on the analytic encounter and shape the particular situation the patient finds him/herself in.

There are a number of contributions in German to the discussion on the *EPP's* tenets, but the majority of them were published in the 1970s and 1980s and were not able to take into account later developments: among them Kapfhammer (1985); Stephanos and Auhagen (1979) and Schneider (1973). Karola Brede's (1974) anthology of position papers in psychoanalytic medicine includes contributions of Marty's. Zepf (2000) shows that critical positions once taken were not necessarily exposed to further literature as the decades went by. In spite of the rather summary dismissal that the French colleagues receive in Thomä and Kächele (2006), based on the discussion of the 1980s, there are also signs of a somewhat more open attitude. Scheidt (2006) sums up the previous reception, emphasises the renewed interest in the alexithymia concept from the 1990s and stresses the wide range and heterogeneous nature of affect pathologies among psychosomatic patients. A more recent passage in a German psychiatric manual (Kapfhammer 2010) shows continuing interest but also some reservations as to the supposed tendency towards mono-factorial presuppositions within the psychodynamic French approach.

On the whole, the French debate seems to have travelled much less well than the American alexithymia and the British mentalisation concepts, hampered, no doubt, by language barriers, but also by the tendency of French psychoanalysts to produce new work at full throttle without spending an equal amount of time delineating the meanderings of the previous debate (although Green and Laplanche, in their different ways, have shown the rich harvest this can bear when applied to Freud and Klein). It has been pointed out that one has to decide whether to interpret *in* the transference or *upon* the transference. It stands to reason that one can, operating a comparable choice, write *in* a tradition without ever finding the time for writing *on* a tradition. So far French psychoanalysis has overwhelmingly opted for the first approach, to mixed quantities of admiration, consternation and dismay among foreign observers.

Given this situation, it is upon favourably disposed, but inevitably somewhat baffled, foreign observers that has most often fallen the task to make sense of what French psychoanalysts have been debating among themselves. One of those who have consistently shown interest has been Otto Kernberg, who has repeatedly pointed out the importance of French contributions, among which – in contradistinction to those who only focus on Marty – he has also included Braunschweig and Fain's (see for instance, Kernberg 1996; 1995). It was Otto Kernberg who encouraged Oliner to proceed with her important work. Curiously, it is nowadays from America, consistently slighted by Lacan, that some very pertinent and intriguing reflection on the French school of psychosomatics has emerged. A continuing interest can be traced in the reports by Emmett Wilson in *The Psychoanalytic Quarterly* on the output of the *Revue Française de Psychanalyse* on an annual basis and in Howard B. Levine's lucid book review essays. In a perspicacious commentary on an article of Pierre Marty's, Richard M. Gottlieb – an author who has repeatedly paid attention to French developments – points out something that might be regarded as obvious, but too often has escaped attention:

> the *psychosomaticien* school has by now been continuously around for more than 50 years and is well into its 'second generation' of theorists and clinicians.... This in turn has resulted in a significant accumulation of clinical experience with their ideas and therapeutic practices. Such an accumulation under one theoretical roof

is unusual if not unique in psychoanalytic psychosomatics today and surely deserves our attention.

(Gottlieb 2010a, p. 365)

Even if this thinking were to contain grievous errors — which would remain to be proven in spite of the condemnation that Siegfried Zepf regarded as conclusive in the early 1980s — no serious consideration of it can take place as long as the examination of it is hampered by an almost total lack of understanding of the internal evolution and adaptation of a thought faced with the continuous challenges of clinical practice in the course of almost six decades. (The reciprocal difficulty: French neglect of developments in the English-speaking world, even in cases where there was an arguable similarity in perspective and interest, was argued by Waintrater 2012.)

There are many indications that suggest that the *opératoire* is a highly context-sensitive phenomenon. Brought to paper as a concept, it gives shape to cogitations on what appears to be woefully lacking in an analytic encounter — a lack that might well be either secondary on the part of the patient (the result of a negative hallucination, as suggested by Pirlot and Corcos (2012), or partly due to the limits of imagination and sensibility of the psychoanalyst. Again, it is R.M. Gottlieb (2010b), who points out that in a conference, in which analysts from different schools shared case material, the analytic potential a situation was deemed to hold varied widely among those present: how could one analyst find almost nothing when another analyst found rich material in the same patient? If 'The Other is an object for the patient's use', as Rina Lazar (2001, p. 284) maintains, would this be true regardless of how this analytic Other inwardly constructs the situation of the encounter?

If we follow Michel Neyraut's (1974) reasoning — and, more recently, Marin (2009) — psychoanalysis always involves an individual (and collective) countertransference on the patient before the latter even enters the consulting room: a theoretically informed expectation of where to look and what to find before the encounter even takes place. Melanie Klein's original objections notwithstanding, neo-Kleinian thinking, on the whole, has regarded countertransference as a source of minable information to be worked through and sifted, not to be set aside or ignored.

What we can take from this is that every proposition has a context and a socially constituted remit. Its implementation is likely to change as it is more widely appropriated and put to use. Not only the individual, but also the professional group requires 'a skin for thought' (Anzieu 1990) which forms a permeable membrane between what is outside and what is inside. This is likely to be even more important in cases that confound professionally honed expectations.

There appears to be consensus that the subject who is thought to be making use of *pensée opératoire* is in a severe impasse, but still conserves residual resources. As psychoanalysis looks at the patient, it is this glance itself that has to be interrogated, especially when confronted with cases in which '*no memory and no desire*' has changed sides and is upheld by patients who seem to be taking a leaf out of Pierre Janet's books instead of Freud's, covertly joining ranks with some of Bion's more disturbed patients.

As Dejours points out:

> Authors, in fact, evolve, sometimes quite brusquely with the experience they acquire while working as analysts, with age and maturity, no doubt, after intellectual encounters, certainly.... But rare are those who strive clearly to lay account of the turning points and diverse stages of their thought. They present it as if this was to be taken for granted, or they forget to speak about it, by tact, calculation or lack of comprehension of the epistemological ruptures they are committing.
>
> (Dejours 2009, p. 18f.)

This requires some persistent tracing of thought which at the moment – as far as the focus of my investigation is concerned – is not likely to come from within France, for what in the last resort may well be quite a simple reason: within French psychoanalysis the highest compliment is to have accomplished an *oeuvre*, rather than to have reflected on one. That is probably the reason why there is a *Prix Bouvet* for those who have in innovative ways excelled in psychoanalysis, but no critical evaluation of the work of Bouvet himself – which on the other hand does exist for Castoriadis, who was also a philosopher, and as such the concern of a discipline that does routinely engage in critical retrospective evaluation.

We will see in the next chapter that the background explains something of the density of the French debates that even their participants might have found difficult to catch up with in all their ramifications.

Sources

Aisenstein, M. and de Aisemberg, E.R. eds (2010), *Psychosomatics today. A psychoanalytic perspective,* London: Karnac Books.
Aisenstein, M. (2018), 'An introduction to Michel Fain's thought', *International Journal of Psychoanalysis* 99(2), pp. 495–509.
Aisenstein, M. (2020), 'A view on patients with somatic or painful conditions', *Romanian Journal of Psychoanalysis* 13(1), pp. 15–28.
Aisenstein, M. and Papageorgiou, M. (2018), 'Mentalisation and passivity by Michel Fain', *International Journal of Psychoanalysis* 99(2), pp. 468–478.
Anzieu, D. (1990) *A skin for thought. Interviews with Gilbert Tarab,* London: Karnac.
Birksted-Breen, D., Gibeault, A. and Flanders, S. eds (2010), *Reading French psychoanalysis,* London: Routledge.
Boucherat-Hue, V., Hulin, A. and Machado, C. (2018), 'Critical and reasoned review of the psychosomatic question in French-speaking psychoanalysts', *International Journal of Psychoanalysis* 99(4), pp. 877–904.
Braunschweig, D. and Fain, M. (1971), *Éros et Antéros,* Paris: Payot.
Brede, K. ed. (1974), *Einführung in die psychosomatische Medizin,* reprint 1980, Frankfurt am Main: Syndikat Verlag.
Bronstein, C. (2011), 'On psychosomatics: The search for meaning', *International Journal of Psychoanalysis* 92(1), pp. 173–195.
Carton, S., Chabert, C. and Corcos, M. (2011), *Le silence des émotions. Clinique psychanalytique des états vides d'affects,* Paris: Dunod.
Chabert, C. (1994), 'Les approches structurales', in: Widlöcher, D. ed., *Traité de psychopathologie,* Paris: Presses Universitaires de France, pp. 105–157.
Chagnon, J-Y. (2012), *45 commentaires de textes en psychopathologie psychanalytique,* Paris: Dunod.
Chemouni, J. (2010), *Psychosomatique de l'enfant et de l'adulte,* 3rd edition, Paris: Editions in Press.
Chiland, C. ed. (1981), *Les ecoles psychanalytiques. La psychanalyse en mouvement,* Paris: Tchou.
Corcos, M. and Pirlot, G. (2011), *Qu'est-ce que l'alexithymie?* Paris: Dunod
Cremerius, J. (1977), 'Ist die "psychosomatische Struktur" der französischen Schule krankheitsspezifisch?', *Psyche. Zeitschrift für Psychoanalyse und ihre Anwendungen* 31(4), pp. 293–317.
Cremerius, J., Hoffmann, S.O., Hoffmeister, W. and Trimborn, W. (1979), 'Die manipulierten Objekte: Ein kritischer Beitrag zur Untersuchungsmethode der französischen Schule der Psychosomatik', *Psyche. Zeitschrift für Psychoanalyse und ihre Anwendungen* 33(9-10), pp. 801–828.

Dashtipour, P. and Vidaillet, B. (2017), 'Work as affective experience: The contribution of Christophe Dejours' "psychodynamics of work"', *Organization* 24(1), pp. 18–35.

de Calatroni, M.T. ed. (1998), *Pierre Marty y la psicosomática*, Buenos Aires: Amorrortu/editores.

Dejours, C. (2009), *Les dissidences du corps. Répression et subversion en psychosomatique*, Paris: Payot.

de Tychey, C. (2010), 'Alexithymie et pensée opératoire: Approche comparative clinique projective franco-américaine', *Psychologie Clinique et Projective* 16, pp. 177–207.

Dodds, J. (no date), 'From Psychosomatics to Neuropsychoanalysis: Contributions of the Paris School, available at: www.npsa.cz/Revue%20Article%20Paris%20School11.pdf

Doucet, C. (2000), *La psychosomatique. Théorie et clinique*, Paris: Armand Colin.

Dumet, N. (2002), *Clinique des troubles psychosomatiques. Approche psychanalytique*, Paris: Dunod.

Fernández, R. (2002), *El psicoanálisis y lo psicosomatico*, Madrid: Editorial Síntesis.

Fischbein, J.E. (2011), 'Psychosomatics: A current overview', *International Journal of Psychoanalysis* 92, pp. 197–219.

Flanders, S. (2018), 'French psychoanalysis and Lacan', in: Bailly, L., Lichtenstein, D. and Bailly, S. eds, *The Lacan tradition. Lines of development. Evolution of theory and practice over the decades*, Abingdon-on-Thames: Routledge, pp. 53–71.

Fonagy, P. (2000), 'L'origine de la sexualité infantile. Réflexions autour de l'article de Daniel Widlöcher Amour primaire et sexualité infantile', in: Widlöcher, D. ed., *Sexualité infantile et attachement,* Paris: Presses Universitaires de France, pp. 83–96.

Fortier, C. (1988), 'À propos de l'école de Paris: quelques repères pour la consultation psychosomatique', *Santé Mentale au Québec* 13(1), pp. 18–33.

Geissmann, C. and Geissmann, P. (2004), *Histoire de la psychanalyse de l'enfant. Mouvements, idées, perspectives*, 2nd edition, Paris: Bayard.

Gottlieb, R.M. (2003), 'Psychosomatic medicine: The divergent legacies of Freud and Janet', *Journal of the American Psychoanalytic Association* 51(3), pp. 857–881.

Gottlieb, R.M. (2010a), 'Commentary on Pierre Marty's "The narcissistic difficulties presented to the observer by the psychosomatic problem"', *International Journal of Psychoanalysis* 91, pp. 365–370.

Gottlieb, R.M. (2010b), 'Coke or Pepsi?: Reflections on Freudian and Relational Psychoanalysis in dialogue', *Contemporary Psychoanalysis* 46, pp. 87–100.

Gottlieb, R.M. (2013), 'On our need to move beyond folk medicine: A commentary on Karen Gubb's Paper, "Psychosomatics Today: A Review of Contemporary Theory and Practice"', *Psychoanalytic Review* 100(1), pp. 143–154.

Green, A. (2010), 'Thoughts on the Paris School of Psychosomatics', in: Aisenstein, M. and de Aisemberg, E.R. eds, *Psychosomatics today. A psychoanalytic perspective*, London: Karnac Books, pp. 1–45.

Holmes, J. (2005), 'Notes on mentalizing – old hat, or new wine?', *British Journal of Psychotherapy* 22(2), pp. 179–197.

Kamieniecki, H. (1994), *Histoire de la psychosomatique*, Paris: Presses Universitaires de France.

Kapfhammer, H.-P. (1985), *Psychoanalytische Psychosomatik. Neuere Ansätze der psychoanalytischen Entwicklungpsychologie und Objektbeziehungstheorie*, Berlin: Springer Verlag.

Kapfhammer, H.-P. (2010), 'Psychosomatische Medizin – Einleitung und Übersicht', in: Möller, H.-J., Laux, G. and Kapfhammer, H.-P. eds, *Psychiatrie. Psychosomatik. Psychotherapie*, volume 2, Berlin: Springer Verlag, pp. 1273–1295.

Kernberg, O. (1995), *Love relations. Normality and pathology*, New Haven: Yale University Press.

Kernberg, O. (1996), 'Differences: psychoanalytic theory and culture in France and the United States, in: Baruch, E.H. and Serrano, L.J. eds, *She speaks, he listens. Women on the French analyst's couch*, New York and London: Routledge, pp. 157–189.

Krystal, H. (1985), 'Trauma and the stimulus barrier', *Psychoanalytic Inquiry* 5(1), pp. 131–161.

Lazar, R. (2001), 'Subject in first person – subject in third person: Subject, subjectivity and intersubjectivity', *American Journal of Psychoanalysis* 61(3), pp. 271–291.

Lebovici, S. and Widlöcher, D. eds (1980), *Psychoanalysis in France*, New York: International Universities Press, pp. vii–xiv.

Levine, H.B (2011), 'Precious ambiguities', *The Psychoanalytic Quarterly* 80(3), pp. 727–740.

Levine, H.B. (2012), 'Review of Psychosomatics Today: A psychoanalytic perspective, Aisenstein, M. and Rappoport de Aisemberg, E. eds, *Journal of the American Psychoanalytic Association* 60(1), pp. 207–216.

Levine, H. (2018), 'The greening of psychoanalysis', *International Journal of Psychoanalysis* 99(2), pp. 535–538.

Marin, C. (2009), 'Au-delà de l'ennui: l'effort pour rendre l'autre intéressant', *Revue Médicale Suisse* 2009(5), pp. 351–353.

Neyraut, M. (1974), *Le transfert,* Paris: Presses Universitaires de France.

Oliner, M.M. (1988), *Cultivating Freud's garden in France,* Northvale, New Jersey: Jason Aronson.

Oliner, M.M. (2010), 'Die zufällige Analytikerin', in: Hermanns, L.M. ed., *Psychoanalyse in Selbstdarstellungen,* volume 8, Frankfurt/Main: Brandes&Apsel, pp. 187–243.

Perelberg, R.J. and Kohon, G. (2017), *The greening of psychoanalysis: André Green's new paradigm in contemporary theory and practice,* Abingdon-on-Thames: Routledge.

Pirlot, G. (2009), *Déserts intérieurs. Le vide négatif dans la clinique contemporaine, le vide positif de 'l'appareil d'ame',* Toulouse: Éditions Érès.

Pirlot, G. (2010), *La Psychosomatique. Entre psychanalyse et biologie,* Paris: Armand Colin.

Pirlot, G. (2011), 'Psychopathologie et psychosomatique psychanalytiques et interculturelles', in: Guerraoui, Z. and Pirlot, G. (2011), *Comprendre et traiter les situations interculturelles. Approches psychodynamiques et psychanalytiques,* Brussels: Éditions De Boeck Université, pp. 145–192.

Pirlot, G. (2013), *Classifications et nosologies des troubles psychiques. Approches psychiatrique et psychanalytique.* Paris: Armand Colin.

Pirlot, G. and Corcos, M. (2012), 'Understanding alexithymia within a psychoanalytical framework', *International Journal of Psychoanalysis* 93(6), pp. 1403–1425.

Pirlot, G. and Cupa, D. (2012a), *Approche psychanalytique des troubles psychiques,* Paris: Armand Colin.

Saada, D. (1972), *S. Nacht,* Paris: Payot.

Scheidt, C.E. (2006), 'Alexithymie und Narzissmus in der Enstehung psychosomatischer Krankheiten', in: Kernberg, O.F and Hartmann, H.-P. (2006), *Narzissmus. Grundlagen – Störungsbilder – Therapie,* Stuttgart: Schattauer, pp. 556–569.

Schneider, P. (1973), 'Zum Verhältnis von Psychoanalyse und psychosomatischer Medizin', *Psyche. Zeitschrift für Psychoanalyse und ihre Anwendungen, 27*(1), pp. 21–49.

Stephanos, S. and Auhagen, U. (1979), 'Objektpsychologisches Modell auf der Basis der französischen psychoanalytisch-psychosomatischen Konzepte', in: Hahn, P. ed., *Psychosomatik (= Die Psychologie des 20.*

Jahrhunderts, volume 9: *Ergebnisse für die Medizin* 1), Zürich: Kindler Verlag, pp. 162–181.

Taylor, J.G. (1990), 'La pensée opératoire et le concept d'alexithymie', *Revue Française de Psychanalyse* 54(3), pp. 769–784.

Taylor, J.G. (1995), 'Psychoanalysis and empirical research: The example of patients who lack psychological mindedness, *Journal of the American Academy of Psychoanalysis* 23, pp. 263–281.

Thomä, H. and Kächele H. (2006), *Psychoanalytische Theorie: Praxis*, Heidelberg: Springer Medizin Verlag.

Ulnik, J.R. (2000), 'Revisión crítica de la teoria psicosomática de Pierre Marty', *Aperturas Psiconalíticas. Revista internacional de psicoanálisis* 5, available at: www.aperturas.org/articulos.php?id=121&a=Revision-critica-de-la-teoria-psicosomatica-de-Pierre-Marty

Waintrater, R. (2012), 'Intersubjectivity and French psychoanalysis: A misunderstanding?' *Studies in Gender and Sexuality* 13(4), pp. 295–302.

Wilson, E. (2012), '"Revue Française de Psychanalyse"', *The Psychoanalytic Quarterly* 81, pp. 505–526.

Young, R.M. (1993), 'Psychoanalytic teaching and research', *Free Associations* 4A, pp. 129–137.

Zepf, S. (2000), *Allgemeine psychoanalytische Neurosenlehre, Psychosomatik und Sozialpsychologie: Ein kritisches Lehrbuch,* Gießen: Psychosozial-Verlag.

Zepf, S. and Gattig, E. (1981), 'Kritik der theoretischen Ansätze: "Pensée Opératoire" und andere Konzepte', in: Zepf, S. (1981), *Psychosomatische Medizin auf dem Weg zur Wissenschaft,* Frankfurt/Main: Campus Verlag, pp. 111–144.

2

BACKGROUND

Both in America and in France, psychoanalysts, as their discipline was asserting its presence in medical institutions, increasingly met with patients who of their own accord would not have set foot in a psychoanalyst's consulting room. When Freud was on his historic journey to America, he – according to what Lacan during his stay in Vienna in November 1955 claimed he had heard from Jung – is thought to have joked, 'Little do they know that we are bringing them the pest' (Lacan 1966, p. 403). If pest indeed it was, its spread was meeting new pockets of resistance. A particularly baffling one of these consisted of opposing a life drained of fantasy and dreams to the psychoanalyst's probing touch. Since people who detest being regarded as dysfunctional only talk to a doctor if they must, a psychoanalyst would only see these kinds of patients if they were suffering from grievous bodily ailments which other doctors could not make sense of. Some of the resulting encounters appear to have come as a cultural shock to both sides; with an emotional profile of the meeting so flat it seemed impossibly unreal. 'It was so boring', Bion (1994, p. 25f.) remarked of an apparently similar case, 'that it made me wonder how he did it'. In France, the wondering, when it came, had a particular background, which we should briefly take a look at to understand the debate unfolding there.

When the *SPP* (*Societé Psychanalytique de Paris*) re-emerged following Liberation in 1944, the challenges facing it were formidable. After the devastations of the years under the swastika, and with important bearers of transmission for French psychoanalysis either gone to America (Rudolph Loewenstein and Heinz Hartmann) or dead (Eugénie Sokolnicka and Sophie Morgenstern), it had to start from scratch. There were, in spite of all the difficulties, signs of a pioneer spirit. Outlawed under Nazi rule, it had lost the premises of its former institute. Not only did it have to look for new quarters, it also had to provide itself with a new framework to administer it. A court case in which a lay member of the *SPP* was accused of the illegal exercise of psychotherapy showed that careful consideration had to be given to the question of how best to provide legal certainty for professional legitimacy. Serious tensions began to emerge about who would direct the institute – for which American subsidies were being sought – and with which agenda. There were five people considered key players in the unfolding events: Sacha Nacht, who wanted to insert psychoanalysis into the medical establishment; Daniel Lagache, professor at the Sorbonne, who wanted to establish it in the university and to provide training for the newly emerging discipline of psychologists, a profession for which a new licence was created; Jacques Lacan, who was keenly interested in the most recent stirrings about town of the intelligentsia; Maurice Bouvet, who was a recognised and gifted clinician interested in object relations theory; and Marie Bonaparte, 'the princess', who had a network of international contacts and who favoured lay analysis. Bonaparte was sympathetic towards Lagache as long as his camp would not include Lacan, whom she loathed. When, after intense debate and in-fighting, a group of rebels, rallying around Lagache, failed to win adequate support against Nacht inside the *SPP*, they left on June 16th 1953 to set up an organisation of their own, the *SFP* (*Societé Française de Psychanalyse*). Lacan, who had been under attack for irregularities in his training analyses (with regard to frequency and duration of the sessions), went with them. Bouvet, who could have moved either way, stayed, and later became the training analyst of a number of young analysts who were to shape the future of the *SPP*, among them André Green. The *SFP* had not fully anticipated an international dimension in what to them was a local dispute and had counted on the aid of the princess to mend any eventual frays with the *IPA*, the *International Psychoanalytic Association*, a support that disappointingly was not forthcoming once it was clear that Lacan was with them. A brief attempt by Lacan to build bridges to Melanie Klein (in his eyes a fellow rebel against the Bonaparte-Anna Freud camp) came to nothing because of a basic incompatibility of personalities. In spite of what was sometimes claimed afterwards, ideology formed no sufficient support for the rupture, which was the first split in the history of psychoanalysis, as de Mijolla has pointed out, that was not based on a major doctrinal dissent but on matters of organisation, training and power as the core issues.

In August 1953, the *SPP* was down to thirteen full members. The new *SFP*, at that stage by no account a Lacanian organisation, drew into its ranks many followers of René Laforgue, a charismatic and ambitious training analyst of the old *SPP* (as the first president of which he served in 1926). Born in Alsace, when it formed part of the German Empire before 1918, he was not without good reason suspected by his colleagues, many of whom had ties to the Resistance, of foul play during the Occupation. Although nothing could be proved at the time (relevant evidence was only to emerge from a Berlin archive in the 1980s, long after his death), Laforgue was being cold-shouldered and sidelined, a situation which was much resented by his training analysands, some of them prominent in cultural life, who took the split as an opportunity to settle accounts with the *SPP*. Even before Lacan's rise to public stardom, pressures were forming within French psychoanalytic culture pushing people to take a stand and to articulate their respective positions clearly. It is difficult to understand the thriving of psychoanalysis in the 1960s if one does not take into account the climate of combat that went back to the 1950s: the fight to gain a hearing and to conquer a public led to a flowering of creative output unprecedented in the history of French psychoanalysis.

When the opposition walked out, Nacht, to whom control of the institute reverted, was free to pursue his project of training a future generation of doctors. The institute gained a good reputation for clinical solidity and proceeded to demonstrate the considerable range of the topics it covered in a showcase publication of 1956. Among those who took up the offer which the *SPP* was extending to them were aspiring young graduates, who, in the course of their psychiatric training in their most formative years, found themselves congregating at the Hôpital Sainte-Anne in Paris, a rather special place as a hospital. Operating somewhat outside the regular system, it offered a setup that encouraged independent reasoning and debate, beyond what was then usual at medical faculties. One of the factors which made the place special were the doctor-scholars who taught there, among them Henry Ey, who, though not a psychoanalyst himself, encouraged the young interns to measure themselves against the best minds of their generation.

As an institution, this hospital existed outside the strife of the rival psychoanalytic organisation, functioning as a structural third, setting a high standard of discussion and promoting a rapprochement with Philosophy and the Humanities. If Nacht's project was to thrive, its participants had to be able to give good account of themselves at Sainte-Anne's, a challenge that in general seems to have been taken up by the younger generation of psychiatrists. Ey also convened what could be regarded as the closest approximative equivalent in France to the London Controversial Discussions (1941–1946): the famous 6th *Colloque de Bonneval* in 1960. Several important differences spring to mind: it came seven years after the split had occurred and so could not possibly avert it; it encompassed philosophers of renown, who had gladly accepted the invitation; and it granted public argumentative space to the 'young lions' of the rival organisations who were eager to leave their mark. Interestingly, psychologists were not invited, nor any senior members of the second French psychoanalytic generation (e.g. Nacht and Lagache). Lacan was denied an exposé but was admitted as a mere participant. In the course of the meetings, there was heated controversy and ferocious, impassioned debate. Green, for one, derived from it the impression of the intellectual weakness of his own camp and decided to attend Lacan's seminar. Green's participation in Lacan's seminar was based on what in retrospect can be recognised as a mutual illusion, the erroneous idea that Green's interrogations in Lacanian thinking-space could somehow lead to interesting convergences. Green followed his teaching until 1967, when Lacan's attempts to bring him to heel failed. Three years after this, Green presented a comprehensive account of the core issue of affect in psychoanalytic theory at the *Congrès des psychanalystes de langues romanes* in Paris, taking into account both the work of Freud and the post-Freudians. It was published in 1973, further augmented, under the title *Le discours vivant*, echo of a dialogue that clearly had broken down between Green and Lacan, but which was to influence further developments. Language, in Green's view, is important, but cannot be held to reign supreme. Lived experience constantly chases after representation without ever catching up with it. What Green did was to provide, as Bion might have put it, a conceptual apparatus for thoughts that had so far largely lacked a thinker in France. Green states (Duparc 1995) that his works could be read as a kind of autobiography. If this is so, it is also representative of the itinerary of a generation, which, in an exciting climate of debate, was faced with another version of Paris' choice between putting a prime on clinical probity (Nacht/

Bouvet), academic possibility (Lagache), or cultural and intellectual prowess (Lacan).

For two young analysts from the *SFP*, Jean Laplanche and Jean-Bertrand Pontalis, the aftermath of the Colloquium led to a number of difficulties with Lacan, who was dissatisfied with the increasingly independent formulations they were proposing. Laplanche, looking back, pointedly remarked that thinking, if it was truly alive, had to be open to emerging problems and could not confine itself to prolonging a master's thought. This was a freedom that, once gained, would have to be defended. He was not alone in his stance: the *SFP* found it increasingly difficult to accommodate Lacan, who continued to take up an ever-increasing number of analysands for ever shorter sessions and with decreased frequency. In 1963/1964 the *SFP* split into the *APF* (*Association Psychanalytique de France*), which joined the *IPA*, and into the *EFP* (the *École Freudienne de Paris*), which Lacan proclaimed with the following words: 'I am [hereby] founding – alone as I have always been in my relation to the psychoanalytic cause – the *École Française de Psychanalyse*' (de Mijolla 1982, p. 101f.). With Lacan on his own path to new peaks of renown, the *APF* in its further course, while mindful of a Lacanian strand to its heritage, successfully continued pursuing Lagache's project of inserting psychoanalysis into academic faculties.

In a rival development, at Louis Althusser's invitation, Lacan held his seminar at the *Ecole Normale Supérieure*, which extended his audience to a non-medical public. The publication of his *Écrits* in 1966 exploded public interest. When, from 1968, Lacan published his own journal *Scilicet*, only his own articles were signed while contributions by others had to remain anonymous. As a consequence of conceptual difficulties with Lacan – who was, as Pierre Marty observed (Marty and Nicolaïdis 1996), given to making fun of everything in human exchange that did not belong to the order of language – a number of French psychoanalysts who were not aligned with Lacan were becoming increasingly interested in British psychoanalysis, which offered an approach worlds apart from Lacan's. When Pontalis founded the *Nouvelle Revue de Psychanalyse* – the first volume was published in Spring 1970 – the editorial board comprised (among others) not only Didier Anzieu (from the *APF*) but also André Green (from the *SPP*), Masud Khan, who provided a link to London, and Jean Starobinski, a renowned scholar from outside the world of psychoanalytic associations. Turning to Winnicott it was easier to make allowances for a 'prequel' to fantasy life, which was required if desire was to be ignited and to find inner representation. Arguing their new insights against Lacan and the Lacanian upsurge, and as their thought was developing, in many cases against each other, they produced publications that were offering a wealth of thought packed into formidably dense presentations.

When Pierre Marty together with Michel Fain, Michel De M'Uzan and Christian David founded the *EPP* (*École Psychosomatique de Paris*) in 1962, this initiative fitted in well with the general outline of the developments portrayed above. Based on the contributions of members of the *SPP*, it can be seen as a logical diversification of Nacht's project to insert psychoanalysis into contemporary medicine, which further developed and reworked pre-existing threads of thinking about the pre-verbal and about relationships between body and mind, which Nacht had already been interested in. It made a meaningful statement on the extralinguistic prerequisites of affect, and it paid attention to the dynamics of the fantasmatic, to which, about the same time, Laplanche and Pontalis were devoting a seminal article in 1964, to be later released in reworked form as a booklet under the title *Fantasme originaire. Fantasme des origines. Origines du fantasme* (1985). While it did not deny the importance of language, it tended to pay more attention to the qualitative framework of early interactions.

The *École Psychosomatique de Paris*, for its part, tried to provide tangible answers to questions addressed to psychoanalysts working in hospitals by their non-psychoanalytic medical colleagues, and followed up issues previously raised by respected figures like Henri Ey and Julian de Ajuriaguerra. It thus offered, albeit in idiosyncratic form, a performative platform, which crystallised a number of concerns important to contemporary French psychoanalysis in its non-Lacanian strands. The *EPP* went about its self-appointed task by looking at cases of personal turmoil sunken into the body without traces of symbolic ripples or even affective storms emerging on the surface. In this way, the *EPP* also claimed territory that Lacan had arguably left unoccupied because it did not partake of the orders of the symbolic. It would tally well with reflections about to be developed by Didier Anzieu (*APF*) that mental activity required '*A Skin for Thought*', a mental epidermis which enabled thought to breathe, as it were.

There was some discernible convergence with concerns pursued by Piera Aulagnier, who together with others in protest about training regulations passed in accordance with Lacan's wishes, left the *EFP* to set up their own group, *Le Quatrième Groupe*, to safeguard what they regarded as the essentials in the transmission of psychoanalytic competence.

As matters were developing, French psychoanalysis from the 1960s went through a crisis fuelled by its unprecedented growth. By the 1970s psychoanalysis in France was reaching an ever-widening public. Its apparent success led Didier Anzieu (1976) to warn that psychoanalysis was becoming a victim of its own success, something that would have been called 'victory disease' by the Japanese in World War II. Reading Anzieu's lines, it is easy to see that some psychoanalysts might have experienced the *opératoire* as a counter-insurgency to a resistance movement they themselves were quite successfully running against a mindless status quo:

> I would also like to say how much psychoanalysis in its very practice constitutes a silent critique and an active resistance to certain aberrations of the industrial civilisation. To set apart three quarters of an hour several times a week for someone to attentively listen to him/her speak about himself/herself in complete freedom is an oasis that it is more and more impossible to find in our century infatuated with speed, output, and the proliferation of material objects.
>
> (Anzieu 1976, p. 145)

In keeping with his approach, Anzieu refers to interdisciplinary discussions between historians and psychologists on the phenomenon of crisis viewed on both a social and a personal level. For a crisis not to be wasted, a stable framework was required that permitted all the various *pulsions* (in individual life) and political movements (in public life) to come into play.

Many psychoanalysts were working long hours. For them contact with those developments was primarily mediated by their patients: 'For years I have been frequenting only psychoanalysts, how should I know what a normal being is?' asked Joyce McDougall (1972, p. 345) somewhat provocatively. If society was changing, it was patients who would most effectively be the message bearers to their analysts. Not all the meetings went according to expectations, or, indeed, made any sense at all.

In *L'Investigation psychosomatique* (1963), the authors described the sort of meeting any psychoanalyst secretly dreaded: a patient, who had been referred by a non-psychoanalytic colleague because something beyond bodily ailments was seriously out of kilter, but whose emotional profile, for all his/her troubles, seemed to be as arid as the desert. Marty, Michel de M'Uzan and David described in 1963 the encounter in a by now classic description:

> The investigator cannot but be struck by how little relational interest – in the usual sense of the term – he seems to arouse in the patient and by the little amount of nuance and differentiation involved in the way in which he is being apprehended by him. Their relation does not give rise to any real elaboration, nor does it seem to be susceptible to being transformed into a dynamic whole which would assure its advancement. It is static and fragmented to a large measure. In its most pure forms the patient tends to respond mechanically, without expecting anything, it seems, but an automatic play of stimulus and response.
> (Marty, Michel de M'Uzan and David, 1963, p. 12)

It is as if the Charlie Chaplin of *Modern Times*, freshly spewn out of the factory conveyor belt, had entered the consulting room. French psychoanalysis was discovering the world of normopathy (or, as Bollas (1987) termed it, the normotic) as if the dire visions of Adorno and Horkheimer (Adorno (1951, p. 57): 'with many people it is already an act of impertinence when they say 'I') had struck their clinical territory with full force.

Incidentally, Marty and his colleagues published their *Investigation* one year before Herbert Marcuse (1964), in a book that at the times enjoyed considerable success, put forward his views on 'one-dimensional man', an individual who lacked critical distance to what existed and seemed to be unaware of the as yet undeveloped potential of the moment: things that might be, which one might toss around in one's mind, although they are not real. Although Marcuse approaches things from a different angle, there is some overlapping territory. How is it possible that a subject is not deeply stirred by what is befalling him/her? It is the many different facets that analysts discern in these encounters that makes the work of the *EPP* so remarkable: the observations they record turn them into cartographers of lost inner worlds at the very opposite of hysteria, dramatic in their resounding absences.

In their goal of mapping these uncharted inner spaces, they developed new conceptual categories, which described strangely un-neurotic morphologies: depression without inner objects that was traceable only through a haemorrhage of energy (*dépression essentielle*); mechanical thinking (*pensée opératoire*) which exhausted itself in compiling, as it were, endless inner shopping lists; and waves of inner destabilisation that overwhelmed all possible defensive points of fixation (*désorganisations progressives*). All of them seemed to be connected to deficiencies in the work of the preconscious and, as a consequence, a striking lack of what they termed *mentalisation*.

In the medium turn, this perspective fitted in well with an increasing concern for inter- and transgenerational phenomena within French psychoanalysis which made itself felt from the 1970s. Clearly, not all of the problems which patients were caught up in started with themselves. François Vigoroux (1993), for one, has provided insight into how a family may be locked into repetitions of a destructive pattern for generations, until one day, changed circumstances permit significant change. It is only then that it becomes possible for an outsider to hear the testimony of the past transmuted.

Over the years, the *Societé Psychanalytique de Paris* developed a network of institutions geared towards providing psychoanalytic consultations and/or treatments, among them the *Centre de consultations et de traitements psychanalytiques Jean Favreau* in Paris; the *Centre de psychanalyse et de psychothérapie E. et J. Kestemberg*, with a special focus on patients presenting with psychoses or grave personality disorders; and the *Centre Alfred Binet*, with a focus on children and adolescents. The latter two belong to the network of services offered by *ASM 13*, the *Association de santé mentale du 13e arrondissement de Paris*. It is not rare to see the children once treated, return, in case of difficulties, as adults. Steven Wainrib (2006) speaks of a *psychanalyse diversifiée*, which has taken up psychoanalytic work not only with individuals but also with families.

Perhaps all of this had an accumulated effect on the nature of the inquiries Marty's group had launched. Although the main emphasis was that some inner interface – the preconscious – was not serving the patient well, there increasingly crept in questions that added another angle: granted an interface *within* the patient was doing strange things, what about the interface *to* the patient? Marty, de M'Uzan and David had thought that matters were sufficiently complicated as they saw them, yet, given some time, they were due to become even more complicated.

Sources

Adorno, T.W. (1951), *Minima moralia*, Frankfurt am Main: Suhrkamp Verlag.
Aisenstein, M. (2018), 'De l'influence implicite de Lacan', *Revue Française de Psychanalyse* 82(4), pp. 1013–1020.
Angelergues, J. (2006), 'Le psychanalyste, consultant de service public?' in: Perron, R. ed., *Psychanalystes qui êtes vous?* Paris: Dunod, pp. 63–68.
Anzieu, D. (1976), 'Devenir psychanalyste aujourd'hui', in: Favez, G., Anzieu, D., Anzieu, A., Berry, N., Pontalis, J.-B. and Smirnoff, V.N., *Être psychanalyste*, Paris: Dunod, pp. 117–147.
Anzieu, D. (1990) *A skin for thought. Interviews with Gilbert Tarab*, London: Karnac.
Baldacci, J-L. (2006), 'La psychanalyse dans la cité', in: Perron, R. ed., *Psychanalystes qui êtes vous?* Paris: Dunod, pp. 49–55.
Barande, I. and Barande, R. (1975), *Histoire de la psychanalyse en France*, Toulouse: Editeur Edouard Privat.
Baranes, J.J. (2002), 'Transgénérationnel et adolescence', available at: www.spp.asso.fr/transgenerationnel-et-adolescence/
Benvenuto, S. and Green, A. (1994), 'Against Lacanism. A conversation of André Green with Sergio Benvenuto', *Journal of European Psychoanalysis. Humanities, Philosophy, Psychotherapies* 2.
Bion, W.R. (1994), *Clinical seminars and other works,* Bion, F. ed., London: Karnac Books.
Birksted-Breen, D. and Flanders, S. (2010), 'General introduction', in: Birksted-Breen, D., Gibeault, A. and Flanders, S. eds, *Reading French psychoanalysis*, London: Routledge, pp. 1–59.
Bollas, C. (1987), *The shadow of the object. Psychoanalysis of the unthought known*, London: Free Association Books.
Chemouni, J. (1991), *Histoire de la psychanalyse en France*, Paris: Presses Universitaires de France.
Chiland, C. ed. (1981), *Les ecoles psychanalytiques. La psychanalyse en mouvement*, Paris: Tchou.
Chiland, C. (1990), *Homo psychanalyticus*, Paris: Presses Universitaires de France.

de Mijolla, A. (1982), 'La psychanalyse en France (1893–1965)', in: Jaccard, R. ed., *Histoire de la psychanalyse*, volume 2, Paris: Hachard.
de Mijolla, A. (1989), 'Documents inédits. Les psychanalystes en France durant l'occupation allemande, Paris, novembre 1943', *Revue Internationale d'Histoire de la Psychanalyse* 2, pp. 463–473.
de Mijolla, A. (1995), 'Les scissions dans le mouvement psychanalytique français de 1953 à 1964', *Topique* 57, pp. 271–290.
de Mijolla, A. (1996), 'La scission de la Société Psychanalytique de Paris en 1953, quelques notes pour un rappel historique', *Cliniques méditerranéennes* 49–50, pp. 9–30, also available at: www.spp.asso.fr/textes/la-scission-de-la-societe-psychanalytique-de-paris-en-1953-quelques-notes-pour-un-rappel-historique/?print=pdf
de Mijolla, A. (2002), 'Psychanalyse et histoire: leur "intérêt" commun', in: Botella, C. ed., *Penser les limites. Écrits en l'honneur d'André Green*, Paris: Delachaux et Niestlé, pp. 294–304.
de Mijolla, A. (2003), 'Psychoanalysis and Psychoanalysts in France between 1939 and 1945', *International Forum of Psychoanalysis* 12, pp. 136–156.
de Mijolla, A. (2007), 'Petite histoire d'une histoire de la psychanalyse en France', *Topique* 98, pp. 37–47.
de Mijolla, A. (2010a), *Freud et la France, 1885–1945*, Paris: Presses Universitaires de France.
de Mijolla, A. (2010b), 'Some distinctive features of the history of psychoanalysis in France', in: Birksted-Breen, D., Gibeault A. and Flanders, S. eds, *Reading French psychoanalysis*, London: Routledge, pp. 60–72.
de Mijolla, A. (2010c), Interview in: '*Tout arrive*' (Radio France Culture), broadcast 8 March 2010.
de Mijolla, A. (2012a), *La France et Freud*, volume 1: *1946–1953. Une pénible renaissance*, Paris: Presses Universitaires de France.
de Mijolla, A. (2012b), *La France et Freud*, volume 2: *1954–1964. D'une scission à l'autre*, Paris: Presses Universitaires de France.
Denis, P. (1971), 'Les sociétés françaises affiliées à l'association psychanalytique internationale', in: Chiland, C. (1981) ed., *Les ecoles psychanalytiques. La psychanalyse en mouvement*, Paris: Tchou, pp. 179–191.
Diatkine, G. (1997), *Jacques Lacan (Psychanalystes d'aujourd'hui* 11), Paris: Presses Universitaires de France.
Diatkine, G. (2006), 'Que doit le succès de la psychanalyse française à Lacan?' in: Perron, R. ed., *Psychanalystes qui êtes vous?* Paris: Dunod, pp. 245–250.
Diener, Y. (2002a), *La psychanalyse*, volume. 1, Paris: ADPF.
Diener, Y. (2002b), *La psychanalyse*, volume. 2, Paris: ADPF.

Duparc, F. (1995), *Une théorie vivante. L'oeuvre d'André Green*, Neuchâtel and Paris: Delachaux et Niestlé.

Duparc, F. (1996), *André Green (Psychanalystes d'aujourd'hui 2)*, Paris: Presses Universitaires de France.

Fages, J.-B. (1996), *Histoire de la psychanalyse après Freud*, Paris: Éditions Odile Jacob.

Fansten, M. (2006), *Le divan insoumis. La formation du psychanalyste: enjeux et idéologies*, Paris: Hermann Éditeurs.

Fansten, M. (2013), 'Présences et absences de la psychanalyse à Cerisy, *Histoire @ Politique* 20, pp. 59–71.

Forrester, J. (1997), *Dispatches from the Freud wars. Psychoanalysis and its passions*, Cambridge, MA: Harvard University Press.

Gekle, H. (1986), *Wunsch und Wirklichkeit. Blochs Philosophie des Noch-Nicht-Bewußten und Freuds Theorie des Unbewußten*, Frankfurt am Main: Suhrkamp.

Gibeault, A. (2006), 'Le centre de psychanalyse et de psychothérapie E. et J. Kestemberg', in: Perron, R. ed., *Psychanalystes qui êtes vous?* Paris: Dunod, pp. 57–62.

Green, A. (1973), *Le discours vivant. La conception psychanalytique de l'affect*, Paris: Presses Universitaires de France.

Green, A. (1994), *Un psychanalyste engagé. Conversations avec Manuel Macias*, Paris: Calmann-Lévy.

Green, A. (2006), *Associations (presque) libres d'un psychanalyste. Entretiens avec Maurice Corcos*, Paris: Albin Michel.

Green, A. (2013), *Penser la psychanalyse avec Bion, Lacan, Winnicott, Laplanche, Aulagnier, Anzieu, Rosolato*, L. Guttierres-Green ed., Paris: Les Éditions d'Ithaque.

Heenen-Wolff, S. (2007), 'Wichtige Strömungen in der französischen Psychoanalyse', *Forum der Psychoanalyse* 23(4), pp. 364–378.

Jackson, J.E. (1991), *De l'affect à la pensée. Introduction à l'oeuvre d'André Green*, Paris: Mercure de France.

Jalley, É. (2006), *La psychanalyse et la psychologie aujourd'hui en France*, Paris: Vuibert.

Jalley, E. (2008), *La guerre de la psychanalyse,* volume 1: *Hier, aujourd'hui, demain*, Paris: L'Harmattan.

Kohon, G. (1999), *The dead mother. The work of André Green*, London and New York: Routledge.

Kristeva, J. (2000), *Le génie féminin*, volume 2: *Melanie Klein*, Paris: Gallimard.

Kurzweil, E. (1989), *The Freudians. A comparative perspective*, New Haven: Yale University Press.

Lacan, J. (1966), *Écrits*, Paris: Éditions du Seuil.
Lagache, D. (1949), 'Institut de Psychanalyse', *Revue Française de Psychanalyse* 13(3), p. 447.
Langlitz, N. (2005), *Die Zeit in der Psychoanalyse. Lacan und das Problem der Sitzungsdauer*, Frankfurt am Main: Suhrkamp.
Laplanche, J. and Pontalis, J.-B. (1985), *Fantasme originaire. Fantasme des origines. Origines du fantasme*, Paris: Hachette Littératures.
Lassmann, W. (2013), 'Intergenerational transmission of influence and family pattern: Some French perspectives', *British Journal of Psychotherapy* 29(1), pp. 75–97.
Lézé, S. (2010), *L'autorité des psychanalystes*, Paris: Presses Universitaires de France.
Marcuse, H. (1964), *One-dimensional man. Studies in the ideology of advanced industrial society*, 2nd edition 1991, Boston: Beacon Press.
Marini, M. (1992), *Jacques Lacan. The French context*, New Brunswick: Rutgers University Press.
Marty, P. and Nicolaïdis, N. (1996), *Psychosomatique. Pensée vivante*, Bordeaux: L'Esprit du Temps.
Marty, P., de M'Uzan, M. and David C. (2003/1963), *L'investigation psychosomatique. Sept observations cliniques*, 2nd edition, Paris: Presses Universitaires de France.
McDougall, J. (1972), 'Plaidoyer pour une certaine anormalité', *Revue française de psychanalyse* 36(3), pp. 345–358.
Nacht, S. ed. (1956), *La psychanalyse d'aujourd'hui*, 2 volumes, Paris: Presses Universitaires de France.
Ohayon, A. (2006/1999), *Psychologie et psychanalyse en France. L'impossible rencontre (1919–1969)*, 2nd edition, Paris: Èditions La Découverte.
Ohayon, A. (2015), 'Psychanalyse et sciences humaines dans les années 1950, débats ouverts, débats clos', in: Perron, R. and Missonier, S. eds, *Sigmund Freud*, Paris: Éditions de L'Herne, pp. 320–326.
Pontalis, J.-B. (1986), *L'amour des commencements*, Paris: Gallimard.
Richard, F. and Urribarri, F. (2005), *Autour de l'oeuvre d'André Green. Enjeux pour une psychanalyse conemporain*, Paris: Presses Universitaires de France.
Roudinesco, E. (1986), *Histoire de la psychanalyse en France 2: 1925–1985*, 2nd edition 1994 Paris: Fayard.
Roudinesco, E. (1993), *Jacques Lacan. Esquisse d'une vie, histoire d'un système de pensée*, Paris: Fayard.
Sparer, E.A. (2010), 'The French model at work: Indication and the Jean Favreau Centre for Consultation and Treatment', *International Journal of Psychoanalysis* 91(5), pp. 1179–1199.

Stephan, J.J. (2002), *Hawaii under the Rising Sun. Japan's plans for conquest after Pearl Harbor*, Honolulu: University of Hawaii Press.
Troisier, H. (1998), *Piera Aulagnier (Psychanalystes d'aujourd'hui* 17), Paris: Presses Universitaires de France.
Turkle, S. (1978/1992), *Psychoanalytic politics. Jacques Lacan and Freud's French Revolution*, New York: The Guilford Press.
Urribarri, F. (2008), 'Après Lacan: père, pacte fraternel et filiation analytique chez André Green', in: Cupa, D. (2008), *Image du père dans la culture contemporaine. Hommages à André Green*, Paris: Presses Universitaires de France, pp. 53–63.
Urribarri, F. (2013), *Dialoguer avec André Green. La psychanalyse contemporaine, chemin faisant*, Paris: Les Éditions d'Ithaque.
Vigoroux, F. (1993), *Le secret de famille*, Paris: Presses Universitaires de France.
Wainrib, S. (2006), 'Subjectivation ou conditionnement?', in: Perron, R. ed., *Psychanalystes qui êtes-vous?*, Paris: Dunod, pp. 13–17.
Widlöcher, D. (1997), *La psyche carrefour*, Genève: Georg Éditeur.
Widlöcher, D. (2004), 'Psychanalyse et psychiatrie française. 50 ans d'histoire', *Topique* 88, pp. 7–16.
Widlöcher, D. (2010), 'What has become of the lines of advance in psychoanalysis? The evolution of practices in France', in: Birksted-Breen, D., Gibeault, A. and Flanders, S. eds, *Reading French psychoanalysis*, London, pp. 73–85.

3

FOUNDATIONS 1
Pierre Marty

In one of his articles, Gerard Szwec recalls having heard Pierre Marty talk about an intervention with a particular patient:

> There was a situation in which I found myself saying to a patient who was telling me how he had refrained from replying to an aggression directed against him, 'You know, I, myself, act in another way; if someone steps on my foot on the underground, I feel like killing him. Sure, I do not kill him! But I am furious, I draw a face, sulk, and after a while, I get angry with myself and find excuses for him. He did not do it on purpose. But no matter what, he did hurt me and I recognise that at this moment I felt like killing him. But that is me, and I am not you.
> (Szwec 2008, p. 25)

Prudently, Marty refrains from suggesting that this is what the patient was feeling, or would have liked to feel, or should better have felt. As Marty sees it, he/she may in fact be quite unable to feel anything of the sort and instead be confounded by his/her inability to come up with a proper response. Telling the patient about himself, he extends the range of possible emotions imaginable without recommending them. Szwec would most likely have heard this vignette in the 1980s or early 1990s, when Marty had had decades of experience and ample time to reflect on the approach he would take with patients hiding fragilities behind a bland surface. His clinical angle, as Szwec stresses, demands of the practitioner no less than adopting the prudence of the mine-clearer.

In this chapter I shall trace how Marty evolved his positions and the way this laid the foundation for the rise and further development of the group that formed around it.

Beginnings and cursus vitae: from neurosurgery to psychoanalysis

As a child, Marty remembers, the illnesses afflicting members of his family had caused him a lot of anxiety. A philosophy professor at school encouraged him to study medicine and then to specialise in psychiatry. He practised neurosurgery with the First Army at the end of the war. As a psychiatrist he started out with an organicist perspective. It was Julián de Ajuriaguerra who one day took him aside, giving him a piece of very straightforward advice: 'Old chap, I say, you will never understand anything without psychoanalysis' (Marty 1996[1991], p. 19). In 1947 Marty entered psychoanalysis with Marc Schlumberger, joined the *SPP*, first as an associate member in 1950, and then as a full member in 1952. Marty married Simone Fain, sister of his friend and colleague Michel Fain, whom he had known from their days at the *lycée*, when they had been schoolmates.

In early 1953 Lacan, president of the *SPP* at the time, chose him as his secretary, a function he held at the time of the historic split. Remaining on Nacht's side, whom he held in great esteem, and yet, until the split, in place as Lacan's secretary on the board, he experienced the most spectacular colitis of his life. A long-time sufferer from allergies, and with close relatives from different branches of the family suffering from asthma, he was always fascinated by what seemed to him their shared characteristics beyond all noticeable differences. Freshly operated on for double cataracts, he had to wear dark glasses, when Lacan, on one occasion wished to see him. Lacan took his changed appearance as a portent in their relationship, while Marty, without much success providing background information, emphasised its separate context, an anecdote perhaps emblematic of their deeper theoretical differences. As he was working on *L'investigation psychosomatique*, his wife, with whom in December 1962 he had prepared a radio feature on *L'art tauromachique et la psychanalyse*, was dying of cancer. Marty did not remarry.

From 1961, he served as vice president of the *SPP*, whose president he became in 1969 (a position he held until 1970). From 1967, having assembled a core of collaborators, Marty ran a centre of psychosomatic consultations in a location in Rue Falguière that had served as a treatment centre for venereal diseases. Its tiled floors had remained in place as a constant reminder of its former function in its battle for hygiene. Now it became a place for teaching, supervision and for seeing psychosomatic patients. Work was organised around the consultations Marty held there twice a week. The team met with Pierre Marty once a week to discuss current patient interviews. This day clinic operated until 1978. One of the inconveniences of the situation was that the previous administration was a continuing source of irritating interference. On the advice of the Directorate for Health and the Paris Prefecture, Marty prepared to set up a non-profit association that would provide a legal framework for further activities. Philippe Paumelle, who, with Serge Lebovici and René Diatkine, had in 1958 put on the rails the *ASM 13* – a pilot project for what later became implemented as the sectorisation policy in psychiatry – assisted in the planning. On 26 December 1972 *l'Institut de Psychosomatique* (*IPSO*) was created. Michel Alliot, former chief of staff of Edgar Faure in the Department of Education, was asked to become president of *IPSO*, and accepted after he had had time to vet the project with the doyens of the Faculty of Medicine, clearing various administrative hurdles that had existed before. In 1978 the *Hôpital de la Poterne des Peupliers* was opened (later named the *Hôpital Pierre Marty*) and Marty was invited to open a care unit for psychosomatic patients. In 2004 their structures were integrated into the *ASM 13*.

Early work: muscular armour and posture control as tools in distance management

At the time of Marty's internship in psychiatry, the only disease that seemed to affect *les aliénés* – as the sectioned patients were called – to a significant degree was pulmonary tuberculosis. Together with Michel Fain, in one of their earliest papers together, Marty looked into what could be gleaned of the psychodynamics and personality structure of more than one hundred post-cure tuberculosis patients. They found that patients who strictly moved only within their personal zone of security healed more rapidly and did not relapse. Physically moving away from the mother was used to supplement more neurotic measures of distance maintenance avoiding a break-up with their families. To maintain a personal equilibrium, they found, was of supreme importance to the individual, more important even than shunning death. Marty and Fain's tentative attempts to connect the development of pulmonary tuberculosis to underlying mental structures were met with little sympathy by at least one important member of the *SPP*: Marie Bonaparte. Her daughter had had pulmonary tuberculosis and this did not predispose her favourably to envisaging connections between somatic disease and mental structure.

Looking at the modulation of physical distance in the face of a difficulty to manage inner distance to an object were difficult to manage was one way to probe the feeble points of an individual's mental conflict management. Soon similar phenomena drew the authors' attention. In studying patients with chronic headaches, Marty and Fain noticed the frequent presence of a painful interdiction of thought. Reading Thomas M. French's 1941 paper, they were struck by the observation that even in their dreams some patients suffering from frontal headaches were loath to envisage the free movement of figures, whom, instead, they had to freeze into motionless states. In an extended congress paper in 1954 they presented, from an object relations perspective, their reflections on the complicated relationship between the exercise of motor skills (*motricité*) and the rise of fantasy. The maturation of motor skills, they reflected, ensures contact, while at the same time permitting the infant progressively to regulate distance. The register of movement is being adapted and fine-tuned in close identification with the moves and glances of the mother. Once internal objects have been established, things complexify further. Social reality usually works towards a heightened amount of interiorisation and social links are shared in reference to a common *idéal du Moi*. Tackling external objects, Marty and Fain suggested, can take pressure off the need to deal with internal objects. Underneath the incorporated images of the satisfying, good object there is likely to be some residual toxic core of frustration. It is vital that early integration under the eye of the mother enable the infant to keep the need for immediate discharge in abeyance. This build-up of a capacity to defer action provides space for the elaboration of thought and fantasy.

As Marty and Fain put it, the primal scene may reverberate through the body, although the cinema of fantasy may still be closed. If things go well for the infant, primary narcissistic identification, also working towards an inner corporal image, will achieve an amount of integration that will make the later elaboration of fantasy more feasible, even though fantasy may at times be hard put to serve as a buffer mechanism sufficiently capable to absorb the excitement generated by object relations. At the most archaic level of defence the subject lives a fantasy by channelling a response directly into motor action. With not enough mental holding structure, nascent fantasy may well be felt to be a useless excrement. This, then, presents a quandary: since impressions cannot be elaborated sufficiently by taking action on them, their continued inflow becomes persecutory. If motor action is the means of choice to process external reality, muscles in an impasse yet have to be restrained in painful contracture. Marty and Fain notice with interest Wilhelm Reich's work on the muscular armour, and importance of the form of expression over its particular contents, but diverge in the ways they put this to use in clinical thinking. Ideally, the authors suggest, their work could be a step towards a *physiologie objectale*, which would place the development of expressive forms in a field in which maturation and object relations interact. In clinical work it may be the identification with the psychoanalyst and his/her interest in the patient's bodily movements that opens them up to increased understanding.

Elements of interactional expression beyond language

In the discussion on the authors' contribution, Sacha Nacht stressed that the dialogue analyst-patient, though language bound, was in reality taking place on a level beyond language, including, notably, emotions, something also noted by Ajuriaguerra, who underlines that the authors permit a glimpse of the first lineaments of tonus and emotion – a 'dialogue body to body' – in the management of distance, an essential precondition for possible identifications that cannot thrive in its absence. René Diatkine regarded it as the task of the psychoanalysts of his generation to integrate their discipline into a larger perspective of neurobiological development and welcomed the authors' contribution as a very interesting step in such integration. Not surprisingly, in a parting shot after his dissociation from the *SPP*, Lacan [1956] singled out Marty and Fain's contribution as an example of what in his view was amiss with his former colleagues' understanding of psychoanalysis: too much attention to the 'real' elements in the relationship that deterred from imaginary constructions pursued by the patient, a line of attack which, despite their personal and ideological antagonism, shared elements with Marie Bonaparte's barbed comments on the paper: to her the interpretation of gestures and postures smacked of 'hyper-interpretation'. In their concluding response to the discussion Marty and Fain explained that they were thinking of clinical examples in which it was not a certain way of thinking that caused a symptom, but rather incapacity to think. It was a Belgian analyst, Fernand Lechat, who in his intervention contrasted patients who refused contact with those who were pathologically incapable of it:

> these types of individuals offer only colourless and monotonous verbal associations, which are nothing but the evocation of memories that seem to belong to another person's history and are only provided to obey the rules of the game.
> (Lechat 1955[1954], p. 291)

This was a problem to which Marty and Fain would return in due course with contributions of their own.

Object capture

If resorting to physical action pre-empts the emergence of fantasies as long as the person is absorbed in this action (Marie Bonaparte (1955[1954]) recalls Henri Bergson's reflection that action clogs representation), striving for near complete fusion with an object is another kind of recourse that enables the subject not to dwell on any shortcomings the moment might otherwise reveal. In his 1958 paper, Marty turns to a particular mode of negotiating distance he has frequently found with patients suffering from allergies: the attempt to merge completely with an object that, once within reach, has to be captured and managed as a quasi-annexed compound of the self. In this instance, distinction between good and bad object does not matter, what is important is the availability of an object that can be assimilated to the personal ideal of oneself. Marty (1958[1957], p. 8) reports the statement of a patient with eczema: 'I cannot live in myself; I cannot live unless united with another person'. There is a crisis if the host object evinces a quality that does not fit the task assigned to it: this is experienced like a loss of oneself. Although the Me may theoretically be weak, it does not appear to be so in practice, as long as there is an object to fuse with. Objects, to some extent, are interchangeable. Often an object is kept in reserve to fall back upon in case of need. Analysis that purely addresses the neurotic screen will not get into contact with the non-neurotic core structure. This situation requires careful consideration on the part of the psychoanalyst.

A new manifesto of psychosomatic investigation in the face of under-investigated lifestyles

In 1963 Pierre Marty, Michel de M'Uzan and Christian David published what was soon recognised as the manifesto of a new approach in psychoanalytic thinking about psychosomatic patients: *L'investigation psychosomatique*. It had a considerable impact and became one of the founding documents of a new clinical platform: the *École de Paris de Psychosomatique* (*EPP*). At its centre the study put the transcripts of interviews with seven patients in a hospital setting in front of an audience of assistants comprising on average six to eight participants. Considerable thought had been invested in the particular setting: no table was placed between doctor and patient; the assistants were seated in clear view of the patient, as was a secretary, who took down what was being said in shorthand. The examination was prolonged, taking always longer than one hour. Patients had been referred to this consultation either by other hospital services or by a local practitioner: seeing a psychoanalyst was not a wish they might have come up with on their own, but was done on doctor's orders. Sometimes, but not always, the patient had been given some preparatory information on the nature and purpose of the consultation. The transcripts of the interviews were provided with copious footnotes to explain what the investigator was doing at each moment. The investigator on occasion addressed the assisting audience directly to point out, in the presence of the patient, what had so far been learned of his/her mental structure. In addition to this, each patient interview was put into further perspective by a commentary at the end of the respective section. An introduction acquainted the reader with the theoretical perspective adopted in the investigations and a conclusion proposed a preliminary take on the yields of the procedure. Early on the authors argued that the material they collected placed types of personality into the centre of scrutiny which had hitherto received too little attention,

> or, more exactly, forms of life, which, as widespread as they may be, as trivial as they may appear, nevertheless, we believe, remain little known and little explored in spite of the human interest they arouse.
>
> (Marty, de M'Uzan and David 2003/1963, p. 3)

To come to terms with this, the investigators probed the subject's defensive style, adaptive means, and capacity for object relations, as evidenced in the unusual situation encountered in the interview. Resorting to established behavioural routines to shield against what could not be mentally digested was understood as but a brittle line of defence that, when breached, had to be bolstered by somatic symptoms. One of the apparent worries of the investigators was that the possible disappearance of a symptom might wreak havoc on the total stability of the subject. To take this into consideration they proposed an economic viewpoint that strove to assess functional equivalents within the energy budget of a person. If well-directed energy was a measure of mobilisation by the outer and inner object world, loss of this level of integration would lead to deterioration in the quality of its articulation. What we might encounter then, in more diffuse form, was a tendency towards muscular contraction or a scanning for sensory stimuli as an external attractor to latch onto. In this view, somatic problems were part of a larger picture: the focus was on the person's habitual ways of handling him/herself and his/her relationships, rather than on the disease as a separate entity. Within a given economy of mental means, even hypochondria might be too organised a state of mind to be within easy reach of the patient. Building on earlier papers of Marty's, there was a noticeable interest in headaches as a conduit for aggressive tension that had not otherwise found expression, and a sensitivity towards fusional tendencies in object relations. Maurice Bouvet, whom we have encountered earlier, had taken an interest in the parameters of 'object distance' that a given patient was most comfortable with: Marty, a lifelong devotee of the *corrida*, the Spanish bullfight, was keenly interested in the way patients made use of the arena they found themselves thrust into, after previous, prolonged exposure to the more familiar behavioural codes of the institutionalised medical care system.

> Everyone tries to understand what the bull does: what it loves and what it seeks, what it flees from, its going quiet, its silences, its brutal discharges, the evolution of its rhythm, its sense of attack and of defence, its means of expression, its reserve or its final fight.
>
> (Marty and Marty 1962, p. 9)

Towards understanding fragile personality structure: business as usual as a front

What could be observed in the context of one particular public hearing was treated as an X-ray picture of the subject's potential to handle him/herself in the inner and outer worlds and as an indispensable guide for therapeutic choices to be made after the session. In these interviews, not only the layers and modes of patients' subjective engagement drew the investigator's attention, but also the camouflaged bypaths that were taken if more neurotic developments remained blocked. What at times appeared a solid character front, put in place to exercise rigid border control on any dealings with the other, might, rather than gradually showing cracks and fissures if put under stress, suddenly collapse without warning in one fell swoop.

In projective reduplication – a term Marty, de M'Uzan and David introduced – the other becomes a replica of one's own persona: without the ability to introject what is different, alterity is a threat that has to be managed by reduplication. The factual in its pressing urgency and the need to manage this takes precedence over everything else. It is the preferential reference to be shared with the interlocutor, with the (dynamic) unconscious largely put out of circuit, and the *magma fantasque* of early childhood having been buried. Understandably, the psychoanalyst confronted with a patient who offered little in the way both of subjective history and personal future was put under considerable strain. There were, it seemed, obscure regions and powerful forces in the patient's life which did not have a configured mental interface. Inasmuch as the most profound interest of the ailing person was absorbed by an inner somatic object, what thought he/she presented was starved of inner resources and battling against exhaustion.

This said, not all of the cases presented showed *opératoire* functioning: the overarching purpose of *L'investigation psychosomatique* was to demonstrate the wide range of psychosomatic structures. Sometimes an early loss of a father had left a determining influence, and, on occasion, a repetition of intergenerational patterns could be spotted. In general, the investigators believed patients played the defensive possibilities at their disposal like a functional keyboard to rise to the challenges their everyday situations faced them with.

When *L'investigation psychosomatique* was published, many of the authors' colleagues had already had the opportunity to acquaint themselves with its basic concepts: at the *23rd Congrès des psychanalystes de langues romanes* in Barcelona in 1962 Pierre Marty and Michel de M'Uzan had given a report on *opératoire* thought. It arrived in print a few months after the *Investigation*. Its publication provided additional reflective depth with a slightly different emphasis. The authors set out by giving Michel Fain and Christian David's keynote congress paper (Fain and David 1963[1962]) a new twist: if fantasy and dream life worked to protect and to further the subject's integration on levels encompassing the somatic, how would a marked lack in this function leave its imprint on the individual's waking thoughts? If there was a fantasy life in minus, they suggested, it could be found in *opératoire* thought – a new colourless term for a bland state – that kept up a front of business as usual but lacked any connection to an inner object really alive. It shadowed and accompanied action, reduced the investigator to his/her professional medical function and offered only a blank relationship in return.

The investigators surmised that this was what the patient was doing all his life, bogged down in actuality. In contradistinction to the obsessional type, he/she did not suffer from an abundance of significant connections that kept him/her from acting. Under his/her vigilant grasp everything transformed into morsels of the present. Bereft of inner directions the person was groping for the safe parameters provided by convention. Contact with the unconscious seemed to be established on a most rudimentary, least elaborated level, beneath the threshold of the *vie pulsionnelle*. The capacity to refrain from routing disquiet into motor discharge was diminished, and dream life was impaired, with a particular propensity to insomnia. If fantasies did develop, they should be appreciated by the therapist in their functional value, given enough slack and not pounced upon in interpretation of their content. The authors emphasised the importance of prophylactic action with children so as to develop their full capacity for fantasy in their lives.

'Essential depression': a fall in tonus without a narrative

Clearly, the role of the object in the development of early fantasy life was decisive. How could Marty and his colleagues come to terms with the apparent disappearance of a vital object in *opératoire* life? In 1968 Marty published a paper in the *Revue Française de Psychanalyse* in which he focused on a particular form of adult depression: *la dépression essentielle*. In it all ability to sustain a libidinal investment of object world and self seemed to have vanished and with it the usual gamut of mechanisms the unconscious uses to keep up links. Libidinal tonus was much diminished, and only obeisance to duty seemed to subsist. The patient was treating himself as just another medical file on the way to just another doctor. It was not so much that the psychoanalyst was kept at a distance by attacks on his/her position, but rather that the potential to maintain links had slipped and vanished. In this dwindling away, Marty saw a similarity to the bleeding away of vitality at the end of life without functional recompensation. If calm was more important than anything else and function was silently disintegrating, Marty pointed out that we were in the territory of the *instinct de mort*. Careful assessment of the situation was needed:

> In doing so, we arrive at a functional evaluation, in which weight is given to [a] mental investments, both pathological and normal, [b] the tendency to employ action and behaviour in a response and [c] the wealth and the mode of object relations. The appearance of a somatic disturbance, in general, follows upon an alteration more or less comprehensive in the aftermath of a conflict.
> (Marty and Fain 1964, p. 616; letters added for clarity)

Counselling divergence from the more customary French tendency of placing a premium on maintaining frustrating distance, Marty stresses it was necessary to keep close to such patients, opening up the possibility for them to identify with a person not too different from themselves.

A launchpad for a new comprehensive system

In 1967, Marty had already observed that progressive disorganisation produced different results from regression in that it did not necessarily gravitate towards a fixation. Faced with the need for differentiation, Marty was looking for systematisation on a larger scale. In *Les mouvements individuels de vie et de mort* (1976) and in *L'ordre psychosomatique* (1980) he attempted to map out his findings in an evolutionary perspective which shared conceptual preoccupations with the neo-Jacksonian perspective proposed by Henri Ey but moved into a different direction. Marty strove to understand how a person in crisis could bodily suffer from a lack of being adequately disturbed in the mind.

With Ey, Marty believed that speaking of disintegration necessitated concepts of hierarchy and evolution. For him, lack of integration was the initial starting point of the newly born: the *mosaïque première*. To the extent cohesion is still lacking, it has to be provided by the functioning of the mother. Gradually, individual rhythms are established, moving from basic *automation* (repetitive patterns) to more sophisticated *programmation* (a differentiation opening up the way to new functional links). As the maturational potential of the child develops, the mother has to scale down her subsidiary help. Depending on the early history of a person, his/her evolutionary trajectory will show a variety of fixations to which he/she can return in case of crisis. There will be parallel or lateral branches of structured response capabilities, split off in their dynamics from mainline development. Among them Marty ranges possibilities such as the processing of stressful situations in certain types of asthma, or manifestations of perverse sexual behaviour, mechanisms that, as varied as they are, take off pressure without being easily amenable to mental perlaboration. Once we are familiar with the individual's fallback positions and available lines of defence (*les paliers de réorganisation*), we can better appreciate his/her defensive depth (*l'epaisseur regressive*).

The central linchpin (*plaque tournante*) to the revitalisation of the subject is the preconscious. Its depth, internal fluidity and retentive capacities keep the subject in exchange with inner and outer worlds. Significantly, Marty believed that an inner life working reasonably well according to Freud's First Topography was not a universal given but came as an acquisition. Only on this basis could those inner structures take shapes that were described in Freud's Second Topography.

Hierarchical structures exposed to traumatic events

When a traumatic event strikes, full mental functioning is threatened. Depending on the previous development of layered, hierarchical structures, the response will come in the form of regression (partial or global) or of progressive disorganisation (temporary or progressive), in which mental response capacity is obliterated. In rising to such a threat, different mental economies command quite different resources, depending on the means they routinely deploy to process tension.

Marty distinguishes neuroses of behaviour – people whose stability strongly depends on their investment in what they are doing – and neuroses of character – which Marty believed to be the most widespread contemporary form of neurosis – from more well-mentalised neuroses capable of a full range of regressive possibilities. In this way of thinking, the *opératoire* constitutes a fragile, precarious response to crisis on a minimal level of resilience, in mental conditions that often do not correspond to the psychoanalyst's expectations.

It is indeed among the neuroses of behaviour and some neuroses of character that the phenomenon of the *opératoire* finds its most conducive structural hinterland according to Marty. With few reserves to draw upon, essential depression more easily sets in, leading to the residual states of the *opératoire* if the destructuring process does not proceed further to severe and increasingly progressive somatic illness. It is a precarious state of affairs, in which there is some stabilisation while cohesion is no longer safeguarded. The individual appears reduced to the agglomeration of autonomous apparatuses and a mosaic of elements of conduct. Survival, instead of having a life worth living, is the order of the day: to the interviewer, in Marty's experience, the patient frequently appears like a dead man walking, a shell of loosely connected templates of conduct, from which any or most of the significance they may have had, has evaporated in the new state of affairs. The phenomenon, though, is Janus faced: as long as automation proceeds, there remains hope of an ultimate restoration of a functional larger whole; it is a ledge the person can cling on to, just, for now.

The importance of careful dosage in therapeutic response and the mothering function

In interviewing the patient, Marty argues, one should not be misled by a flash of mental functioning that cannot be sustained in the long run and proves to be momentary. In an ensuing therapy, it is important that the analyst maintain an active presence. Despite being a relational object of importance, he/she may not be fully invested as an object. It may be destabilising for the patient to be confronted with freedom of mental movement in the person of the interviewer that much surpasses his/her own. Dosage, Marty emphasises, is important and the therapist will have to adjust the relationship so that it supports the maximum level of organisation accessible to the patient while encouraging unconscious articulation. Before antibiotics were available, Marty points out, the institution of the sanatorium attempted to offer a carefully calibrated environment – at a distance to normal daily life – in order to stimulate and support self-healing processes. In a similar vein, Marty enjoins on the therapist a mothering function that builds on the available grasp (*automation*) to stimulate the right amount of farther reach (*programmation*). Again, the psychoanalyst has to be careful so as not unwittingly to bolster a *Moi idéal* pushing towards enablement of the Me to such a degree that it stifles regression.

What is important is to introduce, when needed, an element of reanimation. Once again, the relational form discernible (both to self and others) should be studied carefully and assessed in its functional value before focusing on conflictual content. At the end of the interview a possible sense of being abandoned by the interviewer has to be guarded against.

Marty, on one of his journeys, treated psychosomatic patients in West Africa and relates that in his experience *opératoire* phenomena can frequently be found in families that moved abruptly to a Western way of life. Without a traditional world providing cushions of regression in case of need, and mothers unable to accompany a transition from one culture to the other in early childhood, individuals have to resort to the emergency measures of the *opératoire*.

Layered mentalisation

Behind the loss of structure or apparent in-organisation covered by a bland surface, there may hide considerable complexities: Marty stresses that the sensibility is still working but that the patient's propulsive and expressive capacities are impaired. Marty's (1980, p. 63) often quoted formula for this phenomenon is: 'In terms of the First Topography, the unconscious receives but does not emit', resulting, according to Fain, in a *malaise* without concomitant drama.

From the early 1970s, Marty increasingly used the term *mentalisation* as shorthand for a state of affairs in which a fully functional preconscious was at work. It is the permanent wealth of available representations that makes classical repression of unconscious significance necessary. Despite its inconveniences, it bolsters mental structure, thereby relieving the body of taking the brunt. He uses the example of the doll to show how layer upon layer of meaning creates additional depths to the mental registration of sensory perception: first it is an object to touch and to sight, then an image of a tiny infant, and in the end becomes sexually charged as a girl to dally with. When the object is thought of in adult life, there will be an echo chamber of resonances beyond its mere thingness. If this network of connections cannot be built over time, or collapses under the shock of mental sideration at a later stage, only thingness remains, as such refractory to perlaboration. There are events that seen from the outside should be unsettling but, in fact, barely register.

What seems to reduce mental registration, on the other hand, increases the likelihood of a bodily response to a reality to which a cushion of mental processes is lacking. For all his/her possible mental obtuseness, the individual remains exposed to 'individual movements of life and death'.

'Instinct' as a vector of vitality and its defeat in progressive disorganisation

It has been observed that Marty's use of the word instinct in his later writings does not quite correspond to what is usually understood by it, nor correspond to the usual meaning of the French *pulsion*:

> The Instincts of Life do not reside in a force simply measurable, but in a quality, a virtuality, a potentiality attached to all the functions, which makes life feel better than [just] living matter, the latter being only partially capable of producing an account for this.
> (Marty 1976, p. 11f.)

The Instinct of Life, as Marty employs the term, is manifested by a structure working at peak capacity of its evolutionary potential. The Instincts of Death, on the other hand, show themselves in the failure and disappearance of function, in particular in a counter-evolutionary sense, which reduces vital complexity, rolls back integration and results in disorganisation. This, with Marty, is not, as Freud's *Todestrieb*, an autonomous, albeit negative force; it is rather the undoing of the evolutionary vector producing and sustaining life in a particular individual. Whereas André Green's work on negativity finds its pivotal point in thinking about a mother who, though being physically present, has inexplicably become distant and dead in her feelings for the child, Pierre Marty's starting point is elsewhere: in the progressive wasting away of a person, with little overt drama, in a process medicine can describe but is at a loss fully to comprehend:

> A patient consults a doctor for hyperthyroidism. The doctor is able to heal it. Then diabetes appears, which one puts into equilibrium again with doses of insulin. Pulmonary tuberculosis arises. The cure of the tuberculosis with the help of drugs triggers digestive troubles. One changes therapy and tries other drugs. They bring about a retrobulbar optic neuritis [an inflammation of the optic nerve]. The doctor finds himself truly taken aback, having the impression that all the action on his part produces an unforeseen [somatic] response by the patient.
> One strives in vain to find an anatomo-pathological link between the different affections presented by a 37-year-old man.
> (Marty 1976, p. 69)

Any representation of what is wrong seems to have gone missing in action without the possibility of meaningful closure. If the person suffering mentally may be attacked by terrifying shapes, Marty's patient of reference seems to be hounded noiselessly, but to great effect, by no-shape – brought down by a sudden loss of structure that had previously been reliable enough.

Compared to this silent progressive disorganisation, even mental pathologies seemed to hold the body together. Marty believed it was difficult for psychoanalysts, used to the working of the mental apparatus in which the unconscious and the preconscious were working according to Freud's First Topography, to accept the irregularities offered by the patients of which Marty and his colleagues were striving to take the measure and truly to perceive what they were seeing. It was difficult to come to terms with what was supposed to be there but was not.

Psychosomatic psychosomatics as the heir to Sacha Nacht's project

At the same time, and on another level, Marty's project, which came to fruition in the 1980s, was in many ways the continuation of Nacht's agenda: the insertion of psychoanalysis into medicine as a recognised and legitimate component. Working towards that goal, the phenomenon of affects offered itself as a particularly propitious zone of investigation, an area where interests might converge as efforts by Franz Alexander and his colleagues in America gave reason to hope. This was not, nor could it be, the path of those who had split from the *SPP* in 1953: for different reasons neither Lagache nor Lacan were willing to move into the direction Nacht was favouring, and, in a deeper sense, the split had been just about that divergence. When Pierre Marty, Head of Clinic at Sainte-Anne, was won over to psychoanalysis by no other than Ajuriaguerra, post-war psychoanalysis showed that it was a conceptual force to be reckoned with. Marty's further moves undertaken to establish psychosomatics in France as a legitimate form of investigation, although running into opposition, repeatedly received vital support from the upper echelons within medical and political institutions, without which it could not have been as successful as it was. Conceptually, this project came at a price: to Marty, the psychosomatic viewpoint *included* the psychoanalytic one, a proposition liable to raise doubts about the exact position of psychoanalysis within the suggested unified perspective. André Green, who observed with regret that a controversial debate envisaged with Marty never materialised, once remarked that Marty's system was less geared towards metapsychology than to metasomatics, arriving at an imaginative biologisation of psychoanalytic thought.

From the late 1950s, fresh efforts were being made in France's public health system to reach groups of the population that had previously received too little attention. Parts of this outreach activity were pilot projects like *ASM 13*, the ethnopsychoanalytic service established by Tobie Nathan, and Pierre Marty's psychosomatic clinic. By participating in these efforts, psychoanalysis got into contact with new strata of patients. In Marty's case, this meant close contact with those who had been through all available medical screening, but whose complaints had never been resolved. Marty and Fain noticed that the imputation of repressed meaning as a root cause of these complaints was neither plausible nor helpful. What they also noticed was that these patients were deeply exhausted in their ability to process what had befallen them. In various ways, behind a bland surface, they were at the end of their tether, more on the verge of disintegration than on eruption. The *EPP's* core assumptions, in a way, took a path similar to Freud's observations on the disappearance of higher capacities in a man beset by acute toothache:

> 'Concentrated is his soul', says Wilhelm Busch of the poet suffering from toothache, 'in his molar's narrow hole'.
>
> (Freud 1914, p. 148f.)

Very boldly, they took this one notch further: What if the man's tooth was in rebellion because his bearer had had no sufficient mental space to process his love-sickness?

A social dimension at the margins of perception

There are problems with this approach, something that naturally became clearer as others began to take it up, develop it and work through its implications, at times in a different context than the one originally proposed. This, in hindsight, makes it easy to see that any findings must be highly context-sensitive. A person presenting an irritatingly bland version of him/herself may harbour hidden preferences about where and when best to be bland. His approach, for all its holistic aspirations, shows little noticeable interest in the previous experience of patients with institutions, unless indicative of personal fissure lines. Despite an interest in social conditions, social style as a distinctive element of affiliation is not given much consideration in its own right. Thus, for instance, the frequent use of direct speech rather than indirect speech is primarily understood as a personal trait pointing towards possible difficulties in interiorisation. Yet, when patients met the interviewer, the social frame they suddenly found themselves in will have carried a weight of its own in the encounter.

One of the interviewees showed remarkably little sign of *opératoire* thinking. It may not be quite a coincidence that she was a nurse, familiar with talking to doctors, at ease with the situation and comfortable with showing just the right amount of expected depth. Patients, on the whole, seemed to have experienced these interviews and the presentation that was required of them in different ways – and not all of this was likely to have been a straightforward emanation of their personal pathology. Marty continued a long institutional tradition of seeing patients assisted by a train of junior trainee doctors, which granted little privacy to the conversation between patient and doctor. Yet there was a marked improvement: Marty's interview accorded the individual an extended hearing he would not easily receive elsewhere.

A new terminology

Because this was developing medical practice into a direction heavily informed by experience within the psychoanalytic frame, the way Marty chose to present the sum of his findings (1976, 1980) broke with the conventions of contemporary psychoanalytic language. In its style it seems to have hearkened back to his much earlier discussions with Ajuriaguerra, set in the years of Henri Ey's considerable ascendancy in the psychiatric debate. Somewhat reminiscent of Bion's Grid, Marty developed his own system of classification that tried comprehensively to list factors pertinent to the clinical assessment of psychosomatic patients. Personal preference though it may have been, it also formed part of a strategic choice: only by developing a classificatory system could statistical material systematically be gathered.

Some doubt, even by those who approved the new classificatory grid, remained: were those patients who were classified under the heading of 'character neurosis, *mentalisation* uncertain' by the psychiatrist actually the same as those seen by the doctor of internal medicine? (Andréoli 1996, p. 131). No answer was given to the question and it is easy to see why: if both psychiatrist and doctor of internal medicine were making use of the same grid but interpreting it differently in the context of their separate patient encounters, how would one discern those differences that were neither registered nor taken into account by the shared classification?

Marty's legacy

On the whole, Marty's thinking, beyond its reception in France, fell on fertile ground in the Spanish speaking world, to which Marty felt close ties, mastering the language himself. Marty himself noticed that his thinking fared better where discourse had developed from Latin structures and travelled less well in English.

One of his lasting contributions to the debate was a sense of the depths of mental exhaustion hiding behind relentlessly functioning facades, an exhaustion that was not due to the working of classic repression, but something much closer to life slowly ebbing away that could easily escape attention behind the bland, undramatic surface. While he was very influential in raising the problem, the ensuing discussion went beyond the theoretical system he personally suggested.

We shall see that Michel Fain, Marty's friend, brother-in-law and long-time collaborator, who outlived him by almost fifteen years and remained productive for quite some time, was thinking along the lines of inner scenes produced by social interactions, where Marty was building carefully crafted conceptual cathedrals dedicated to the understanding of the rise and fall of an evolutionary *élan vital* expressed in individual structure. Although Marty integrates presuppositions about early interactions, his main focus is on structure. Fain subtly shifts focus: he is drawn to speculate on the hidden dramas of which a given structure may be the ossified mute memorial. This difference of style, emphasis and nuance had further consequences for the ramifications of their clinical thinking.

If Marty's take on complexities was quite multi-layered as can be seen in his reflections on the significance of the doll, Fain was prepared to ask questions that distinctly added further dimensions in questioning the imaginings of the mother: what if the mother's inner eye could not take in the ruddy infant before her, but could only see its potential to be transformed into an inanimate doll to be handled at will? It is to Michel Fain's contributions we have to turn now to understand another long-term effect of Pierre Marty's legacy.

Sources

Aderhold, M. (1994), 'Bibliographie complète des œuvres de Pierre Marty', *Revue Française de Psychosomatique* 6, pp. 209–217.

Aisenstein, M. (1994), 'Plaidoyer pour un certain inachèvement', *Revue Française de Psychosomatique* 6, pp. 71–74.

Aisenstein, M. (2020), 'La "pensée opératoire", de Pierre Marty et Michel de M'Uzan', *Revue Française de Psychanalyse* 84(5), pp. 1263–1278.

Aisenstein, M. and Smadja, C. (2017), 'Destins d'une rencontre', *Revue Française de Psychosomatique* 52, pp. 5–28.

Andréoli, A. (1996), 'Intervention', in: Marty, P. and Nicolaïdis, N. (1996), *Psychosomatique. Pensée vivante*, Bordeaux-Le-Bouscat: L'Esprit du Temps, pp. 131–132.

Angulo, F. (1994), 'Pierre Marty, Barcelone et la psychosomatique', *Revue Française de Psychosomatique* 6, pp. 167–172.

Asséo, R. (1994), 'L'allergie, un concept psychosomatique. Allergie et Moi-idéal, deux concepts en rapport avec la notion de "caractère" chez Pierre Marty', *Revue Française de Psychosomatique* 6, pp. 53–62.

Asséo, R. (2002), 'allergique (relation d'objet −)', in: de Mijolla, A. ed., *Dictionnaire international de la psychanalyse,* volume 1, Paris: Calmann-Lévy, pp. 55–56.
Asséo, R. (2009), 'La prudence du démineur', *Revue Française de Psychosomatique* 35, pp. 113–120.
Bergson, H. (1907), *L'évolution créatrice*, 5th edition, Paris: Presses Universitaires de France, in English translation: Bergson, H. (1911), *Creative evolution*, translated by Mitchell, A., London: Macmillan.
Bernier, M.-C. (1994), 'Pierre Marty et la naissance de l'*IPSO*. Quelques souvenirs', *Revue Française de Psychosomatique* 6, pp. 163–166.
Bonaparte, M. (1955[1954]), 'Intervention' on Marty, P. and Fain, M. (1955[1954]a), *Revue Française de Psychanalyse* 19(1–2), pp. 285–286.
Brown, T.M. (2000), 'The rise and fall of American psychosomatic medicine', available at: www.human-nature.com/free-associations/riseandfall.html
Clervoy, P. (1997), *Henri Ey 1900–1977. Cinquante ans de psychiatrie en France,* Le Plessis-Robinson: Institut Synthélabo.
David, C. (1967), 'Intervention', *Revue Française de Psychanalyse* 31(5-6), pp. 1127–1128.
David, C. and de M'Uzan, M. (1994), 'Origine et travaux initiaux', *Revue Française de Psychosomatique* 6, pp. 13–22.
de Ajuriaguerra, J. (1955[1954]), 'Intervention' [on Marty, P. and Fain, M. (1955[1954]a)], *Revue Française de Psychanalyse* 19(1–2), pp. 295–299.
de Calatroni, M.T. ed. (1998), *Pierre Marty y la psicosomática,* Buenos Aires: Amorrortu/editores.
de M'Uzan, M. (2008), 'L'École psychosomatique de Paris', in: Denis, P. ed., *Avancées de la psychanalyse,* Paris: Presses Universitaires de France, pp. 25–29.
de M'Uzan, M. (2009), 'Cinquante ans après …', *Revue Française de Psychosomatique* 35, pp. 9–15.
Debray, R. (1994), 'L'influence et le rayonnement des conceptions de Pierre Marty', *Revue Française de Psychosomatique* 6, pp. 105–109.
Debray, R. (1996), *Clinique de l'expression somatique,* Lausanne: Delachaux et Niestlé.
Debray, R. (1998), *Pierre Marty (Psychanalystes d'aujourd'hui* 16), Paris: Presses Universitaires de France.
Debray, R. (2002), 'Pierre Marty', in: de Mijolla, A. ed., *Dictionnaire international de la psychanalyse,* volume 2, Paris: Calmann-Lévy, pp. 1020–1021.
Diatkine, G. (1994), 'Pierre Marty', *Revue Française de Psychosomatique* 6, pp. 159–161.

Diatkine, R. (1955[1954]), 'Intervention' [on Marty, P. and Fain, M. (1955[1954]a)], *Revue Française de Psychanalyse* 19(1-2), pp. 305–307.
Fain, M. and David, C. (1963[1962]), 'Aspects fonctionnels de la vie onirique', *Revue Française de Psychanalyse* 27, special number, pp. 241–343.
Fain, M. and Marty, P. (1965[1964]), 'A propos du narcissisme et de sa genese', *Revue Française de Psychanalyse* 29(5–6), pp. 561–572.
Fain, M. and Marty, P. (1959), 'Aspects fonctionnels et rôle structurant de l'investissement homosexuel au cours des traitements psychanalytiques d'adultes', *Revue Française de Psychanalyse 23*(5), pp. 607–617.
Fernández, R. (2002), *El psicoanálisis y lo psicosomatico*, Madrid: Editorial Síntesis.
Fine, A. (1994), 'Quelques points clés de l'oeuvre de Pierre Marty', *Revue Française de Psychosomatique* 6, pp. 39–52.
Fine, A. (2004), 'Enjeux du "caractère" et vicissitudes de la "névrose de caractère" dans l'oeuvre de Pierre Marty', in: Bouhsira, J., Dreyfus-Asséo, S. and Fine, A. eds, *Caractères*, Paris: Presses Universitaires de France, pp. 109–128.
Fine, A. and Smadja, C. (2000), 'Interview [avec] André Green', *Revue Française de Psychosomatique* 17, pp. 149–171.
Freud, S. (1914), 'Zur Einführung des Narzissmus', in: *Gesammelte Werke*, volume 10, London: Imago Publishing [1940–1952], pp. 137–170.
Garrabé, J. (1997), *Henri Ey et la pensée psychiatrique contemporaine*, Le Plessis-Robinson: Institut Synthélabo.
Green, A. (1998[1994]), 'Théorie', in: Fine, A. and Schaeffer, J. eds, (1998), *Interrogations psychosomatiques*, Paris: Presses Universitaires de France, pp. 17–53.
Green, A. (2007b), 'La psychosomatique de Marty', in: Green, A. (2007), *Pourquoi les pulsions de destruction ou de mort?* Paris: Èditions du Panama, pp. 125–130.
Indepsi, ed. (2013), 'Pierre Marty (1918–1993)', Newsletter Indepsi 27, available at: www.indepsi.cl/newsletter/News-27/terapeutas-27.html.
Jaeger, P. (2015), 'Winnicott et l'École psychosomatique de Paris, convergences?', *Revue Française de Psychosomatique* 47, pp. 13–36.
Jorda, P. (1994), 'Hommage à Pierre Marty', *Revue Française de Psychosomatique* 6, pp. 173–177.
Kreisler, L. (1984), 'De la pédiatrie à l'économie psychosomatique de l'enfant', *Revue Française de Psychanalyse* 48(5), pp. 1243–1258.
Krzysztof, F. (2009), 'Le dialogue tonique dans la psychothérapie analytique de relaxation', *Psychothérapies* 29, pp. 33–38.

Lacan, J. [1956], 'De l'analyse comme *bundling*, et ses conséquences' (19. December 1956), in: Miller, J-A. ed., (1994), *Le séminaire de Jacques Lacan IV, La relation d'objet*, Paris: Éditions du Seuil, pp. 77–92.

Lê, M.G. (1994), 'Statistique et psychosomatique: incompatibilité absolue ou approche cohérente', *Revue Française de Psychosomatique* 6, pp. 99–103.

Lechat, F. (1955[1954]), 'Intervention' [on Marty, P. and Fain, M. (1955[1954] a)], *Revue Française de Psychanalyse* 19(1-2), pp. 289–295.

Marty, P. (1951), 'Aspect psychodynamique de l'étude clinique de quelques cas de céphalalgies', *Revue Française de Psychanalyse* 15(2), pp. 216–252.

Marty, P. (1952), 'Les difficultés narcissiques de l'observateur devant le problème psychosomatique, *Revue Française de Psychanalyse* 16, pp. 339–362; in English translation: Marty, P. (2010[1952]), 'The narcissistic difficulties presented to the observer by the psychosomatic problem', *International Journal of Psychoanalysis* 91, pp. 463–468.

Marty, P. (1955), 'Intervention' [on 'A propos de musique' de H. Racker], *Revue Française de Psychanalyse* 19(3), pp. 402–405

Marty, P. (1956), 'Clinique et pratique psychsomatiques', in: Nacht, S. ed., *La psychanalyse d'aujourd'hui*, volume 2, Paris: Presses Universitaires de France, pp. 532–573.

Marty, P. (1957[1956]a), 'Intervention' [on 'Essai sur la situation analytique et le processus de guérison (la dynamique)' de B. Grunberger], *Revue Française de Psychanalyse* 21(3), pp. 448–452.

Marty, P. (1957[1956]b), 'Intervention' [on 'A propos d'un cas d'hypertension artérielle' de M. Fain], *Revue Française de Psychanalyse* 21(4), pp. 479–481.

Marty, P. (1958[1957]), 'La relation d'objet allergique', *Revue Française de Psychanalyse* 22(1), pp. 5–29; in English: 'The allergic object relation', *International Journal of Psychoanalysis* 39, pp. 98–103.

Marty, P. (1960), 'Maurice Bouvet familier', *Revue Française de Psychanalyse* 24(6), pp. 709–710.

Marty, P. (1962[1961]), 'Intervention' [on 'Les identifications précoces dans la structuration et la restructuration du moi' de P. Luquet], *Revue Française de Psychanalyse* 26, special number, pp. 293–300.

Marty, P. (1967), 'Régression et instinct de mort: hypothèses à propos de l'observation psychosomatique', *Revue Française de Psychanalyse* 31(5–6), pp. 1113–1126.

Marty, P. (1967[1965]), 'Intervention' [on 'A propos de la sublimation' de Sandler, J. and Joffe, W.G.], *Revue Française de Psychanalyse* 31(1), pp. 22–25.

Marty, P. (1967/2003), 'Aspects psychosomatiques de la fatigue', *Revue Française de Psychosomatique* 24, pp. 9–32.

Marty, P. (1968[1966]), 'La dépression essentielle', *Revue Française de Psychanalyse* 32(3), pp. 595–598.
Marty, P. (1968[1967]), 'A major process of somatization: The progressive disorganization', *International Journal of Psychoanalysis* 49, pp. 246–249.
Marty, P. (1969), 'Intervention sur l'exposé de Sami Ali suivi de Notes cliniques et hypothèses à propos de l'économie de l'allergie', *Revue Française de Psychanalyse* 33(2), pp. 243–253.
Marty, P. (1970), 'Allocution', *Revue Française de Psychanalyse* 34(5-6), pp. 751–752.
Marty, P. (1972), Intervention, *Revue Française de Psychanalyse* 36(5-6), pp. 805–816.
Marty, P. (1976), *Les mouvements individuels de vie et de mort. Essai d'économie psychosomatique*, volume 1, Paris: Payot.
Marty, P. (1980), *L'ordre psychosomatique* [= *Les mouvements individuels de vie et de mort. Essai d'économie psychosomatique*, volume 2], Paris: Payot.
Marty, P. (1981[1980]), 'Intervention', *Revue Française de Psychanalyse* 45(2), pp. 293–294.
Marty, P. (1984a), 'Des processus de somatisation', in: Fain, M. and Dejours, C. eds, *Corps malade et corps érotique*, Paris: Masson, pp. 101–115.
Marty, P. (1984b), 'A propos des rêves chez les malades somatiques', *Revue Française de Psychanalyse* 48(5), pp. 1143–1162.
Marty, P. (1990a), *La psychosomatique de l'adulte,* Paris: Presses Universitaires de France.
Marty, P. (1990b), 'Psychosomatique et psychanalyse', *Revue Française de Psychanalyse* 54(3), pp. 615–624.
Marty, P. (1991[1990]), 'Genèse des maladies graves et critères de gravité en psychosomatique', *Revue Française de Psychosomatique* 1, pp. 5–21, also available in: Nicolaïdis, N. and Press, J. (1995), *La psychosomatique hier et aujourd'hui*, Paris: Delachaux et Niestlé, pp. 155–178.
Marty, P. (1991/2013), *Mentalisation et psychosomatique*, Le Plessis-Robinson: Institut Synthélabo, reprinted in: Press, J. ed., (2013), *Rêver, transformer, somatiser,* Geneva: Georg, pp. 13–31; original edition Marty, P. (1991), *Mentalisation et psychosomatique*, Paris: Les Empêcheurs de penser en rond.
Marty, P. (1996[1991]), 'Entretiens avec Pierre Marty', in: Marty, P. and Nicolaïdis, N. (1996), *Psychosomatique. Pensée vivante*, Bordeaux-Le-Bouscat: L'Esprit du Temps, pp. 15–81.
Marty, P. (2001[1981], 'La psychosomatique en 1981. Les processus de somatisation', *Revue Française de Psychosomatique 19,* pp. 161–171.

Marty, P. (2006[1987]), 'Introduction à la psychosomatique', *Revue Française de Psychosomatique* 30, pp.165–167.
Marty, P. and de M'Uzan, M. (1963[1962]), 'La pensée opératoire. Intervention sur le rapport de M. Fain et Ch. David: Aspects fonctionnels de la vie onirique' [23e Congrès de psychanalystes de langues romanes, Barcelona 1962], *Revue Française de Psychanalyse* 27, special number, pp. 345–356.
Marty, P. and Fain, M. (1954[1953]), 'Notes sur certains aspects psychosomatiques de la tuberculose pulmonaire', *Revue Française de Psychanalyse* 18(2), pp. 244–275.
Marty, P. and Fain, M. (1955[1954]a), 'Importance du rôle de la motricité dans la relation d'objet', *Revue Française de Psychanalyse* 19(1-2), pp. 205–284.
Marty, P. and Fain, M. (1955[1954]b), 'Réponse de Pierre Marty et Michel Fain', *Revue Française de Psychanalyse* 19(1-2), pp. 318–322.
Marty, P. and Fain, M. (1964), 'Perspectives psychosomatiques sur la fonction des fantasmes', *Revue Française de Psychanalyse* 28(4), pp. 609–622.
Marty, P. and Marty, S. (1962), *L'art tauromachie et la psychanalyse*, typed and bound manuscript of the radio feature broadcast in December 1962, unpublished, in possession of the author of this book.
Marty, P. and Nicolaïdis, N. (1996), *Psychosomatique. Pensée vivante*, Bordeaux: L'Esprit du Temps.
Marty, P. and Parat, C. (1974), 'De l'utilisation des rêves et du matériel onirique dans certains types de psychothérapie d'adultes', *Revue Française de Psychanalyse* 38(5-6), pp. 1069–1076.
Marty, P., de M'Uzan, M. and David C. (2003/1963), *L'investigation psychosomatique. Sept observations cliniques*, 2nd edition, Paris: Presses Universitaires de France.
Marty, P., Fain, M., de M'Uzan, M. and David, C. (1968[1967]), 'Le cas Dora et le point de vue psychosomatique', *Revue Française de Psychanalyse* 32(4), pp. 679–714.
Moreau, F. (1998), *Écoute psychosomatique. Deux situations cliniques de Pierre Marty*, Bordeaux-Le-Bouscat: L'Esprit du Temps.
Nacht, S. (1955[1954]), 'Intervention' [on Marty, P. and Fain, M. (1955[1954] a)], 'Importance du rôle de la motricité dans la relation d'objet'], *Revue Française de Psychanalyse* 19(1–2), pp. 286–289.
Nicolaïdis, N. (1996a), 'Introduction', in: Marty, P. and Nicolaïdis, N. (1996), *Psychosomatique. Pensée vivante*, Bordeaux-Le-Bouscat: L'Esprit du Temps, pp. 7–14.

Nicolaïdis, N. (1996b), 'Complément aux entretiens', in: Marty, P. and Nicolaïdis, N. (1996), *Psychosomatique. Pensée vivante*, Bordeaux-Le-Bouscat: L'Esprit du Temps, pp. 137–164.

Parat, C. (1994), 'Pour dissiper quelques malentendus …', *Revue Française de Psychosomatique* 6, pp. 23–28.

Ribas, D. (1998), 'Le lieu perdu des traces retrouvées', *Revue Française de Psychanalyse* 62(5), pp. 1607–1612.

Rouart, J. (1981), '"L'ordre psychosomatique" par Pierre Marty', *Revue Française de Psychanalyse* 45(2), pp. 417–427.

Szwec, G. (2008), 'Le psychodrame avec des patients somatisants', *Le Carnet PSY* 127, pp. 24–29.

Ulnik, J.R. (2000), 'Revisión crítica de la teoria psicosomática de Pierre Marty', *Aperturas Psiconalíticas. Revista internacional de psicoanálisis* 5, available at: www.aperturas.org/articulos.php?id=121&a=Revision-critica-de-la-teoria-psicosomatica-de-Pierre-Marty

Wiener, P. (2011), 'La consultation psychosomatique avec Pierre Marty, rue Falguière', *Le Coq-héron* 207, pp. 147–149.

Zubiri, M. (1994), 'L'usage de la classification psychosomatique à l'Institu Pierre Marty de médecine psychosomatique de Bilbao', *Revue Française de Psychosomatique* 6, pp. 179–183.

4

FOUNDATIONS 2

Michel Fain with Denise Braunschweig

In April 1998, not long after Michel Fain had turned 80, on the occasion of colleagues coming together to honour the import of his life's work by debating it with verve, there was a moment when he was noticeably struck by the presentation of one of the participants. Listening to the exposition of François Duparc, who, based on remarks of Fain's, was identifying four major lines of development in early mother-child interaction, the reminder struck Fain as if out of the blue. It caused him, he avowed, something akin to an attack of anxiety: he had forgotten all about this particular germ of thought and had failed to develop it any further. As painful as this realisation was to Fain, it is a fitting illustration of a tenet pivotal in Michel Fain's thinking: every event, according to him, unfolds its personal significance in three stages: (a) original incidence within a given relational field, (b) latency, (c) configuration of its ultimate personal meaning and impact. This, he holds, is not only true of the symptom, but also of the effects of an interpretation given in a session, or, more generally, the vicissitudes of scientific discovery and psychoanalytic discourse. In this chapter we shall see how much Michel Fain's thought added to the original propositions by Pierre Marty.

Marty's original hunch in a different frame: the mother and the lover

Taking its cues from Freud, Fain's line of thinking not only gives a new guise to Marty's thought, but also takes it to new directions. Discontinuing Marty's attempts at a metabiology, Fain places the focus much more squarely on the interactions of a concrete child with a concrete mother. In contradistinction to any approach privileging the outwardly observable, Fain takes a keen interest in the fantasies affecting the mother as she is handling her child. Important parts of his work were developed together with Denise Braunschweig between 1970 and 1981, at a time when they formed a couple.

In its ideal-typical form, the early foundations of a rich fantasy life, according to Braunschweig and Fain, might be laid as follows: after a period during which the mother's attention is intensely centred on the newborn child, there comes a time when she wants to return to the life she had before and in particular her love life. To turn *femme* again she has to take periodic leave from her functions as mother. As she is holding the child, her mind strays elsewhere: how can she put her child to undisturbed sleep so that she can turn into the arms of her lover? In a series of exchanges with her infant, investment is withdrawn within a safe enough framework, which permits the child to glide into sleep and into more auto-erotic modes. In such an early affective ambiance in the gravitational pull of a triadic field, the hysteric potential of the child and its capacity for bi-sexual identification is gradually developed to the rhythm of continuously repeated discontinuities of investment. It is such an environment in which the hallucination of desire can find its place.

In its early form (Fain 1971a), Braunschweig and Fain's concept of the *censure de l'amante* – their term for the vital, structuring role of the mother turned lover – predates André Green's concept of the Dead Mother, to which it yet forms the flip side of a coin. In Green's version, the mother, who had previously taken delight in her child, has become absorbed by an unspeakable loss, which, inexplicably to the child, has transformed her presence into a permanent mental absence. In vain the child tries to reinsert him/herself into a story that would make sense of this brutal eclipse of the sun, in a world which had, just a short while before, been full of colour and warmth and light.

As in Green's template, yet separated from it as if by an abyss, the much more fortunate child in Braunschweig and Fain's situation of reference senses that something important has happened to his/her mother.

> When the desire for her male partner reappears with a mother, a message gets transmitted to her child by way of a modification of her bodily contact, a message that points to an object of desire in

another location. The body of the mother, as it extricates itself 'mentally' from the one of the child, confers autonomy to the latter. In this regard we have used the image that the mother takes back her narcissistic investment from the child 'to put it on as make up' [*pour s'en farder*].

(Fain 1999[1980], p. 209f.)

the *femme* takes back, for her own dispositions, all the investment, in which it had enveloped her child, and in doing so becomes fascinating. This fascination gets displaced on this *femme*'s object of desire.

(Fain 1991b, p. 1132)

The early bath of affects and the role of stimulating discontinuities

This, if circumstances are sufficiently good, is embedded in a kind of lullaby, drenched in affects addressed to the child and attaching itself to the animistic worlds of the child. The mood music, which is deeply sunk into the unsaid that underlies the quality of the gently rocking movements with which the mother lulls the baby cradled in her arms into sleep, is crucial for future developments. Maternal tenderness nurtures a link between a wholesome, indispensable narcissism it confers and the quality of the infant's sleep: 'my sleep loves me just as my mother does' (Fain 1996a, p. 56).

Handling her baby in this way, enrobing it in the projection of her own narcissism, the mother enthrones it as 'his majesty the baby'. Yet, the wish to put her child to sleep is not a purely altruistic act – she has to take leave of her child to resume those parts of her life that exclude it. In a partnership this means putting functioning as a parent on hold and leaving family concerns aside so as to turn to each other as lovers. It is the *censure de l'amante* mentioned above, a contact barrier between their moments as lovers and their function in the family, which permits the parents for the time of their lovemaking to forget that they are parents. For the child it is important that the sexual relationship between the parents is working out well enough. On it depends the way primal fantasies are organised and the functional quality of the preconscious.

When the mother puts her child to bed, withdrawing the protective cover of her full libidinal investment in it, she rarely leaves it with a sufficiently functioning defensive shield. This exposes the child to stimuli from the realms of raw, non-symbolised reality, which impact on its sensibility. Fain likens the resulting fragile situation to the paranoid-schizoid position. Counter-availing to these forces of fragmentation there is the pull to what the child vaguely senses as the mother's desire directed to an absent third that reinforces its auto-erotism. It identifies both with the desiring mother and with the desired third, and within this framework the perception of lack serves as an architect for future dreams. Contact with the reality of the parents' reciprocal sexual desire sets off differentiations within the child's id and stimulates an elaboration of animistic thought. Since it springs from the loss of the mother's palpable physical presence, nascent desire contains strong masochistic elements. The loss of the position as the centre of the mother's universe combines with emerging fantasies about the putative beneficiary of the mother's changed focus to create a sense of riches lost and to be rediscovered.

The infant's fantasy life against the background of the parents' relationship

This is a very important experience, but itself part of a larger gamut of mutual relations in which the unconscious fantasies of the parents play an important part: the fantasies awakened in the mother when she touches the child; the way the father responds to the spectacle of the unfolding relationship between mother and child; the jealousy with which the mother responds to the unconscious identification with the mother, which shapes the counter-oedipal aspects of the father's position; the ways the parents talk or behave when they believe the child cannot comprehend them; the degree to which the father himself experienced an investment of good quality by his own mother; the narcissistic cover of a texture, different from the mother, which the father 'of good quality' early on provides for his daughter; or the paths on which the boy arrives at a possible positive identification with his father; all contribute to infinitely complex individual variations. Particular circumstances are liable to complicate pre-existing structure. Braunschweig and Fain argue that *pulsion* comes into being on the basis of successive inscriptions of memory traces constituted by various registers of language intimately and erotically linked to the body – a perspective, they contend, that, by situating the sources of erogenous excitement outside the infant, is able to provide an explicative hypothesis to the mysterious concept of *pulsion*.

Early on the mother transmits an unconscious message of inquietude to her child with regard to its continued well-being, when she is faced with auto-erotic behaviour and her responses to it. This unspoken exchange, understood by Braunschweig and Fain as the first stage of the structuring of the castration complex, receives its interpretation only in retrospect, creating the myth, almost akin to a primal fantasy, that the mother had in fact issued a verbal warning to the child. It is deeply steeped in the mother's own unconscious fantasies, a manifestation of her own oedipal conflicts.

Abandoned to its own devices, the subject exhausts itself in vain attempts to discover workable means to discharge excitement. Experiences are needed that give form to dream symbolism, making use of the mediating force of primal fantasies. These experiences are provided by the alternation of periods of retention interspersed with periods of satisfaction. In Freud's understanding of the First Topography, the unconscious, Fain points out, maintains a constant pressure towards the preconscious, aided and directed in this push by preconscious content previously put into latency. If this is so, the time of latency required has to be of a particular quality, a quality that will to some extent be shaped by cultural factors.

Thus, despite Marty's reticence to envisage this, his concept of evolution necessarily contains a cultural perspective, which as Fain argues, is patently included, in particular, in the phenomenology of the *opératoire*. Fain conceptually differentiates the non-symbolised 'real' from a subjectively accessible reality that may be grasped, passed on in codified form and which supplies incentives to action models. Since reality, in this perspective, is an interim notion as defined by a given group, it is of particular importance to which extent a family and their ways of dealing with the spoken and the unspoken provides a framework for the emergence of animistic thought in a child: will there be sufficient space for an oscillation between the 'baby of the night', the baby of fantasies, and the 'baby of the day', the infant in its material existence and its social significance?

In this context, the mother's membership of a wider social group affects the messages she transmits to her child. If the way the parents live their sexuality does not provide building blocks for the child to organise his/her fantasy of the primal scene, the image of an erotic father will find itself excluded, with damaging effect for the future development of the child. A good deal depends upon fine balances in the dealings between the mother and the child. Early trauma does not necessarily point towards objective flaws in a mother but might as well spring from a mismatch between the subject and the ambient framework into which various factors, some of them conceivably of hereditary nature, may enter, putting at risk the emergence of a field of integration complexified enough within a developed mental economy. Reflecting on the experience of the child's encounter with his/her own mirror image, which entered psychoanalytic discourse with Lacan, Braunschweig and Fain characteristically contextualise it: the image results from a complex history, which is particular to each and every one, and in which the individual appropriates a series of figurations emerging from the latent thoughts of others.

A question of fine balances which can easily be disturbed

Serge Lebovici, one of the pioneers of the psychoanalytic study of the child in France, in 1965 encouraged Michel Soulé, a paedopsychiatrist, and Michel Fain, known for his psychosomatic research, to undertake a study of the somatic disorganisations of early childhood, a work group which was then joined by Léon Kreisler, a paediatrician and clinical director of the department of child and adolescent psychiatry at the hospital Saint-Vincent-de-Paul. The discussions seem to have deepened Fain's interest in the plight of the very young child suffering from insomnia. For this baby, the fine balances necessary for drifting safely into sleep have been severely disturbed and the mother, emitting discordant messages, has not been able to protect it against an excess of excitement in her arms, of which she herself is the source – a quandary that becomes a crucial point of reference in Fain's thinking.

Continuous rocking, pitting itself against any emergent discontinuity, is employed to force the child into sleep, a sleep which, when it does eventually come, is not conducive to the development of a wholesome dream life. The place a satisfying mother might have occupied has been lost to a mother hyperactively intent on instilling calm, reducing to nought any auto-erotic tendencies: sometimes this leads to violent spasms of sobbing in presence of the mother, in which unconsciousness is sought by induced anoxia. Fighting agitation by persistent mechanical rocking, the mother tries to fight fire with fire in an attempt not only to run down excitement but also to dull sensibility. There are instances in which what gets transmitted seems to be *une pure culture d'instinct de mort* pushing towards the extinction rather than the transformation of excitement. One might say, Fain muses, taking his cue from Bion, that the holding frame has lost its capacity to dream the subject: it is as if a bad fairy had been sitting at the infant's bedside.

Premature maturity as a heavy burden

To come to terms with the chronically unsafe environment, in which passivity does not procure any pleasure, the infant prematurely strives for a maximum of attainable mastery: to make up for what he/she does not receive, the child does everything to construct his/her own bunker.

> In fact, under the impact of an excitement receiving an insufficient holding structure within a balanced family organisation, there may from the outset develop a primal disequilibrium between the processes of mastery and that excitement.
> (Fain 1982, p. 19)

Sensory perceptions cannot easily be put to rest or transformed into *pulsion*. Animistic thinking finds no favourable conditions to blossom. There is little resonance for double layers of meaning in language. Early suffering does not give rise to an abundance of representations. To develop quickly becomes the supreme imperative, with less space accorded to complexification and mental sophistication. As a result, the development of the Me suffers a distortion, a condition, which may, but need not, be an antecedent of a future obsessional neurosis. One cannot, Fain points out, endlessly put oneself to bed all alone, as it were, especially if one has no illusions.

Although one or the other line of development is more pronounced with each individual, traces of the imperative of prematurity and the imperative of complexification co-exist in everyone. What will vary is the degree to which a child is exposed to distorting influences in his/her early childhood. Braunschweig and Fain, in one of their quirky musings, give a twist to Lacan's formula of the foreclosed by connecting it to a meaning it has in legal transactions: a right forfeited because not laid claim to within a stipulated period. Coming too late to exercise it, the claimant finds the service desk closed and the clerk asleep protecting himself against the disturbance by producing dreams.

Transitionality provided or impeded by the parents

When parents leave their children so as to spend time as lovers, they do not quite close the service desk abruptly: the transitional objects described by Winnicott are provided by the parents to be deployed in a space from which they are going to become absent. The ability to put playful distance to the world is embedded in the ability of the parents to disengage from their social obligations and their duty to larger groups. On this disengagement depends their time as lovers and, if they are able to experience this, their sleep in each other's arms, an echo of the sleep of the baby whom its mother has helped to let go of daytime object investments.

> In this way, the Sandman, bringing about the child's slumbers, closes its eyes on the things it should not know, while at the same time protecting the parents from a return of the repressed that would confer to their vigorous lovemaking a forbidden character. He thus condenses the barrier of censorship and the protective shield systematically deployed by each family.
> (Braunschweig and Fain 1971, p. 198)

In Fain's multi-layered reading of the dream of the burning child there are echoes of Lacan's (1973[1964]) emphasis on the intrusion of 'the real' into the dream. Fain imagines a prequel to the child's death: exhausted by the long watches at the son's sickbed, the father at a certain point had repressed indications of his son's worsening fever so as to be able to sleep. The son's death not only caused the re-emergence of the perception in a traumatic dream, it shed doubt on the quality of the compromise – and its wisdom – effected to enable sleep. Though periodically turning one's back on reality is important, we may conclude, the environment has to be free of serious threat to make the act of distancing safe enough.

In constant tension with the mandates of vigilance, being able to take a step back from the flood of perceptions so as to negate the clamours of reality is an important prerequisite for adaptation. It permits regression in treatment, it prevents complete exhaustion for the person who has fallen sick, and it is a feature which is woven into humour. Put to use like this, negation opens space for the imaginary by keeping reality at a distance from which it does not have to be expunged. This, Fain holds, should be differentiated from a form of denial that has no fantasmatic use for reality but tries to root it out as a persistently traumatic source of excitement. It is as if someone, unable to shield oneself from the sunlight by wearing sunglasses has to go one-eyed. What is thus rejected will no longer provide representations or give fantasies, as disturbances are weeded out at the source by dulling perceptions. Since repeatedly processing small quantities of trauma is an important condition for staying alive, denial like this shares goals with *l'instinct de mort*.

Denial as a shared bond

Turning one's back on becoming too curious about reality is most efficiently done in a group, in the exercise of shared identifications and reduced sensibilities. In its most radical form it is much more substantial than wearing socially agreeable blinkers: it is a process that very early denies mental space to the child in a way that pre-empts any defensive action against it. In its implicit maternal message, it locks the child into an idealised image that does not correspond to anything which it has a chance to develop on its own and uses the infant as a prop to provide figuration to the mother's latent thoughts in a denial of oedipal loss and refusal of mourning. It pushes the child into what Fain terms an identification in a community of shared denial (*identification dans une communauté de déni*): it is something that is present in the parents' unspoken attitudes (often contradictory to their manifest verbal declarations) and finds itself articulated in mundane everyday activities. As a consequence of something that did not happen – contact with a mother whose desires go beyond the child and can be satisfied – there is a segment of the Me that has been exposed to the impact of a lack, a lack that has to be denied in unconscious identification with a member of the family. What should, according to Freud's First Topography, show evidence of an irresistible push of a dynamic unconscious becomes a phenomenon belonging instead to collective psychology: the subject is not so much driven to something as merged into something.

Muscular masculinity as a group ideal

Fain discusses possible ramifications of this in an article. There he gives a thumbnail sketch of groups in which lads come together to venerate the shared ideal of invincible toughness: *les rouleurs de mécaniques*. Being part of such a group means it is not enough to be tough today: one has to be seen to get better at this, every single day. It is as if an erection had to be maintained in permanence, without any implied reference to an eventual orgasm that might provide release. In Fain's perspective, these are individuals locked into a mother's glance that turns the child into an imaginary, timeless adult who is there to remedy her narcissistic and erotic deficiencies. Their early relationship is determined by being handled like a small girl's doll straight out of the mother's dreams and her unconscious aspirations. It forms a transitional object for a person who does not transit anywhere. His/her persona has been dreamt up by another's unconscious. This is covered up by the mother's defensive measures that conceal what the child really means to her. They are bound into a community of denial with the mother, instrumentalised in effacing the traces of the mother's exclusion of the father as a sexual object. Once they have become members of the group united by a shared code of conduct, there surfaces the need permanently to safeguard against turning into a woman. Though at first contact presenting with a classically neurotic personality, placed in psychotherapy they are deprived of the protective cover which their usual behaviour provides and they succumb to what Marty terms *dépression essentielle*. Moving in an environment in which they are constantly perceived and acknowledged is indispensable to them for the continued working of mental processing, evidence of a relatively shallow subjectivity, despite all activity, asleep on its feet and unable to dream. Interpreting as closely as possible to the Me can be quite a tall order for the analyst when the Me in question can hear only a recognition of failure, while the analyst would like the person to see a glimpse of hope.

Artificially engendered needs that prop up the Me's economy

Fain pays close attention to the transformation of the libidinal economy that takes place when new needs pre-fabricated by the cultural environment take hold of the subject. Building on an illustration he and Braunschweig provide, and integrating further reflections of theirs in their highly complex chapter on the *néo-besoins*, it is as if a group of teenagers congregating at a tram stop were to use the wait to light their cigarettes while facing a huge billboard that enticingly links the consumption of the right brand of cigarettes to the flavour of adventures in the wild, true nonchalance and boundless erotic opportunities. What they are doing is not about entertaining fantasies where the tram might take them but about soaking up the tension of living through empty time. They resort to a social practice that bolsters group life in an affirmation of shared style. It holds out promises of transit but its true transitional value has to be seriously put into doubt. The space it arrogates is one that has been lost to the latency of a desire that would have taken time to develop: Braunschweig and Fain argue that a mother who abusively keeps her child at her breast causes harm to the development of his/her auto-erotism. Artificially closing gaps of discontinuity, the *néo-besoin* has to be constantly renewed to remain effective. The authors stress that this is a mechanism everyone is familiar with to some extent. What is important is what kind of wider economy of functioning it is embedded in.

Fain points to the work of Paul Federn on the shrinking of the borders of the Me under the impact of trauma, a reduction of territory which leaves outside zones that used to belong to it but are no longer invested as Me. Braunschweig and Fain, in keeping with this line of thinking, argue that important splits do, not as Kleinian authors assume, originate from a mechanism within the subject, but from a reality it is exposed to.

Going militant with nothing else to cling to

In 1982, Fain organised one chapter of his *Le désir de l'interprète* around the case of a young girl, who is wedged into a story that leaves her limited space to manoeuvre. In the interview with the mother the following emerges: weary of having to accompany the eldest sister to school on top of a multiplicity of professional and domestic tasks, the mother agreed to the wish of the girl to have a bicycle. On her first trip the girl was killed by a car. Following the tragic accident, the parents dedicated all their time to saving children from an unhappy childhood – as if, by virtue of their efforts, somehow, their eldest child could still be saved. By doing so, they left their remaining two children in such a state of neglect that they might easily have fallen victims to accidents. It is not that these efforts were not crowned by social success, the problem was that their charity work was part of a dogged work of denial, indicative of the fact that they could not absorb the shock by falling back on more classically neurotic means like obsessional neurosis. If the parents had not become militants in a good cause, another possible route for them might have been going *opératoire*, being reduced to perfunctory mental routines on the verge of bodily illness.

The effects of this turn of events on the surviving daughter, whom Fain saw in consultation, were, as might be expected, withering. She showed identity confusion, finding it difficult to maintain a sense of being separate from her elder sibling, whom she idealised and kept alive in her fantasy. She suffered from camouflaged depression and from agoraphobia, did badly at school, and had the impression of being followed. Fain argues that within her personality there existed a contradiction, with two aspects pitted against one another in mutual denial. On the one hand, there was an identification with the family unit built on shared denial of what had happened – a position which made it impossible for her to take over the place of the sister kept artificially alive by the parents. This produced a stalemate, denied her something to make sense of and dragged her into depression. At the same time, there were, on the other hand, traces of a hysterical elaboration of the event, which turned the crushing to death of her sister into a substitute for the primal scene. Producing symptoms centred around an identity confusion constituted a defensive reaction, which was constructive because it pointed towards the parents' madness and by this permitted the girl to recover her own identity.

As for the parents, they found, as we have seen, recourse in permanent moral action, applying themselves with an amount of exertion they had shrunk back from earlier, when they granted the eldest daughter her wish of a bicycle. Fain has an acute sense of how a certain turn of events may wreak havoc on balances that had previously worked well enough but, in retrospect, throw into relief the limited defensive depth of individuals and families within an overall economy of ways and means. If a child falls sick, the family environment may lack sufficient supporting qualities. When a family is confronted with a child's problems, it does matter, Fain points out, what their social resources are, because this will determine which links they are able to establish and who they will turn to when they are in trouble. If a mother is enveloped in a traumatic neurosis with her child, there is a need for a level of symbolisation provided from outside that helps to break the loop.

Sinking into Chronos

There are occasions when it is the proverbial straw that breaks the camel's back. If a juncture of external and internal factors eventually leads to a crisis, the *opératoire* person acts *as if* he had a defensive potential he is, in fact, sorely lacking. To carry on, he falls back on whatever mental cover his membership of a group provides. This remedy is a two-edged sword: while it grants some mental stay, it swallows up the subjective dimensions of time traversed:

> Chronos, who gave his name to time in its social dimension [*temps social*], to what devours the life of humankind, counter-investment to the timelessness of desire, is he not also the god who devours his children?
> (Braunschweig and Fain 1975a, p. 100)

For the interlocutor talking to a person disappearing into the social background it is a mystery why he/she does not feel as depersonalised as the listener does. Again, almost in passing, Fain gives an interpersonal twist to Marty's formula that the *opératoire*'s unconscious receives but does not emit: the psychoanalyst's unconscious, in session, has emitted but no response has come back. The psychoanalyst finds his existence as a dreamer rejected and his own professional reality negated.

Fain, as we have seen, traces this (non)response back to antecedents in the person's personal history: there is a fundamental difference between everything transmitted by contact with the real body of the mother and things which in their unmediated suchness envelop the subject in indifference. What is held in check in its raw form by being put to calm is vulnerable to coming forcefully to the fore if external reality breaks the truce that, while it lasts, sustains the efficacy of the tension reducing measures employed as a stand-in.

Being swaddled in indifference

Though Fain does not directly make this argument, there is some evidence that child raising in the past engaged in practices that provide rich illustrations for what he addresses as the workings of the *instinct de mort* by proxy. Edward Shorter (1975) relates that peasant nurses in the region of Auvergne in France would tightly swaddle their children to suspend them from a nail when they wanted to go about their work. In the early 19th century there are numerous complaints from Central Europe that children are knocked into the sleep of insensibility. In Fain's use, the *instinct de mort* or *pulsion de mort* is like a cold, dank shroud of insignificance the child gets swaddled in at a time when all resistance is futile. In contrast to the reverberations of the hysteric nucleus, which unfold in two phases, separated by latency, the sequels of having been 'suspended from a nail' in indifference or turned into an inanimate doll tend to be refractory to elaboration, chronic and thus mono-phasic. Liable to be subject to denial, they foment sectors that are split off and are not even open to masochistic elaboration. This creates very complex relations not only between denial and non-perception, which are difficult to keep apart, but also between loss and non-acquisition.

Fain contrasts an understanding of the death instinct that follows Freud in emphasising the noiseless waning and bleeding away of mental life with the noisier manifestations of the death instinct in the tradition of Melanie Klein. The contrast, however, he points out, may be starker in theory than in practice. A child having been exposed to the *instinct de mort* of the early environment is forced into premature development. It will have to come to terms with impulses of a kind of hatred that will do nothing for the proper construction of his/her Me because it has to combat what is lacking, which cannot be named and has to be covered up. Destruction is the reverse side of the imperative of supreme calm.

Fain as a reader of puzzles left by Freud

To come to terms with the challenging clinical landscape, Fain does not move towards synthesis – as Pierre Marty did – but rather traces some of the puzzles left by Freud in the different strata of his thinking without ever coming to a comprehensive solution. In doing so, Fain creates puzzles of his own. Can one maintain, he asks, that Freud's metapsychology as presented in 1915, and in which the unconscious constantly pushes towards the preconscious, has not perceived within its horizon the repetition compulsion as described in 1920? Does one not perceive what one has not thought yet? As Bion has Alice, one of his characters in *A Memoir of the Future*, say: 'My headache is no dream I can tell you' (Bion 1991, p. 221). It is difficult to perceive, we may conclude, what one has not yet dreamt.

Not surprisingly, Fain pays particular attention to the *Massenpsychologie und Ich-Analyse*, which appeared between *Jenseits des Lustprinzips* and *Das Ich und das Es*. The Me analysed on the basis of collective psychology depends, above all, on an exterior organisation pivoting on what Freud terms the object of the Me. The complexity of the Me, Fain concludes, depends on the complexity of the object, in as much as it takes shape not in contact with reality but with reality as codified by the object. This is a juncture, we have to surmise, based on what Braunschweig and Fain write elsewhere, at which the permanently *opératoire* person possibly misses an important turn and gets locked out of his /her subjective future. In Freud's thinking after 1920, reality is a traumatic source of excitement, with the death instinct trying radically to run down the sensibility that at the same time offers the chance to turn reality into lived through experience. The seduction of unfortunate children by adults, as discussed around 1900, now finds a complement in the incapacity of the same adults to construct a symbolic holding frame around the child, or in other words, to construct the primal fantasy around the seduced child. It is unfortunate both for the patient and the child constantly to compensate for the supposed or real unreliability of a holding frame, as if it had to bootstrap his/her environment in the manner of Baron Münchhausen's famously bogus exploit of having successfully pulled himself out of the swamp by his own hair.

For the early psychoanalytic movement, including Freud, Fain points out, the introduction of the new economy of mental functioning with all the questions it raised was experienced as nothing short of traumatic. Freud's work, which in itself seemed to be taking shape as a discontinuous process, was subjected to reinterpretations that worked like catastrophes hitting the individual. To get back a sense of control, simple formulas were subsequently developed that facilitated the teaching process. Yet, getting things into too much of a delimiting frame could have its drawbacks: if Melanie Klein had been part of a task group working within a pre-established methodological framework, Fain argues, she might still have been a talented child psychotherapist but would have been unable to achieve anything out of the ordinary.

The psychoanalyst as a refugee from worlds drenched in 'banality'

In one of his many asides, Fain reflects that recoil from banality may originally have led many to choose psychoanalysis as their profession. If he included himself in their number, as seems plausible, it must have come as a shock to him to discover that psychoanalysis might be capable of developing *opératoire* versions of itself. One glaring instance of this, in his view, was one brand of American psychoanalysis, very successful at the time, which gave pride of place to the ego as an autonomous agency. As with *opératoire* patients, one would look in vain for the work of the preconscious. Fain concedes that he arrives on different paths at a number of conclusions that are similar to Melanie Klein's. What she catches well, in Fain's view, is the dynamics of the primal process. Everyone, Fain believes, is likely to have developed elements of a premature Me. This means that believing it is an innate trait, which he does not but Klein does, produces no divergence on a practical level. If only theoretical considerations were to matter, it would be difficult to explain why he worked well with Marty, who was a firm believer in the evolutionary process, something quite alien to Fain's perspective.

One of the marks of *opératoire* language is that it lacks depth to the listener, is rather dry and does not cause reverberations. This is a complaint that occurs with noticeable frequency once language borders are crossed by the reader, especially if the translation used is reasonably accurate. Fain seems to have a corresponding experience with English as used in psychoanalytic texts, which he finds devoid of subtleties and indicative of a pragmatic, 'hands-on' approach, intent on distancing itself from mere 'literature'. Taking a leaf out of Fain's own book one might argue that whenever ideas cannot be put into abeyance, having been rendered amenable to negation, a shared imaginary becomes very difficult.

Unfinished shape, unmourned by the mother

Translating Bion for himself, Fain notices that he does not remember well what he has read, and has difficulties to absorb it, until it comes back years later. One of the ideas that attract his interest is Bion's thinking about pre-conceptions. Although there is no evidence he ever came across it, we can safely assume he would have approved of the temporal onion layers in Bion family crest's motto *Nisi dominus frustra* in allusion to Psalm 127:1: *Nisi dominus aedificaverit domum in vanum laborant qui aedificant eam* [Vulgata: 126:1].

In typically stenographic fashion, Fain in one passage refers to a patient who arrives like an *ours mal léché* (a bear badly licked). The expression, in French popular usage designing an uncouth person, stems from a passage in Isidor of Sevilla's *Etymologies* (XII.ii.22). There, the author suggests that the bear (*ursus*) has received its name because it is said to lick its offspring, to which it gives birth after a very short period of gestation as raw packages of meat, unformed, into shape with its mouth (*ore suo*).

Fain adds that for bears to have been properly treated, the mother has to disinvest them in just the right way so that dreams can take shape. What to do with those patients who have not experienced this? The psychoanalyst, like the mother, transmits a culture that injects elements of symbolism and provides another chance for discontinuity to give rise to dreams. For this it is important that the consulting room of the psychoanalyst is clearly demarcated from a medical setting, and perceived to be so, in discontinuity to what else is going on in the life of the patient.

In a footnote he stresses the importance of the secondarily original narcissism imparted to the child: something not born with but born into that should come as a self-evident right: an inalienable claim made to an environment that should be able to fulfil a promise. Once turned adolescent, the group the individual belongs to may be a decisive element in how the subject handles him/herself.

If we look at what Fain brings to Marty's original observations, it is the role of the other in the individual's mental economy that becomes much more conspicuous; how the parents were navigating their own unconscious, what the mother's inner eye was occupied with as she looked at her child, is central to the development of the child's desires.

In the next chapter we turn to Nicolaïdis and his suggestion of a basic toolkit transmitted to the child by the mother's culture and the quality of the necessary cushion of regression offered by myths available at the time.

Sources

Aisenstein, M. (1999), 'Valeur économique et texture de la vie fantasmatique', in: Duparc, F. ed., *La censure de l'amante et autres préludes à l'oeuvre de Michel Fain*, Paris: Delachaux et Niestlé, pp. 25–33.

Aisenstein, M. (2000), *Michel Fain (Psychanalystes d'aujourd'hui* 28), Paris: Presses Universitaires de France.

Aisenstein, M. (2018), 'An introduction to Michel Fain's thought', *International Journal of Psychoanalysis* 99(2), pp. 495–509.

Aisenstein, M. and Papageorgiou, M. (2018), 'Mentalisation and passivity by Michel Fain', *International Journal of Psychoanalysis* 99(2), pp. 468–478.

Asseo, R. (2005), 'Le traumatisme dans ses fonctions organisatrices et désorganisatrices', in: Brette, F. and Emmanuelli, M. and Pragier, G., *Le traumatisme dans ses fonctions organisatrices et désorganisatrices*, Paris: Presses Universitaires de France, pp. 57–68.

Barney, S.A., Lewis, W.J., Beach, J.A. and Berghof, O. (2006), *The etymologies of Isidore of Seville*, Cambridge University Press.

Bion, W.R. (1991[1975–1981]), *A memoir of the future*, London: Karnac Books.

Braunschweig, D. (1967), 'Intervention' [on Luquet-Parat, C.-J. 'L'organisation œdipienne du stade génital'], *Revue Française de Psychanalyse* 31(5–6), pp. 853–857.

Braunschweig, D. (1982), 'Introduction', in: Fain, M. (1982), *Le désir de l'interprète*, Paris: Éditions Aubier Montaigne, pp. 7–13.

Braunschweig, D. (1984), 'Psychosomatique et psychanalyse', in: Fain, M. and Dejours, C. eds, *Corps malade et corps érotique*, Paris: Masson, pp. 116–122.

Braunschweig, D. and Fain, M. (1970), 'Intervention' [on Green, A., 'L'affect'], *Revue Française de Psychanalyse* 34(5-6), pp. 1175–1182.

Braunschweig, D. and Fain, M. (1971), *Éros et Antéros*, Paris: Payot.

Braunschweig, D. and Fain, M. (1974), 'A propos du rêve symptôme', *Revue Française de Psychanalyse* 38(5–6), pp. 1041–1046.

Braunschweig, D. and Fain, M. (1975a), *La nuit, le jour. Essai psychanalytique sur le fonctionnement mental*, Paris: Presses Universitaires de France.

Braunschweig, D. and Fain M. (1975b), 'Le messianisme en psychanalyse', *Revue Française de Psychanalyse* 39(1–2), pp. 195–224.

Braunschweig, D. and Fain M. (1976), 'Réflexions introductives à l'étude de quelques facteurs actifs dans le contre-transfert', *Revue Française de Psychanalyse* 40(3), pp. 483–540.

Braunschweig, D. and Fain, M. (1977), 'Des mécanismes communs à l'auto-érotisme et à l'interprétation', *Revue Française de Psychanalyse* 41(5-6), pp. 993–1002.

Braunschweig, D. and Fain, M. (1979), 'Quelques réflexions à propos du livre de Michel Neyraut "Les logiques de l'inconscient"', *Revue Française de Psychanalyse* 43(2), pp. 343–348.

Braunschweig, D. and Fain, M. (1981a[1976]), 'Un aspect de la constitution de la source pulsionnelle', *Revue Française de Psychanalyse* 45(1), pp. 205–226.

Braunschweig, D. and Fain, M. (1981b), 'Bloc-notes et lanterne magiques', *Revue Française de Psychanalyse* 45(5), pp. 1221–1242.

Braunschweig, D. and Fain, M. (1983), 'Symptôme névrotique, symptôme de transfert: commentaire basé sur les conférences réunies sous le nom "Introduction à la psychanalyse"', *Revue Française de Psychanalyse* 47(2), pp. 567–590.

Braunschweig, D. and Fain, M. (1983[1975]), *I ritmi della vita mentale* [= *La nuit, le jour: Essai psychanalytique sur le fonctionnement mental*], translated by Pavan G., Rome: Edizione Borla.

Braunschweig, D. and Fain, M. (2010/1974), 'Du démon du bien et des infortunes de la vertu', *Revue Française de Psychosomatique* 37, pp. 151–171; first published in *Nouvelle Revue de psychanalyse* 10, pp. 161–178.

Chervet, B. (2020), '"Aspects fonctionnels de la vie onirique", de Michel Fain et Christian David', *Revue Française de Psychanalyse* 84(5), pp. 1247–1261.

Cosnier, J. (1978), 'Analyse de: Braunschweig D., Fain M., La nuit, je jour. Essai psychanalytique sur le fonctionnement mental. Paris, PUF, 1975', *Revue Française de Psychanalyse* 42(1), pp. 123–146.

Donabédian, D. and Fain, M. (1995/1993), 'Psychosomatique et pulsions', *Revue Française de Psychosomatique* 7, pp. 141–152; previously published in 1993 in *Cahiers du Centre de Psychanalyse et de Psychothérapie* 26, pp. 11–21.

Dufour, J. (2008), 'Un legs de Michel Fain: entre négation hystérique et déni traumatique', *Bulletin du Groupe Lyonnais de Psychanalyse* 63, pp. 27–31.

Duparc, F. (1999c), 'L'enfant et son corps: les lignées psychosomatiques', in: Duparc, F. ed., *La censure de l'amante et autres préludes à l'oeuvre de Michel Fain*, Paris: Delachaux et Niestlé, pp. 73–86.

Fain, M. (1962), 'Intervention' [on Grunberger, B., 'Considérations sur le clivage entre le narcissisme et la maturation pulsionnelle'], *Revue Française de Psychanalyse* 26(2-3), pp. 204–205.

Fain, M. (1965), 'Le dialogue de sourds', *Revue Française de Psychanalyse* 29(1), pp. 105–108.

Fain, M. (1965[1964]), 'Intervention' [on 'Aperçus sur le processus de la création littéraire' de M. de M'Uzan], *Revue Française de Psychanalyse* 29(1), pp. 71–72.

Fain, M. (1966a), 'Régression et psychosomatique', *Revue Française de Psychanalyse* 30(4), pp. 451–456; also in: *Revue Française de Psychosomatique* 9, pp. 197–202.

Fain, M. (1966b), 'Intervention' [on Kestemberg, E. and Kestemberg, J, 'Contribution à la perspective génétique en psychanalyse'], *Revue Française de Psychanalyse* 30(5-6), pp. 720–728.

Fain, M. (1967), 'Intervention' [on Marty, P., 'Régression et instinct de mort: hypothèses à propos de l'observation psychosomatique'], *Revue Française de Psychanalyse* 31(5-6), pp. 1129–1133.

Fain, M. (1968), 'Intervention' [on Barande, I., 'Le vu et l'entendu dans la cure'], *Revue Française de Psychanalyse* 32(1), pp. 86–88.

Fain, M. (1969a), 'Laurence ou le labeur statufié. Commentaire sur le cas exposé par Mme Loriod', *Revue Française de Psychanalyse* 33(2), pp. 273–284.

Fain, M. (1969b), 'Intervention' [on 'Une observation d'agoraphobie "pour raisons de famille"'], *Revue Française de Psychanalyse* 33(4), pp. 599–606.

Fain, M. (1969c), 'Ébauche d'une recherche concernant l'existence d'activités mentales pouvant être considérées comme prototypiques du processus psychanalytique', *Revue Française de Psychanalyse* 33(5-6), pp. 929–962.

Fain, M. (1970), '"A partir de Freud" par Francis Pasche. Un modèle de réflexion psychanalytique', *Revue Française de Psychanalyse* 34(4), pp. 709–719.

Fain, M. (1971a), 'Prélude à la vie fantasmatique', *Revue Française de Psychanalyse* 35(2-3), pp. 291–364.

Fain, M. (1971b), 'A propos du processus psychanalytique', *Revue Française de Psychanalyse* 35(5-6), pp. 1087–1095.

Fain, M. (1973), 'Quelques remarques sur l'humour', *Revue Française de Psychanalyse* 37(4), pp. 529–538.

Fain, M. (1974a), 'Avant-propos', in: Fenichel, O. (1945/1953), *La théorie psychanalytique des névroses*, volume 1, 2nd edition, Paris: Presses Universitaires de France, pp. vii-xiii.

Fain, M. (1974b), 'A propos d'un "Souvenir d'enfance de Léonard de Vinci"', *Revue Française de Psychanalyse* 38(2-3), pp. 315–322.

Fain, M. (1976), 'Une conquête de la psychanalyse: "Les mouvements individuels de vie et de mort" de Pierre Marty', *Revue Française de Psychanalyse* 40(4), pp. 741–755,

Fain, M. (1977), 'A propos de l'exposé introductif de L. Kreisler', in: Kestemberg, E. ed., *Le devenir de la prématurité*, Paris: Presses Universitaires de France, pp. 79–84.

Fain, M. (1981a), 'Vers une conception psychosomatique de l'inconscient', *Revue Française de Psychanalyse* 45(2), pp. 281–292.

Fain, M. (1981b), 'Diachronie, structure, conflit oedipien: quelques réflexions', *Revue Française de Psychanalyse* 45(4), pp. 985–998.

Fain, M. (1982), *Le désir de l'interprète*, Paris: Éditions Aubier Montaigne.

Fain, M. (1982[1980]), 'Biphasisme et après-coup', in: Guillaumin, J. ed., *Quinze études psychanalytiques sur le temps. Traumatisme et après-coup*, Toulouse: Privat, pp. 103–124.

Fain, M. (1983), 'Réalité du fétiche, réalité de la castration', *Revue Française de Psychanalyse* 47(1), pp. 325–332.

Fain, M. (1984a), 'Des complexités de la consultation en matière psychosomatique', *Revue Française de Psychanalyse* 48(5), pp. 1209–1227.

Fain, M. (1984b), 'Ouverture du congrès', *Revue Française de Psychanalyse* 48 (special number), pp. 7–10.

Fain, M. (1986[1983]), 'Rôle de la sexualité des parents', in: Sztulman, H., Barbier, A. and Caïn, J. eds, *Les fantasmes originaires: les origines du commencement*, Toulouse: Privat, pp. 99–103.

Fain, M. (1986), 'A propos des réflexions de M. Ody sur noyau dépressif, noyau hystérique', *Revue Française de Psychanalyse* 50(3), pp. 973–978.

Fain, M. (1987[1986]), 'Psychanalyste, un métier impossible? Rome et Londres', in: Fain, M., Cournut, J., Enriquez, E., Cifali, M. and de Mijolla, A., *Les trois métiers impossibles*, Paris: Les Belles Lettres, pp. 9–39.

Fain, M. (1988), 'Les "ouatères" et leurs verrous', in: Soulé, M. ed., *L'enfant et sa maison*, Paris: Les éditions ESF, pp. 113–117.

Fain, M. (1989a), 'Lettre de Michel Fain à Jean Bégoin', *Revue Française de Psychanalyse* 53(5), pp. 1271–1275.

Fain, M. (1989b), 'Symbolisation', *Revue Française de Psychanalyse* 53(6), pp. 1999–2001.

Fain, M. (1990a), 'Virilité et antihysterie. Les rouleurs de mécaniques', *Revue Française de Psychanalyse* 54(5) pp.1283–1291.

Fain, M. (1990b), 'Psychanalyse et Psychosomatique', *Revue Française de Psychanalyse* 54(3), pp. 625–637.

Fain, M. (1991a), 'Lettre aux rapporteurs', *Revue Française de Psychanalyse* 55(1), pp. 193–196.

Fain, M. (1991b), 'A propos des fantasmes originaires', *Revue Française de Psychanalyse* 55(5), pp. 1131–1134.

Fain, M. (1991c), 'A propos du sujet, du soi et du self', *Revue Française de Psychanalyse* 55(6), pp. 1721–1723.

Fain, M. (1991d), 'Préambule à une étude métapsychologique de la vie opératoire', *Revue Française de Psychosomatique* 1, pp. 59–79.

Fain, M. (1992a), 'Le schibboleth', *Revue Française de Psychanalyse* 56(2), pp. 329–333.

Fain, M. (1992b), 'Banalités à propos de certains facteurs poussant à la régression au cours des cures', *Revue Française de Psychanalyse* 56(4), pp. 1109–1113.

Fain, M. (1992c), 'Emprise et pensée animique', *Revue Française de Psychanalyse* 56(5), pp. 1445–1447.

Fain, M. (1992d), 'La vie opératoire et les potentialités de névrose traumatique', *Revue Française de Psychosomatique* 2, pp. 5–24.

Fain, M. (1993a), 'Nécessité d'un référent au cours de l'étude de l'interprétation', *Revue Française de Psychanalyse* 57(2), pp. 157–160.

Fain, M. (1993b), 'Maladies de la civilisation', *Revue Française de Psychanalyse* 57(4), pp. 1087–1094.

Fain, M. (1993c), 'Face à face', *Revue Française de Psychosomatique* 3, pp. 121–125.

Fain, M. (1993d), 'Spéculations métapsychologiques hasardeuses à partir de l'étude des procédés autocalmants', *Revue Française de Psychosomatique* 4, pp. 59–67.

Fain, M. (1993e), 'Théorie de la technique de la cure psychanalytique de la névrose obsessionnelle', in: Brusset, B. and Couvreur, C. eds, *La névrose obsessionnelle*, Paris: Presses Universitaires de France, pp. 127–142.

Fain, M. (1993f), 'Le pénis-emblème', *Revue Française de Psychanalyse* 57 (special edition), pp. 1703–1708.

Fain, M. (1994a), 'Premiers pas en psychosomatique', *Revue Française de Psychosomatique* 6, pp. 7–11.

Fain, M. (1994b), 'La névrose de comportement selon Pierre Marty', *Revue Française de Psychosomatique* 6, pp. 151–158.

Fain, M. (1994c), 'Tout analyser?, *Revue Française de Psychanalyse* 58(4), pp. 1041–1046.

Fain, M. (1994d), 'Troubles somatiques et remaniements psychiques. Introduction, *Revue Française de Psychosomatique* 5, pp. 7–16.

Fain, M. (1995a), 'Régression ou distorsion?', *Revue Française de Psychanalyse* 59(3), pp. 737–743.

Fain, M. (1995b), 'A propos de la transitionnalité', *Revue Française de Psychanalyse* 59(5), pp. 1547–1549.

Fain, M. (1996a), 'Quelle pure culture?', *Revue Française de Psychanalyse* 60(1), pp. 55–63.

Fain, M. (1996b), 'Intervention' [on 'L'enfant et son corps, vingt ans après la publication du livre], *Revue Française de Psychosomatique* 9, pp. 35–43.

Fain, M. (1996c), 'Lettre à Marta Calatroni', *Revue Française de Psychosomatique* 10, pp. 135–138.

Fain, M. (1997a), 'Névrose de caractère et mentalisation', *Revue Française de Psychosomatique* 11, pp. 7–17.

Fain, M. (1997b), 'La goutte d'eau', *Revue Française de Psychosomatique* 12, pp. pp. 69–76.

Fain, M. (1997c), 'La machine à remonter le temps', *Revue Française de Psychanalyse* 61(5), pp. 1685–1687.

Fain, M. (1997d), 'Entretien avec Diane L'Heureux Le Beuf et Georges Pragier (à partir de questions élaborées par les rédacteurs)', in: Le Goues, G. and Pragier, G. eds, *Cliniques psychosomatiques*, Paris: Presses Universitaires de France, pp. 137–146.

Fain, M. (1998a), 'Réflexions sur la rencontre et son histoire', *Revue Française de Psychanalyse* 62(1), pp. 25–29.

Fain, M. (1998b), 'Quelques réflexions sur la masculinité et le monothéisme', *Revue Française de Psychanalyse* 62(2), pp. 425–428.

Fain, M. (1998c), 'Commentaire sur l'opératoire', *Revue Française de Psychanalyse* 62(5), pp. 1493–1497.

Fain, M. (1998d), 'Brève introduction à une discussion sur le système sommeil-rêve', *Revue Française de Psychosomatique* 14, pp. 7–13.

Fain, M. (1998e), 'Commentaire de "La vie onirique chez l'enfant" de Gérard Szwec', *Revue Française de Psychosomatique* 14, pp. 107–111.

Fain, M. (1998f), 'Vie et impératif de désinvestissement', in: Schaeffer, J., Cournut-Janin, M., Faure-Pragier, S. and Guignard, F. eds, *Interrogations psychosomatiques*, Paris: Presses Universitaires de France, pp. 145–149.

Fain, M. (1998g), 'À propos de son itinéraire personnel et de sa pensée', available at: http://www.spp.asso.fr/wp/?vimeo-video=michel-fain-a-propos-de-son-itineraire-personnel-et-de-sa-pensee.

Fain, M. (1999[1980]), 'Introduction à la régression dans la cure', in: Duparc, F. ed., *La censure de l'amante et autres préludes à l'oeuvre de Michel Fain*, Paris: Delachaux et Niestlé, pp. 191–214.

Fain, M. (1999[1987]), 'Psychopathologie de la vie quotidienne et délire', in: Duparc, F. ed., *La censure de l'amante et autres préludes à l'oeuvre de Michel Fain*, Paris: Delachaux et Niestlé, pp. 215–227; also available in: *Revue Française de Psychosomatique* 43, pp. 87–94.

Fain, M. (1999[1989]), 'Une sémiologie du rêve?', in: Duparc, F. ed., *La censure de l'amante et autres préludes à l'oeuvre de Michel Fain*, Paris: Delachaux et Niestlé, pp. 229–251.

Fain, M. (1999[1990]), 'À propos de l'hypocondrie', in: Duparc, F. ed., *La censure de l'amante et autres préludes à l'oeuvre de Michel Fain*, Paris: Delachaux et Niestlé, pp. 253–264, also available as Fain M, (2010/1999[1990],

'À propos de l'hypocondrie', *Revue Française de Psychosomatique* 37, pp. 177–184.
Fain, M. (1999[1992]), 'Le message', in: Duparc, F. ed., *La censure de l'amante et autres préludes à l'oeuvre de Michel Fain*, Paris: Delachaux et Niestlé, pp. 265–275.
Fain, M. (1999a), 'Réponse aux exposés de M. Aisenstein et J. Press. Discussion', in: Duparc, F. ed., *La censure de l'amante et autres préludes à l'oeuvre de Michel Fain*, Paris: Delachaux et Niestlé, pp. 51–61.
Fain, M. (1999b), 'Réponse aux exposés de M. Ody et F. Duparc. Discussion', in: Duparc, F. ed., *La censure de l'amante et autres préludes à l'oeuvre de Michel Fain*, Paris: Delachaux et Niestlé, pp. 87–97.
Fain, M. (1999c), 'Réponse aux exposés de B. Chervet et J. Dufour. Discussion', in: Duparc, F. ed., *La censure de l'amante et autres préludes à l'oeuvre de Michel Fain*, Paris: Delachaux et Niestlé, pp. 139–154.
Fain, M. (1999d), 'Table ronde', in: Duparc, F. ed., *La censure de l'amante et autres préludes à l'oeuvre de Michel Fain*, Paris: Delachaux et Niestlé, pp. 155–187.
Fain, M. (1999e), 'Autour de l'enfant battu', *Revue Française de Psychanalyse* 63(5), pp. 1737–1740.
Fain, M. (1999f), 'La fonction maternelle selon Pierre Marty', *Actualités Psychosomatiques* 2, pp. 97–103, also available in: *Revue Française de Psychosomatique* 20, pp. 47–52.
Fain, M. (1999g), 'Interview de Michel Fain par Claude Smadja et Gérard Szwec', *Revue Française de Psychosomatique* 16, p. 185–193.
Fain, M. (1999h), 'Un avatar du pénis', in: Schaeffer, J., Cournut-Janin, M., Faure-Pragier, S. and Guignard, F. eds, *Clés pour le féminin. Femme, mère, amante et fille*, Paris: Presses Universitaires de France, pp. 163–167.
Fain, M. (2000a), 'Transfert négatif et faillite du cadre', *Revue Française de Psychanalyse* 64(2), pp. 419–423.
Fain, M. (2000b), 'Á propos du masochisme érogène primaire, dialogue imaginaire avec Benno Rosenberg', in: Aisenstein, M., *Michel Fain* (Psychanalystes d'aujourd'hui 28), Paris: Presses Universitaires de France, pp. 65–71.
Fain, M. (2000c), 'Quelques réflexions sur le rêve et le clivage à la lumière de l'École psychosomatique de Paris', in: Aisenstein, M., *Michel Fain* (*Psychanalystes d'aujourd'hui* 28), Paris: Presses Universitaires de France, pp. 72–80.
Fain, M. (2001a), 'Mentalisation et passivité', *Revue Française de Psychosomatique* 19, pp. 29–37.

Fain, M. (2001b), 'Préface', in: Smadja, C., *La vie opératoire. Études psychanalytiques*, Paris: Presses Universitaires de France, pp. 11–21.

Fain, M. (2001c), 'La fonction maternelle selon Pierre Marty', *Revue Française de Psychosomatique* 20, pp. 47–52.

Fain, M. and David, C. (1963[1962]), 'Aspects fonctionnels de la vie onirique', [23e Congrès de psychanalystes de langues romanes, Barcelona 1962], *Revue Française de Psychanalyse* 27, special number, pp. 241–343.

Fain, M. and Guignard, F. (1984), 'Identification hystérique et identification projective', *Revue Française de Psychanalyse* 48(2), pp. 515–528.

Fain, M. and Kreisler, L. (1970), 'Discussion sur la genèse des fonctions représentatives à propos de deux observations pédiatriques', *Revue Française de Psychanalyse* 34(2), pp. 285–306.

Fain, M. and Marty P. (1965[1964]), 'A propos du narcissisme et de sa genese', *Revue Française de Psychanalyse* 29(5–6), pp. 561–572.

Fain, M. and Marty, P. (1959), 'Aspects fonctionnels et rôle structurant de l'investissement homosexuel au cours des traitements psychanalytiques d'adultes', *Revue Française de Psychanalyse* 23(5), pp. 607–617.

Green, A. (2010b), 'Rencontre avec Michel Fain', *Revue Française de Psychosomatique* 37, pp. 115–117.

Jaeger, P. (2008), 'Excitation et pulsion de mort dans l'oeuvre de Michel Fain: un parcours de l'excitation à partir de l'insomnie précoce du nourrisson', *Revue Française de Psychosomatique* 38, pp. 45–66.

Kamieniak, I.M. (2017), 'Éros et Antéros – Réflexions psychanalytiques sur la sexualité [Eros and Anteros – Psychoanalytic Reflections on Sexuality] by Denise Braunschweig and Michel Fain, Éditions In Press, Paris, 2013', *International Journal of Psychonalysis* 98(1), pp. 277–282.

Kreisler, L., Fain, M. and Soulé (1974), *L'enfant et son corps. Etudes sur la clinique psychsomatique du premier âge*, Paris: Presses Universitaires de France.

Lacan, J. (1973[1964], *Les quatre concepts fondamentaux de la psychanalyse*, ed. Miller, J.-A., Paris: Éditions du Seuil.

Maupas, A. and Prudent-Bayle, A. (2016), 'La censure de l'amante', in: Danon-Boileau, L. and Tamet, J-Y. eds, *Des psychanalystes en séance. Glossaire clinique de psychanalyse contemporaine*, Paris: Gallimard, pp. 497–501.

Ody, M. (1999), 'L'apport de la théorie de Michel Fain à la pratique de l'analyse d'enfants', in: Duparc, F. ed., *La censure de l'amante et autres préludes à l'oeuvre de Michel Fain*, Paris: Delachaux et Niestlé, pp. 63–71.

Ody, M. (2000), *Denise Braunschweig (Psychanalystes d'aujourd'hui 30)*, Paris: Presses Universitaires de France.

Ody, M. and Danon-Boileau, L. (2002), 'censure de l'amante', in: de Mijolla, A. ed., *Dictionnaire international de la psychanalyse*, volume 1, Paris: Calmann-Lévy, pp. 303–304.

Riolo, F. (2018), 'Comment on 'Mentalisation et passivité' by Michel Fain', *International Journal of Psychoanalysis* 99(2), pp. 485–486.

Shorter, E. (1975), *The making of the modern family*, Glasgow: William Collins Sons & Co.

Simpson, R. (2018), 'On being consoled: Engaging with Michel Fain's paper 'Mentalization and passivity', *International Journal of Psychoanalysis* 99(2), pp. 487–494.

Szwec, G. (2013c), 'Préface à la réédition d'*Éros et Antéros*', in: Braunschweig, D. and Fain, M. (1971), *Éros et Antéros*, new edition, Paris: Éditions in Press, pp. 5–21.

5

BASIC MECHANISMS 1

Nicos Nicolaïdis

In his inquiry, Nicos Nicolaïdis picks up threads from Pierre Marty, Michel Fain and Denise Braunschweig about the prerequisites for infantile desire. As befits French psychoanalysis, the resulting work is relentlessly dense, rich in thought and material. To understand his work, it is essential to grasp the dialectic between absence and desire implied, but not spelled out, in Nicolaïdis' thought. Since he does not provide vignettes, following French precedent, I make use of an example from Literary History to illustrate this. Let us consider the following situation: While courting Elizabeth Barrett in her father's house, Robert Browning showed her lines that gave poetic voice to his strong sense of what the English landscape, gradually awakening to Spring, must be looking like at a time when the persona of the poem, a sojourner wandering the continent, cannot actually witness this. In *Home-Thoughts, from Abroad* (published in 1845 in *Dramatic Romance and Lyrics*) memory steps in and provides impressions garnered in the past to be arranged into a vivid mental picture of what is currently beyond his grasp. Every minute little detail, quite possibly lost to a casual rambler traversing a landscape familiar to him/her, bespeaks the magnitude of loss inflicted by its physical absence. It is the poignancy of feeling, coming to him like an unsolicited visitor at an untoward moment, and for which the poetic persona in Browning's lines may have been ill prepared upon leaving England, that reveals to him who he is to himself in his solitude and to where a sense of unbidden belonging is now drawing him from afar. Not long after this, Robert Browning eloped with Elizabeth, taking her from England, the country *for* which his poetic alter ego had felt such acute pangs of nostalgia, to

Tuscany, the place he had experienced this *from*, in this translocation famously curing his newly wedded wife – after her marriage without further ado disinherited by her father – from the illness that had beset her and had rendered her a fragile invalid whilst at home.

It is some of such complexities that Nicos Nicolaïdis – straddling Greek and French culture in his own way while working in Switzerland – addresses in his studies on perception, representation and the blocking force of mentally indigestible presence, topics to which we now turn.

On the tracks of disorganisation

In one passage, Nicolaïdis reminds us that Henry Ey, the influential mentoring spirit of a generation of young French psychiatrists, held it against psychoanalysis that it inadequately accounted for mental disorganisation. He argued that any attempt to draw on the forces of 'libido and destrudo' was incapable of explaining the phenomenon of disorganisation, thus making the important point that a lack of mental organisation might neither be indicative of a hidden wish nor constitute a covert attack. This chimed in with earlier positions, not referred to by Nicolaïdis, by Pierre Janet, who stressed deficiencies in organisation over the dynamics of the unconscious, positions with which Ey's own thought reverberated in critical tension. Although we shall see that disorganisation does play some part in Nicolaïdis' thought, it is to the disastrous consequences of insufficient differentiation that he turns when he presents his psychoanalytic reading of the Gaia–Ouranos myth.

The drama of Gaia and Ouranos

From the primal abyss, Gaia (Earth) emerges. In parthenogenesis, she gives birth to Ouranos (the Sky), who covers her entirely and has incessant intercourse with her, reflecting himself in her image. In this constant mating, in which the generational difference is swept aside, respite from mirroring is none: rare will be perceptually unsaturated moments, little can give rise to the mental anticipation of pleasures yet to come. Gaia and Ouranos are caught in a sensory-perceptual forcefield entrapping them in a degree of homeostasis that is detrimental to the further development of the Kosmos. To countermand this, Gaia sets an end to this relationship, which is exhausting itself in driven repetitive action and is lacking in representation. She orders her son Kronos to cut off the testicles of his father-brother Ouranos. It is, in Nicolaïdis' view, the 'No' of a mother renouncing completion by her child, the son-lover to be pried off her in this act of castration, that opens up the necessary space for differentiation and the establishing of a new timeline and a new rhythm. This permits her to reposition herself in the undoing of a tight dyadic fit marinated in stale satiety beyond measure. From the cut-off testicles fallen to Earth, the Erinyes, the Furies, spring into existence establishing a first law of talion. The *originaire* has to pass and wane before even the primary can set in.

Escape from oppressive presence

Greek theogony, Nicolaïdis points out, presents the world of humans as a realm owed to the rise of displeasure. He sees strong inner connections between the mythemes of Hesiod and the psycho-sexual development of the child as described by Freud. Is there, Nicolaïdis asks, an early perceptive-sensorial force field that provides a primitive voltage supply for the organisation of an as yet fragmentary self – the *mosaïque prèmiere* hypothesised by Marty – a force field which, if unduly strong and protracted, impedes hallucination and the onset of the imaginary? Instead of coming to terms with absence, distance and delay, Nicolaïdis suggests, images of a surfeit of the same will exert their unbridled magnetic attraction. Perception of raw sensory reality will freeze numb what could otherwise have served as later contact points to the symbolic. This early hoar frost descending on the nascent subject will paralyse affect, while at the same time conserving it in shrivelled form, shunted off from representation. Meaningless perception will go on offering a nucleus of anti-fantasmatic potential set beneath the threshold of fantasy. If crises later in life throw the subject back to its early defences, and they were to prove unstable, it is the sheer force of perception that will offer a rallying point by drawing the subject magnetically towards the unthinkable image of the early object, in which residual excitement remains symbolically undigested, and pre-symbolic perception frames the subject.

The sway of early reality unprovided with a representational handle

As Nicolaïdis relates, it was Winnicott's work on breakdown, and in particular his words about 'breakdown' to describe the unthinkable state of affairs that underlies the defence organisation' (Winnicott 1974, p. 103) that provided the germ for his initial reflections on the *objet référent*, an (early) object. This, we may gather, is the vital place which in the subject's foundational groundwork can neither be experienced nor thought of. The *référent*, in Nicolaïdis' thought, is the form under which the early object imposes itself if and when there are the prodromes of a breakdown, elusively escaping the grasp by a subject who was not really there when its foundations were laid, '*en deça de l'appareil psychique*'.

Nicolaïdis derives the term *référent* from Ferdinand de Saussure's structural hierarchy of linguistic classification, a means to denote a concrete, nameless quiddity without linguistic significance. In a paper in the *Revue Française de Psychanalyse*, based on a course he gave at the Psychological Faculty of the University of Geneva in the 1978/79 winter term, Nicolaïdis sets out to connect this to psychoanalytic theory and practice. Like Saussure's *référent*, the object which Nicolaïdis hypothesises is comparable only to itself and does not point to anything else. Although there is a Gestalt (or rather Pre-Gestalt) to it, it is situated on a pre-objectal level, before even the appearance of partial objects. It cannot be hallucinated, does not lend itself to either figurability or metaphor and does not produce dream images, although it may give rise to something akin to a *trompe l'oeil*, a two-dimensional near approximation to hallucination. Echoing Piera Castoriadis-Aulagnier, Nicolaïdis sees in this *référent* an early form of the *pictogramme* that expresses the lasting sensory attraction of the irreplaceable original, for which no representational substitute is acceptable, a reality that cannot be told and against which one has to fling oneself relentlessly. It belongs to the realms of Ananké, at this stage unvisited by desire.

Since separation has not occurred, lack is not experienced as something caused by the doings of the object, an object, to which at this stage the baby, make or break, is totally fused in a symbiosis that may yet come to haunt it in future shapeless blanks. Perception that cannot be invested in subverts the psychic apparatus, sweeping the mindscape with a cold wind. Granted the individual is born with a given constitution, a considerable weight lies on the development of the newborn's relational interactions – something Nicolaïdis terms synaptic in the original Greek sense of the word: a function of elements touching in liaison.

The advent of language into a world shaped by interaction

Much as the good breast in Kleinian psychoanalysis provides a comprehensive metaphor for what is wholesome, the Lacanian term *signifiant phallique* (phallic signifier) is used by Nicolaïdis as short hand for an indispensable ingredient in mental development: a signal of separation, a harbinger of asymmetries to be dealt with, a portent of differentiation to come, transforming by its vigorous insistence the early dyad. As this is happening, and the earlier scaffolding is left behind, a world beyond is opening up: language, as a movement towards the world, significantly extends the scope of reference and sentiment beyond immediate lack and survival: more fully fledged representation under the impact of separation spells out the early hieroglyphic presence of the mother in more freely mobile elements analogous to the transit from Linear A/B script to the alphabet. If it is in place, there is the increased possibility a rich multiplicity of meanings and representations can be processed more easily, crucially enriching the preconscious. Whereas the early 'hieroglyphs' conserve a link with bodily movement, condensation, displacement and figuration now take advantage of the new possibilities provided by language to furnish the world of dreams, and in doing so finds new means to evade censorship. Language joins the subject to a community of speakers and, to boot, gives access to a galore of stories drenched in fantasies. It is the capacity of illusion passed on by the parents that determines how long the desert of meaninglessness will have to last.

The power of historically contingent myth

In contrast to Lacan, as Nicolaïdis himself says, he does not believe that we are faced with supposedly invariant, universally valid structures. Rather we deal with historically grown myths shaped by the experiences and desires of a particular society, group or family and in considerable flux. With the preconscious in development, mythologies into which the mother and her world are embedded come more forcefully into play, offering to the infant culturally engendered dream equivalents, of which he/she will make selective use according to the shape and the needs of his/her particular infantile neurosis. Myth selects from the historical experience of a people to present an imaginary continuity grounded in desire, whereas regular history accounts present a line-up of facts and events, which corresponds to the imperatives of desire only in discontinuous bouts. Myth gives form to desire by offering a screen, thus unifying experience. Beyond the structuring of content, it shapes the very container for what escapes the conceptual framework of the times.

A potential crisis of transition

Into this pre-existing space the child enters, finding in it, as Nicolaïdis suggests in allusion to words ascribed to Aristotle, in nascent subjectivity a position to learn, to suffer, as well as getting involved in a process of being made ready for a disposition. Transitions have to be negotiated and for this the infant needs to meet with the right conditions accorded by both the mother and her world, a world in which important choices as to which symbolic screens are to be privileged have already been made. Although individual myth and collective myth have to be differentiated, there is a permanent interaction between the two.

Leaving behind early sensory worlds of *pictogrammes* is fraught with hazards: early idiom has to find a translation into the new worlds of meaning, mediated by language, delimiting the role of the mother and giving an inkling of her desires pointing beyond the dyad. If the mother is not able to connect to a preconscious sufficiently structured by triangulation, provided with freely mobile elements, with a good regressive potential grounded in her personal and her group's myths, the effects on the infant will likely be deleterious: whatever tinder there is in the child will find it uncommonly difficult under these conditions, to meet with the indispensable spark.

Although there is territory that will never be indexed in networks of meaning, Nicolaïdis, in contrast to Lacan, does not believe that foreclosure, once it has occurred, has to be deemed an irreversible structure: what once was excluded may still be re-inserted into the realms of the symbolic.

In critique of supposedly supra-historic structures

Considering Nicolaïdis' strong interest in the mutability of specifics and their evolution, it is not surprising that he takes exception to Melanie Klein's view of phantasy, which in his view tends to assign a supra-historic statute to it, and which, he says, erects a wall around the dyad. He accuses her of confusing, and conceptually merging, a potential for symbolisation with its actual manifest functioning. Nicolaïdis regards culture – like the psychosexual development of the child – as work in progress, linked to civic space, social developments and cultural processes. The *roman culturel* of a specific time and place opens up or hinders, as the case may be, specific forms of mental elaboration. In this his view he is closer to Winnicott, to whose understanding of the importance of culture and the environment he repeatedly refers, than to the structuralism of Lacan, as a theory less accommodating to refractory specifics and the tides of change. Within a French context there seems to be, in this point, some unstated proximity to his fellow Greek-French psychoanalyst Cornelius Castoriadis' understanding of the social imaginary as *magma*, not a structure but something in movement, which can take different shapes.

If the concept of affect does indeed include, as Nicolaïdis acknowledges with André Green, aspects of perception, it is important that it finds mental representation early enough. Both perception and affect are solicited by fantasy linked to the mythological potential of the times. Cuts in the cohesion of affective tissue will form scars that spur the individual to responding perceptively and not by way of representation.

The importance for flexible building blocks for fantasy

Borrowing from Lacan, Nicolaïdis refers to the processes of transformation from crude to elaborate, which meaning and language distil from early asymbolic experience, under the term algorithm. For a workable result the distance between the element to be transformed and the element into which it is translated should neither be tantalisingly great nor stultifyingly small, lest the voltage flow of desire be impaired. To bolster this productive tension, there have to be freely mobile elements of form (an alphabet of combinable elements) accessible to the subject to express nuances of sentiment and to bind them into a gamut of meaning. To return to our initial vignette, Robert Browning himself would not have been able to produce his poems in hieroglyphic script (or have them, anachronistically, replaced by photographs) to the same effect and, thus restricted, would not have been able to woo Elizabeth Browning in the way he did, playing on the tension between what is, what is not and what might be. In order for lack to be able to register as loss with the individual, absence from the object of desire has to work on the mind and be provided with elements of a configuration breathed upon and quickened by language.

In such manner, Jeanette Winterson, adopted into an oppressively religious family in Lancashire, for all the mental shackles her mother attempted to put on her, found yet the language of the King James Bible, echoed in local vernacular use, a source of rich cadences and a treasure trove of verbal space. In her experience, it was capable of empowering the hearer and reader to enter a world beyond the confines of the family, in a wealth of connectivity which the more facile, lexically refurbished new versions, cutting links to four hundred years of poetry, could not offer. With all acceptable form put beyond the pale, on the other hand, things to be said may have to be kept *en souffrance* (waiting for realisation), in at best, a twilight of stasis unable to carry investment.

Potential dis-differentiation: sensitivity reduced, complexity on hold

Insertion into and investment of the symbolic, desirable as it is, remains liable to be put at risk by the archaic *référent*, threatening not just the fruit of translation but the very process itself: a disruption instead of a productive discontinuity within a continuum, 'affect without a skin'. To all intents and purposes, the realms of Nicolaïdis' *référent* bear close relationship to E.M. Forster's fictitious Marabar caves, used to great effect in *A Passage to India*, in which meaning falls prey to much more archaic forces and composure succumbs to the inchoate.

Not surprisingly, Nicolaïdis shows little faith in the workings of the *pulsion de mort* posited to be striking the psyche of the individual as a force of nature unconnected to his/her concrete moorings, in this joining André Green's doubts on the justification of assuming an auto-destructive function that were to articulate itself primitively, spontaneously or automatically from innate sources. This does not keep Nicolaïdis from finding himself in agreement with Michel Fain's non-metaphysical use of the *pulsion de mort* in describing forces leading to disorganisation. These processes, he believes, typically work in silence, much less spectacularly than the majority of phenomena described by Kleinians under this heading, and act as a shield against an overflow of excitement, striving to reduce it to nothing.

Michel Fain, as Nicolaïdis points out, imperceptibly rehabilitates the death instinct as a force opposing death, when he reminds his readers that Freud considered living matter as typically clothed in a defensive coating provided by a deadened – more obtuse – layer which protected the narcissistic capital of the subject from exposure to the world in raw, as if skinned alive.

If we connect this with the potentially disruptive effect of the *référent*, a complex picture emerges, in which the *caveat* lodged by Henri Ey (and Pierre Janet) can be given its due. Integration may have been jeopardised because differentiation was arrested in too prolonged an *avant coup*. For all the resulting deficiencies, dead insensitive layers of the individual may find secondary use in defensive and life sustaining purposes. Attempts to 'mentalise' what owes its function to being mentally deaf could have potentially destructive consequences.

Référent: a state of affairs that cannot be resolved in a crisis

In the effects of prolonged exposure to the *référent* – perhaps loosely to be translated as a state of affairs in which things are as they are and only as they are, without anything pointing to a beyond – Bion's 'unsaturated element' seems to find a dark cousin: whereas with Bion it seems to be a factor impelling onwards, urging new solutions to previous arrangements, the *référent* has a more sinister side to it, potentially putting at risk all translation into meaning. It is as if in Bion's (1990) parable of an egg hatching out, faced with a crack but not knowing of the chicken it will turn to, the natural causeway leading from egg to chicken were to be put into doubt. Just as with Bion, we find crises of transition with Nicolaïdis, but in some of them form cannot adequately be invested in, constrained by the limited horizons of an environment that does not take kindly to the kindling of desire and in which little, if anything, points beyond the mandates of sheer necessity.

The *référent* as a retardant of sublimation

This is, of course, in many ways the reverse of what has traditionally been discussed under the heading of sublimation, a term much less frequently used outside the Francophone zone within the psychoanalytic world today. Yet, as Valdre (2014), in her extensive study, points out, it seems that 'reparation', which has to some extent replaced it, only partially covers the territory vacated by its disappearance in psychoanalytic discourse, with Winnicott's 'potential space' admittedly recovering important stretches of it. With an author like Hans W. Loewald (1988) we find sublimation as a means to overcome alienating differentiation on a higher level, which would not have been sought for if no sharp loss had been felt. In an interesting comment by Antonio Di Benedetto (1993) sublimation is seen as a move from the causal order of things to the realms of the aesthetic.

Psychoanalytic aesthetics as a domain receptive to the restraints of the material

It is in the department of psychoanalytic aesthetics, indeed, that the questions raised by Nicolaïdis seem to have received closest attention within British psychoanalysis, which in its Kleinian articulation has been more inclined to see the subject as naturally equipped – and preyed upon – by an abundance of formative, if problematic, forces and thus has had no good reason to doubt their continued operation. Although Melanie Klein in her paper *On Identification* (1955), offering her comments on Julian Green's novella *Si J'étais vous*, accepts that the shape of the host character taken over by the protagonist severely limits the sensibilities of the transmigrating 'soul', the further developments initiated by Bion's concept of the container do not seem to have led to an extensive literature on the social morphology and texture of form, beyond what can be asserted about the naturally somatoform. This, perforce, cannot apply to aesthetics, which by its very nature has to ask questions about the interplay between dark urge and available material form.

Available remedies contingent on the times

What Nicolaïdis' thinking throws into relief is that the form needed to process inner life may or may not be available. Nicolaïdis does not expatiate on this but what happened to John Stuart Mill in the 19th century may well serve as an example. As we know from his autobiography, when John Stuart Mill went through a deep crisis in the latter half of the 1820s, he felt as if stranded, 'with a well-equipped ship and a rudder, but no sail; without any real desire' (Mill 1873, pp. 139). He was saved from his wretched state by reading in the autumn of

1828, as he recalls, for the first time in his life, the poems of William Wordsworth, which turned out to be 'medicine for my state of mind' (1873, p. 148). Mill's crisis had been taking place in an environment in which antidotes to the idolatry of the factual were both available and accessible to him. What objects can be put to service to increase mental space seems to vary considerably. What is self-appropriated has often been present in waiting, as it were, to be found and put to use by the subject. Yet, the means to do so have to be present in the mental environment and will change with the times.

The sensation of lack mediated by the inner worlds of the mother

Nicolaïdis, in tackling the imagination (conceptualised as representation), concedes almost Wordsworthian status to the power of the preconscious regressing to memory traces 'in tranquillity' as it were, yet grounds this not in universal capability and natural endowment but in the stimulus offered by access to the phantasms of others, often mediated by a halo of words. Although there is an acknowledgement of the libidinal kick and push in the individual, there is also an interpersonal, object related element, which finds its inter-generational pivotal kingpin in the preconscious of the mother.

It is not lack as such that creates desire but lack to which a trajectory of desire is opened by the mother's own desires, taking the child from a reverie within the dyad to a reverie beyond the dyad, and bridging the dry sands of what is continually at hand to intimations of what might possibly be. Demand for form has to be complemented by a supply of building blocks of form – the more freely mobile the better – if the preconscious is to develop and thrive. Infantile object seeking should be given the chance of meeting an object that herself is given to the seeking of pleasure, whatever the duty she has signed up for. Images saturated with presence could dampen the representative imagination, which, on the other hand, if permitted to amble into, and lose itself in, family myth, will work its way towards pictures sponsored by both language and absence, as happening in dream life.

Yet, as myth shows, there are times when it is useful to lose oneself in non-differentiation so as to better survive the crisis: Thus, Odysseus, confronted with Polyphemos determined to devour him and his comrades, retreats into a 'I am nobody', a wily move employed to best the Cyclops.

Attention to concrete interactions as a step beyond Lacan

In the positions of Nicolaïdis, sketched above, he deviates from Lacan – whose thoughts he does not reject, but whose group he does not belong to – along remarkably similar lines as Winnicott does from Melanie Klein. Both were willing to take into account the goings-on in the concrete mother to an extent thought unwarranted by those with whom they were parting company.

We shall see with César and Sára Botella, who do not belong to Nicolaïdis' more immediate group, that his inquiries into the hazards of figurability were addressed afresh from a somewhat different angle. His interest in motricity as a substitute for representation (used as a blueprint by Ouranos in the Gaia myth) finds more detailed treatment in the work of Gérard Szwec on the contemporary epidemic of 'voluntary galley slaves', rowing towards release from tension, a matter to which we turn in the next chapter.

Sources

Bion, W.R. (1990), *Brazilian lectures* (1973–74), London: Karnac Books.
Bromberg, P. (1998), *Standing in the spaces. Essays on clinical process, trauma, and dissociation*, New York: The Analytic Press.
Chazaud, J. (2004), 'Place et influence des conceptions de Pierre Janet dans l'élaboration de l'œuvre d'Henri Ey', *L'Information Psychiatrique* 80, pp. 403–406.
Di Benedetto, A. (1993), 'La sublimazione nella prospettiva di Bion e Matte Blanco: La sublimazione come arte della "trasformazione" e della "formalizzazione"', *Rivista di Psicoanalisi* 39(1), pp. 65–82.
Ey, H. (1950), *Études psychiatriques*, volume 2, Paris: Desclée de Brouwer.
Gálvez, M.J. (2002), '"Alphabet et psychanalyse" de Nicos Nicolaïdis', *Revue Française de Psychosomatique* 22, pp. 175–181.
Loewald, H.W. (1988), *Sublimation: Inquiries into theoretical psychoanalysis*, London: Yale University Press.
Masciangelo, P.M. and Racalbuto, A. (1987), 'Nicolaïdis sulla rappresentazione: l'evoluzione freudiana', *Rivista di Psicoanalisi* 33, pp. 529–540.

McNay, L. (2000), 'Psyche and society: Castoriadis and the creativity of action', in: McNay, L., *Gender and agency. Reconfiguring the subject in feminist and social theory*, Cambridge: Polity Press, pp. 117–154.

McNay, L. (2008), *Against recognition*, Cambridge: Polity Press.

Mill, J.S. (1859), *On Liberty*, 3rd edition 1864, London: Longmans, Green, Reader and Dyer.

Mill, J.S. (1873), *Autobiography*, 3rd edition 1874, London: Longmans, Green, Reader and Dyer.

Nicolaïdis, G. and Nicolaïdis, N. (1977), 'Jeu d'ombre et sujet-objet mélancolique', *Revue Française de Psychanalyse* 41(1–2), pp. 281–286.

Nicolaïdis, G. and Nicolaïdis, N. (1994), *Mythologie Grecque et Psychanalyse*, Paris: Delachaux et Niestlé.

Nicolaïdis, G. and Nicolaïdis, N. (1997), 'La mythologie la plus proche de la fantasmatisation symbolique', in: Clancier, A. and Athanassiou Popesco, C. eds, *Mythes et psychanalyse*, Paris: In Press, pp. 23–31.

Nicolaïdis, N. (1971), 'La réalité du "mythe" dans la cure psychanalytique', *Revue Française de Psychanalyse* 35(5–6), pp. 1011–1013.

Nicolaïdis, N. (1972), 'Intervention', *Revue Française de Psychanalyse* 36(5-6), p. 973.

Nicolaïdis, N. (1973), 'Proto-Oedipe et Oedipe oedipifié. Une "mutation" sur-moïque. A propos de Oedipe sans complexe de J.P. Vernant', *Revue Française de Psychanalyse* 37(3), pp. 473–490.

Nicolaïdis, N. (1975), 'La psychanalyse survivra-t-elle en "1984"? L'Hybris kleinienne (du côté de Clytemnestre)', *Revue Française de Psychanalyse* 39(1-2), pp. 247–272.

Nicolaïdis, N. (1977), 'L'auto-érotisme instantané: dédoublement phallique: une aventure apollinienne', *Revue Française de Psychanalyse* 41(5-6), pp. 1107–1112.

Nicolaïdis, N. (1979a), 'Oedipe: Le message de la différence', *Revue Française de Psychanalyse* 43(3), pp. 409–419.

Nicolaïdis, N. (1979b), 'Aspects de représentation psychanalytique (De l'objet référent à l'axe phallique de la représentation significante)', *Revue Française de Psychanalyse* 43(5-6), pp. 1031–1064.

Nicolaïdis, N. (1980a), 'Proto-Oedipe et Oedipe oedipisé. Une "mutation" sur-moïque. A propos de Oedipe sans complexe de J.P. Vernant', in: Anzieu, D., Carapanos, F., Gillibert, J., Green, A., Nicolaïdis, N., and Potamianou, A. (1980), *Psychanalyse et culture Grecque*, Paris: Société d'Édition des Belles Lettres, pp. 159–182.

Nicolaïdis, N. (1980b), 'Mythes et écriture, moyens d'approche de l'appareil psychique', in: Anzieu, D., Carapanos, F., Gillibert, J., Green, A.,

Nicolaïdis, N., and Potamianou, A. (1980), *Psychanalyse et culture Grecque*, Paris: Société d'Édition des Belles Lettres, pp. 197–214.

Nicolaïdis, N. (1981), 'Le coté "hieroglyphique" de la langue maternelle résistance aux changements du processus psychanalytique', *Revue Française de Psychanalyse* 45(4), pp. 1029–1033.

Nicolaïdis, N. (1982a), 'Du meutre du savoir et de l'inceste (Questionnements et ambiguïtés)', *Revue Française de Psychanalyse* 46(4), pp. 857–865.

Nicolaïdis, N. (1982b), 'La créativité à l'intérieur de la langue', in: Nicolaïdis, N. and Schmid-Kitsikis, E. eds, *Créativité et/ou symptome*, Paris: Éditions Clancier-Guénaud, pp. 199–206.

Nicolaïdis, N. (1984a), *La représentation. Essai psychanalytique. De l'objet referent a la représentation symbolique*, Paris: Bordas.

Nicolaïdis, N. (1984b), 'Homosexualité, culpabilité inconsciente ou préconsciente?: du "cratylisme" avec Freud' *Revue Française de Psychanalyse* 48(3), pp. 731–744.

Nicolaïdis, N. (1985), 'Fixations synchroniques et négations diachroniques: à propos de René Girard', in: Flournoy, O. ed., *Psychanalyse 1985*, Schweizerische Gesellschaft für Psychoanalyse, pp. 197–214.

Nicolaïdis, N. (1987), 'Un préconscient extra-territorial (L'historien objectif doit mourir), *Revue Française de Psychanalyse* 51(2), pp. 775–780.

Nicolaïdis, N. (1988), *La théophagie. Oralité primaire et métaphorique*, Paris: Dunod.

Nicolaïdis, N. (1989a), 'Le sujet perdant', *Revue Française de Psychanalyse* 53(2), pp. 231–234.

Nicolaïdis, N. (1989b), 'Le fonction symbolique dans le processus dissociatif et les désorganisation contre-évolutives', *Revue Française de Psychanalyse* 53(6), pp. 1871–1877.

Nicolaïdis, N. (1989c), 'Hésiode et Freud, chemins parallèles: l'infrastructure mythique inaugurale', *Topique* 43, pp. 101–114.

Nicolaïdis, N. (1990), 'Le langage, élément neg-entropique', *Revue Française de Psychanalyse* 54(6), pp. 1635–1638.

Nicolaïdis, N. (1991), 'Fantasmes originaires et fantasmes "historico-mythologiques"', *Revue Française de Psychanalyse* 55(5), pp.1185–1188.

Nicolaïdis, N. (1992), 'De la "mère symbiotique" à la renonciation pulsionnelle', *Revue Française de Psychanalyse* 56(5), pp. 1639–1642.

Nicolaïdis, N. (1993), *La force perceptive de la représentation de la pulsion*, Paris: Presses Universitaires de France.

Nicolaïdis, N. (1995a), 'Perception et reconnaissance', *Revue Française de Psychanalyse* 59(4), pp. 565–569.

Nicolaïdis, N. (1995b), 'Temps cyclique et temps linéaire', *Revue Française de Psychanalyse* 59(4), pp. 1189–1196.

Nicolaïdis, N. (1995c), 'Le langage, appareil d'action', *Revue Française de Psychanalyse* 59(5), pp. 1695–1698.

Nicolaïdis, N. (1995d), 'Introduction', in: Nicolaïdis, N. and Press, J. eds, *La psychosomatique hier et aujourd'hui*, Paris: Delachaux et Niestlé, pp. 9–30.

Nicolaïdis, N. (1995e), 'Psychosomatique un concept limite', in: Nicolaïdis, N. and Press, J. eds, *La psychosomatique hier et aujourd'hui*, Paris: Delachaux et Niestlé, pp. 259–293.

Nicolaïdis, N. (1995f), 'Analyse de: Green, A. – Le travail du négatif. Paris: Les Éditions de Minuit, 1993', *Revue Française de Psychosomatique* 7, pp. 211–217.

Nicolaïdis, N. (1996a), 'Introduction', in: Marty, P. and Nicolaïdis, N. (1996), *Psychosomatique. Pensée vivante*, Bordeaux-Le-Bouscat: L'Esprit du Temps, pp. 7–14.

Nicolaïdis, N. (1996b), 'Complément aux entretiens', in: Marty, P. and Nicolaïdis, N. (1996), *Psychosomatique. Pensée vivante*, Bordeaux-Le-Bouscat: L'Esprit du Temps, pp. 137–164.

Nicolaïdis, N. (1996c), 'Préface', in: Athanassiou-Popesco, C., *Penser le mythe*, Lausanne: Delachaux et Niestlé, pp. 9–17.

Nicolaïdis, N. (1997a), 'La crise "solution de continuité" de l'organisation défensive', *Revue Française de Psychosomatique* 12, pp. 143–149.

Nicolaïdis, N. (1997b), 'De la perception au moi-idéal', in: Schmid-Kitsikis, E. and Sanzana A. eds, *Concepts limites en psychanalyse*, Lausanne: Delachaux et Niestlé, pp. 329–341.

Nicolaïdis, N. (1998a), 'Argument: L'unité fondamentale de l'être humain', *Actualités Psychosomatiques* 1, pp. 11–19.

Nicolaïdis, N. (1998b), 'Argument', *Actualités Psychosomatiques* 1, pp. 73–78.

Nicolaïdis, N. (1998c), 'Le cheminement de l'AGEPSO', *Actualités Psychosomatiques* 1, pp. 151–154.

Nicolaïdis, N. (1998d), 'La "poupée" de Pierre Marty et les Barbies de notre époque', *Revue Française de Psychanalyse* 62(5), pp. 1579–1581.

Nicolaïdis, N. (1998e), 'Le "modèle Marty": pré-psychique ou près-psychique?' in: Fine, A. and Schaeffer, J. eds, *Interrogations psychosomatiques*, Paris: Presses Universitaires de France, pp. 125–135.

Nicolaïdis, N. (1999a), 'Introduction', *Actualités Psychosomatiques* 2, pp. 3–11.

Nicolaïdis, N. (1999b), 'Le langage rend "l'amour plus fort que la mort"', *Revue Française de Psychanalyse* 63(5), pp. 1899–1904.

Nicolaïdis, N. (1999c), 'Le langage infraverbal: une "transfusion" olfacto-gustative', *Revue Française de Psychosomatique* 16, pp. 173–178.

Nicolaïdis, N. (2000a), 'Questionnement et apories', *Actualités Psychosomatiques* 3, pp. 3–8.
Nicolaïdis, N. (2000b), 'Esquisse d'une réponse à René Roussillon', *Actualités Psychosomatiques* 3, pp. 115–117.
Nicolaïdis, N. (2001a), *Alphabet et psychanalyse. Suivi de Une séance de supervision avec Jaques Lacan*, Bordeaux-Le-Bouscat: L'Esprit du Temps.
Nicolaïdis, N. (2001b), 'Esquisse du travail du rêve', *Actualités Psychosomatiques* 4, pp. 3–6.
Nicolaïdis, N. (2003a), *Angoisse, dépression, dépression essentielle*, Paris: Delachaux et Niestlé.
Nicolaïdis, N. (2003b), 'Surmoi et religions (Une mutation surmoique)', *Actualités Psychosomatiques* 6, pp. 159–173.
Nicolaïdis, N. (2004), 'Aux confins de la représentation', *Actualités Psychosomatiques* 7, pp. 9–22.
Nicolaïdis, N. (2005), 'Réflexions à propos de la dépersonnalisation', *Revue Française de Psychosomatique* 27, pp. 163–176.
Nicolaïdis, N. (2006), 'Modes de défenses qui protègent le fonctionnement mental: hypothèses de travail', *Actualités Psychosomatiques* 9, pp. 5–9.
Nicolaïdis, N. (2009a), 'Mes réflexions sur le petit-a de J. Lacan', *Actualités Psychosomatiques* 12, pp. 139–159.
Nicolaïdis, N. (2009b), 'Réflexions sur le livre d'André Green: Le Premier Commandement de J. Conrad', *Revue Française de Psychosomatique* 35, pp. 183–190.
Nicolaïdis, N. and Abraham, G. (1989), 'Sur l'économie du désir', *Evolution Psychiatrique* 54(4), pp. 787–801.
Nicolaïdis, N. and Andréoli, A. (1986), 'Discutants', *Revue Française de Psychanalyse* 50(1), pp. 337–370.
Nicolaïdis, N. and Cornu, F. (1976), 'Etude du signifiant psychanalytique à travers les "Cinq psychanalyses" de S. Freud', *Revue Française de Psychanalyse* 40(2), pp. 325–350.
Nicolaïdis, N. and Papilloud, J. (1988), 'Une langue privée pour combler le manque', *Revue Française de Psychanalyse* 52(2), pp.523–531.
Nicolaïdis, N. and Press, J. (2004), 'Un regard sur le parcours de l'AGEPSO', *Actualités Psychosomatiques* 7, pp. 5–7.
Roux, M-L. (1985), 'La représentation, essai psychanalytique de Nicos Nicolaïdis', *Revue Française de Psychanalyse* 49(6), pp. 1594–1597.
Thanopulos, S. (1997), 'Il vuoto di rappresentazione e la destrutturazione del pensiero', *Rivista di Psicoanalisi* 43(3), pp. 385–411.
Valdre, R. (2014), *On sublimation. A path to the destiny of desire, theory and treatment*, London: Karnac Books.

Warnock, M. (1976), *Imagination*, Berkeley: University of California Press.
Winnicott D.W. (1974), 'Fear of breakdown', *International Review of Psychoanalysis* 1, pp. 103–107.
Winterson, J. (2011), 'The King James Bible's Language Lesson', available at: www.jeanettewinterson.com/journalism/the-king-james-bibles-language-lesson/

6

BASIC MECHANISMS 2

Gérard Szwec

Being able to draw on flexible building blocks for representation may, as we have seen, be of great importance to the subject: it determines what can be processed. At the same time, having at one's disposal a protective layer capable of reducing the amount of incoming stimuli – Nicolaïdis reminded his readers of Freud's image of the outer peel of the vesicle – can keep the individual up and running in the face of adversity. This, apparently, can work both ways: There are those who have to keep on running until they drop so as to generate the only means known to them to process tension. It is to these devotees of a Sisyphos agenda unbeknownst to them that Gérard Szwec turns his attention in his study *Les galériens volontaires*, which has received attention and acclaim within a wider public beyond a strictly professional readership.

> Some people appear like convicts chain-ganged to repetition beyond the pleasure principle. They are fascinated by their own functional [*opératoire*] robotisation. Sometimes it is this that they count upon to pull them out of the shipwrecks of their distress to which, however, they return compulsively and which they re-edit to exhaustion. They row, run, and swim, to the limit of their forces; and then they recommence. Adventure repeated *ad nauseam* does not make them dream any more. For a long time it [this way of dealing with things] has been nothing but constraint to them, constraint automatically to repeat behaviour exactly identical, without repose, without respite. They have turned themselves into voluntary galley slaves.
>
> (Szwec 1998a, p. 9)

Self-imposed drudgery in quest for inner calm

Gérard Szwec points out that his focus is not on individuals who love adventure or who develop a taste for risk but specifically on those who use fright as a paradoxical means to soothe themselves and to bring about radical inner calm. He refers to interviews with solitary, long distance rowers published in the journal *Libération*, already in the public domain. One of the interviewees, Gérard d'Aboville, sustained on average seven thousand oar strokes per day over a distance of ten thousand kilometres at a rate of seventeen strokes per minute. To keep up this amount of programmed regularity he inwardly had to go on automatic pilot. Szwec quotes d'Aboville:

> Always the same tune, always the same metronome rhythm … the body works like a machine and the spirit functions like a calculator.… Minutes are hours, hours are days, days are months.… It is another world that resembles hell.
> (Szwec 1998a, p. 19)

Szwec provides other examples of extreme sportsmanship in which the athletes deliberately take their psyche off-line by resorting to regular counting and making an effort of focusing on pre-programmed automatic bodily movement. In the world of work this is not a matter of choice; with rowers like d'Aboville it is. Why do people eagerly enter a hell of their own making? One rower interviewed by *Libération* stated that rowing had quickly become a terrible drug to him, impossible to renounce. Once the behaviour has been established, tension is not routed into the psyche but soaked up by the activity and laid to rest in pre-established patterns. There seems to be little pleasure and satisfaction involved. A new need has been created; the realms of *Ananke* have been ingeniously extended. Mastery, not desire, is the order of the day, as new states of helplessness are ushered in to be repeatedly overcome in a desperate struggle for survival engineered on purpose. To hold fast to the helm, the muscular apparatus is solicited to the full. Perception of pain becomes a substitute for the object. Emptiness offers its folds into which to sink as fickle relief, if the body is not ready to succumb to illness as yet.

Some may be pushed to extreme feats by a group ideal that seeks excellence in the quest to provide incontrovertible evidence for a bullet proof masculine identity. No one will be able to mistake those clad in it for a weakling, a woman or a person terminally at the end of their tether. Szwec refers to Fain's words on the *rouleurs de mécaniques*, the swaggering lads, who need to show off their virility. Living this ideal, though, is something that, once attained, has to be put to the test repeatedly to be topped again and again in ever new ordeals. Touching rock bottom raises the animal that will respond, d'Aboville explains, a response that, we must assume, has been coveted all along: 'I am a resistance fighter in a war I have invented for myself' (d'Aboville 1992, p. 76). Anguish and despair welling up on the razor edges of the abyss' brink perform a function nothing else will. Only perception confronted with concrete, stark reality can provide what the imagination cannot stand in for, offering to bind together in action what cannot liaison in fantasy. Focused pain is better than formlessness, fright better than distress without an object.

For others, the environment they seek uncannily replicates important features of the dungeons of their daily drudgery, this time however, self-inflicted as a pastime. One of Szwec' patients, approaching his fifties, runs a commerce, in which he works without a break upwards of thirteen hours a day, with no time to lean back. He dumbs himself down into a brutish existence (*s'abrutit*), as he says, by thinking of concrete tasks only. Among his customers there are violent petty criminals who think nothing of getting out the knife. He accepts a fight when he has to and sees it as a chore that goes with the job. To occasionally break out of the routine, he goes on solitary full marathons for which he is not in near enough acceptable bodily shape. Chronological lists of sometimes serious accidents, which he has survived, attempt to glue together morsels of his life, which do not feel like he has really lived them, into a semblance of a pretended whole.

A lack of being unconscious

Understandably, against the background of his case material, Szwec shows interest in Jean Cournut's (2006) studies on the inwardly broken inhabitants of psychic deserts (*les désertiques et défoncés*), but he does not believe that an unconscious identification with a mother who has not been able to grieve her losses – and which the patient would subsequently feel tied to in a secret crypt according to the famous suggestions by Nicolas Abraham and Maria Torok – goes very far in explaining the problems of his Rowing Dutchmen, inwardly chained to their oars. Patients like these, he believes, present with problems that turn on a lack of the very ability of being unconscious.

They do not strive to lodge a forceful, if painful, message in the other. Instead, they want to lay to rest any excitement emerging from the object and have substituted vigorous activity for an object relationship. If anything has been lodged outside the subject, it has been deposited in the activity. Under these circumstances it becomes impossible for the individual to establish links of sufficient quality; psychic activity is not usually tinged with erotic hues, and leaning back into passivity is extremely difficult. Indefinite repetition, sought for the sake of the exhaustion it will eventually bring, does not produce symbolic content. Given more leeway to develop into links with the object world, the states forestalled by the seeking of supreme calm – in itself a substitute for erogenous masochism – could further develop into inhibition or phobia.

While the psychosomatic sufferer in a quandary will respond with a somatic crisis so as to take off unbearable pressure, the individuals whom Szwec discusses have to resort to a particular type of extreme behaviour to reduce tension, a stop gap measure that does not produce pleasurable rest and which has to be employed repeatedly to achieve, again and again, the required effect, as if scooping out water from a leaking boat. As long as you keep up action you have a chance not to be traumatically overwhelmed and sink.

Early interactions out of kilter

Szwec comes to his deliberations from his own background as a psychoanalyst working with children both within the framework of *IPSO*, where in 1993 he was heading their unit for children at Paris, and within the *Centre médico-psycho-pédagogique* at Trappes, a child guidance institution which he directed as a paedopsychiatrist and which was offering consultations to families challenged by behaviourally disruptive children. He served as president of *IPSO* and, from 1990 to 2016 was the medical director of the *Centre de psychosomatique de l'enfant Léon Kreisler* (*Institut de Psychosomatique, IPSO/ASM 13*). In the light of his experience he establishes links between the traumatophilia among the athletes he read about, hellbent to put themselves in harm's way, and the situation of the baby that is not cuddly and does not affectionately invite caresses (*non câlin*):

Those babies that are unstable refuse to be cuddled by their mother and seemingly prefer living in the solitude of a nightmare rather than in the traumatising anxiety against which they do not find appeasement on the part of the woman who is the very source of it.
(Szwec 1994a, p. 749)

Something in the early interactions is seriously out of kilter with how the child ticks and, consequently, does not lead to the development of an ample enough regressive potential in the infant, a letting go without losing the libidinal object world. In the face of unsatisfactory early balances, the future 'slaves of quantity' do not turn to hallucination but to behavioural devices that prematurely provide self-help without taking recourse to an object. They have, in a sense, become guerrilla fighters of the nursery, already gearing up towards a future indefatigable survivalism. In many cases, Szwec was able to observe that children whose mothers experienced difficulties to touch them, in response, tried to keep her at a distance early on by becoming hyperactive, falling into uncontrollable fits of rage, taking refuge in noise and avoiding her lap. Whatever physical skills they had acquired was put to service in a determined attempt to steer clear of unwanted contact with her. Not just the physical contact skin to skin but vital elements in the transmission of unconscious messages from mother to baby have been seriously compromised: the libidinal sensibilities of the child are not furthered by the qualities of a mother's fond touch, nor does the skin, in this instance, fully develop its essential role at the crossroads of self love and object love.

Often the ability of the mother to disinvest the imaginary ideal child of her dreams is impaired, which has detrimental effects on the necessary oscillations between periodic investment and disinvestment of her real child. Fantasmatic interaction between mother and infant becomes a secluded locked room, and the future fault lines of the child's defensive organisation take shape under this darkening star. Early development may for different reasons come to harm if the mother's dream worlds cannot protect the baby against disruptive hospitalisation and/or prolonged pain. In this case maternal care is not enough to permit the child to acquire enough of an illusion of narcissistic invulnerability. Szwec relates that mothers who talk about their babies in a consultation may abruptly become matter-of-fact and *opératoire* in a limited sequence of the conversation when their words touch a traumatic event that has never ceased stalking them.

Excitement which a mother cannot shake off may goad her to an effort to shake, rather than lull, the baby to sleep. Another one may habitually throttle any nascent desire of the infant by offering her breast pre-emptively. In a contribution to a panel discussion, Szwec mentioned that he had found that a number of mothers coming for consultation with babies presenting alimentary difficulties had previously been active sportswomen. During pregnancy they had been deprived of their habitual ways of channelling tension into exercise: being forced to be more passive had led to important imbalances in the way they handled themselves, an imbalance that apparently made it difficult for them to regress with their babies. In some cases this led them to excessively stimulating their children into early motricity.

Szwec, following Michel Fain, believes that essential things happen when a baby is put to sleep. In letting her baby glide into sleep, the mother's unconscious, if things go rather well, will be conveying a dual message: the moment has come when it is right for the child to go to sleep, unalarmed and with no need for heightened vigilance, so as to, in slumbering, be taken on a safe path into pleasurable and wholesome becoming; it is equally time for the mother to see to other investments of hers now, be it pleasure or work. For the child the way it finds sleep is vital for the quality of its dreams. It is indeed the 'imaginary appetite' of the mother that colours, beyond the sensations offered by her presence, the quality of her absence and which establishes early possibilities for identification both with herself and the object of her desire, thus laying early foundations for psycho-sexual affectation. Thus the constitution of the first kernel of the unconscious and the work of primary repression depend heavily on the role of the mother in the early dyad. Children who are locked into an immutable position assigned to them in their parents' prefabricated fairy tales lack necessary stimulating discontinuity and find it difficult to find satisfactory balances between primary and secondary processes.

Striving for premature independence as an escape route

In a number of papers, Szwec grapples with different emergency arrangements that prematurely try to make do without the mother, who is either unavailable or far too much present in a disturbing way.

Depending on inner and outer factors and their interplay, this may result in different clinical arrays, the composite parts of which may, to some extent, intermingle. Encounters with small children often show a co-existence of different modes and a recourse to the *opératoire* if and when a function insufficiently libidinalised fails to provide support.

Focusing on possible destructuring effects of early depression veering into the traumatic, Szwec reminds us that René Spitz insisted that anaclitic depression was contingent on a reasonably good relationship with the mother predating disruptive separation. If the nascent Me and its object links are still too precariously developed, hallucination and auto-eroticism cannot carry the weight of the mother's too prolonged absence. The emergent state, Szwec argues, will go beyond depression. Not only has the object gone missing, but its inner representation, not yet safely established, will slip and be rejected once re-established. If this happens, the developing subject's capacity for investment in the object world (including inner objects, be it good or bad) will receive a dire blow, with consequences for vital tonus and representative function. Mourning will be impeded because mental life was struck at a structurally fragile moment by a non-event: something failed to happen, leaving a gap rather than a memory. A destructuring push against the grain of progressive development impairs further processing. Loss cannot be represented and distress does not turn into anxiety; there is no phobia of strangers because everyone, in a sense, is a stranger and projections falter. Pain may be solicited to defend against what cannot be processed mentally. There is a comprehensive 'failure to thrive' (Szwec 1999b). To come to terms with what is not there, the child turns to an early form of *opératoire* functioning, in place of hallucination. In doing so it is trying to defend itself against the consequences of an earlier even more basic defence, when object links slipped/were cut, a process which one must assume, remains ambiguous because the subject is not fully differentiated from the object and the environment, having just about reached the threshold of this process.

Alimentary disorder as an attempt of demarcation

There are babies that, practically from the first days after birth, find it difficult to establish a workable balance between hunger and satisfaction. Szwec (2002a) relates the case of Nina, who presented with a severe case of alimentary disorder. Despite all medical intervention, she seemed determined to let herself die of hunger. The case was addressed to Szwec by a paediatric unit when Nina was eleven months old. What emerged from the very challenging treatment of Nina – and her family – was that her oldest brother in his early infancy had to receive hospital treatment for anorexia. The mother had lost her father when she was an adolescent and her own mother, whose first name she had given to her daughter, had died after a long, painful fight against her disease three years before the first interview with Szwec took place. Nina was beset by an incredible amount of consecutive illnesses: influenzas, rhinopharyngites, anginas, fatigues of various origin, and most of all, gastroenterites. The mother's every concern was centred on her daughter's weight, with all conceivable means pressed into service to make her eat. Her ability to play with Nina was restricted, especially with regard to playing hide-and-seek. She had great difficulty to accept that her daughter had nightmares and pressurised doctors vigorously, but in vain, to prescribe nighttime sedation. Even when Nina grew and was putting on weight, her mother kept fretting she was still worryingly slim. Hankering after measurable weight increase, the mother had become indentured as a 'slave of quantity': every gram Nina did not put on threatened her mother's narcissism. Things began to take a turn when the mother's worries changed and began focusing on her growing conviction that she herself was developing cancer: becoming a hypochondriac in her own right – and thus reaching a personal holding point of sorts – she released her grip on her daughter.

Calling in medical support, to some extent, had worsened the problem because it further tampered with the establishment of autonomous cycles of hunger and satisfaction. The hospital, in fact, was at risk of being made complicit in a Munchausen syndrome by proxy. The combination of mother and machine (Nina was put on feeding tubes) left Nina with very little in the way of Melanie Klein's oral sadism, splitting into good and bad objects, introjection of the object and re-introjection of her projections. In all of this, worrying for the integrity of the corporeal envelope of the child, the only acceptable evidence for which was corpulence, constituted a protective shield for the mother, who was not able to provide this protection for herself in replacing her own mother. What could not turn hypochondriac anxiety on her own behalf, was burdened onto the daughter, with *opératoire* measures to stand watch over both her and the traumatic wounds the mother herself had received.

Absence of Stranger Anxiety as a warning signal

Under the circumstances, it is not surprising that Nina, deadlocked into her mother's investment of her, was not able to find relief in another arrangement, studied by Szwec, to deal with early environments: fusion with an archaic object, especially in children suffering from early asthma. Much depends on how the infant negotiates the crucible of Stranger Anxiety, originally described by René Spitz as a normal phenomenon appearing with infants suddenly around eight months after birth. As Szwec points out, the presence of fright at this age, while indicating that a hallucinatory solution has failed, also bears witness to a certain degree of successful mental organisation: it provides evidence of a Me sufficiently differentiated from an object to be struck by the thought of the possible loss of a libidinal object clearly constituted. Absence of anxiety at this stage, far from being an encouraging sign of self-confidence, points to a development that has not run its regular course, with apparently problem-free serenity deceptively masking a structural deficiency. Szwec takes up Claude Le Guen's reflections on the impact of the non-mother as a precursor of triangulation in a very early form: infant – mother – non-mother, a basic form later fantasies can successively build upon. Before this important watershed of differentiation, extreme situations are lived as unmitigated distress but not, properly speaking, as anxiety anticipating loss.

In children whose environment does not suffer separation lightly, this necessary development is impeded by a mother whose continued hovering presence gradually becomes a disorganising burden for the infant, and who may smother in the very plenitude of her loving, gratifying care the emergence of necessary auto-erotic behaviour in the infant. Absence is nullified. In many children troubled by early asthma, on the other hand, objects seem to have remained interchangeable. Defence mechanisms more archaic than repression and projection are resorted to: expulsion, reversal into the opposite, and turning things round upon the subject's own self carry the brunt in the process. Conflict is thinned out and a choice between different objects shunned. Szwec reminds us that Pierre Marty thought it possible that the avoidance of conflict seen in these children was not primary but the consequence of even earlier prenatal conflictual disbalances between the foetus and the mother on a hormonal level. In these infants an attack of asthma is likely to appear when a surcharge of tension cannot be processed. Phobia is circumnavigated at a high price: identification remains bound to the mimetic, whereas the hysterical position and auto-erotism are difficult to reach. The occurrence of fusional relationships, however, does not mean a given patient cannot show several registers of mental functioning, one, for instance, at the moment of crisis, and another one in the intervals between crises. In some cases, moments of regression comprising asthma (and the negating of object distance), can alternate with bouts of insomnia, raging fury and hypermotricity. Until the end of adolescence things will remain in flux, so that in spite of early fixations, any assessment of the best inner arrangement to be arrived at has to remain provisional.

Camouflaged early fault lines

What many of the asthmatic children whom Szwec has studied seem to share with some of his extremist sportsmen is that they have difficulties in reaching a stage at which they are able to experience object anxiety. In at least one way, however, they show extreme opposites: if the analyst strays into limiting him/herself to a superficial treatment, patients given to allergic relationships can appear to be the patients their analysts have always dreamt of, adroitly morphing towards any expectation unconsciously directed at them, open to a generously free flow of associations. This sets them, in appearance, miles apart from the *opératoire* patient who quickly becomes his/her analyst's countertransferential nightmare. While the 'allergic' patient will shape shift into fusion with the threat, turning the object into a host of him/herself, the hyperactive person will act as if affected by invisible *Epidermolysis bullosa*, a state, in which he/she, the 'Butterfly Child', has to avoid unthinkingly all contact with a mother that does not hold and soothe but excites and irritates. If there is compromise, it will have to be reached by establishing a balance between the traumatophilic and the traumatophobic tendencies.

No easy access opens for them towards a recognisable variety of W.R. Bion's self-holding experience in World War I under extreme duress (Bion 1997). The children who show what in Szwec's view is the prototype of the experience do not cradle themselves soothingly but, sometimes, have to head bang themselves into oblivion against the cradle's wooden frame. For them the mother's investment in them is a vessel of death, an offshoot of the maternal *pulsion de mort*, which, according to Denise Braunschweig, is emanating from the mother's superego. In this context, laying a baby to rest is a crucial moment, in which the mother's reduction of the intensity of her child-directed awareness (including manifestations of her *pulsion de mort*) has to be offset by the safe – and well-enough satisfied – regression of the child into a fantasy space not frantically imposed upon it.

Substitutes for impossible 'no's

If the early environment with its tug-of-war between balances and disbalances – played out on a turf fully soliciting the mother's fantasmatic object relations – happens to jar with the infant's nascent subjectivity, his/her possibilities effectively to say no to what is on offer will, at an early stage, be limited. What can be raised in place of 'no' will have to be predicated on the body. We have seen that eating disorders may develop as a consequence. They often set in during the first six months, when the early object relation has been constituted. In its eating behaviour, the anorexic infant displaces a first conflict that it cannot successfully transfer from the mother to the face of a stranger. Dramatic sobbing spasms often appear between six and eighteen months and typically eclipse consciousness for the duration of the crisis. Children who show difficulties early on are likely to provoke negative responses from their parents that give rise to further crises. It is within this field of early interactions that the responses of babies *non câlins* find their particular place. By their hyperactive behaviour they try to escape from a form of relationship that does not provide them with an adequate protective shield but threatens them with an ever-present source of trauma, giving rise to an internalised image of insecurity. If disconnecting from it by ordinary means is not possible, ramping up the volume of sensations that can be actively procured acts as a barrier against the source of unacceptable sensations – the mother – that can neither be dealt with nor fused with. Putting up screens of mobility and/or noise carves out a habitat that will not be meddled with. It attempts to self-cradle in a hostile environment on a precarious ledge. Though resistance may well be futile, surrender is not an option: succumbing passively to the given environment on offer would be inconceivable. By these devices, which shun any passive position, the path to the constructive build-up of a protective masochism is impaired. The only form of relaxation available is that produced by exhaustion. If the child has directly or indirectly been exposed to adult violence, a sense of self may coalesce around pain, which may in cautious therapy be re-linked to its lost masochistic potential.

If the hyperactive child tries to flee the intolerable, sometimes by producing barrages of noise, the prematurely 'wise' child has found a different way to disappear from the locus of pain by merging into the more impersonal background of social noises regurgitating received wisdom. Turned adult, his position is aphoristically characterised by Szwec (2009a, p. 17) as 'My father has died, my wife has left me, what is it now people do in such a case'. In spite of their obvious, impressive surface differences, the restless warrior infant and the quiescent child Stoic, Szwec seems to suggest, present different faces of an *opératoire* use of the world of physical and social data to constantly re-edit the traumatic. While the hyperactive child turns to strenuous exercise, the prematurely 'wise' child uses suppression to obliterate any potentially dangerous connection between affect and mental representation by the vigorous exercise of premature ego function. What the 'wise child' certainly has learned is to avoid unwelcome attention by nipping, one might say, subjectivity in the bud.

Putting a stop to the capacity to form saturated links

Szwec's use of the term suppression builds on previous discussion. In the very first issue of the *Revue Française de Psychosomatique*, Catharine Parat (1991) pertinently pointed out that a close reading of Freud suggests that there is a difference between *Verdrängung* (English: repression, French: *refoulement*) and *Unterdrückung* (English: suppression, French: *répression*) and that this was of clinical relevance. According to Parat, suppression obliterates affect while keeping the representation intact but separate and neutralised at the level of the preconscious, pre-empting the need for perlaboration in an act in which volition plays an important role. Parat, following previous work by Sami Ali, envisages a suppression of the capacity to have a working imaginary that enters into character formation. She concedes that an important part of reality is constituted by acts of suppression brought to bear upon the child by its immediate family environment. A loss of a privileged channel of discharge for tension can in further life lead to a critical disbalance which can make the person more vulnerable. Szwec, as we have seen, shows that alimentary arrangements that do not work on an elementary level are a heavy burden for a subject's future development. What if the mental diet fed to a child produces a recoil from sinking back into levels of the unconscious provisioned by the way the parents handle the child? We have seen that Pierre Marty believed that too quick a transition in West Africa from tribal cultures to the modern life in cities left children exposed to modes of the *opératoire* as a fall-back coping mechanism.

Disappearance into conformity

Szwec notes that the particular link the fully fledged *opératoire* person is likely to entertain to the social dimension differs from what Freud described as a tendency of behaviour in crowds: It is not the identification with or attachment to a leader that is moving the *opératoire*, but a quest for functional conformity, an identification with no one in particular but with what people say and with the realm of time-hallowed recipes. To behave as if motivated by the self-same forces that drive others enables them to gloss over the sorry state of their inner worlds. If the allergic child can be a gifted imitator of prominent politicians, the *opératoire* has a knack of assimilating the critically unscrutinised broad consensus. This acts as a kind of prosthesis for what would otherwise be kept malleable by the various strata of the preconscious. With shallow identificatory processes and attempts to deal with their problems by way of projective reduplication, they are, we have to conclude, moles without a spymaster to liaison to, in a brittle way vulnerable to being exposed in the difficulties they face and constantly challenged to produce the same evidence for 'depth' of psychic functioning as others.

In at least one of his contributions, Szwec (1996d) seems to echo approvingly a comparison between Hannah Arendt's description of the totalitarian domain and the mind exposed to infantile distress. Although the connection may not be stringent, one can see that fault lines in the individual could easily be re-enforced by larger forces in the socio-cultural domain. At any rate, the individual formerly exposed to childhood trauma will try to find and maintain a social location, in accordance with his/her needs for a protective shield against the onslaught of tension difficult to process, buttressing an ideal Me comforted by the existence of overwhelming might, and be it that of facts, outside its psyche.

Cultural toolkits for quick steps into mindlessness

When Szwec's 1998 book *Les galériens volontaires* was released in a new edition in 2013, it had, in the meantime, inspired further studies on the implementation of self-calming procedures as described by Szwec, among them a study of the *clochards* of Paris. In a new preface, Szwec introduces what at first seems to be a further clinical vignette. It focuses on a runner of ultra-marathons in pursuit of his goal to run 100 kilometres and who describes his ordeal based on notes shortly after completion of his course. The world, as described by him, shrinks and is reduced to the ground three meters ahead. 'I run to attain emptiness', the runner confesses. Szwec finds ample echoes of the patients he described in the previous edition, who try to install vigorously anobjectal regimes and who reduce tension by exhausting themselves while concentrating on their exertion. Then he reveals the identity of the runner: it is Haruki Murakami, the celebrated Japanese writer, who runs every morning to empty his mind and who has written an essay about his experiences as a runner. Can one be able to function on a high level of symbolisation and be capable of being *opératoire* at the same time, Szwec asks. Can one be a part-time *opératoire*? Can there be a cyclical division of labour between the *opératoire* and the fully mentalised, an occasional binging on the *opératoire*, as it were?

Apparently, Szwec concedes, there are people who can function in more than one register. Szwec is willing to envisage the possibility of a highly performative split in the way Murakami functions. Everyone, in the course of his individual psychopathology of daily life, can pass through transitory *opératoire* moments, by, for instance, mechanically doing crossword puzzles, or by counting sheep so as to fall asleep more easily. In passing, he notes that Murakami mentions the 'mantras' he recites and without which he believes he would not be able to be up to his task. Szwec suspects there are elements of ancient non-integrated distress that move him to his runs. Although Szwec does not explicitly address the matter, this raises the question whether some of these transitory *opératoire* moments may be grounded in a locally accessible range of cultural practices: it would not be too difficult to find cultural equivalents in attaining nothingness by the persistent reciting of a mantra in Japan. In other places, local culture seems to have developed special techniques to put the flavour of fancy into the dullness of repetitive labour, depriving routine behaviour of some of its *opératoire* potential.

It is indicative of a certain distance between psychoanalysis and cultural studies that Szwec does not seem to be aware of the work of Ian Hacking on people who, in France, in the latter part of the 19th century felt driven to take to their feet to escape the constrictions of their immediate environment and became part of a widely commented upon cultural phenomenon of the times. Hacking pays close attention to the consequences of medical attention and classification on the people set on going on a *fugue*, but tries to stay close to the feeling of events:

> One reader of my story wanted more history – of the politics of psychiatry, for example, and how it fitted into nineteenth-century French politics. Instead I added more about buildings, more about the sense of being in provincial, closed-in Bordeaux, where Albert went mad. I am no novelist, but I hope to have invited the reader into the mean dark streets of a town that suffocates under its own pride or into the spacious cloister of the hospital where my compulsive walker found a safe place.
> (Hacking 1998, p. 5)

A mother certainly can be inept to deal with infantile trauma. But what about cultural environments? Does it make any difference how they are marked by trauma or whether they have set apart ways of dealing with it?

Concluding his preface fifteen years after the first publication of *Les galériens volontaires*, Szwec reveals that in writing the book he realised he had spent his childhood immersed in an environment in which *galériens du travail* (galley slaves chained to their work) were very much in evidence. In the Ashkenazi surroundings in which he grew up after World War II, hard work from morning to evening was the rule. What people advanced as arguments, when asked, was related to economic reasons, but what he personally knew of these men and women makes him, looking backwards, believe they were in a state of trauma. Writing about one of his patients made him remember one person in particular, of whom he had vivid childhood memories. Bent all day over his clattering sewing machine, bathed in an ambience of furious sound, with a radio he did not listen to booming away in the background, this was the way he passed the day, all of his days. He had had to leave his family and to work at the machine when he was ten years old, before finding himself tumbled into the cauldron of war and revolution. He had survived famine first, then wartime persecution. He justified his constant work by arguing that it was either 'March or die' in life. One can easily understand that Szwec believes it is clinically useful to keep the registers of trauma and masochism separate because they follow different developmental lines. To this galley slave, to whom memory took him back, and to some others he has known, Szwec dedicates the new edition of his book, a book deeply engaged with the reverberations of trauma in seemingly erratic behaviour.

Object distance in an environment inculcating self-impingement

Szwec, in the footsteps of Marty, Fain, Braunschweig and Léon Kreisler, continues Maurice Bouvet's interest in object distance, the spatial position the subject tries to occupy in relation to the object. The infantile positions described so far try to make do without having to acknowledge the presence of a concrete, distinct object into whose fantasy life the subject entered even before birth. True to Fain and Braunschweig's suggestions, Szwec considers the *pulsion de mort* to originate from outside the infant, with the mother. Granted some of this may always be present, what will vary is the mixture, the fusion and the patterns of periodic oscillation between calming down and stimulation. If calming down is the standard fare, there will be little in the way of a fantasmatic catalyst present to stimulate the imagination of the child. In Jean Laplanche's General Theory of Seduction the focus is on libidinal subversion. In Szwec' reflections there is a dark cousin to this, in the possible undermining of the nascent fantasmatic potential of the child in the family he grows up in: it is not the dark sinful desire of the vampire that threatens the child here, so to speak, but the dementor's horrid kiss. Mothers who reduce the infant in their care to a functioning thing spur the baby to set in motion a range of emergency measures. The attempt to run down tension, using too forcefully the *pulsion de mort*'s reductive tendencies to defend and shield oneself at all costs, is a means born of distress rather than of object anxiety. In a number of very difficult cases there is not enough object link to envelop this early distress in a mesh of masochism in which object relations are at least implied.

The mechanisms which Szwec discusses address what Winnicott would have considered negative impingement, a reduction of the available expanse of mental space in which the child is free to move. Using a desperate stratagem, the child combats archaic distress by deploying an emptiness of its own, with the *opératoire* as a mode to disengage when no other disconnect is ready to do the job, measures that will likely, at later stages, be embedded in cultural practices and the world of work. Not everyone can find it in his heart to go insane like King Lear: for those not sufficiently predisposed to disengage psychotically, going *opératoire* can be something seemingly within their conscious grip. Lebovici (in Lebovici and Castarède 1992) speaks about the early 'bath of affects' that turns proto-representations into fantasies: Szwec shows that that the fantasmatic worlds of the mother determine not only the temperature of this bath but the dimensions and the positioning of the tub the baby encounters it in. His approach, open to meaningful nuance, takes an interest in early fantasmatic interactions so as to better understand such resulting arrangements that leave the subject libidinally and narcissistically ill prepared to face the moment of crisis when it arrives. We shall see with Anna Potamianou in our next chapter how the Me is likely to respond in the face of such emergencies.

Sources

Bion, W.R. (1997), *War memoirs 1917–19*, Bion, F. ed., London: Karnac Books.
Cournut, J. (2006), 'Les défoncés', in: Aubert, N., ed, *L'individu hypermoderne*, Toulouse: Éditions Érès, pp. 59–71.
Cramer, B., Denis P., Henny, R., Nicolaïdis, N., and Szwec, G. (1999), 'Discussion', *Actualités Psychosomatiques* 2, pp. 13–19.
d'Aboville, G. (1992), *Seul*, Paris: Éditions Robert Laffont.
Declerck, P. (2001), *Les naufragés. Avec les clochards de Paris*. Paris: Plon.
Fine, A. (1995), '"La psychosomatique de l'enfant asthmatique" de Gérard Szwec', *Revue Française de Psychanalyse* 59(3), pp. 935–939.
Hacking, I. (1998), *Mad Travelers. Reflections on the reality of transient mental illnesses*, Cambridge, Massachusetts: Harvard University Press.
Kamieniak, I. (2015), 'Les Galériens volontaires de Gérard Szwec', *Revue Française de Psychanalyse* 79(3), pp. 895–901.
Korczynski, M., Pickering, M. and Robertson, E. (2013), *Rhythms of labour: Music at work in Britain*, Cambridge: Cambridge University Press.
Lebovici, S. and Castarède, M.-F. (1992), *L'enfance retrouvée*, Paris: Flammarion.

Nayrou, F. (2014), 'Les galériens volontaires de Gérard Szwec', *Revue Française de Psychosomatique* 46, pp. 173–180.

Palacio Espasa, F. (2002), 'répression', in: de Mijolla, A. ed., *Dictionnaire international de la psychanalyse*, volume 2, Paris: Calmann-Lévy, pp. 1537–1538.

Parat, C. (1991), 'A propos de la répression', *Revue Française de Psychosomatique* 1, pp. 93–113.

Sirjacq, M. (2017), 'La psychosomatique de l'enfant', in: Nayrou, F. and Szwec, G. eds, *La psychosomatique*, Paris: Presses Universitaires de France, pp. 133–154.

Sitbon, A. (2002), '"Les galériens volontaires" de Gérard Szwec', *Revue Française de Psychanalyse* 66 (1), pp. 283–289.

Smadja, C. (1999b), 'Les galériens volontaires de Gérard Szwec', *Revue Française de Psychosomatique* 16, pp. 211–218.

Szwec, G. (1989a), 'Figure de l'étranger, langage et régression formelle', *Revue Française de Psychanalyse* 53(6), pp. 1977–1987.

Szwec, G. (1989b), 'Les mots dans l'image', *Revue Française de Psychanalyse* 53(6), pp. 1989–1992.

Szwec, G. (1991), 'De la crise d'asthme à la crise de fou rire', *Revue Française de Psychosomatique* 1, pp. 115–136.

Szwec, G. (1992), 'Psychothérapie d'une enfant chauve au seuil de l'adolescence. Réflexions sur les relations entre la pelade et le traumatisme', *Revue Française de Psychosomatique* 2, pp. 43–67.

Szwec, G. (1993a), *La psychosomatique de l'enfant asthmatique*, Paris: Presses Universitaires de France.

Szwec, G. (1993b), 'Faudra mieux surveiller les petits!', *Revue Française de Psychanalyse* 57(2), pp. 591–603.

Szwec, G. (1993c), 'Les procédés autocalmants par la recherche répétitive de l'excitation. Les galériens volontaires', *Revue Française de Psychosomatique* 4, pp. 27–51.

Szwec, G. (1994a), 'Adultes naufragés – nourrissons en perdition. (Réflexions sur l'utilisation autocalmante du danger et de l'effroi), *Revue Française de Psychanalyse* 58(3), pp. 743–761.

Szwec, G. (1994b), 'L'enfant dans l'adulte dans la théorie de Pierre Marty', *Revue Française de Psychosomatique* 6, pp. 63–70.

Szwec, G. (1995a), 'Relation mère-enfant machinale et procédés autocalmants', *Revue Française de Psychosomatique* 8, pp. 69–89.

Szwec, G. (1995b), 'Le retour de l'expérience traumatique', *Revue Française de Psychanalyse* 59(5), pp. 1629–1633.

Szwec, G. (1996a), 'L'enfant et son corps, vingt ans après la publication du livre', *Revue Française de Psychosomatique* 9, pp. 7–13.

Szwec, G. (1996b), 'Pathologie fonctionnelle néonatale, mosaïque première et comportement défensif prématuré', *Revue Française de Psychosomatique* 9, pp. 69–77.

Szwec, G. (1996c), 'Subversion érotique et subversion autocalmante: une double potentialité pour les fonctions somatiques', *Revue Française de Psychosomatique* 10, pp. 47–58.

Szwec, G. (1996d), 'La psychanalyse ne rend pas éternel (à propos de l'article de Natalie Zaltzman', *Revue Française de Psychanalyse* 60(4), pp. 1137–1142.

Szwec, G. (1997a), 'Devenir d'une dépression de la première enfance génératrice de somatisations et conséquences psychosomatiques de la maltraitance', in: Le Goues, G. and Pragier, G. eds, *Cliniques psychosomatiques*, Paris: Presses Universitaires de France, pp. 67–90.

Szwec, G. (1997b), 'La vie onirique chez l'enfant', in: Decobert, S. and Sacco, F. eds, *L'enfant, le rêve et le psychanalyste*, Toulouse: Érès, pp. 39–60.

Szwec, G. (1998a), *Les galériens volontaires*, Paris: Presses Universitaires de France.

Szwec, G. (1998b), 'La vie, mode d'emploi', *Revue Française de Psychanalyse* 62(5), pp. 1505–1517.

Szwec, G. (1999a), 'Présentation d'un cas clinique: conduites dangereuses à la suite d'une désorganisation somatique grave', *Actualités Psychosomatiques* 2, pp. 21–41.

Szwec, G. (1999b), 'La fonction maternelle du thérapeute, la mère morte, l'amante', *Revue Française de Psychosomatique* 16, pp. 7–18.

Szwec, G. (2000a), 'A propos d'une situation extrême de la pratique psychanalytique', in: Cournut, J. and Schaeffer, J. eds, *Pratiques de la psychanalyse*, Paris: Presses Universitaires de France, pp. 87–94.

Szwec, G. (2000b), 'A propos de l'observation d'une somatisation grave à la fin d'une psychanalyse', *Revue Française de Psychosomatique* 17, pp. 25–35.

Szwec, G. (2000c), 'Sa Majesté, le bébé, et le bébé en non-majesté', in: Joly, F. ed., *Sa majesté, le bébé*, Toulouse: Érès, pp. 119–135.

Szwec, G. (2001), 'La désorganisation de l'état dépressif chez le bébé, à l'origine de la dépression essentielle', *Revue Française de Psychosomatique* 20, pp. 7–27.

Szwec, G. (2002a), 'L'enfant – organe hypocondriaque de sa mère', *Revue Française de Psychosomatique* 22, pp. 65–83.

Szwec, G. (2002b), 'La mére "surintricante"', *Revue Française de Psychanalyse* 66(5), pp. 1789–1797.
Szwec, G. (2003a), 'Argument', *Revue Française de Psychosomatique* 23, pp. 5–8.
Szwec, G. (2003b), 'La fatigue qui ne joue plus son rôle de signal', *Revue Française de Psychosomatique* 24, pp. 37–43.
Szwec, G. (2003c), 'À propos d'un petit insatiable', in: Blin, D., Soulé, M. and Thoueille, É., *L'allaitement maternel: une dynamique à bien comprendre*, Toulouse: Érès.
Szwec, G. (2004), 'L'épuisement activement recherché', *Revue Française de Psychosomatique*, Hors-série, pp. 81–89.
Szwec, G. (2005a), 'Plutôt fou que malade?', *Revue Française de Psychosomatique* 27, pp. 7–16.
Szwec, G. (2005b), 'Avant-propos', *Revue Française de Psychosomatique* 28, pp. 5–11.
Szwec, G. (2006a), 'Les maladies de peau dans quelques modèles psychosomatiques', *Revue Française de Psychosomatique* 29, pp. 31–49.
Szwec, G. (2006b), 'Une pratique psychanalytique avec de très jeunes enfants à risque somatique', in: Perron, R. ed., *Psychanalystes, qui êtes-vous?* Paris: Dunod, pp. 153–160.
Szwec, G. (2008a), 'Discussion d'un cas de céphalalgie', *Revue Française de Psychosomatique* 34, pp. 79–85.
Szwec, G. (2008b), 'Le psychodrame avec des patients somatisants', *Le Carnet PSY* 127, pp. 24–29.
Szwec, G. (2008c), 'Je vais en parler à ton père', in: Cupa, D. ed., *Image du père dans la culture contemporaine. Hommages à André Green*, Paris: Presses Universitaires de France, pp. 141–144.
Szwec, G. (2008d), 'La construction dans l'analyse avec des enfants, un passage à l'acte de l'analyste?', *Revue Française de Psychanalyse* 72(5), pp. 1661–1665.
Szwec, G. (2009a), 'Capacité à dire "non" et désorganisations psychosomatiques', *Actualités Psychosomatiques* 12, pp. 3–19.
Szwec, G. (2009b), 'Hommage à Léon Kreisler', *Revue Française de Psychosomatique* 35, pp. 7–8.
Szwec, G. (2010a), '"L'enfant dormira bien vite..."', *Revue Française de Psychosomatique* 37, pp. 81–95.
Szwec, G. (2010b), 'Le symptôme psychosomatique est bête', in: Bayle, G. ed., *L'inconscient freudien. Recherche, écoute, métapsychologie*, Paris: Presses Universitaires de France, pp. 215–220.
Szwec, G. (2010c), 'Defaillance de la psychisation du corps chez le bébe non-câlin', *Revue Française de Psychanalyse* 74(5), pp. 1687–1691.

Szwec, G. (2012a), 'Grandir avec une rectocolite (commentaire de l'article de Claire Rojas)', *Revue Française de Psychosomatique* 41, pp. 37–42.
Szwec, G. (2012b), 'Une conduite anorexique après de graves somatisations chez un adolescent (commentaire de l'article d'Irène Nigolian)', *Revue Française de Psychosomatique* 41, pp. 65–70.
Szwec, G. (2012c), 'À propos d'une psychothérapie mère-bébé (commentaire de l'article de Pascale Blayau)', *Revue Française de Psychosomatique* 41, pp. 101–106.
Szwec, G. (2013a), 'Sex machine. Néo- besoins et pseudo-pulsions', in: André J., Chabert C. and Coblence F. eds, *Le corps de Psyché*, Paris: Presses Universitaires de France, pp. 67–84.
Szwec, G. (2013b), 'Preface', in: Szwec, G. (1998a), *Les galériens volontaires*, new edition, Paris: Presses Universitaires de France, pp. i–xx.
Szwec, G. (2013c), 'Préface à la réédition d'*Éros et Antéros*', in: Braunschweig, D. and Fain, M. (1971), *Éros et Antéros*, new edition, Paris: Éditions in Press, pp. 5–21.
Szwec, G. (2015), 'Les travaux forcés de la répétition autocalmante', in: André, J. and Chabert, C. eds, *Les travaux forcés de la répétition: obsessions, addictions, compulsions*, Paris: Presses Universitaires de France, pp. 95–112.
Szwec, G. (2016a), 'Enfoncer un trou plutôt que de le contempler...', *Revue Française de Psychanalyse* 80(3), pp. 684–699.
Szwec, G. (2016b), 'Perception et transfert dans la pensée de Pierre Marty. Réflexions sur le texte de Sara Botella', *Revue Française de Psychosomatique* 49, pp. 45–58.
Szwec, G. (2016c), 'Les procédés autocalmants', in: Danon-Boileau, L. and Tamet, J-Y. eds, *Des psychanalystes en séance. Glossaire clinique de psychanalyse contemporaine*, Paris: Gallimard, pp. 413–419.
Szwec, G. (2017a), 'Introduction', in: Nayrou, F. and Szwec, G. eds, *La psychosomatique*, Paris: Presses Universitaires de France, pp. 1–6.
Szwec, G. (2017b), 'La psychosomatique, quelques débats après...', in: Nayrou, F. and Szwec, G. eds, *La psychosomatique*, Paris: Presses Universitaires de France, pp. 7–45.
Szwec, G. (2017c), 'Les identifications à l'œuvre dans l'interprétation', *Revue Française de Psychanalyse* 81(5), pp. 1445–1454.
Szwec, G. (2018), 'Absence de négation, rage destructrice et déséquilibres psychosomatiques', *Revue Française de Psychosomatique* 54, pp. 67–84.

7

CONFIGURATIONS 1
Anna Potamianou

In the last chapter we followed Gérard Szwec study the desperate lengths the subject might go to in order to find a modicum of transient calm. In this chapter I shall present Anna Potamianou's approach, who views this situation from yet another angle. For many of the patients Potamianou reflects upon, transition to a land of meaningful hopes has stalled. What is left of one's personal future has been deposited and locked into action. The territory remaining to the Me is defended with tooth and claw.

This is indicative of an overall situation that leaves much to be desired.

The subject marooned in fallow lands sustained by routines

The individual in the centre of Potamianou's interrogation has been cut off from vital resources in what otherwise might have constituted his/her self, following a process the history of which has fallen beyond reach. Within the remaining impaired repertoire of defensive possibilities, much is loaded on a mechanism that once helped the nascent Me to feel reasonably secure within established perimeters: repetition. As Freud suggested, repetition compulsion opens a window to a world beyond the pleasure principle. Since this is territory the *mode opératoire* clearly transverses, the detailed look Potamianou takes at processes of repetition helps to understand more fully an important ingredient of robotic functioning as portrayed by Marty and his colleagues.

This follows its own logic, patiently traced by Potamianou: of old repetition served to produce building blocks of the familiar, giving rise to rememoration and underscoring testable lines of demarcation between Me and non-Me. While granting apprenticeship in manageable skills, it also has entrenched borders that, for all their being to some extent artificial, can be put to use in warding off the turmoil of exposure to the unknown. Although repetition often appears to be a pliant servant of the conservative status quo, Potamianou believes there is also a mesh of possibly quite discrete potential that links it to former theatres of the libido. What the individual who makes extensive use of repetition does is to deposit as much of his/her core history for safekeeping directly in the enactment of the actual without passing the realms of fantasy. With no other elaboration accessible, motricity provides a shell, thereby protecting mental life from the threat of extinction, faintly echoing times the link to which has slipped and putting into deep storage remaining supplies of libido.

Repetition as a deposit of relationship: forgetfulness as a ritual offering

Concomitantly, as Potamianou points out, objects fade in vitality and lose their own proper texture. It seems the subject has become impervious to any urge to realise his/her fuller potential. Myth constructs stories around this: banished by the gods, the only sustainable relationship Sisyphos can enter into is to his stone. In this shrinking of the world the Me has ceded territory in what Potamianou discusses as an often-unconscious act of quasi-sacrificial offering, re-enforcing his/her links to a social environment to which this *kenosis* – self-emptying – is offered as a gift and as a binding contract. To illustrate this, Potamianou draws our attention to the ancient rites at the temple of Trophonios, in ancient Boiotia, Greece, in which the pilgrims to the sanctuary were administered special potions by the officiating priests so as to make them forget their previous lives and to remember more poignantly what happened in the ceremony. In the patients whom Potamianou considers, this transaction – effected to gain access to the lived values of a rite in exchange for the seal of oblivion on antecedent history – has not worked in their favour and has given rise to mental habitats not easy to live in, in which the urge not to wish for more than what circumstances seem to permit shores up the status quo in but a threadbare fashion: repetition churns on dust. Administering to death a refusal to expand into the world, it attempts to keep a lid on any surge of excitement, the understanding of which, deprived of a context in retrievable memory, has become exceedingly difficult.

Attractors embedded in force fields detrimental to thriving

In the downsized mental economy envisaged by Potamianou, external reality has gained ground as an organiser for the impaired inner dynamics: the weakened psychic apparatus is being drawn to what, following the work of Georges and Sylvie Pragier (1990), Potamianou terms attractors, positioned outside the subject, powerful force fields that distract and disperse rather than equip with nuclei of nascent cohesion. Unless the individual finds within himself/herself the inner vertebrae to stand up to the vortex, alloplastic vicissitudes, not autopoiesis, occupy the foreground largely vacated by the subject, with the regulatory system of the subject struggling to deal with the effraction of his/her defensive shields by what he/she experiences as barrages of the aleatory. The subject is drawn into the fissures opened up by the primal object's deficiencies, especially if early tendencies towards non-differentiation remain strong. Wishes for fusion and a turning against the self may provide protection against the painful realisation that the maternal object is, in effect, failing the subject. This is significantly different from the attraction exercised by objects invested in by desire (which, Potamianou suggests, may well work like the *pregnance* postulated in the theories of René Thom). Potamianou posits a continuing, gravitational pull of the original lack of representation — a forcefield of representative nullity, omnipotent in absence of something conceptually tangible — to which the individual is exposed in crisis. In the effort to maintain a threatened balance at all costs, Potamianou suggests, the attraction of an inner pre-conceptual abyss makes itself felt, a chasm that alluringly calls out to the subject bidding it to bury all painful conceptual differentiations in it. The subject becomes susceptible to being magnetically drawn towards the dark gulf of early experience never really given up, beckoning with intimations of a fusional potential and a possible potency beyond common measure, a constellation that does not favour figurative work. Precariously perched on a brink, beset by a painful silence of memory, the implicit continuities of the non-dynamic parts of the id provide solace against a background in which the more elaborated strata of mental life thin out and fray, with the id drawing on a pool of restive, non-qualified, indifferent energy that has never entered into feeding the *pulsion* (*montage pulsionnel*) and which makes liaisons to mental work difficult: the individual's capacities for binding tension into representational and symbolic thinking is put at risk. Interested in the work of César and Sára Botella on the catastrophic dangers of non-representation, Potamianou emphasises the possibility that the gap between perception and representation could also originate in an early act of renouncement on the part of a Me not previously exposed to the right degree of seduction. Entire zones of its territory are being shed, leaving them, as a consequence, fallow.

Repetition as part of a residual shock absorption system

For all the difficulties this creates for analytic work, repetition compulsion should not, Potamianou argues, be seen as an unalloyed articulation of the *pulsion de mort*: neither the slipping of links nor the withdrawal of erotic interest will ever be total. It offers to the subject a Janus-faced means of last resort to fix boundaries when nothing else holds, although this emergency measure further tears and frays the mental web it was meant to conserve. It is, the reader understands, a desperate measure like calling in the Goths to save Rome. In spite of the considerable collateral damage its use causes, it may in its frantic drive to establish a grip on things (*prise sur*), nevertheless, enshrine hope for a future new take on things (*re-prise*), if the analyst manages to work with it and can discover in dreary repetition the potential for promoting an amount of change that has so far been put beyond the pale. In some cases, the new amount of mobility made available by the treatment becomes unbearably terrifying to the patient because it smacks of a loss of control and poses an unacceptable threat to how things have been run so far.

As Kaswin-Bonnefond (2004) remarked, Potamianou tends to understand the sequels of the traumatic as a dynamic process rather than as a static structural deficit. Potamianou refers to Jean-Claude Ameisen's exploration of *apoptosis* – programmed cell death – that is sculpting recognisable form in a constant interplay of construction and destruction, which keeps and conserves only what is bound into vital exchange. For new forms of inner life to arise, tendencies to break up and to detach oneself play an important part. Potamianou stresses that Freud's *pulsion de mort* disaggregates larger units and sees libidinal disentanglement and disinvestment as consequences of this within the mental apparatus.

In a 2001 monograph of hers, the author comes to develop her topic further, grounding it more deeply in her reflections on trauma. The traumatic, she argues, is inevitably present at the beginning of our existence: it is a vein that runs through all psychic territory. Yet, this territory does not always have the same extensions:

> More than once Freud alluded to the capacity of the mental apparatus to open or to tighten up, to restrict or, on the contrary, to widen its processual aptitude and its mobility.
> (Potamianou 2001, p. 87)

With the subject under duress, the traumatic forms a link of last resort when the subject finds itself plunged into disarray. It is then that an emergency boot up of agency, marshalling residual self-states, steps in to connect to an otherwise no longer tangible object world: 'The frozen [in the original: *fixé*] time of traumatism shatters and upholds at the same time' (Potamianou 2001, p. 40). Dissatisfaction, lack and loss weave a string of frustrations which does not attach to symbolising nodes. Repetitions usually address knots of tension, in quest of a link escaping the mental apparatus. When disobjectalisation threatens, holding fast to the traces of the traumatic constitutes is all there can be held to. It conserves what can be salvaged by employing behavioural rather than mental means. In some instances, traditionally connected to severe cases of the *mode opératoire*, the unconscious seems to have fallen mute altogether: it still receives but has ceased all discernible emission, according to Marty's (1980, p. 63) classical formula ('*L'inconscient reçoit mais n'émet plus*'). The propulsive and directional guidance provided by the working of the *pulsions* disintegrates. Fantasy falls silent and mental activity tumbles head down, drowning, into the shallows of stagnant waters. Response to stimuli becomes an overweening concern, dragging the subject through cycles from tension to exhaustion. What has been ceded/foreclosed, Potamianou concedes, may well return from the outside. If no cushion of the imaginary dampens the effects of exterior reality, its impact may be violent. Perceptions cannot sink into a mental cushion where they can become latent thoughts but are clung to so as to provide subsidiary anchorage. For figurative work to take place and comprehensible desires to emerge there would have to be a dialectic between the Me that represents itself and the Me that lets itself go, something that evidently does not happen in the case of the *opératoire*. There are also indications, Potamianou points out, that the subject's psycho-sexuality has not solidly enough been established along hysterical lines.

With Neyraut (1997), Potamianou understands repetition compulsion as a pivotal element of an anti-traumatic protective shock absorption system. In broad accord with him, she remains attentive to the amount of sexual co-excitation occasioned by trauma and the position in which the defensive measures adopted place the Me vis-a-vis the id. In more amenable cases masochism will attempt to liaison with the unsupportable. Potamianou refers to Benno Rosenberg's (1991) work on the two versions of masochism: life saving as opposed to death procuring. If masochism as a guardian of life comes into play, it will meaningfully connect the woes the subject finds itself in to the worlds of infantile sexual fantasy, assigning suffering a legitimate place in the experience of the individual.

Pain as an envelope to contain a breach

In another solution, further removed from the object world, the puncturing of the protective shield, signalled by pain, will be ring-fenced by narcissism, as an emblem of the hope that the affliction can be contained locally: pain becomes a sign that there is still something alive to respond to it beyond the devastated zone. It compacts the Me, as it were, in routines in which repetition compulsion is an important factor. To be able to survive may become a triumph as such, witnessed by the ability to co-exist with pain, nurturing ideals of narcissistic empowerment. Embracing pain and an envelope of suffering will become a way of life and support for one's sense of self. Potamianou takes as an example Philoctetes, a Greek soldier in the Trojan war marooned on an island by his erstwhile comrades for the unbearable stench of his festering wound incurred whilst in service. Following Michel Fain, Potamianou considers the possibility that the narcissistic investment hemming in the wound and hurt may constitute a protective, quasi erogenic, zone in its own right designed to form a second protective shield against traumatic neurosis.

The fewer of these links of last resort can be entertained, the more repetition will be conserving residual links that increasingly reach out into empty space. If nothing else serves as a remedy, somatic episodes could constitute attempts to take off pressure from having to come to terms with the unsupportable.

Identification sickness

In all these processes the role of identifications should not be neglected. In 1984, Potamianou devoted a book to the subject, to which she came back in her later studies. Although it is not directly focused on the *mode opératoire*, it has clear repercussions on it. Potamianou reminds us that identification at the oedipal stage serves as an antidote to desire in the face of overwhelming obstacles – in the form of an interdicting powerful third – to its realisation. More generally, it also appropriates and attempts to assimilate the fascinatingly and disturbingly powerful which cannot be dealt with in other ways. As it disposes of – and to some degree neutralises – desire to which an immediate outlet is blocked, it also dispenses considerable violence in the process of laying hold on the object to be hauled in for identification. In case of a mentally disturbed relative on whose frighteningly unbridled power a part of the subject's Me may unconsciously model itself, there may open an insufferable gap between conscious and unconscious self-representations. Attracted by the gaping void at the origin of our existence bare of representation, the subject is drawn to representations of violence that others exercise on us or on themselves. Following Alain de Mijolla's (1981) work on 'visitors in the Me', including the presentation of the disquieting case of Arthur Rimbaud – part of a very vivid discussion on alienating unconscious identification in France from the late 1970s – Potamianou highlights the possibility of 'identification sickness'. In a passage particularly relevant to an understanding of possible pre-histories to the *opératoire*, she suggests that the way the preconscious gains shape takes its cues from the inner image of persons of particular significance to the subject. Often enough, things develop sufficiently well and identification can open up meaningful futures and zones of desire. In other cases however, identification closes mental space and obliterates desire, with no language at hand to offer solace and sustenance, a situation in which compulsive repetition has to stand in for the inexpressible.

Hope gone rancid

Even if the subject still feels entitled to hope, there are cases in which this hope is little more than a fetish, tenaciously clung to, opening up a semblance of future that on closer inspection proves to be a dead end. In a 1992 monograph, Potamianou describes a shield of stagnant hope, sometimes used by borderline patients, which nurtures a gratifyingly soothing confidence in the ultimate arrival of transformative change, which, however, is continuously adjourned *ad calendas graecas*. One of its important functions is to put the present into stasis, isolating it against mutative change and the necessity of choice at a crossroads, in this its working reminiscent of Winnicott's concept of 'fantasying', an activity 'absorbing energy but not contributing either to dreaming or to living'. Potamianou evokes the myth of Pandora and reminds us that hope is not always a good thing for the person who entertains it. Keeping hope detached from all possible realistic attempts at realisation, the patients Potamianou has studied spare themselves the mental mobilisation necessary to invest libidinally in objects and self, which would require, they say, an amount of energy which they simply do not possess. Potamianou refers to André Green's term 'the object's other' (the one the object's inner gaze is directed to if it does not purely dwell on the subject): what if the space on offer by the primary care giver were to deny any potential to thriving and force the subject in the straits of enforced self-sameness? Others are necessarily closely involved in what the subject comes to experience as hope: functionally hope shares traits with the *idéal du Moi*, whose receptability for influences from the grandparents has been discussed by de Mijolla. Potamianou approvingly sums up Janine Chasseguet-Smirgel's (1973) position on the importance of a sense of promise in the *idéal du Moi*. In case of threatening helplessness, various sub-projects undertaken in search of a Graal, as it were, may serve as an anti-phobic screen that protects against a loss of all hope. Even if everything is blocked, there is comfort in feeling that hope is still there, secured in a locked strong box, enough to keep some inner flame flickering lest the glacial night of non-desire covers everything.

In Pandora's case it was her curiosity that caused her to open the lid to the box. Neither curiosity nor hope, be it in the particularly stagnant form Potamianou portrays, have been regarded as hallmarks of the *opératoire*. Nor are oscillations between desire and lack of desire, which Potamianou finds with borderline cases something the *opératoire* seems inclined to. Flights of hopeful fancy and any extravagant flourish, on the whole, appear to be alien to their mode of being and functioning. Creative illusions are not their genre. Whatever safety buckle they have is formed by an investment in facticity and activity.

Resilience at a rock bottom level: the *opératoire* as a process in a field of shifting forces

When Anna Potamianou addresses problems of the *opératoire*, she strongly emphasises, as has been pointed out, the processual as an important complement to any structural considerations. If a person has at his/her disposal a network of mental representations of sufficient depth and flexibility, his/her psyche will have the ability to oscillate. These oscillations will be set in a field of shifting (inner and outer) equilibria in an economy of forces, an 'entanglement', as Potamianou writes 'of defensive arrangements exposed to the ripples of incessant vibrations' whilst integrating experiences of the past (Poatamianou 1986, p. 254). Such a person will be able to apply regulatory brakes without grinding to a halt: neither excitement nor exhaustion will easily wreak havoc on his/her mental economy. In contrast to this the *opératoire's* situation is characterised by an inordinate amount of violence, not only exercised against the psychic apparatus (by early or later traumatisms and by narcissistic hurts) but also within the psychic apparatus. The platform of *opératoire* functioning actively takes things in hand, operating an intra-systemic strategy which brutally knocks about the functionality of the Me. The Me is shrunk violently so as to offer as little as possible vulnerable surface to be pierced in its protective tissue. Mounted from a reduced basis, defence consumes a lot of energy. In this perspective, the Me is not so much exhausted as such, but working at the limits of its defensive capacity. Without quoting him, Potamianou shows how Michel Fain's caustic remarks to the effect that the *opératoire* patient is a person demonstrating too successfully that the Me can go autonomous could work out in a situation in which bearing up is all there is left to the subject.

In Potamianou's delineation, the *opératoire* person's situation is, indeed, to all intents and purposes reminiscent of a wartime economy. As in every war, questions of the exact make up of core territories and remaining resources at a given moment are crucial to any assessment of future viability. In line with her general approach that privileges nuanced differences, she contends there may be quite a range of varieties of the *opératoire*, not all of them covered in the original identikit provided by Pierre Marty and his colleagues. Some of the patients Potamianou has in mind do not show the heightened degree of disorganisation postulated by Marty but rather a massive tightening of mental life around a hard narcissistic core, in a situation in which boundaries waver and the defensive organisation of the Me falters. Under these circumstances *opératoire* functioning, which operates with reduced tonus over a shrunken mental surface, in Potamianou's view, takes on the character of a substantial, defensive counter-investment.

As a defence against afflictions in dire straits is it only directed against an external lack or is there a fifth column of the negative, striking from within when the mental apparatus is weakened by crisis? In the problematic response the subject musters in the face of adversity, we may well find a dysfunctionality on the level of the unconscious, but what emerges on the surface, under the conditions, is an iron curfew which the weakened Me clamps down on what arrives from within and without. Transformation is put on hold in a sclerosis of free mental movement and relational zest. It is a pathology of the Me we are confronted with, which may or may not be linked with psychosomatic illness and *dépression essentielle*. There are, probably, different paths, involving an interplay of inner and outer factors that drive people into a corner, to which the *opératoire* is an emergency response. In the varieties described by Potamianou there is resilience but at a rather basic level and at appalling costs. The Me that is in place emerges as a rather securitarian establishment, relentlessly patrolling the perimeter with all the manpower available, an action quite possibly in tacit obeisance to a cult of supposedly archaic power. There will be bread, more frequently stale than not, but no amenities and, in particular, very little in the way of games. If they are held at all, they are a serious affair in which neither man nor beast will be spared.

Personal myth as a force of irrigation

Piera Aulagnier – whom we have met earlier in Chapter 2 – quoted by Potamianou on various occasions, held that it was not really the unconscious that was constructed like a language, as Lacan taught. Rather this was something that might be said about the (unconscious) Me, for the constitution of which identification plays an important role (Aulagnier 1974). Potamianou moves into related territory when she speaks of cases in which inscriptions fail to take place because morphemes that would be needed to give shape to psychic events are not available to the individual. Myth, to some extent, steps in to fill the gap:

> repression leaves gaps in perception and memory which allow for omissions in the historical continuity of the subject's life. The gaps are filled by the mythical morphemes that shape the self-image and influence the perception and understanding of the surrounding world.
> (Potamianou 1985b, p. 294)

Personal myth, Potamianou believes, aids the differentiation between inner and outer world and constitutes an individual's 'most personal mode of shaping his or her own reality' (Potamianou 1985b, p. 292f.). It 'irrigates analysis with the flow of desires' and contributes 'to the structuring and maintenance of the invididual's unique inner world' (Potamianou 1985b, p. 292), a territory which, as we have seen, finds itself under intense pressure in the varieties of the *opératoire*. In her treatment of the figure of Helena in various strands of old lore she draws an implicit comparison between mythical morphemes and dream work, which supports the mental economy of the subject. As with the appearance of dreams, the emergence of personal myth in analysis should not be used single-mindedly to ferret out the 'real' history of the patient: it is the only way he/she has to deal with the derivatives of the unconscious. What is important is to help the patient to live with the fact that his/her ego 'can never acquire complete control over the primary processes' (Potamianou 1985b, p. 294).

It is interesting to note the importance she accords the myth of Prometheus: would Oedipus have found himself at the triple cross-road, she asks, if in some part in him a Prometheus had not made himself heard? Although Potamianou emphasises the invariant necessity of psychic conflict, she is very sensitive to the social and cultural conditions that shape the work of the great Greek tragedians: conditions push the poet who uses myth to develop in his work the stuff dreams are made of (*la fantasmatique*). What she writes of Prometheus seems to be applicable as much to the great playwright as to the average citizen:

> deliverance will come when Prometheus will be able to imagine the effort, the ordeal, and acknowledges the conflict to step up to it [*assumer le conflit*].
>
> (Potamianou 1979, p. 384)

Ambition is nothing less than setting one's sights at changing the way things are ordered in this world. It is this both libidinal and aggressive fire that Prometheus brings to mankind, which, if held and kept within a furnace, can be used by artisans and craftsmen, a fraternity of which Prometheus becomes, in acknowledgement of this gift, the protective deity in the city of Athens.

What if a story like Prometheus had never come to the fore and, in addition to this, tragedy as an art form had never developed in Greece? Would there have been a difference if a person had tried to work out his personal matters not in Athens but in Sparta, a society finding an important backbone of its collective identity in the ritually repeated choreography of the oppression of helots?

Civic space under consideration

If one's access to participation in an arena of shared projects is very much at risk, how much can individuals process what is befalling them? In a written response of his own to the article in which Potamianou uses Philoctetes' story to reflect on what it means to hold fast to one's pain, Jacques Press points out

> the wound and the pain of Philoctetes contain, un-thought, both un-formulated and incapable of formulation [*non formulables*], all the elements which appear, in contrast, with great abundance in the tale of Neoptolemus.
>
> It is incapable of decryption as such, were it not through the putting into representative form undertaken by his *vis-à-vis*, with the supplementary paradox that this is at first of no use whatsoever to Philoctetes.
>
> (Press 1999, p. 73f.)

It takes more than one person, Press suggests, to give voice to, and be able to process, pain and grief, just as Greek myth considered Prometheus instrumental in bringing fire to the furnace. Though Potamianou has an emphasis different from Press, she acknowledges the importance institutions and the framework they provide play in aiding or discouraging people to accommodate the unfamiliar. As a psychoanalyst in touch with the work of Serge Lebovici and René Diatkine at *ASM 13* in Paris, she shows sensitivity to the concrete cultural and social conditions in existence at a given time, an awareness perhaps also sharpened by her work with children and the difficulties to find proper space for this work in Greece. Her contributions to the *Yearbook of the International Association for Child and Adolescent Psychiatry and Allied Professions* show her thematically connected to a wide-ranging international network of research on child therapy, within which her work for the *Centre of Mental Health and Research*, founded by her in 1956 in Athens must have been of considerable relevance.

The voice of Anna Freudians as background chorus

Perhaps mediated by these connections and concerns, she shows more echoes than can usually be found in other French language publications of topics of importance to Joseph Sandler and to Anna Freud: the safety principle and restriction of the Me. As happened on a more public stage in Spartan society and culture, a subject about which Potamianou published an article (1998c), an individual tempted to the thrust of *opératoire* measures, will feel his/her sense of security threatened from without and from within. Potamianou points out that it is not just ego restrictions that hamper the subject in his/her dealings with the outside world, there is also the possibility of fissures within, 'cavities bored into the flesh of the ego' (Potamianou 2006b), a situation that admits a number of variants which might include the 'crypt' – containing a dead embalmed object tenaciously clung to – described by Abraham and Torok (1987). In the constellation envisaged by Potamianou there is an 'incrustation in the ego of an object', which becomes 'a source of encapsulated excitation' (Potamianou 2006b). The resulting impairment, however, may well be partial, depending on the overall organisation.

Though events in the past may have long lasting effects, they have to be considered within an overarching inner economy of ways and means. A radio interview with Stephen Grady, who as a boy was active in the French Resistance, illustrates some of the variants Potamianou repeatedly explores in her work. Deeply traumatised by his earlier experiences, he spent his later years in a remote spot in the Greek islands in a house which he surrounded with trip wire so as to feel safer. At a later stage, he took down the tripwire, because, as he said in the radio interview, he got prone to tripping himself up with increased age. In doing so he showed, for whatever reason, an amount of flexibility that was apparently not available to him earlier on.

Can fire be admitted to the house without a furnace?

The turn that security measures take in this illustration throws into relief Potamianou's approach to them. In her writings there is a dialectic between the frighteningly unrepresentable and the frame charged to deal with it that is constantly put to the test within an overall economy of ways and means. Potaminaou emphasises that we should bear in mind the differences between a valid frame wilfully not made use of and a frame not fit for use. This is an important distinction, it seems: While some patients engage in attacks on figuration, there are others who have not been able at their own good time safely to reject what was foisted on them as an impingement. The necessary work of differentiation, we may conclude, leads to another consideration: was there at any point in the subject's early development a crisis that had gone wasted because there was no proper space for it? Potamianou shows interest in Piera Aulagnier's reflections on pre-forms of the symbolic that have not been able to develop more fully. In a recent contribution Potamianou (2015) points to Levine, Reed and Scarfone (2013) for the gaps that open between what can be taken in by the senses and what can be provided with a mental handle. Some of the sensory footprints of the past may eventually, given the opportunity, serve as pre-forms of fantasy.

Theory as an aid to gauge the potential of situations

If this is to happen, words have to be highly time sensitive: there are, as Potamianou says, ports that are not navigable at all times. In this enterprise to find the right moment for the right move, theory does not only protect against being submerged by the chaotic, it also suggests where to look. The elements of clinical theory which

Potamianou assembles into a whole attempt to accompany the analyst, as Athanasios Alexandridis (2012) has observed, like a watchful mother sensitive to every half felt stir. Potamianou, in the corpus of her work, introduces possibilities to fine tune the concept of the *opératoire* by offering points of contact with existing stretches of theory on ego restriction and, to some extent, the clinic of trauma. Anna Potamianou's contributions on repetition compulsion, mental pain, identification as a strait jacket and the bunker of false hopes occupy an important position in understanding the *mode opératoire*. Although her thinking is firmly grounded in the work of the *EPP*, she has shown, as we have seen, a noticeable interest in perspectives on ego pathologies informed by Anna Freud's work, while at the same time integrating this with strands of French thinking on the *opératoire*.

With Potamianou we have seen a beleaguered Me threatened in its territory employ all regulatory means at its disposal. In the next chapter we shall see Jean Benjamin Stora, while being very much interested in the aspect of regulation, introduce further concerns: a sense that for a person to keep a lifeline open to the world a shared imaginary may be required and, flowing from this, an interest in and respect for ethnopsychoanalysis.

Sources

Abraham, N. and Torok, M. (1987), *L'écorce et le noyau*, Paris: Flammarion.

Alexandridis, A. (2012), 'Aspects du maternel dans le travail avec des enfants polytraumatisés (à partir de l'exposé de Claire Rojas)', *Revue Française de Psychosomatique* 41, pp. 27–35.

Anzieu, D., Carapanos, F., Gillibert, J., Green, A., Nicolaïdis, N., and Potamianou, A. (1980), *Psychanalyse et culture Grecque*, Paris: Société d'Édition des Belles Lettres.

Aulagnier, P. (1974), 'À propos de la réalité: savoir ou certitude', in: Aulagnier, P. (1986/2001), *Un interprète en quête de sens*, Paris: Payot, pp. 271–297.

Carapanos, F. and Potamianou, A. (1980), 'Langage, désir', in: Anzieu, D., Carapanos, F., Gillibert, J., Green, A., Nicolaïdis, N., and Potamianou, A. (1980), *Psychanalyse et culture Grecque*, Paris: Société d'Édition des Belles Lettres, pp. 53–100.

Chasseguet-Smirgel, J. (1973), 'Essai sur l'idéal du Moi'. Contribution à l'étude de "la maladie d'idéalité"', *Revue Française de Psychanalyse* 37(5-6), pp. 735–929.

Clair, M.A. (2003), 'Le traumatique, répétition et élaboration', *Canadian Journal of Psychoanalysis* 11, pp. 229–233.
de Mijolla, A. (1981/2003), *Les visiteurs du moi*, Paris: Les Belles Lettres.
Fine, A. (1995c), '"Un bouclier dans l'économie des états limites" d'Anna Potamianou', *Revue Française de Psychanalyse* 59(3), pp. 922–927.
Grady, S. (2013), *Gardens of stone: My boyhood in the French Resistance*, London: Hodder & Stoughton.
Guignard, F. (1998), 'Anna Potamianou, Processus de répétition et offrandes du Moi', *Revue Française de Psychanalyse* 62(4), pp. 1297–1303.
Guillaumin, J. (1992), 'Jugement de non-représentabilité et renoncement à la maîtrise de la pensée', *Revue Française de Psychanalyse* 56(1), pp. 9–21.
Kaswin-Bonnefond, D. (2004), 'Le traumatique, répétition et élaboration d'Anna Potamianou', *Revue Française de Psychanalyse* 68(1), pp. 273–278.
Lebovici, S. (1988), 'Les enfants de la folie: By Anna Potamianou. Toulouse: Privat. 1984', *International Journal of Psychoanalysis* 69, pp. 564–565.
Levine, H.B., Reed, G.S and Scarfone, D. eds (2013), *Unrepresented states and the construction of meaning. Clinical and theoretical contributions*, London: Karnac Books.
Marty, P. (1980), *L'ordre psychosomatique* [= *Les mouvements individuels de vie et de mort. Essai d'économie psychosomatique*, volume 2], Paris: Payot.
McDougall, J. (1994), '"Un bouclier dans l'économie des états limites: l'espoir": Anna Potamianou. Collection Le fait psychanalytique. Presses Universitaires de France, Paris, 1992', *Canadian Journal of Psychoanalysis* 2, pp. 271–273.
McDougall, J. (1996), '"Un bouclier dans l'économie des états limites: l'espoir": Anna Potamianou. Collection Le fait psychanalytique. Presses Universitaires de France, Paris, 1992, 160pp., FF. 128', *Journal of the American Psychoanalytic Association* 44, pp. 1295–1298.
Midweek: Owen Sheers, Stephen Grady, Michael Ball, Ffion Jones, broadcast on BBC Radio 4, 20th February 2013.
Müürsepp, P. (no date), 'Semiophysics as a theoretical basis for scientific creativity', available at: www.academia.edu/715209/Semiophysics_as_a_Theoretical_Basis_for_Scientific_Creativity
Neyraut, M. (1997), *Les raisons de l'irrationnel*, Paris: Presses Universitaires de France.
Patrick, M. (1999), 'Hope: A shield in the economy of borderline states', *Psychoanalytic Psychotherapy* 13, pp. 91–93.
Paul, P.I. (1997), 'Processes of repetition and offerings of the ego', *International Journal of Psychoanalysis* 78, pp. 1037–1039.

Potamianou, A. (1973), 'A propos du développement de l'idéal du Moi', *Revue Française de Psychanalyse* 37(5–6), pp. 1169–1174.
Potamianou, A. (1974), 'Illusion du rêve et de la connaissance', *Revue Française de Psychanalyse* 38(5–6), pp. 1127–1132.
Potamianou, A. (1975), 'Réflexions sur le transsexualisme féminin', *Revue Française de Psychanalyse* 39(5–6), pp. 1053–1064.
Potamianou, A. (1977a), 'Le deuil de Prométhée', *Revue Française de Psychanalyse* 41(1-2), pp. 205–216.
Potamianou, A. (1977b), 'Mouvement auto-érotique de la pensée', *Revue Française de Psychanalyse* 41(5–6), pp. 1117–1124.
Potamianou, A. (1978), '"Comme on l'utilisera …": sur la fonction de l'analyste', *Revue Française de Psychanalyse* 42(1), pp. 111–122.
Potamianou, A. (1979), 'Réflexions psychanalytiques sur la "Promethia" d'Eschyle: rapports entre l'omnipotence et la dépression', *Revue Française de Psychanalyse* 43(3), pp. 375–400.
Potamianou, A. (1980), 'Vécu de l'enfance, défenses du moi et rencontre avec le psychanalyste', *Revue Française de Psychanalyse* 44(5-6), pp. 990–998.
Potamianou, A. (1982a), 'On ego defenses', *Psychoanalytic Study of the Child* 37, pp. 421–432.
Potamianou, A. (1982b), 'Sur le travail analytique', *Revue Française de Psychanalyse* 46(2), pp. 371–376.
Potamianou, A. (1983a[1978]), 'Discussion' in: Anthony, E.J. and Chiland, C. eds, *L'enfant dans sa famille*, volume 5: *Parents et enfants dans un monde en changement*, Paris: Presses Universitaires de France, pp. 104–107.
Potamianou, A. (1983b[1978]), 'Quelques commentaires sur le changement social en Grèce', in: Anthony, E.J. and Chiland, C. eds, *L'enfant dans sa famille*, volume 5: *Parents et enfants dans un monde en changement*, Paris: Presses Universitaires de France, pp. 179–185.
Potamianou, A. (1983c[1978]), [untitled, separate contribution to] 'Visites sur le terrain en Israël: juillet 1976', in: Anthony, E.J. and Chiland, C. eds, *L'enfant dans sa famille*, volume 5: *Parents et enfants dans un monde en changement*, Paris: Presses Universitaires de France, pp. 308–310.
Potamianou A. (1983d), 'Propos sur quelques modalités de la régression', *Topique* 31, pp. 91–104.
Potamianou, A. (1984a), *Les enfants de la folie. Violence dans les identifications*, Toulouse: Edition Privat.
Potamianou, A. (1984b [1980]), '"Une bonne pluie connaît sa saison …"', in: Anthony, E.J. and Chiland, C. eds, *L'enfant dans sa famille*, volume 6: *Prévention en psychiatrie de l'enfant en un temps de transition*, Paris: Presses Universitaires de France, pp. 529–531.

Potamianou, A. (1985a), 'Concerning the second drive movement', [= 'Propos sur l'autre courant...'], *Bulletin of the European Psychoanalytic Federation* 25, pp. 97–102.

Potamianou, A. (1985b), 'The personal myth: points and counterpoints', *Psychoanalytic Study of the Child* 40, pp. 285–296.

Potamianou, A. (1986), 'Des origines du refoulement et de l'agencement des défenses', *Revue Française de Psychanalyse* 50(1–2), pp. 521–524.

Potamianou, A. (1987), 'De vortex et de volcans. Toujours sur le parcours des identifications', *Topique* 39, pp. 49–61.

Potamianou, A. (1988a), 'Figurations du Nirvâna et réaction thérapeutique négative', *Revue fraçaise de psychanalyse* 52(4), pp. 917–935.

Potamianou, A. (1988b), '"Episkepsis": pensées autour de la visite d'Anna Freud à Athènes', *Revue Internationale d'Histoire de la Psychanalyse* 1, pp. 247–254.

Potamianou, A. (1990a), 'Somatization and dream work', *Psychoanalytic Study of the Child* 45, pp. 273–292.

Potamianou, A. (1990b), 'Réflexions et hypothèses sur la problématique des états limites', in: Le Guen, C. ed., *La psychanalyse: questions pour demain*, Paris: Presses Universitaires de France, pp. 171–179.

Potamianou A. (1990c) 'Rêves et somatisation', *Topique* 45, pp. 49–62.

Potamianou, A. (1991), 'D'un reste irréductible', *Topique* 47, pp. 57–67.

Potamianou, A. (1992a), *Un bouclier dans l'économie des états-limites*, Paris: Presses Universitaires de France.

Potamianou, A. (1992b), 'Inquiétudes au sujet d'une étrange familiarité', *Revue Française de Psychanalyse* 56(2), pp. 121–129; also available in: Denis, P. and Schaeffer, J. eds (2001), *Devenir psychanalyste?*, Paris: Presses Universitaires de France, pp. 121–129.

Potamianou, A. (1992c), 'Note sur un avant-coup', *Revue Française de Psychanalyse* 56(4), pp. 1101–1104.

Potamianou, A. (1992d), 'Emprise et dé-prise: une combinatoire', *Revue Française de Psychanalyse* 56(5), pp. 1519–1525.

Potamianou, A. (1992e[1988]), 'Le processus d'identification chez les enfants soumis à un stress causé par la psychose de la mère', in: Anthony, E.J. and Chiland, C. eds, *L'enfant dans sa famille*, volume 8: *Le développement en péril*, Paris: Presses Universitaires de France, pp. 73–79.

Potamianou, A. (1992f), 'Etre par procuration', in: Gros, F. and Huber, G. eds, *Vers un anti-destin? Patrimoine génétique et droits de l'humanité*, Paris: Odile Jacob, pp. 309–315.

Potamianou, A. (1992g), 'Approche psychanalytique de la tragédie grecque', *Psychanalyse dans la civilisation* 7, pp. 29–40.

Potamianou, A. (1993a), 'Insuffisance des procédés autocalmants', *Revue Française de Psychosomatique* 4, pp. 87–95.

Potamianou, A. (1993b), 'En exil de langue maternelle', *Canadian Journal of Psychoanalysis* 1(2), pp. 47–59.

Potamianou, A. (1994a), 'Réflexions sur le processus désinvestissants', *Revue Française de Psychosomatique* 5, pp. 101–105.

Potamianou, A. (1994b), 'Sur le thème du "tout analyser"', *Revue Française de Psychanalyse* 58(4), pp. 983–987.

Potamianou, A. (1995), *Processus de répétition et offrandes du Moi*, Lausanne: Delachaux et Niestlé.

Potamianou, A. (1997a), 'De crises et de maladies', *Revue Française de Psychosomatique* 12, pp. 7–22.

Potamianou, A. (1997b), 'Faits mythiques, évènements historiques, réalité psychique', in: Clancier, A. and Athanassiou Popesco, C. eds, *Mythes et psychanalyse*, Paris: In Press, pp. 33–39.

Potamianou, A. (1997c), 'Working the borders', *Bulletin de la Fédération Européenne de Psychanalyse* 48, pp. 32–38.

Potamianou, A. (1997d), 'L'angoisse de mort', in: Cournut, J., Israël, P., Jeanneau, A. and Schaeffer, J. eds, *Le mal-être (angoisse et violence). Débats de psychanalyse*, Paris: Presses Universitaires de France, pp. 45–56.

Potamianou, A. (1998a), 'Les contraintes de l'opératoire', *Revue Française de Psychosomatique* 13, pp. 49–62.

Potamianou, A. (1998b), 'En dehors du temps ... dans les figures du mythe: Hélène: brillance et éblouissement du désir', *Revue Française de Psychanalyse* 62(3), pp. 947–955.

Potamianou, A. (1998c), 'Parricide et inceste: la solution de Sparte', in: Le Beuf, D., Perron, R. and Pragier, G. eds, *Construire l'histoire*, Paris: Presses Universitaires de France, pp. 53–61.

Potamianou, A. (1999a), 'Avoir la douleur', *Revue Française de Psychosomatique* 15, pp. 51–63.

Potamianou, A. (1999b), 'Le temps de l'interprétation', *Revue Française de Psychosomatique* 16, pp. 49–57.

Potamianou, A. (1999c), 'Croisements', *Revue Française de Psychanalyse* 63(5), pp. 1703–1709.

Potamianou, A. (2000a), 'Dans les sillons du traumatique', *Actualités Psychosomatiques* 3, pp. 119–138.

Potamianou, A. (2000b), En contre-ordre de la mort, in: Guillaumin, J., Potamianou, A., Roussillon, R., Kaës, R., Lamothe, C., Vasseur, C., Vermorel, M. and Vermorel, H., *L'invention de la pulsion de mort*, Paris: Dunod, pp. 55–69.

Potamianou, A. (2001), *Le traumatique. Répétition et élaboration*, Paris: Dunod.
Potamianou, A. (2002a), 'Mouvoir. En revenant sur l'analité primaire', in: Botella, C. ed., *Penser les limites. Ècrits en l'honneur d'André Green*, Paris: Delachaux et Niestlé, pp. 523–529.
Potamianou, A. (2002b), 'Fixations psychiques, liages somatiques', *Revue Française de Psychosomatique 22*, pp. 151–174.
Potamianou, A. (2002c), 'Pathways of pleasure: The channel of primary anality', *International Journal of Psychoanalysis* 83(3), pp. 609–621.
Potamianou, A. (2003), 'Attaches métapsychologiques de la fatigue', *Revue Française de Psychosomatique 24*, pp. 45–60.
Potamianou, A. (2004a), 'Ouverture psychique – souffrance somatique', *Actualités Psychosomatiques 7*, pp. 141–158.
Potamianou, A. (2004b), 'Discussion of Robert Asséo's Report', *Bulletin de la Fédération Européenne de Psychanalyse* 58, pp. 118–123.
Potamianou, A. (2005), 'Excitante hybris', *Revue Française de Psychanalyse* 69(1), pp. 169–186.
Potamianou, A. (2006a), 'Violence dans la vie opératoire et dans les somatisations', *Actualités Psychosomatiques 9*, pp. 37–47.
Potamianou, A. (2006b), 'In the space of the lost footsteps', *Bulletin de la Fédération Européenne de Psychanalyse* 60, pp. 51–60.
Potamianou, A. (2007), 'Témoignages et questionnements', *Revue Française de Psychosomatique 32*, pp. 89–105.
Potamianou, A. (2008a), 'Épimythion au négatif', *Revue Française de Psychanalyse* 72(1), pp. 63–74.
Potamianou, A. (2008b), 'Frappes et battements d'excitation', *Revue Française de Psychosomatique 33*, pp. 8–29.
Potamianou, A. (2008c), 'The part of the shadows', *Bulletin de la Fédération Européenne de Psychanalyse* 62, no page numbers.
Potamianou, A. (2010a), 'Calmer, s'abstenter, veiller', *Revue Française de Psychosomatique 37*, pp. 97–108.
Potamianou, A. (2010b), 'De flux et de reflux. En discutant le rapport de Françoise Coblence', *Revue Française de Psychanalyse* 74(5), pp. 1357–1366.
Potamianou, A. (2010c), 'En poursuivant', *Actualités Psychosomatiques* 13, pp. 163–175.
Potamianou, A. (2011a), 'Aux carrefours des passions et de la toute-puissance', *Revue Française de Psychanalyse* 75(2), pp. 501–515.
Potamianou, A. (2011b), 'Une fois de plus … la culpabilité', *Revue Française de Psychosomatique 39*, pp. 77–90.
Potamianou, A. (2013), 'Destins et carillons de la culpabilité', *Revue Française de Psychosomatique 44*, pp. 93–109.

Potamianou, A. (2015), 'Amnemonic traces: traumatic after-effects', *International Journal of Psychoanalysis* 96(4), pp. 945–966.

Potamianou, A. (2016), 'Donner forme, figurer, représenter. Quelques réflexions', *Revue Française de Psychosomatique* 50, pp. 207–223.

Potamianou, A. (2017a), 'Revisiting the destiny compulsion', *International Journal of Psychoanalysis* 98(1), pp. 55–69.

Potamianou, A. (2017b), 'Pour le temps d'une amitié', *Revue Française de Psychosomatique* 52(2), pp. 151–162.

Pragier, G. and Faure-Pragier, S. (1990), Un siècle après l'"Esquisse": nouvelles métaphores?: Métaphores du nouveau', *Revue Française de Psychanalyse* 54(6), pp. 1395–1500.

Press, J. (1999), 'A propos de l'article d'Anna Potamianou' [Potamianou 1999a], *Revue Française de Psychosomatique* 15, pp. 65–77.

Rosenberg, B. (1991), *Masochisme mortifère et masochisme gardien de la vie*, Paris: Presses Universitaires de France.

Steiner, J. (1993), ' "Un bouclier dans l'economie des etats limites l'espoir"', *International Journal of Psychoanalysis* 74, pp. 846–849.

Talfanidis, K. and Maniadakis, G. (2014), 'Studying the archives of the Hellenic Society of Psychoanalytic Psychotherapy: An outline of its historical course', *International Forum of Psychoanalysis* 23(2), pp. 127–132.

Vaneck, L. (1985), ' "Les enfants de la folie. Violence dans les identifications" par Anna Potamianou', *Revue Belge de Psychanalyse* 7, pp. 127–130.

Vlachakis, I. (2004), 'La tradition psychiatrique en Grèce et la transmission de la psychanalyse: La paradigme historique du Centre d'Hygiène Mentale à Athènes', *Topique* 89, pp. 103–109.

8

CONFIGURATIONS 2

Jean Benjamin Stora

Jean Benjamin Stora, who worked with Pierre Marty, and from 1989 to 1992 was president of *IPSO* introduces further dimensions to the reflection on the *opératoire*. Born, like André Green, in an Arab country into a Jewish family, he brings to his work an acute awareness of the importance of affect and the enormous difficulties that accrue if this finds no adequate support in the shared imaginary of the environment.

Among the cases Jean Benjamin Stora presents in his 1999 study there are at least two in which the subject's capacity to sustain a working defensive shield against adversity, without warning, takes a devastating hit at a nodal point. Turning the immediate environment into helpless bystanders, the event shows all reparatory efforts *post hoc* to be dramatically futile.

Shocks that kill

The first of these stories is one that Stora witnessed as a small child. It set him on a lifelong course of inquiry leading him to his work in psychology, psychoanalysis and psychosomatics. It happened to his grandfather, at a time when the family was still living in the province of Constantine (present day Algeria). Stora's grandfather, a veteran of the Great War, in which he had lost his left arm, had been hit by Vichy's pernicious antisemitic legislation. His possessions had been expropriated and handed over to a 'trustee' appointed by the state. A sister, whom he had loved very much, had died about the same time. Then came another shock: an army truck ran over and killed a cousin of Stora's in the streets of the quarter. His grandfather's health deteriorated steadily. He sought solace in the *Tehillim*, the Book of Psalms, the traditional sustenance of those fallen on hard times, in which he immersed himself night and day. The child, who observed all this, had the impression that this practice did indeed provide a modicum of help to his grandfather, but then, to his surprise, became aware of a change in quality and daily rhythm, when local magical healers, whose charms to him seemed to be little in consonance with the spirit of Judaism, began to be admitted to the house. Their efforts, too, proved to be in vain. Stora's grandfather died of a cancer, of which he had not been told, but of which he somehow knew.

A second case, related in one important point, came to Stora's attention, mediated by a source somewhat unusual for a French psychoanalyst. He found it quoted by Jon Kabat-Zinn (the American pioneer of the mindfulness-based stress reduction programme) in his book *Full Catastrophe Living*. It derived from the recollections of a renowned American cardiologist, Bernard Lown, who as a young doctor witnessed an incident which, even at a distance of some thirty years, still caused him to shudder. Lown had a post-doctorate fellowship with S.A. Levine, professor of cardiology at Harvard Medical School. In one of his first clinics Lown had Mrs. S. as a patient, a middle-aged librarian who had low grade congestive heart failure. What follows merits to be quoted *in extenso* because it reflects the incredulity of the shocked observer looking back at the course of events:

> Dr. Levine, who had followed her in the clinic for more than a decade, greeted Mrs. S. warmly and then turned to the large entourage of visiting physicians and said, 'This women [sic] has TS', and abruptly left.
>
> No sooner was Dr. Levine out of the door than Mrs. S.'s demeanor abruptly changed. She appeared anxious and frightened and was now breathing rapidly, clearly hyperventilating. Her skin was drenched with perspiration, and her pulse had accelerated to more than 150 a minute. In reexamining her, I found it astonishing that the lungs, which a few minutes earlier had been quite clear, now had moist crackles at the bases. [...]
>
> I questioned Mrs. S. as to the reasons for her sudden upset. Her response was that Dr. Levine had said that she had TS, which she

knew meant 'terminal situation' [what the doctor really had done was to use the medical acronym for 'tricuspid stenosis'. […]. I tried to reach Dr. Levine, but he was nowhere to be located. Later that same day she died from intractable heart failure.

(Kabat-Zinn 1990, p. 189)

In both cases, as Stora observes, there is an onslaught of excitement, well beyond the capacity of the subject to process. With the arrival of an unforeseen piece of information, the imagination takes fright and balks at the fuller implications of the new scenario, before it can be herded back into the safer confines of previously established networks of meaning. On impact, the mental apparatus goes into a state of disconnect. It is as if the subject were to 'bleed to death in his own tissues' (Bion 1970) – those tissues, we have to remember, that a person considered to be *opératoire* is deemed not to have.

Shared symbolic universes as a precondition for communication in depth

Stora takes care to point out the relevance of the imagery developed by the patients that is embedded in the universe of symbolic meaning they have been moving in. He goes as far as saying that psychoanalysis is counter-indicated for first generation immigrants and possibly has to be adjusted for second generation immigrants. If this extra caution is neglected, there is the danger that the patient's and the psychoanalyst's inner worlds will irremediably run on separate rails. In such a case, a large, if not major, part of the patient's imaginary life risks escaping treatment. It is therefore requisite for the psychoanalyst to be conversant with the patient's cultural universe of reference. The wealth of the patient's imaginary life can only be appreciated if there is sufficient knowledge of the myths implied in it. Repeatedly, Stora refers to Tobie Nathan's work in ethnopsychoanalysis, pointing out that there are cultures in which the individual does not strive for a degree of separation from the group, but in which the individual Me forms part of a group Me to an extent unusual in Western society. Images of what forces the patient believes to be at work in his/her inner life – and be it of supposedly demoniacal nature – have to be taken into consideration. If this is not heeded, the patient may erroneously be classified as *opératoire* not because he/she is constitutionally unable to connect to others on an emotional level, but because he/she cannot do so under present circumstances.

Stora (1999; 2013) also relates the case of Nina, a young woman from the Maghreb, a patient who was referred to him by a GP, who found her lacking in the rudiments of the imagination. Stora discovered that, by inferring links from his personal familiarity with the patient's cultural background, which were not being made explicit, he was gradually able to gain access to a rich inner universe. In it a belief in evil spirits at odds with Western thinking was central to the patient's assumptions, which she had been keeping secret. Reading the case description, one understands that Nina, in turning a bland surface towards the world around her, was attempting to adapt as best as possible to the place in which she found herself.

Entering hospital, Stora believes, patients leave behind a world of previous arrangements and have to come to terms with a situation in which clinical success may depend on their capacity to stay passive in the face of extended waiting. Being enveloped by an all-encompassing institution may further regression, encourage drawing on a masochistic core, and offer a certain protective shield to patients. At the same time, they will also be confronted with a medical system that comprises numerous complex examinations, in which they may feel as if they were a loose confederacy of facts and functions, part of an elusive whole, in which importance is expressed in numbers and conversations with doctors can take a turn that is experienced as Kafkaesque. Stora warmly recommends Marie-Christine Pouchelle's anthropological studies on hospital culture. In them she observes styles of interaction strangely reminiscent of what psychoanalysts have described as *opératoire*:

> From the first moments of my investigation in this centre, I was surprised by the 'surgical' style of interpersonal relations, widespread among the medical caregivers [*les soignants*]: whatever the sympathy and the warmth connecting two people speaking with each other, one of them is capable of abruptly breaking up contact and turning away without employing any of the forms of disengagement usual in daily life. [...] As if the 'soft tissue' ... of interpersonal relations had been sacrificed to the benefit of a hard core of a communication reduced to the essential.
>
> (Pouchelle 2003, p. 16)

Adaptive measures put to the test

If an excessive investment in work might serve as an anti-traumatic measure outside hospital, turning oneself into a highly invested collection of facts, a medical file on two legs as it were, must offer benefits to certain patients, some of whom may be able to protect their own subjective belief systems in this way. The inability to translate inner worlds into language accepted as valid currency in hospital culture is at its most conspicuous in cases in which patients who are considered inveterate hypochondriacs are eventually, on insistence, given the benefit of doubt, re-examined and, to the doctors' surprise, diagnosed with cancer. Clearly, the atmosphere of the hospital and the interactions taking place there colour the responses to anything that touches the patient's mental life and should be taken into account when we assess a person's psychological functions. Also, it is important to gauge the response of the family to what is happening to the patient.

As we have seen with Stora's grandfather, a fully functional symbolic universe may not be enough to restore patients at the end of their tether to a working equilibrium (not even *après coup*). Both Stora's grandfather and Mrs. S. were not without resources when we find them struck by disaster: Stora's grandfather was intimately familiar with the tradition of a discourse of the soul with itself; the librarian diagnosed with TS had a background of long familiarity with the treatment supervised by a trusted professor. Yet, under the impact of a sudden shock the network of inner and outer objects was no longer providing adequate support. The patients fell through the mesh of the network of links that had hitherto sustained them. Emergency measures attempted both by the hospital and by the traditional magical healers came to nothing. Apparently, even a sufficiently rich inner world is of no avail if it cannot sustain its buffer function at crisis point in a given environment. Stora, in his study on stress, in line with Marty's and Fain's thought, emphasises the importance of a preconscious of sufficient depth, fluidity and of spontaneous availability to absorb shock in case of need.

Buffer zones invigorated by the imaginary

Stora refers to Anzieu's concept of a psychic envelope structured like a multilayered skin, comprised of different strata separated from each other, which protects from the outside and relays signification inside. If there is a sufficiently demarcated distance between the surface of excitability and the surface of communication and signification, there is a transitional intermediary zone that transforms stimuli into meaning. If the distance between the two collapses, layers get glued to one another and mental function is lost, constituting, according to Anzieu, another description of the *mode opératoire*. Work, under the circumstances, can serve an anti-traumatic function.

From other information Stora provides, we have to gather that the inner leeway a person possesses can, to some extent, depend on the social imaginary he/she is able to tap into. Stora draws on studies that found that individuals who thought to be in control at the workplace felt less stress and more of a sense of well-being than those who did not. Countries which favoured an individualist culture produced a greater number of people who felt on top of the situation than those in which collective culture was emphasised to a greater extent. Since this perception is culturally mediated and does not correspond to an increased level of measurable social security, we have to assume that the magma of socially available imaginary performs buffer functions in any judgement upon circumvailing reality: illusionary though it might be, the culturally mediated but personally claimed imputation of self-efficacy and liberal agency will show tangible results nonetheless if there is a cultural frame for it and conditions do not deteriorate.

Aridity of mental links as a fire-door shut on fright

What seems to be so destructive to the equilibrium of some patients we have to conclude is the eruption of inflammatory meaning of an event which incontrovertibly presents itself to the psyche as a portent of ill, a meaning for which an *opératoire* person might not be susceptible because he/she does not spend much time in the realms of the imagination. Although the shock waves of an event will reach the *opératoire* eventually, most likely on a bodily level, we cannot see the *opératoire* as a person who takes fright easily. There is a measure of stolidity to be derived from an overwhelming preoccupation with stark unadorned reality and this, although Stora does not specifically mention it, has been an ideal held out by a number of cultures. Stoic thinking, in particular, has traditionally suggested we should adjust our imagination so that bursts of bad fortune will not unsettle it and should make judicious use of the world as it is without giving too much slack to the vagaries of what is seen as vain desire.

Rehearsals of trivia of material culture as a re-affirmation of shared bonds

There is gain to be derived from an intense investment in fact, which offers ties to a shared community of practice and remembrance inaccessible to the uninitiated observer. Stora shows interest in the work Marcel Mauss, whose seminal work, *Essai sur le don*, examined the various dimensions of the gift. If what appears as perfunctory mental functioning in some patients were to tie into a communality of material culture, social bonds and transgenerational transmissions, what would its implicit exchange value as a gift be both to the subject and to others? Granted it might in some particular cases be a quest for the non-desire of the other, as Stora quotes André Green (1983), its meaning, as Stora's work amply shows, will have to be considered on various levels and in different contexts: it remains polyvalent in its opaqueness. Stora himself points towards Antonio Damasio's work (1994) on potential representations.

Repression of emotion as a corollary to a body having to establish new equilibria

Stora reflects on the possibility of specific physiological and neurological impediments to the expression of their emotions encountered by heart transplant patients for some time after the operation; points out that the repression of emotions and their re-routing into the body is not necessarily the equivalent of alexithymia; and notes the alleviation of emotional repression inculcated in a severe education after a heart transplant has re-established bodily integrity.

In the patients whom he sees both progressive adaptation and a drifting into residual robotic functioning remain possible outcomes. After having earlier on worked with Pierre Marty, Stora was able to examine more than 3,000 patients as a psychosomatic consultant attached to the Pitié-Salpêtrière hospital's department of endocrinology, whose help was made accessible to patients from all departments of the hospital. Drawing on his experience, he was able to establish a university diploma course in *Psychosomatique intégrative*.

The work of the psychosomaticien in the institution as an enfranchised outsider

In his interviews with patients he seems to enjoy a unique intermediary – and paradoxical – position of an esteemed and well-connected outsider inside the institution, who is able to engage patients from an angle that both breaks their hospital routine and draws their attention. He wears a white blouse and the badge of doctors with additional reference to his psychosomatic competence but is not part of any *grande visite* and takes along on his visits one of his students at most, in a conscious break with the large academic audiences present at the interlocutions with patients in the tradition from Charcot to Marty. A significant number of the patients he writes about have a linguistic or childhood background outside France.

With both his cross-cultural patients and some of his neurological patients, he has to inject quantities of the imaginary and to propose chains of association, with which patients are made aware they are at liberty to disagree, in an effort to re-animate mental processes. With some patients who lack adequate gratification in sublimatory activities, lateral transference in new fields of self-assertion and exploration are actively encouraged. At times the release of previously inhibited aggression, even if directed against hospital staff has to be understood as a sign of improvement, an assessment that puts the psychosomatician into a somewhat delicate position vis-a-vis his medical colleagues.

Working with the submerged potential of patients

Stora habitually enquires about his patients' spiritual beliefs and practices so as better to assess the recourse available to them, in cases of distress, to face up to adversity. He also shows interest in belief-based cultural constructions feeding into research. The symbolic potential of a person, in part, depends on the way his/her culture provides him/her with accessible meaningful structure in his/her preconscious. Apparently, there has to be a shared dimension of the imaginary for the analyst to become tangible to the patient – the mental space of the encounter cannot simply be taken for granted.

On one occasion Stora met a former patient of Marty's, whose long road to treatment is probably representative of more than just her own personal experience. At one point she consulted a psychologist at a big Paris hospital because she wanted to receive help better to observe her diet. This psychologist interrogated her, did not communicate his findings to her, but recommended psychotherapy to her. He also, and this becomes very important, wrote a letter of reference to the medical head of *IPSO* for her:

> She keeps this letter in her bag for a year, and after some reflection, she goes to make the visit to the Institute of Psychosomatics, where she is received warmly [*de façon chaleureuse*] by Pierre Marty in his office; of which encounter she still keeps a vivid, warm memory [*un souvenir ému*].
> (Stora 2005, p. 193)

The way she was received by Marty made it possible for her to begin therapy with him. There was a bridge between her world and the idea that therapy might be something important for her.

Stora avows having been influenced by the thought of Thure von Uexküll, from which he retains a vivid interest in the patient's ways to inhabit his/her world and his/her transformation of input into autopoiesis. Yet, as the case of Stora's grandfather shows, there are times when autopoiesis fails, when existent form can no longer be invested in to keep up a good enough defensive screen and the threads of libido fray.

Regulatory ways of dealing with tension

Stora privileges the economic point of view that takes a deep interest in the vicissitudes of mental energy, although he concedes that energy in this context is a metaphor to deal with states of the mental apparatus in its dealing with stimuli of excitement and tension. How much this apparatus has been developed may vary considerably between different individuals. If pain sets in and life trickles out of whatever remains, behaviour and character try to hold the line as elements of composure. Stora postulates a series of auto-regulatory oscillations, island-like zones of stability in a whole in which instability predominates. They work within certain limits like catchment basins, at times competing to attract currents. If the mental apparatus is overwhelmed, Stora believes, there is a latency of at least 24 to 48 hours before elaborative work can be resumed. If this does not happen, stimuli are passed on to other neuronal subsystems which attempt adaptation to what by then has become a threat to the organism. Stora quotes David Ruelle's (1991) image of the faucet that regulates the flow of water: if opened too wide there will be turbulence. If shut tightly – as we have to take the *opératoire* to be against any surprising outbursts of the imagination – can we assume the pipes, once pressure builds up, will have a tendency to burst at default lines of greatest fragility? Stora does not expatiate upon this in his lines on Ruelle, but, with Jaak Pans*epp*, distinguishes four sub-systems that control emotion at a neuronal level – another base line of integration to assist at processing stimuli: seeking, rage, fear and panic. Stora discusses the circuit of seeking from the point of view of its exploratory and auto-conservatory functions: under-stimulation of this sub-system results in loss of interest in the world, consummation of its basic goals extinguishes its activity. Libido, as a concept, is here replaced with appetite. Both a lack of *pregnance* of form, as Thom would have put it, and a lack of lack (a satiety) – to which we can safely add lack of basic security – will impede exploratory behaviour. What integrates all the different mental and physiological sub-systems is the overarching necessity to process whatever stress is impacting on the subject: 'Complete freedom from stress is death', Stora (2005) quotes Hans Selye.

Illusion conducive to the inception of form?

Stora places his approach, derived from Pierre Marty, within a larger theoretical framework of, as he terms it, a bio-psycho-social approach. Stora believes that it is impossible to develop a science of the interrelations of the different levels of life by only referring to psychoanalysis, which reflects Pierre Marty's own emphasis.

His main concern is the psychoanalytically informed psycho-somatic treatment of the severely ill, or post-operational, patient. Although his main focus is not on the *mode opératoire*, his observations, as we have seen, contain important reflections pertinent to it. He shows sustained sensitivity to the states of the patient's imaginary as an access point to his/her condition. This personally appropriated imaginary, rooted in culture, forms a barrier against disintegration; it also makes the person vulnerable to imaginary ills a person short on fantasy might not similarly be exposed to. Among other concerns, Stora raises the question how much of the imaginary specific to the patient has to be shared for effective treatment to be able to start.

His approach to the situation of the patient's economy of mental energy presupposes a concept of cathexis – mental investment – which seems to imply that a given patient may be out of budget to entertain a fantasy. This fantasy out of reach would then have to be considered as something akin to a faint, pale, distant beckoning of a form without a self-supporting force field to go with it. If this – the absence of fantasy – were the possible plight of a patient, we would then have to see in it the reverse of what Ferenczi (1909; 1912) proposes as a habitual mode of enrichment of the Me: the constant introjection of elements of non-Me to extend the subject's mental realms. The question is whether for this to happen this process has to be sustained by what Winnicott termed illusion (in this diverging from Freud's use of the word) as a feeling for the yet unproven potential the future might hold in store. Seen in this way, the French use of *investissement* (cathexis) and *intrication* (libidinal entanglement), on the one hand, and Winnicott's use of illusion, on the other hand, may be approaching the same problem – how enchantment with the world is produced and what it is contingent upon – from different access points.

It may not be enough for a person to have a cultural imaginary to tap into if this does nothing or little to sustain the person at the end of his/her tether. In the case of Mrs. S., Dr. Levine's patient, a basis of trust in her doctor was not enough when his presence would have been required.

In our next chapter we will see how César and Sára Botella put a particular emphasis on the work of figurability stalled if not for a double, in whose inner presence it can take place.

Sources

Anzieu, D. (1990), *L'Épiderme nomade et la peau psychique*, Paris: Editions Apsygée.

Bion, W.R. (1970) *Attention and interpretation*, London: Karnac Books.

Correale, A. (2007), *Il campo istituzionale*, 3rd edition, *Prospettiva della Ricerca Psicoanalitica*, Roma: Edizione Borla.

Damasio, A. (1994), *Descartes' error. Emotion, reason and the human brain*, London: Vintage Books.

Ferenczi, S. (1909), 'Introjektion und Übertragung', *Bausteine zur Psychoanalyse*, volume 1: *Theorie*, Frankfurt/Main: Ullstein, pp. 9–57.

Ferenczi, S. (1912), 'Zur Begriffsbestimmung der Introjektion', *Bausteine zur Psychoanalyse*, volume 1: *Theorie*, Frankfurt/Main: Ullstein, pp. 58–61.

Foehl, J.C. (2010), 'The necessity of shared illusion in the creation of "reality": commentary on paper by Christopher Bonovitz', *Psychoanalytic Dialogues* 20, pp. 642–653.

Green, A. (1983), *Narcissme de vie, narcissime de mort*, Paris: Les Éditions de Minuit.

Harvey, W.P. and Levine, S.A., (1952), 'Paroxysmal ventricular tachycardia due to emotion; possible mechanism of death from fright', *Journal of the American Medical Association* 150(5), pp. 479–480.

Kabat-Zinn, J. (1990), *Full catastrophe living. Using the wisdom of your body and mind to face stress, pain and illness*, New York: Random House.

Kull, K. and Hoffmeyer, J. (2005), 'Thure von Uexküll 1908–2004', *Sign System Studies* 33(2), pp. 487–491.

Lown, B. (1983), 'Introduction', in: Cousins, N. (1983), *The healing heart*, New York: W.W. Norton, p. xi ff.

Nathan, T. (1994), *L'influence qui guérit*, Paris: Odile Jacob.

Nussbaum, M.C. (1994), *The therapy of desire. Theory and practice in Hellenistic ethics*, Princeton: Princeton University Press.

Pouchelle, M-C. (2003), *L'hôpital corps et âme. Essais d'anthropologie hospitalière*, Paris: Éditions Seli Arslan.

Ruelle, D. (1991), *Hasard et chaos*, Paris: Odile Jacob.

Stora, J.B. (1991/2005), *Le stress*, Paris: Presses Universitaires de France.

Stora, J.B. (1999), *Quand le corps prend la relève. Stress, traumatismes et maladies somatiques*, Paris: Odile Jacob.

Stora, J.B. (2004), 'The French group of psychoanalysis, medicine, and psychosomatics: Nouveaux horizons psychosomatiques', *Neuropsychoanalysis* 6, pp. 123–124.

Stora, J.B. (2005), *Vivre avec une greffe. Accueillir l'autre*, Paris: Odile Jacob.

Stora, J.B. (2006), *La neuro-psychanalyse*. Paris: Presses Universitaires de France.

Stora, J.B. (2010), 'Troubles psychosomatiques, des maladies imaginaires?' *Les Grands Dossiers des Sciences Humaines* 20, p. 31.

Stora, J.B. (2011), *Neuropsychanalyse. Controverses et dialogues*, Paris: MJW Fédition.

Stora, J.B. (2013), *La nouvelle approche psychosomatique: 9 cas cliniques*, Paris: MJW Fédition.

Stora, J.B. (2018), 'Psychosomatique integrative', at http://www.psychosomatique-integrative.net/

Turner, J.F. (2002), 'A brief history of illusion: Milner, Winnicott and Rycroft', *International Journal of Psychoanalysis* 83(5), pp. 1063–1082.

von Uexküll, Th. (1963), *Grundfragen der psychosomatischen Medizin*, Reinbek bei Hamburg: Rowohlt.

Weber, F. (2007), 'Présentation', in: Mauss, M. (1923/24), *Essai sur le don. Forme et raison de l'échange dans les sociétes archaïques*, Paris: Presses Universitaires de France.

9

INQUIRIES

The work of César and Sára Botella

As we saw in the last chapter, Stora offers material that shows that, for treatment to work, a shared imaginary between patient and doctor/therapist can be indispensable. Yet, this may not be easy to come by. There are encounters that give rise to the suspicion that people plodding through the wastelands of the absorbingly functional are unlikely to be beset with unexpected visitations from beyond their horizon: no mirage lights up for them taunting them with delights tantalisingly out of reach. Like the colour blind who are not easily taken in by camouflage, no trick of the light or lay of the ground will distract them into vain hopes. It appears as if their crushing lack has been barred from tapping into sources of hallucination open to others.

Given this particular configuration, it comes as no surprise that member of the *EPP/IPSO* have on a number of occasions entered into discussion with César and Sára Botella, from outside their more immediate circle and who, inspired by Fain among others, have produced a cohesive body of work on the inner connections between traumatic potential, psychic configuration and hallucinatory capacities.

The vital difference between figurability and presentability

Pivotal to their work is a concept that appears prominently in the *Interpretation of Dreams*, where it is accorded the dignity of a section title and is being treated as a baseline concept: German *Darstellbarkeit*, which is reduced to presentability in Strachey's translation and to which the Botellas have striven to restitute some of its original texture by turning to French *figurabilité*. This they take to designate the manner and extent to which what exercises the mind lends itself to being given shape, in ways to be found and created in conformity with the material. César and Sára Botella, with good reason, contend that the word employed by Freud does not exhaust itself in mere goal-oriented presentability – an act of rendering to the purview of social recognition a reasonably functional exhibit. Instead it connects to the inherent messiness of a terrain from which cohesive form must eventually arise, somewhat akin to the working field of a potter modelling from clay. Not surprisingly, they deplore the choice of the editorial collective in charge of publishing the *Œuvre Complètes de Freud* to diverge in their new edition from previous French usage so as to now uniformly employ *presentabilité*, sacrificing in this step a considerable amount of cultural context, both French and German, to the rigorously closed lexis mandated by their editorial policy.

Figurability, they suggest, is most properly conceived against a backdrop of absence, just as Isaac Luria thought, when he tried to come to grips with an emptiness from which plenitude had first to be withdrawn graciously in an act of *tsimtsum* (contraction, withdrawal) in order to make room for the act of creation. The Botellas, without reaching back quite as far into history, provide a glimpse into mutual Franco-British bafflements when they reproduce ironical reflections of Voltaire's on the difference between Paris and London:

> A Frenchman who arrives in London, will find matters in philosophy, like everything else, very much changed there. He has left the world a plenum, he now finds it a vacuum … in Paris … according to your Cartesians, everything is performed by an impulsion of which we have very little notion; according to Mr. Newton, things work by attraction, of which one does not any better understand the cause. […] What a ferocious contradiction. At last, the better to resolve, if possible, every difficulty … [Newton] proves or at least makes it probable … that it is impossible there should be a plenum; and brings back the vacuum, which Aristotle and Descartes had banished from the world.
>
> (Voltaire 1733, Letter XIV and XV)

For Voltaire, the Botellas go on to say, leaving Paris is like turning one's back on an established repertory of pattern recognition, which makes one see only what is bound into it. Instead, one moves to a place in which the mind, bereft of one's bearings, its inner lantern of calibrated insight extinguished, finds itself disturbingly exposed to what is uncertain, doubtful and strange against the backdrop of an infinite void. Thinking, the Botellas suggest, is always something of a ceaseless to-and-fro between Paris and London, as it were, a movement again and again repelled by emptiness and in itself a substitute for hallucinatory desire.

The dynamic potential of the void held in a dialectical relationship

In this perspective the developments of Freud's position in his later years are of particular importance. What has earlier been established as a central nexus: drive – repression – fantasm, closely connected to the First Topography – takes a new turn with the discovery of traumatic neurosis, which escapes dream perlaboration and grants a new status to external events. In his theoretical revision of 1920, Freud introduces the death drive as a means to tackle negativity, and the introduction of the id emphasises a primitive foundation rooted in motion, act and raw discharge. These developments decentre previously established theory towards a new axis object-reality-denial, complementing the previous one.

To show how momentous this new direction is, the Botellas turn to Hegel, who at a time when, as they say, Newton's notions of the void had fallen by the wayside, was rethinking the prodigious power of the negative to kick things into motion and to confer vitality to whatever puts itself into opposition. It has pertinently been pointed out that there are considerable differences in the ways Hegelian negativity has been interpreted and put to use in France over the last century. What springs to mind from the Botellas' treatment, who clearly follow the general lines of Alexandre Kojève's interpretation, is that the dynamic potential of the negative is developed in sustained opposition to something set against it, to which tension is run up in a contained field. Much as in a water pump, which uses vacuum to counteract gravity, water will only be displaced as long as the integrity of the duct holds. Thus even severe lack may not inevitably produce desire. It will only do so if it forms part of a dynamic relatedness within which Hegelian *Aufhebung* – a new combination of elements on higher levels of integration, entailing the destruction of previous form – becomes conceivable. In order to enable negativity to become productive, enveloping form and dynamic force have to come together, a precondition that should not too lightly be taken for granted. While Freud's first model of psychic functioning would follow the trace of what has been repressed, his later reflections show much more interest in what has left no memory trace and yet keeps lurking in the absence of such inscription. There are evidently zones beyond the pale of liaisoning, not even bound into antagonism. They remain mutely averse to taking part in the libidinally infused Queen Mab-like dance vividly described by Hegel:

> The true is such a bacchantic dizzying waltz (or: frenzy: *Taumel*), in which no member is not intoxicated and since each [member], in differentiating itself, thereby also dissolves [into the whole], it is equally fully transparent and simple tranquility.
>
> (Hegel 1807, p. 46)

What strikes us as trauma, however, is a negative that puts into question any possible *Aufhebung* capable of creating productive fusion on a higher level, a void that on encounter declines to be harnessed into anything obligingly dialectical.

While the Botellas do not in the least deny the range of clinical challenges posed by the unconnected negative, their work shows an acute interest in the negative as a potential engine of dialectic movement and as an incentive to shaking the mind from the confines of too narrowly conceived certainty and too settled habit. With Alexandre Koyré, they admire in Newton his ability to oppose, and at the same time bring together into one, the discontinuity of matter and the continuity of the void, a mode to think attraction in empty space. With Sami Ali, following the well-known lead in Freud's 1910 work, *The Antithetical Meaning of Primal Words*, on similar expressions, they also show curiosity for the *addâd*, Arab words that hold several mutually exclusive meanings in abeyance, like *dûn* (below and above as well as in front and behind), words that, as they say, are apt to throw down a gauntlet to quick and easy understanding. Koan-like, these words kick away the scaffolding of secondarised thought and may even push the mind to quasi-hallucinatory realisation. If transferred to the psychoanalytic turf with whatever degree of necessary creative misunderstanding, Hegel's *unité supérieure négative* plays in the same league as Bion's unsaturated element, albeit emerging from a different philosophical pedigree: from one angle it banks on the future dynamic potential of the provisionally contained contradiction, from another one it opens frontier space to the emergence of the unexpected, in rupture with zones of previously settled thought.

Coherence one level up

In the Botellas' view, the *unité supérieure négative*, uniting while separating, finds its early laboratory in the mother–infant relation, in which object representation and self representation are intimately and inextricably entangled. Any new superior level is also a condensation, which simplifies both structure and function in a new array of coherence. The Botellas build on Francis Pasche's work to consider that the seemingly unitary concept of object representation is a composite traversed, of old, by two contradictory movements: an anti-narcissistic one setting into motion the centrifugal thrust of desire in its inexhaustible quest for the object, and an auto-erotic one, leading to a return to the self. Reflections of the erogenous body self and perceptions of the external object both leave their mark on the representation of the object. Dark undercurrents to this development are constituted by the traumatising and disorganising forces fed by non-represented chaos and non-perception returned by the sense-organs.

If the object is gone, this will not have a traumatic impact as such, as long at its inner representation is kept alive by the pleasure self. According to the Botellas, the supreme threat for the nascent subject is not the absence of the object, but the loss of its representation. Against this unspeakable menace, raising the threat of a possibly implosive emptiness, the subject will defend itself at all costs, even if this means enlisting the sensory plenitude of a nightmare to protect itself against an empty regard. To be scared out of one's wits might well be preferable to losing oneself in the infinite aridities of indifference, in which the subject has to contend with the non-represented, and to defend itself against the spectre of psychic death itself.

What strikes the authors in the bobbin reel game of *Fort/Da* that Freud's grandson invented for himself (in French, famous as *jeu de la bobine*) is that the baby, who at the moment of the play, is outside the cot, is throwing the bobbin inside. Although the bobbin certainly represents the mother, it evidently also stands in for the baby itself, who is exerting himself to master his own possible disarray in the game of the absent mother. Playing the game, it seeks to keep at bay the threat of exhausting his inner capacities of holding fast to an object representation on which hinges the possibility of keeping alive his own self-representation. Engaging in this activity, the infant also enacts the burial of the early mother, coming to terms with the body memory her holding left on the body, to create the image of another one in the present, a process to which Freud's grandfatherly presence provides the necessary framework. One angle of looking at infantile sexual theories is to appreciate that they maintain a link to absent parents and keep up the child's investment in them. Fairy tales, even if peopled with monsters, are preferable to figurative destitution.

With Thom, the Botellas believe that early salience for the baby is linked to the perception of a qualitative discontinuity. Representation, in tension with perception, comes into being as a projection on the void left behind by the object. Only when the hallucinatory solution fails, does the distinction between outside and inside turn hallucinatory continuity into sensorial discontinuity and absence becomes real. Words emerge to signify what is not there and which cannot otherwise be pointed to in place of former hallucinatory continuity. This loss produces a *pulsion*, carries a charge and ultimately establishes a link, where else there would have been none.

For the baby, hallucinatory stages mark the transition from mere states of tension to a new order of psychic functioning, slowing down the onrush of raw urge. Consciousness thus unfolds against a backdrop of a hallucinatory response to lack and cannot be understood as being solely based on what arrives via the sense organs. In the magical moments at which mental life ignites, the matrix of all reflexivity is configured by the triad perceiver – perceived – lost object, in which the perceiver is not yet a subject but close to a corporeal Me.

A primal trace of lack

The Botellas feel compelled to postulate the existence of a primal trace of lack in the interstices between the loss of the object and hallucinatory satisfaction. This primal trace leaves a mark on further developments, reorganising the whole of investments and offering an explanatory point of reference for every emergent lack. Infantile trauma and non-representation are closely tethered to the primal trace and its vicissitudes. What has never been represented is not, they stress, necessarily a result of the work of denial or foreclusion. Every night, as we sink into sleep, the psyche has to navigate its self-preservation between a wish for narcissistic regression without bounds and the dangers of non-representation. Exposed to non-representation, we are closer to the primal trace of absolute distress and prone to taking fright at a possible loss of representation and object investment.

So, the primal trace has to be tamed by a return to one's self under the auspices of the object: if we look at ourselves auto-erotically this glance will always bear the marks of being looked at by the object. Two productive negatives combine paradoxically, the Botellas suggest, to keep the psyche at work: represented, the object is considered to be physically absent; perceived, its hallucinatory presence is kept in abeyance. Just as a piece of magnet, if divided, will produce both a north and a south pole in its individual fragments, the psyche is maintained by a comparable field, which, by virtue of its dual, symmetrically constituted negativity, grants coherence to the whole. As long as this field holds, perception is constantly re-linked to infantile sources of fantasy. It is non-representation that is apt to rend asunder the dynamic symmetry, producing sterile perception and devitalised representation, cut off from their archaic animistic sources. Our complexes, on the other hand, bound to sexual infantile theories, promote an investment of object representations, suggest explanations for absence and difference and obscure the negative face of infantile trauma, which receives its force from the infant's incapacity to transform early states of tension that are unlinked and unbound.

Perception as an anchor

Beyond questions of psychic structure, the problems of transformation, put on the agenda by Bion, have become a concern to psychoanalysts. The conceptual terms of Freud's First Topography, in the Botellas' view, do not suffice to think about this. What Freud in 'On Narcissism: an Introduction' terms *das aktuelle Wahrnehmungsmaterial* (Strachey: 'currently active perceptual material') resists integration and witnesses to the flaws in the narcissistic cohesion of the subject. If sensations perceived cannot become part of a dream working towards a realisation of desire, they become hyper-invested and transformation is impeded. The Botellas advance the hypothesis that there exist precursors of liaison to be found in movements of perception that carry their own track record of a quest for satisfaction with them. When representational links are suddenly ruptured, there is a turning to perceptive form and a regression to a condensed, overdetermined, basic representation deeply clinging to the sensation. On the trace of the hallucinatory, the old bulwark against primordial distress, we find ourselves beyond the established pathways of infantile neurosis in territory on which the webbing and weaving of psychic causality is still in *statu nascendi*.

The Botellas use Arthur Koestler's experience of a quasi-mystic bliss, which he strayed into unawares when imprisoned by the Fascists during the Spanish Civil War and under threat of imminent death. He had extracted a piece of iron spring from the wire mattress and found himself lost in contemplation of a mathematical problem he had scratched with it on the prison walls, drifting into a wordless trance.

This mirrors, to some extent, the experience of Zoran Music, referred to by the Botellas. Music, when imprisoned at Dachau concentration camp, felt a paradoxical state of exaltation while drawing on scraps of paper, which he had furtively managed to lay his hands upon, sketches of the horror of corpses piled up in the camp. In this disappearance of limits, the Me fuses with something larger. When the hallucinatory erupts into the realm of perception it is in retrospect seen as a happy state of union with an immaterial object that is being idealised in place of an investment of object and self. On an even more basic level, abandoned babies turn towards whatever, in place of a more permanent object, provokes sensations in them – movement, light, contrasts, smells, sound, contact – to find some sort of coherence and sustenance.

Imageless states of terror

In contrast, the Botellas report the case of a patient, who wakes up at night in the grips of a raw panic in complete absence of any image, unable to link this brutal shock to any event. Even a terrifying image, arising from the depths of a nightmare gives the subject something to latch onto, as it wards off even deeper levels of distress beyond any representation. Although a dream springing from traumatic neurosis confronts us with a memory of sorts, it is not amenable to dream perlaboration. Rather, it is heir to a sensory trace of a perception that has not found inscription in memory. If it becomes conscious at all it does so in a hallucinatory fashion bypassing both the preconscious and the established nexus of infantile neurosis. For some patients – including the one mentioned above – investment in the object increases the threat of a loss of all representation because it activates a primal trace of distress. If early tendencies to immediate discharge, emanating from an inchoate id, are not modified in the organisation of an unconscious capable of condensation and displacement, offering a chance to complexification and growth, there will be no psychoanalytic version of the Hegelian *unité supérieure négative*, something that coalesces on a higher level. Running counter to the psyche's tendency to work towards coherence and convergence, traumatic potentiality is not limited in its presence to individuals with particularly fragile structures, but exists also in those Marty would have regarded as well-mentalised. In case of emergency, a regression to perception traces will attempt to mend the tissue of ruptured psychic links in hallucinatory fashion and work towards coherence. To take into account both structure and the as yet unstructured, the Botellas have found it useful to focus on what is in process.

The work of the double

If the environment is in a shape propitious to the thriving of the subject, this regression to the sensory trace will not occur in a relational void: alterity and sameness will be kept in productive tension in what the Botellas term the work of the double. In the beginning, the body of the mother is the first mirror of the child: investing in it, the infant assembles its own disparate parts into a whole and by doing so imitates the model of the mother in which it seeks its reflection, basking in her libidinal and narcissistic satisfaction. The Botellas understand this early function of the mother as a primitive, composite double of the child, a stage at which being looked at, erogenous body and perception of the double are closely linked, establishing the basis for a future auto-erotic regard on one's own self. This experience provides the foundations for a continuous sense of one's own existence.

To explore this role of the double, the Botellas turn to Freud, looking at both his investment of Fliess as a supposedly ideal addressee, functioning as a catalyst in the gradual unfolding of his thought and at his later reflections on the disturbingly familiar stranger. In Freud's, *The Uncanny*, the double, understood as a creation that harks back to mentally archaic times, is at the outset regarded as benevolent. It belongs to an animistic world, in which everything around seemed to be a reflection of one's own psyche. Representation and perception are not markedly separate and inner and outer have not definitely parted ways as yet. In the Botellas' hypothesis, the need to create a double can be understood as a means to deal with the shocking perception of absence and to cope with an encounter with the empty regard of indifference by a psyche avid in its search for complementarities: it surges to rise up against the fear of mental death.

> the negative foundation of every infantile trauma resides, in short, in the impossibility for the child to imagine himself non-invested by the object of desire; to imagine the irrepresentable character of his own absence in the object's eyes.
> (Botella and Botella 2005, p. 131)

At a first stage, the baby uses thumb-sucking to self-appropriate the motherly object as a pre-representational substitute for the relationship to the mother in a basic, minimal organisation of the libido. As the development of auto-eroticism proceeds, the animistic double is enriched, as an interplay between being passively observed and taking on the role of an active observer permits the infant's self image to deepen. At this stage the auto-erotic double, the Botellas hold, constitutes an inner mirror, which, like the shield of Perseus in the face of the Gorgon, bounces off the fatal threat of non-representation. In times of crisis this internal mirror can turn dark and leave the subject destitute, casting around for a material external replacement, a narcissistic double that will come to the rescue.

Giving shape to nightmares in the psychoanalytic session

For the Botellas, the psychoanalytic session, when free association, figurability and use of words prove to be insufficient to discharge tension, a situation close to actual neurosis emerges. An uncomfortable strangeness creeps in, and the patient, to avoid a breakdown of all accessible representation, needs to make use of the analyst as a double, a step in which the figurability solicited in the analyst is both reflection and complement to the psychic functioning of the patient.

What conveys to this its specificity is the quasi-hallucinatory character of the disturbing, seemingly unconnected images that surge in the analyst and against which he/she at first will try to defend himself/herself. It is from the rifts and flaws within the densely knitted tissue of links and investments that a work on what has never been representable emerges if the chance is being seized upon. César Botella reports a session with Florian (Botella and Botella 2001a), in which the patient referred to a previous dream. There he had been together with his analyst but not followed him into the shower, a dream that did not give rise to any associations. The analyst somewhat reluctantly refrained from an interpretation on the homosexual elements in the scene and after further listening found himself saying 'The shower is the gas chamber'. While the first interpretation might have been quite plausible, it was the latter that proved pivotal to further work with the patient by giving shape to a nightmare that had been beyond any conceivable representation before.

> the quality of the analyst's psychic functioning [*la calidad del psiquismo del analista*] consists of reaching the capacity to hallucinate, which is a process whereby unconscious representation acquires a quasi-perceptive quality, as an act of psychic survival of the analyst faced with the patient's disruptive and destructive unrepresented.
> (Botella C. [1999] quoted in 'Discusion a la conferencia de Cesar Botella', Salamanca, May 2005, p. 3)

Under the circumstances,

> the new task of the analyst is not so much to discover, but to confer meaning to what had forever been lost, buried and 'without memory', and of which a suffering, deprived of represented content, can often be the sign.
> (Botella C. 2015a, p. 222)

A ghostly potential of form and the role of conviction

Taking inspiration from Winnicott, the Botellas propose the possibility of trauma in a negative key: the lasting effect not of what took place in the past but of what did not when it should have. Of this the subject has neither perception nor representation. No trace left in memory can be an object of repression or rejection. If we know that the traumatic impact of an event confronts the subject with a rupture in psychic coherence, the traumatic impact of a non-event must likewise be understood to produce much the same effect on the subject's mental territory. Refractory to a reparatory grasp by the Me, primordial narcissistic wounds are yet liable to produce an inveterately figurative punch that will seek hallucinatory realisation in a quest for transformation.

The Botellas point out that with Freud, from 1937, rememoration finds itself dethroned in his work not just, as is widely known, to admit subsidiary construction in absence of memory. There is another turn as well: conviction becomes a factor worthy of metapsychological consideration. It is now accorded attention as a state of mind emerging from the psychoanalytic process in quasi-hallucinatory fashion and in prolongation of a past that had psychically been non-existent. It is, the Botellas write, using a surrealist image of André Breton's, as if, before biting the hook offered by the analyst in his work at figurability, the *négatif* had been a 'trauma-fish' in diluted, shapeless manifestation at large in the vast seas of the id, existing in some places in more dense concentration than in others, a ghostly potential of form, so to speak.

In its confrontation with both memory and doubt, conviction (which permits form to solidify) has roots in animistic thought. It carries qualities of affect and representation without being either the one or the other. The Botellas advance the hypothesis that reality testing needs to pass through the contradictory position of doing away with outside reality and vigorously denying it by insisting that the object exists only inside. If this is so, space for representation and thought may open up, and the object can be held internally. Because it exists, as if by magic, inside, it can be found outside – 'only inside, also outside' is the paradoxical formula that by virtue of its dynamics grants a sense that what is being perceived is indeed real. Perception alone cannot carry conviction: we cannot deeply hold as real something in the creation of which we have not ourselves participated – perception of the world remains intimately linked to the hallucinatory. It is to this primitive level, to which the perceptive elements of hallucination provide access, that psychoanalysis has to accede, if memory alone cannot be relied upon to provide the necessary clues.

Regredience to untamed memory

For this to work, a community of regression needs to be available, as the Botellas show in a case vignette (Botella and Botella 2001a).

Jasmine, a girl from Vietnam, now in latency, was adopted by non-Vietnamese French parents. Her own parents had been killed in a massacre together with all the other villagers during the wars and the small child, who may have been two years old at the time, had been found close to the corpse of her mother, at the side of whom she had been lying for an indeterminate period of time. She knows her past but cannot believe in it, and is condemned to live in a present confined to the immediate. When she sees her own image in a mirror she is struck as if having encountered a ghost. Only when she is able to persuade herself that her analyst, like her, was born in Vietnam (which is patently untrue) does the quasi-hallucinatory image of her village resurge in a shared link of regression to a sense impression that had previously not properly been part of memory.

The Botellas remind us that Freud is aware of 'untamed memory': a *Niederschlag* of the past leaving a lasting dent on the present, but not a properly constituted memory trace. Construction in a psychoanalytic session is always related to a regression in thought shared by the two partners in the psychoanalytic enterprise. In this way, access to a hallucinatory actualisation of pre-symbolic traces of the perceptive may become possible, leading to a sentiment of psychic reality based on shared experience. The figurability contributed by the analyst – attentive to what is going on beyond the levels of memory and symbolisation in the session – represents both the reflection and the complement of the psychic functioning of the patient. This means the analyst will have to be prepared to follow the absence of thought in the patient rather than the contents in evidence, in a movement of regredience that permits itself to be disturbed in its freely floating state and attracted by non-represented zones of disturbance.

The impact of child psychoanalysis

As Sára Botella points out, a sense of the non-separability between mother and child has been kept alive in the United Kingdom, where adult and child psychoanalysis have not been running on separate rails, as they did elsewhere, including France. This has meant that the accumulated experience of psychoanalytic work with children, in which attention to the perceptions of the moment is very important – just as it is with psychosomatic patients – has perhaps been unduly slow in being taken up by the main stream. Only because a bridge between British psychoanalysis and French psychoanalysis was facilitated by André Green was it possible for some of the old sterile dichotomies to be overcome in a move in which Winnicott's and Bion's ideas were brought into contact with both structuralist tendencies and those that favour economic and dynamic models in French psychoanalytic thought.

The work of the double between 'projective identification' and 'partners in thought'

César Botella himself, who had left Franco's Spain to go to France, had grounding in Bion before he began a thorough reading of Freud, as he explains in an interview in Brazil. His and his wife's interest in figurability started when a child, in therapy with Sára Botella, would not respond to any intervention until she confronted him with the image of a wolf that had risen up in her mind. César Botella believes that there are cases when projective identification is not an ideal guide to the process of figurability because the structuring image does not really originate with the putative 'sender'. Donnel B. Stern, who had dedicated his earlier book *Partners in thought* to 'unformulated experience', not without good reason groups the Botellas' work with Bionian field theory – together with Antonino Ferro – and points out there is some common ground with interpersonal/relational psychoanalysis (*IRP*) in the apparently shared assumption that the symbolic experience emerging in the session does not pre-date it. Ferro and Civitarese, on their part, see an important divergence to *IRP* analysts in the amount of active investigation resorted to in the session. This is exactly the reservation Botella and Botella have raised with regard to inter-subjectivist practice: in their view regression is given too little scope, if compared to Winnicott's practice in this matter, which has remained the reference of choice for them. For their part, they are happy with André Green's suggestion that psychic work is sometimes incomplete without the work of two psyches involved.

The non-communicating central self

Although the Botellas' endeavour, if successful, will ultimately give rise to new symbolic meaning in session, their more immediate call might be best caught by those lines of Milton's to which Bion was fond of returning:

[Light] Shine inward, and the mind through all her powers irradiate, there plant eyes, all mist from thence Purge and disperse.
(Paradise Lost, Book III, lines 52ff.)

This, the Botellas believe, will only happen in the darkroom of regredience (a conceptual relative of Bion's 'negative capability'). James Rose (2014), in a reflection on figurability, establishes a connection to a passage by Winnicott:

I have tried to state the need that we have to recognize this aspect of health: the non-communicating central self, for ever immune from the reality principle, and for ever silent. Here communication is not non-verbal; it is like the music of the spheres, absolutely personal. It belongs to being alive. And in health, it is out of this that communication naturally arises.
(Winnicott 1963, p. 192)

If this non-communicating central self is there as a tacit retro-scene of psychic life, something very important has already been achieved. What if this sustaining quality is missing or has been badly damaged?

Building transitional space for survivors

Given this conundrum, it comes as no surprise that some of the echoes of the Botellas' concept of a necessary 'work of the double' come from practitioners familiar with survivors of the Shoah (Fohn and Heenen-Wolff 2011; Moore 2009). It may well be, as Devoto has put forward in a different context, that 'representational enrichment', in a transitional space that was previously not available, is much needed in some therapies. Yet, it has also to be considered that, for this to happen, intermediary steps towards the symbolic have to be facilitated, which will require the analyst to be willing to stay in the unrepresented. External reality may well have wrought considerable havoc, which has to find means of transformation in a work of the double before it can turn into words.

Negativity thus has to be contained by the quality of presence of the psychoanalyst, who as an animistic double favours regression and with it elicits a hallucinatory response to the track of traumatic lack that has not left a memory but rather an indelible dent in the psychic cohesion of the subject. What then are we to make of the fact that *L'investigation psychosomatique* regards projective reduplication as one of the hallmarks of the *opératoire*? Would not this be close to the ability of the patient to seize the analyst as a double, postulated by the Botellas? It seems that, like the traumatic dream that tries to work its way towards linking, this mechanism seeks from the other something which it has great difficulties in finding. César Botella finds with Marty great attention to what can be perceived in the manner the patient handles him/herself and, in the tradition of Bouvet, of the way the patient positions him/herself in relational space. Taking into consideration the mental economy of the patient, the analyst may have to bear in mind what is beyond representation (and has to remain there) at a given moment. In the case study of Jasmine the Botellas, following Marty, reflect on the narcissistic difficulties of the analyst to regress and identify with a certain patient beyond his/her reach, which, in a way, renders the analyst *opératoire*:

> one might think that, at the end of the day, the analyst has a deficient mental apparatus, unendowed in that it does not possess the mental plasticity necessary to accompany his/her patient. And, one would conclude, that it is as difficult for the analyst to be the mirror of his/her patient as it is difficult for the patient to recognise him/herself in his/her analyst. It might well be that taking into consideration this mutual strangeness is the first step of a move that would join our experience in the therapy of Jasmine.
> (Botella and Botella 1999, p. 132)

Poverty in theory and the non-inevitability of Hegelian 'Aufhebung'

If theoretical work in recent years has received new impetus it is because it has become clear that the aridity of some patients finds an equivalent in the psychoanalyst's own theoretical and technical poverty faced with the opacity of the cure of the *opératoire*, in the light of his lack of tools to seize such a functioning. This, one would assume, is another instance of negativity, leading to a further push for a new, more satisfactory solution, hopefully in a contained field of theory.

While this is a desirable development, can it be said to be inevitable? Claire Pagès (2015) has pointed out the inconveniences of the fact that Hegelian negativity is always in league with an *Aufhebung* (a surpassing on a higher level), a perspective which creates difficulties for its use in psychoanalysis. Hegelian negativity is an element in a contradiction, which starts as difference to become opposition, as part of a whole. With Hegel, negativity does not lead to nothingness but to mediation. Is it not, Pagès, asks, possible to conceive of a psychic negativity which does not lead to any secondary benefits for the psyche, a derivative of the *pulsion de mort* without any positive structuring effect?

It seems that André Green, a pronounced proponent of a hardy implementation of the concept of negativity in psychoanalytic thought was aware of unresolved problems. In 2011, after his summer vacation, he said he had spent time reflecting on *le négatif du négatif*. He wanted to develop his reflections in a seminar but his deteriorating state of health prevented this. Nietzsche, who had criticized Hegel, figured prominently among his reading that summer but we do not know what results he might have arrived at if he had had more time and been able to transmit them. Whatever he might have emerged with, he would not, given his clinical and intellectual trajectory, have chosen Goethe's Mephistopheles as his guide (who as part of his self-advertisement claims to be part of the forces that always plotting evil always manage to contrive good). Neither have the Botellas: coming to terms with infantile trauma with them is contingent on the availability of the work of a double that permits a vacuum to produce results.

Possible sense that is not latent

If we follow this line of thought, an important part of mental development depends on the accessibility of an encounter of substantial quality. *Avant-coup*, the subject may not have an idea of what to expect because, as Sára Botella reflects, it does not express a *latent* but a *possible* sense. Thus, it may not even be denied, rejected or repressed, although lack may well give rise to a system of defence. Denial and non-representation may look similar, and yet they will have arrived on different paths.

These paths will inevitably be linked to developments in surrounding society and culture. In Erik Erikson's (1965[1950]) observations of Sioux children it is produced by cultural responses: the rage of the frustrated child is linked by observers to his future strength as a hunter and as a warrior within the tribe, a narrative that may work to contain some, but possibly not all, of the early distress. With Nicolaïdis we may well take interest in cushions of possible regression facilitated or denied by a given culture.

A cultural frame to hold potential space

Most difficult of all, there remains the assessment of processes that have fatally failed to happen. Psychic structures remain vulnerable to the impact of what was not registered when it did not happen, a 'negativity' that has never found a sufficiently performative enveloping field. Just as the psychoanalytic debate of trauma has always had to take into consideration what the subject's psyche cannot generate by itself, any therapeutic action will try to add something crucial previously not available in the environment, in an encounter which can be had or missed. Only when it has taken place it can be experienced that something indispensable had been lacking.

The Botellas' counsel in the face of this difficulty, certainly relevant to our understanding of the *opératoire*, is to crank up disciplined creativity within psychoanalysis, while opening gates of exchange between different strands of thinking. In his 2007 interview with the *Revista Brasileira de Psicanálise* César Botella quoted with some relish the statement by an unnamed colleague of his that something Darwinian must be done in psychoanalysis to make it stronger. A response from Brazil pointed out that the function of an author always exceeded his own contribution because it permitted its readers to give to work on their own understanding in permanent confrontation with the creative ideas of others. Perhaps, if things turn out well, interregional exchange in psychoanalysis can perform what Barros points out will be the result of successful work on dreams: a perlaboration of the symbolic foundations helps the mind to enhance its ability to think.

In recent work, César Botella writes,

> Freud never conceived of psychoanalysis as a sum of ideas that aspire to becoming, one day, a theory that is complete and closed. On the contrary, and this is my basic hypothesis, the continuous development of the work [of psychoanalysis] cannot be grasped if not in a permanent movement of opening up, a movement in which the present state is there to support what follows upon it. This is the image of a person walking, every step of whom is only possible in a constant [change from] dis-equilibrium to re-equilibrium owed to the next step just initiated.
>
> (Botella, C. 2018b, p. 732)

For this to happen, a certain distance has to be taken from the immersion in a feeling of self-evidence. Our next chapter will show Claude Smadja's look back at the beginnings of the *EPP* in a break with available interpretation and his attempts to integrate this in a perspective not available at the time.

Sources

'Colour blindness and camouflage', *Nature* 146, 17 August 1940, p. 226.

'Discusion a la conferencia de Cesar Botella' ("Consideraciones sobre verdad, memoria, e interpretación en la practica psicoanalitica"), *Jornada Anual de S.E.P.I.A*, Salamanca, 21 May 2005, available at: http://www.sepia-psicosomatica.org/%20Revistas%20SEPIA/R5-4.pdf

'Rencontre à la librairie Tschann mai 2013': 'Penser la psychanalyse', d'André Green – (26th June 2013, Ithaquesmedia), available at: www.youtube.com/watch?v=bPKamQKEMsM

Ali, S. (1997), *Le rêve et l'affect. Une théorie du somatique*, Paris: Dunod.

Baranes, J.J. (2002), 'Penser le double', *Revue Française de Psychanalyse* 66(5), pp. 1837–1843.

Barros, E.M. da Rocha (2007), 'Botella, Ogden, Green, Ferro, Bion: comentário à entrevista de César Botella, *Revista Brasileira de Psicanálise* 41(1), pp. 33–45.

Belliard, S. (2012), *La couleur dans la peau: Ce que voit l'inconscient*, Paris: Albin-Michel.

Botella, C. (1991), 'La memoire sans souvenirs', in: *Avancés metapsychologique. L'enfant. La famille*, Paris: Apsygée, pp. 121–126.

Botella, C. (1997a), [Contribution to 'Discussion de la conférence d'André Green'], in: Piñol-Douriez, M. ed., *Pulsions. Représentations. Langage*, Lausanne: Delachaux et Niestlé, pp. 67–70.

Botella, C. (1997b), [Contribution to 'Discussion de l'exposé de G.Gimenez'], in: Piñol-Douriez, M. ed., *Pulsions. Représentations. Langage*, Lausanne: Delachaux et Niestlé, pp. 128–132.

Botella, C. (1999), 'Entrevista con César Botella', *Revista Uruguaya de Psicoanálisis* 90, pp. 238–253.

Botella, C. (2001), 'À propos du livre de Jacques Press. La perle et le grain de sable (Traumatisme et fonctionnement mental): Essai psychanalytique', *Revue Française de Psychosomatique* 19, pp. 181–190.

Botella, C. (2002), 'Motifs et raisons: la pensée psychanalytique en question', in: Botella, C. ed., *Penser les limites. Écrits en l'honneur d'André Green*, Paris: Delachaux et Niestlé, pp. 21–32.

Botella, C. (2003), 'Propositions pour une recherche psychanalytique fondamentale', in: Green, A. ed., *Le travail psychanalytique*, Paris: Presses Universitaires de France, pp. 27–41.

Botella, C. (2005a), 'Enjeux pour une psychanalyse de demain', in: Richard F. and Urribarri F. eds, *Autour de l'œuvre d'André Green. Enjeux pour une psychanalyse contemporaine*, Paris: Presses Universitaires de France, pp. 11–31.

Botella, C. (2005b), 'Levels of memory and truth: Their interpretation', *Bulletin de la Fédération Européenne de Psychanalyse* 59, pp. 36–43.

Botella, C. (2006), 'Reflexion conclusive', in: Green, A. ed., *Unité et diversité des pratiques du psychanalyste*, Paris: Presses Universitaires de France, pp. 185–192.

Botella, C. (2007), 'Entrevista', *Revista Brasileira de Psicanálise* 41(1), pp. 19–29.

Botella, C. (2008), 'Œdipe et Don Juan. À propos de l'image du père chez quelques fils célèbres, in: Cupa, D. ed., *Image du père dans la culture contemporaine. Hommages à André Green*, Paris: Presses Universitaires de France, pp. 396–406.

Botella, C. (2011a), 'Sur les "limitations" de la méthode freudienne', *Revue Française de Psychosomatique* 40, pp. 109–132.

Botella, C. (2011b), 'Préface. Nous sommes tous des exilés', in: Lussier, M., *Terre d'asile, terre de deuil. Le travail pychique d'exil*, Paris: Presses Universitaires de France, pp. 1–5.

Botella, C. (2014a), 'De l' "attention flottante" de Freud à l' "expression associative" de Marty. Une nouvelle perspective dans la méthode psychanalytique', *Revue Française de Psychosomatique* 45, pp. 83–102.

Botella, C. (2014b), 'L'œuvre de Green et l'évolution de la pensée analytique', in: Chervet, B. ed., *Hommage à André Green*, Paris: Societé Psychanalytique de Paris, pp. 31–37.

Botella, C. (2015a), 'Sur la remémoration: la notion de mémoire sans souvenirs', *L'Année psychanalytique internationale 2015*, Paris: Éditions in Press, pp. 197–231 (= Botella C. (2014), 'On remembering: The notion of memory without recollection', *International Journal of Psychoanalysis* 95, pp. 911–936).

Botella, C. (2015b), 'Meutre et transmission. Préhistoire et psychanalyse. Quelle rencontre?', in: Chervet, B. ed., *Le meurtre fondateur. L'acte psychique par excellence*, Paris: Presses Universitaires de France, pp. 75–79.

Botella, C. (2016), 'Mémoire sans souvenirs. Cas limites et psychosomatique', *Revue Française de Psychosomatique* 50, pp. 183–206.

Botella, C. (2018a), 'Simultanéité en séance/Diachronie du processus', *Revue Française de Psychanalyse* 82(1), pp. 26–38.

Botella, C. (2018b), 'L'évolutivité primordiale de la psychanalyse. Diversification théorique et tendance unificatrice – Dialogue avec Jorge Canestri', *Revue Française de Psychanalyse* 82(3), pp. 719–739.

Botella, C. and Botella, S. (1984), 'L'homosexualité inconsciente et la dynamique du double en séance', *Revue Française de Psychanalyse* 48(3), pp. 687–708. [in English available as: Botella, C. (2010/1995), 'Working as a double', in: Birksted-Breen, D., Gibeault, A. and Flanders, S. eds, (2010), *Reading French psychoanalysis*, London: Routledge, pp. 367–387.]

Botella, C. and Botella, S. (1988), 'Trauma et topique (Aspects techniques de l'abord du trauma en séance)', *Revue Française de Psychanalyse* 52(6), pp. 1461–1477.

Botella, C. and Botella, S. (1990), 'La problématique de la régression formelle de la pensée et de l'hallucinatoire', in: Le Guen, C. ed., *La psychanalyse: questions pour demain*, Paris: Presses Universitaires de France, pp. 63–90.

Botella, C. and Botella, S. (1992a), 'Le statut métapsychologique de la perception et l'irreprésentable', *Revue Française de Psychanalyse* 56(1), pp. 23–41.

Botella, C. and Botella, S. (1992b), 'Névrose traumatique et cohérence psychique', *Revue Française de Psychosomatique* 2, pp. 25–36.

Botella, C. and Botella, S. (1995a), 'La dualité négative du psychisme', in: Green, A., Favarel-Garrigues, B., Guillaumin, J. and Fédida, P., *Le négatif. Travail et pensée*, Le Bouscat: Édition L'Esprit du temps, pp. 63–82.

Botella, C. and Botella, S. (1995b), 'Sur le processus analytique: du perceptif aux causalités psychiques', *Revue Française de Psychanalyse* 59(2), pp. 349–366.

Botella, C. and Botella, S. (1995c), 'A propos du processuel: automate ou sexuel infantile?', *Revue Française de Psychanalyse* 59(5-6), pp. 1609–1615.

Botella, C. and Botella S. (1995d), 'La dynamique du double: animique, auto-érotique, narcissique: le travail en double', in: Couvreur, C., Fine A. and Le Guen, A. eds, *Le double*, Paris: Presses Universitaires de France, pp. 65–82.

Botella, C. and Botella, S. (1996), 'La tendance convergente de la régression narcissique', *Revue Française de Psychosomatique* 9, pp. 109–125.

Botella, C. and Botella, S. (1997a), 'L'inachèvement de toute analyse: le processuel: introduction à la notion d'irréversibilité psychique', *Revue Française de Psychanalyse* 61(4), pp. 1125–1144.

Botella, C. and Botella, S. (1997b), 'Pulsions, représentations, langage', in: Piñol-Douriez, M. ed., *Pulsions. Représentations. Langage*, Lausanne: Delachaux et Niestlé, pp. 179–194.

Botella, C. and Botella S. (1998), 'Pour un monisme sexuel psyché-soma', *Revue Française de Psychanalyse* 62(5), pp. 1483–1492.

Botella, C. and Botella S. (1999), 'La thérapie de Jasmine, une communauté dans la régression de la pensée', *Actualités Psychosomatiques* 2, pp. 121–132.

Botella, C. and Botella, S. (2001a), *La figurabilité psychique*, Lausanne: Delachaux et Niestlé.

Botella, C. and Botella, S. (2001b), 'De la recherche en psychanalyse', in: Green, A. ed., *Courants de la psychanalyse contemporaine*, Paris: Presses Universitaires de France, pp. 355–372.

Botella, C. and Botella, S. (2001c), 'Figurabilité et régrédience', *Revue Française de Psychanalyse* 65(4), pp. 1149–1239.

Botella, C. and Botella, S. (2005), *The work of psychic figurability. Mental states without representation*, London: Routledge.

Botella, C. and Botella, S. (2006), 'Pour une métapsychologie de la remémoration', in: Green, A. ed., *Les voies nouvelles de la thérapeutique psychanalytique. Le dedans et le dehors*, Paris: Presses Universitaires de France, pp. 709–731.

Botella, C. and Botella, S. (2007), 'Préface à la deuxième édition: "Figurabilité", embarras du traducteur et du psychanalyste', in: Botella, C. and Botella S., *La figurabilité psychique*, 2nd edition, Paris: Éditions In Press.

Botella, C. and Botella, S. (2013), 'Psychic figurability and unrepresented states', in: Levine, H.B, Reed, G.S and Scarfone, D. eds, *Unrepresented states and the construction of meaning. Clinical and theoretical contributions*, London: Karnac Books, pp. 95–121.

Botella, C. and Botella, S. (2020), 'Les états intermédiaires dedans/dehors. Rêve et réalité', *Revue Française de Psychosomatique* 57, pp. 35–48.

Botella, C., Botella, S. and Haag, G. (1977), 'En deça du suçotement', *Revue Française de Psychanalyse* 41(5-6), pp. 985–992.

Botella, S. (1997), [contribution to 'Discussion de la conférence d'André Green'], in: Piñol-Douriez, M. ed., *Pulsions. Représentations. Langage*, Lausanne: Delachaux et Niestlé, pp. 73–78.

Botella, S. (2002), 'Une approche psychanalytique de la langue maternelle', in: Botella, C. ed., *Penser les limites. Écrits en l'honneur d'André Green*, Paris: Delachaux et Niestlé, pp. 79–86.

Botella, S. (2003a), 'L'élaboration autour de l'objet perdu', in: Green, A. ed., *Le travail psychanalytique*, Paris: Presses Universitaires de France, pp. 195–201.

Botella, S. (2003b), 'Une "théorie implicite" de la pratique analytique', *Revue Française de Psychanalyse* 67(4), pp. 1173–1184.

Botella, S. (2004), 'Quelques réflexions après le Colloque: "Autour du champ dépressif"', *Revue Française de Psychanalyse* 68(4), pp. 1299–1304.

Botella, S. (2005a), 'L'Œdipe du ça ou Œdipe sans complexe', *Revue Française de Psychanalyse* 69(3), pp. 717–729.

Botella, S. (2005b), 'Racines traumatiques du complexe d'Œdipe', in: Richard, F. and Urribarri, F. eds, *Autour de l'œuvre d'André Green. Enjeux pour une psychanalyse contemporaine*, Paris: Presses Universitaires de France, pp. 343–359.

Botella, S. (2007), 'La naissance de la pulsion. Les processus originaires et la pratique analytique', *Revue Française de Psychanalyse* 71(1), pp. 27–39.

Botella, S. (2010), 'De la mémoire du Ça', in: Bayle, G. ed., *L'inconscient freudien. Recherche, écoute, métapsychologie*, Paris: Presses Universitaires de France, pp. 161–170.

Botella, S. (2013a), 'La mémoire du rêve. Un conflit épistémique dans la théorie freudienne', *Revue Française de Psychanalyse* 77(1), pp. 160–169.

Botella, S. (2013b), 'À propos des processus transformationnels dans la théorie freudienne', in: Press, J. ed., *Rêver, transformer, somatiser*, Chêne-Bourg: Georg Editeur, pp. 141–147.

Botella, S. (2014a), 'La valeur psychanalytique du "procédé d'investigation" de Pierre Marty. Notes en marge de la relecture aujourd'hui d'une investigation psychosomatique publiée en 1963', *Revue Française de Psychosomatique* 45, pp. 77–81.

Botella, S. (2014b), 'Sur le négatif psychique dans l'œuvre d'André Green', in: Chervet, B. ed., *Hommage à André Green*, Paris: Societé Psychanalytique de Paris, pp. 39–43.

Botella, S. (2018), 'De "L'Interprétation du rêve" à "L'Homme Moïse": La liberté de penser chez Freud', *Revue Française de Psychanalyse* 82(2), pp. 499–508.

Botella S. (2020), 'Le "perceptif" en psychanalyse', *Revue Française de Psychanalyse* 84(3), pp. 765–780.

Delourmel, C. (2003), '"La Figurabilité psychique" de César et Sara Botella', *Revue Française de Psychosomatique* 24, pp. 183–190.

Devoto, T. (2006), 'El desarrollo del espacio transicional en la técnica analítica con pacientes psicosomáticos', *Psicología y Psycopedagogía, Revista Virtual del Instituto de Investigaciones Psicológicas. Facultad de Psicologia y*

Psicopedagogia, available at: http://p3.usal.edu.ar/index.php/psico/article/view/1285/1646.
Erikson, E.H. (1965[1950]), *Childhood and society*, Harmondsworth: Penguin Books.
Ferro, A. and Civitarese, G. (2015), *The analytic field and its transformations*, London: Karnac.
Fohn, A. and Heenen-Wolff, S. (2011), 'The destiny of an unacknowledged trauma: The deferred retroactive effect of après-coup in the hidden Jewish children of wartime Belgium', *International Journal of Psychoanalysis* 92(1), pp. 5–20.
Habermas, T. (2014), 'Dreaming the other's past: Why remembering may still be relevant to psychoanalytic therapy, at least in some traditions', *International Journal of Psychoanalysis* 95(5), pp. 951–963.
Hebbrecht, M. (2005), 'Het onvoorstelbare verbeelden', *Tijdschrift voor Psychanalyse* 11(4), pp. 293–294.
Hegel, G.W.F. (1807), *Vorrede zur Phänomenologie des Geistes*, Moldenhauer, E. and Michel, K.M. eds [1970]. Frankfurt am Main: Suhrkamp.
Jung, J. (2012), *Le double transitionnel. Trajectoire identitaire et organisation réflexive*, Thèse de doctorat de Psychologie, Université Lumière Lyon 2.
Koestler, A. (1954), *The invisible writing*, London: Collins.
Levine, H.B. (2008), 'The work of psychic figurability: Mental states without representation', *The Psychoanalytic Quarterly* 77(2), pp. 639–648.
Mancia, M. (2004), 'Cesar e Sara', *Rivista di Psicoanalisi* 50(4), pp. 1285–1291.
Moore, Y. (2009), 'Thoughts on representation in therapy of Holocaust survivors', *International Journal of Psychoanalysis* 90, pp. 1373–1391.
Pagès, C. (2015), 'Le travail du négatif: Freud avec Hegel?', *Revue Française de Psychanalyse* 79(3), pp. 809–823.
Parsons, M. (2005), 'Introduction', in: Botella, C. and Botella, S., *The work of psychic figurability. Mental states without representation*, London: Routledge, pp. xvii–xxiii.
Pasche, F. (1965), 'L'anti-narcissisme', *Revue Française de Psychanalyse* 29(5-6), pp. 503–518.
Priel, B. (2009), 'The transformation of sociogenic autistic defences in the lives of others', *International Journal of Psychoanalysis* 90(2), pp. 387–393.
Roche, R.C. (2004), 'Presentación del libro "La figurabilidad psíquica" César y Sara Botella', *Revista de Psicoanálisis, Madrid* 42, pp. 165–171.
Rose, J. ed. (2007), *Symbolization. Representation and communication*, London: Karnac Books.

Rose, J. (2014), 'The isolate and the stranger: Winnicott's model of subjectivity and its implications for theory and technique', in: Spelman, M.B. and Thomson-Salo, F. eds, *The Winnicott tradition: Lines of development – Evolution of theory and practice over the decades*, London: Karnac, pp. 175–184.

Stern, D.B. (2010), *Partners in thought. Working with unformulated experience, dissociation, and enactment*, London: Routledge.

Stern, D.B. (2013), 'Field theory in psychoanalysis, part 2: Bionian Field Theory and contemporary Interpersonal/Relational Psychoanalysis', *Psychoanalytic Dialogues* 23(6), pp. 630–645.

Stern, D.B. (2015), *Relational freedom: Emergent properties of the interpersonal field*, London: Routledge.

Stroczan, K. (2002), 'Zoran Music: zwischen Abstraktion und Konkretismus', *Psyche. Zeitschrift für Psychoanalyse und ihre Anwendungen* 56, pp. 505–525.

Voltaire, F.M.A. de (1909–14[1733]) *Letters on the English*, volume 34, Part 2. The Harvard Classics. New York: P.F. Collier & Son.

Winnicott, D.W. (1963), 'Communicating and not communicating leading to a study of certain opposites', in: Winnicott, D.W., *The maturational processes and the facilitating environment*, London: Hogarth, pp. 179–192.

Zilkha, N. (2004), 'La figurabilité psychique', *International Journal of Psychoanalysis* 85, pp. 225–228.

10

SECOND THOUGHTS

Claude Smadja

As pointed out by Denise Bouchet-Kervella (2001) in her review of articles by the *Revue Française de Psychosomatique*, the second generation of members of *IPSO* has shown a marked tendency to move away from Pierre Marty's conceptual hierarchies towards a stronger appropriation of Freud's Second Topography, often in dialogue with André Green's contributions. Though in contradiction to Marty's own theoretical edifice in its final form, this has often been in continuation of reflections by Marty's colleagues, Denise Braunschweig and Michel Fain.

Among those most visibly engaged in integrating these new directions in systematic fashion has been Claude Smadja, long-time president of the *Association Internationale de Psychosomatique Pierre-Marty (AIPPM)*, medical director of the *Institut de psychosomatique de Paris* (since 2004 part of *ASM 13*) and founding editor, with Gérard Szwec, of the *Revue Française de Psychosomatique*, an important publishing platform of *IPSO*.

Marty's divergence from previous models reconsidered 40 years later

In his key paper on *opératoire* functioning as encountered in psychosomatic practice at the 58th *Congrès des Psychanalystes de Langue Française* in 1998, he adopts an approach in agreement with a maxim once employed by André Green: *Reculer pour mieux sauter* – if in the midst of an intractable problem, get some distance to gather force in dealing with it. Altogether, he traces the major lines of psychoanalytic engagement with somatic illness to show how disenchantment with the available approaches led a group of young French psychoanalysts to a new approach which had long-term consequences that become clearer in hindsight. In their meeting with a new group of difficult patients they started to take a closer look at what they did *not* find in these encounters.

Previously, various attempts had been made to assign covert meaning to bodily disease. With Georg Groddeck, psychic and somatic affections are, on par, considered manifestations of a powerful id. To him everything is a symbol, generated by an id exuding signification like a plant producing oxygen in photosynthesis. In this view, the creation of symbol does not necessitate a psychic structure of particular quality involved in its creation. Bodily complaints are accessible to interpretation in much the same way as typical dreams are and do not require the patient's associations so as to be intelligible to the analyst.

Smadja groups this approach together with that of others, like Ángel Garma or Jean-Paul Valabrega, who, he contends, would be hard-pressed to differentiate the meaning of an illness in one case from its non-meaning in another case. While their approach finds coherence by understanding the body as a front end of the soul's quest for expressive means, another school of thought, quite influential in postwar France, moves in the opposite direction. Franz Alexander and his colleagues in the Chicago Psychoanalytic Institute – building on the work of Walter B. Cannon and, later, of Hans Selye – considered the preservation of homeostatic equilibria and adaptation in the pursuit of this goal as the organising principle that permitted a unified perspective on mind-body disorders. In a meeting of minds between hospital medicine and a psychoanalytically inspired psychiatry, physiological processes were regarded as crucial for the development of somatic disease in a conflicted individual, with emotions as the subjective face of the process. The key terms they employed, like adaptation and emotion, but also energy, were used somewhat ambiguously, slanted towards the biological but appearing to be loaded with psychological meaning. Seemingly with frictionless borders, Smadja argues, psychoanalytic interpretation was patched on as an extra to a stock of received medical perspectives. In the last resort, a difference between conversion neurosis and a vegetative neurosis – a concept which Alexander developed from Ferenczi's organ neurosis – depended on neurophysiological criteria and not on any specific psychological process of transformation. In addition to this, Alexander's Theory of Specificity introduced constant conjunctions between a certain type of unresolved emotional conflict and a specific organ liable to bear the brunt of this aggravation, irrespective of the particular psychohistory of the individual. Flanders Dunbar attempted to identify personality types that were most likely to be at risk from certain diseases.

Although this approach had its limitations, it contributed important elements, further developed by French analysts who were to form the core of the later *EPP/IPSO*. Reflecting on the detrimental effects of certain physiological states, Alexander pointed out that, in these cases, the individual was suffering from an excess of defence, an observation Michel Fain found of great interest for understanding impoverished mental states. There is something else: with Alexander's vegetative neurosis the possibility that an illness rooted in a subject's personality might altogether lack a hidden symbolic agenda was squarely on the agenda again.

It is this aspect that seemed to engage Pierre Marty from early on. He had met Franz Alexander in 1950 and exchanged views with him on the subject of gastric ulcers. One year later he presented to the *SPP* the case of Marie, a patient suffering from headaches, which caused him to reflect on the inhibition of thought and the failure of dream work. This, followed up in a 1952 paper, led him to question both the concept of generalised symbolisation and the idea of a close correlation between illness and personality profile and to focus, instead, on the narcissistic difficulties of the psychoanalyst in his encounter with the patient. In analogy to libidinal regression, the idea of somatic regression arose during those years.

Increasingly, a new generation of French psychoanalysts saw the somatic as a field to which Freudian metapsychology could fruitfully be applied if the patient was regarded as a whole and the relationship to him/her was shifted to centre stage. Moving the main emphasis from wishing to investigate a given disease to understanding what happened in the encounter with a sufferer, among whose problems evidently ranged a serious disease, they had to propose a new angle to this meeting, in a change of focus that in a typically French way was buttressed by theory. In this sense, the publication of *L'investigation psychosomatique* was the founding document, and rallying cry, of a new school. From this new perspective, perhaps for the first time in the institutional context that formed its starting point, it was possible to sense the strangeness of meetings with hospital patients who presented themselves as nothing more than the incarnation of their medical files, a kind of behaviour that might have seemed perfectly rational to another generation of doctors but which seemed very peculiar to psychoanalysts at this time. Against the new conceptual background, set in an object relations perspective inspired by Bouvet's work, what was not happening in the meeting was regarded as an important part of the way the patient was handling him/herself and integral to how he/she dealt with any emerging blankness resulting from non-meaning. This, they thought, gave important indications as to the libidinal economy of the subject in which the somatic disease and his/her response to it was set.

A need to address simplifications

While Claude Smadja builds on Pierre Marty's work, he gives it, as mentioned, a new turn by more fully taking into account Freud's Second Topography, following both Fain's and Green's leads on this. He suggests the *opératoire* could suitably be understood as a pathology of the Me within Freud's Second Topography and sets out to make the case for this. In taking another look at the various layers of *EPP/IPSO* conceptualisation in the course of this venture, he also points out that the public image of *opératoire* life has been shaped by collective assumptions that need to be opened to critical re-examination.

The first simplification of this type is the idea that *opératoire* life emphasises its chronicity. To say someone is *opératoire* tends to be a judgement on the likely irreversibility of this state based on an interpretation of the patient's structure and constitution. Marty himself was of two minds on this and clinical experience shows that the *opératoire* can be found in different forms, some of which seem to be better understood in terms of process rather than in terms of structure. Though it can appear as a permanent condition, it can also show up as a transitory phenomenon in daily life, moments at which, Smadja suggests, the subject takes a nap from his/her subjectivity, retiring into a convalescence of being. Since the Me has need to put down its burdens in periodic withdrawal of investment, these states ultimately serve to bolster the person's narcissistic resources. An overall understanding of the *opératoire* has to take the whole gamut of variants into account, from the most deeply entrenched to the most transitory.

A second popular over-generalisation posits the well-nigh complete lack of the imagination as central to *opératoire* life. If this were the case, as radically as suggested, the person, Smadja points out, would have to be dead on arrival to qualify. Treatment often finds that a potential was present at one time but not developed and thus without reach of the individual.

A third collective idea regularly associates the *opératoire* with a severe somatic affection that puts the patient's life at risk. As with the other two assumptions there is some truth to this stereotype but it covers only one part of clinical experience. Over the years the number of *opératoire* patients with whom no somatic disorder is found seems to have increased. It is possible to see these patients as close to tipping towards somatisation, a point which, however, in their case has not been reached. It is moreover likely that no single patient vignette will show the whole range of qualities with which the discussion of the phenomenon has associated the 'ideal type'.

The Me turned pauper

To find suitable angles of attack we have to look at the practical concerns that have been raised in dealing with *opératoire* patients. *L'Investigation psychosomatique* emphasised the difficulties of the psychoanalyst in identifying with the patient as well as the latter's great narcissistic fragility. It used the image of a wall that is more likely to crumble than to show cracks. Once the connection between a liability to somatic disintegration and a lack of fantasy had been made, the investigation moved to an increased interest in the ground on which facades facing on to a busy street were built with little living space behind. Smadja finds early hints in an aside of Freud's, in which he envisages states in which melancholy is not directly object related.

Smadja traces the various attempts by Marty and his colleagues to understand this inexpressive depression. He links the mute complaint, without a proper inner addressee, to further layers of thought which situate the narcissistic depletion and lack of vital tonus in evidence in an early relational field not accessible to the patient: because of problems of her own, the mother did not elect her baby to be enthroned in majesty. Smadja sees considerable convergence with Green's reflections on negativity. As Green's work on the Dead Mother shows, transgenerational influences may have to be reckoned with, in particular to what is not there. If things were out of kilter at a time when mother and child were not yet experienced as separate, the Me is not a place that is continuously replenished with investments flowing from the id. The Me itself has been turned pauper and has gone missing as a valid object of predilection.

Low 'subjective density' and low levels of aversion

Considering that Freud saw early hatred emerge from the infant's narcissism, averse to the world's demands, Smadja finds it striking how many *opératoire* patients do not show a propensity towards hatred, lacking the requisite 'subjective density': there is not enough of a Me in evidence to kick back against what should better not be tolerated. If thwarted, they show diffuse signs of excitement instead, as they fall prey to something Smadja likens to an inflammatory process. Whenever circumstances permit, there seems to be an attempt to harvest perception for all it can deliver in place of hallucinatory wish fulfilment and to self-cradle as much as possible in stark reality. Since this process is essential to their stability, it is not surprising that there can be a surplus of vigilance found with them, amounting to a veritable 'hypochondria of the real'. If they are mad from the psychoanalyst's view, they are 'mad' in having gone hyper-real to an uncommon degree, having seemingly consented to having their lives cut down to size as teleguided front ends of a reality they unflinchingly affirm and which they are determined to inhabit without divergence from others.

The *opératoire* subject as a crowd unto him/herself

Smadja believes that too little attention has been paid to the relationship between the *opératoire* and collective psychology. For *opératoire* patients, the world runs on well discernible rails, which precludes doubt, hesitation and having to feel one's way into the future. They are a crowd unto themselves, losing their individuality in it, and yet cannot derive the profit from this act of immersion that Freud envisages in his study on crowd psychology: Affectivity is not heightened, intellectual activity is not diminished, and libidinal investments are not in evidence. If Freud suggests that the ego ideal opens up a significant path to the understanding of the psychology of crowds, Smadja proposes looking at what crowds can teach us about the Me. In the state of affairs Freud discusses, crowds put the subject into a state of relative narcissistic abundance: it is when he reflects on those extraordinary moments in which a mass disintegrates, wreaking havoc on the libidinal economy of its members, that we get closer to the narcissistic subsistence economy the *opératoire* must make do with. If there is an identification with the ways of the world on the part of the patient, it is the image of a social ecosystem under extreme pressure that is being conjured up by Smadja's descriptions: whatever function the social collective has for others, his/her own standing in it may be closer to the voyage of a third-class passenger on the Titanic who spent all his/her meagre means to make it on board.

A narcissism invested in codes of behaviour

Following Michel Fain, Smadja speaks of a *narcissisme de comportement* and, with Green, of a *narcissisme d'emprunt*, something borrowed and propped up by a certain type of behaviour designed to ward off passivity at any cost. While identifications usually serve to appropriate mental territory, and are, indeed, of considerable importance to the *opératoire* patient, they seem to be particularly unhelpful to sustain and enrich his/her inner life. One way of looking at this is to posit deficiencies in the quality of primary identification in a patient whose mother may not have been able to invest her child in a way that permitted enough of a hysterical potential to be developed. Another way to tackle this is to probe into the patient's apparent need not to be found out of step with the social group of reference: would an offence against the norms of the group make the patient feel guilty or rather ashamed? This is quite a different form of inner organisation from the the patient suffering from a powerful superego in melancholia. Apparently, the relationship of the *opératoire* to his/her superego is of a different nature: somehow the superego has lost its object, the Me. The ideal, the faceless norm takes the place of the superego. Breaking the ranks would matter, being a subject does not, or at least not that much. In this sense the *opératoire* is also a *maladie du Surmoi*. Carrying oneself well is of paramount importance. Tensions between one own's norms and those of the collective are experienced as very painful and receive a lot of attention. Perhaps, then, it should come as no surprise that some patients feel a sense of relief at falling sick: now, at least, something that concerns them personally, in a certifiable way, does matter. Being cared for in a medical institution may permit an amount of regression that might have been regarded as improper before.

Actual neuroses revisited

Although Freud at one time explicitly stated that the study of actual neuroses offered no angle of attack to psychoanalysis, the situation looks different today. Smadja, building on developments in Freud's thought, argues for their close connection to narcissistic and traumatic neuroses and the importance of this for an understanding of somatosis. After Freud's theoretical innovations of 1920 actual neurosis has to be seen in a new framework: any traumatic event is liable to interrupt the dynamics of psycho-sexuality and to engender an actual neurosis. Recent hurt joins ancient trauma to drain the subject of the possibility to liaison libidinally with either object or self. Mental organisation, when and if it exists, acts as a protective shield for the body. With this shield failing, aggressive forces that can no longer be tethered to a subject's vital projects, unleashed, become destructive and turn inward as the capacity of the subject to keep working links intact is put to risk.

> When the erotic investments placed in objects fall away, the narcissism of the subject becomes the ultimate barrier before the body is affected. When the narcissistic investments fall away as well, auto-destruction spreads within the organic domain.
> (Smadja 2009, p. 19f.)

Regression impeded by an ambient *'pure culture d'instinct de mort'*

Ambient reality against which the individual defends itself seems to be reeking of a *pure culture d'instinct de mort*, reducing to nothing all strivings of the individual in undifferentiated, impersonal, administrative procedure. Against the background of increasing exhaustion, the *opératoire* mode is being used to brace and shore up the floundering subject. What has not fallen silent by itself, as yet, is put under the strict curfew of a self-calming agenda that has to serve, under the terms of the command economy imposed, as *Ersatz* for more luxurious means of regression currently unavailable. Staying active is a way of keeping things together. This is not limited to patients seen within a psychosomatic consultation: when the psychic survival of an individual brought to the brink of death is at stake, as Smadja points out – be it towards the end of life weighed down by progressive illness or under the extreme conditions of a Nazi extermination camp – the *opératoire* is one last line of defence.

Self-inflicted compliance with an imperative of calm

When Michel Fain was reflecting on the ideal type of the toxic mother, the image he came up with, as we have seen, was in the likeness of a fairy tale, stepmotherly, Ice Queen, who does everything within her means to reduce her child to a mere object, a thing, to be handled efficiently. Working from the outside – but with much the same effect as Freud thought the death instinct might achieve from the inside – she would clamp down on her child, sending cascades of 'terminate all' signals, both covert and overt, to its boisterousness so as to induce compliant and swift enough calm. Thrown upon him/herself, in dire straits, the *opératoire* patient, according to Smadja, comes up with similar recipes when handling him/herself. What cannot be transformed within mental space has to be brought to a definitive stop: there must be, there will be, silence. If this is not successful, or insufficiently successful, the diffuse anxieties well up without a distinct image. Together with Szwec (for which they received the *Prix Maurice Bouvet* in 1996), Smadja early on focused on the particular self-calming processes used in absence of tangible modes of inner processing, as a last resort, if the projection of destructivity outwards is no feasible option.

The problem, under the conditions, is what to do with an excitement that has no history, no project and no memory, in contradistinction to a *pulsion* that has both a history and a project. If tension cannot be absorbed, it has to be reduced by any means at hand, applying emergency measures which are bound to draw heavily on perception, physical movement and codes of behaviour. Running dry on both hope and desire leaves quantities of destructive energy unbound, only precariously taken care of by self-calming measures. Paradoxically, excitement can also be fought by further excitement which is marshalled to procure a plenitude of sensation in absence of other anti-traumatic resources. If this is the case, masochism has failed to act as a sufficient binding mechanism of excitement/tension.

Smadja speculates that exposure of a baby to the will of an adult who does not act in accordance with the child's needs can place the infant in a zone not only beyond contradiction and conflict, but also beyond the pleasure principle and thus beyond masochism. Some patients indeed give the impression of having been, under total maternal domination, locked out from their own subjectivity and denied access to territory much needed for affects to take shape. Smadja refers to René Roussillon's contributions to point out that for an affect to acquire its particular quality three requirements have to be met: it has to be capable of being shared at a primitive stage with the primary object to gain its ultimate form; it has to be regulated by the meeting with the object; and it has to become individualised by becoming distinct and separate from the mother's own response. If the nascent subject is denied this process, his/her affective future will bear the marks of this missed opportunity. There will still be the raw material for affect but it will not have been bound into processed form yet. Using *opératoire* procedures may be an attempt at self-healing in a situation in which the Me is fragile, and disappearing in the crowd is grasped upon as a means to avoid surveillance by an oppressive inner mother.

Links to revitalisation disrupted in conjunctures of hurt

In more recent work, Smadja reconfirms his view on what he believes to be the most likely road to somatisation: a conjuncture of circumstances reawakens the traces of ancient hurt and re-activates previously established lines in radical defence against it, among which splitting of the Me and denial take pride of place. The already stretched narcissistic capital of the individual is further depleted, with what is left flowing from the libidinal to the auto-conservative pole of the inner economy. *Déliaison*, a cutting off from libidinal ties, not conflict, is the order of the day. With this turn away from the world of objects, destructivity is set free and directed towards the subject. Together with Marilia Aisenstein, Smadja recalls the work of the renowned French biologist Jean-Claude Ameisen on the mechanisms of cell death. If a neuron drops out of vital exchange with other neurons, its programme of auto-destruction gets activated.

> Their survival permanently depends on the nature of the interactions upon which they enter with the community that surrounds them, interactions that are indispensable to the repression of their auto-destruction. A new, more dynamic perspective of our body begins to emerge: our continued existence depends

on a permanent balance between the processes of deconstruction and reconstruction, of auto-destruction and renewal.

(Ameisen 2007, p. 22)

In his reflections on fatigue, Smadja – without reference to Ameisen – produces his own parallel to the above lines. He invites his readers to imagine they return home from work one evening and their only wish in mind is to go to rest. But an evening invitation to friends is on the programme. So, despite the fatigue, it is time to go out again. A few hours later, on return, one notices that far from adding to one's fatigue, the evening with friends has spirited it away. If this ability to liaison pleasurably is lost, not only is the likelihood of fatigue increased, but a lack of flexibility and immobility creep in, affecting the way the flow of time is experienced. All lightness of touch is gone, the future does not beckon with new possibilities. If perception does no longer evoke hope and desire, the relentless repetition of the same sets in. Fatigue is spreading. What Ameisen's passage shows, but Smadja does not particularly emphasise, is that the ability to liaison is a two-way traffic. Smadja, in the above example, certainly has to be willing to leave his house, but for this to happen there needs to be an invitation.

Somatic diseases: cause or effect of narcissistic depletion

Absence of this possibility for interaction, if not compensated by other means, will, one has to suppose, wear down the body in the long run. Smadja, following this line of thought, posits the depletion of narcissistic resources of the Me as the most likely root cause of somatisation. Szwec, with whom he had introduced the investigation of self-calming measures in 1993, is not convinced. In his contribution to the 1998 congress, he points out that Freud was comparing the redistribution of libido found in hypochondria to the *consequences* of somatic disease. What metapsychology may help us to understand are the consequences of somatic disease not its causes.

Somatic illness as the only point of contact with psychoanalysis

As Roussillon observes, Smadja's *maladie du Moi* confronts us with 'a failure and inability to be' rather than an act of repression, extra-territoriality to the subject's Me rather than an unconscious that dwells in him/her. Jean Guillaumin emphasises that the group of people showing *opératoire* traits seems to extend much beyond the psychosomatic patients in whom Pierre Marty and his colleagues showed such interest. In fact there seems to be a fair number of them in present day society, Guillaumin reflects, but they do not seek psychoanalysis. The only professional point of contact psychoanalysts are likely to have with them is established if they fall sick and are referred to them in the course of their medical treatment. People in long term medical treatment for severe illnesses will, as observation has shown, lean towards *opératoire* behaviour the more vigorously they are subjected to medical treatment and the more chronic their state becomes. In these cases hyper adaptation to 'reality' is the consequence of a mortal threat against which the subject tries to find a valid line of defence. Inner and outer reality, of which the therapist is deemed to form part, is no longer safe, and the subject tries to gain some distance by objectifying itself. If there is disinvestment, it is partial and functional: preconscious dimensions lose importance because all the energy is needed to man the Me's defence perimeters. What we observe as *opératoire* behaviour is a last-ditch defence against a catastrophic loss of inner organisation. In agreement with Smadja, Guillaumin regards Freud's Second Topography as well suited to describe the position of a Me vis-à-vis superego, ego ideal and id, who must subjectively experience this within his/her own intimacy as an encounter with extraterritorial forces.

In a recent contribution Smadja returns to the precarious situation of a subject exposed to the *actuel*, the raw forces of mentally undigested inner reality in a situation where he/she finds himself on a precarious ledge between inner, yet extraneous, forces and a social reality into which he/she is bound. Smadja takes up the question posed by Jacques Mauger:

> What are we to make of that excess of heat and noise that assails from outside psychoanalytic working space supposedly at shelter, by its silence and is rhythm, and without an oculus.
> (Mauger 2014, p. 1501)

How are we to deal with lives in which what impacts on them can find only little subjective narrative, does not reverberate in figurative shapes and does not easily admit transformation? Smadja refers to a passage by Maurizio Balsamo (2014):

> The problem appears when we are confronted with mental functioning where chance and noise are excluded from the field of the possible or are present in excess, with structures and lifestyles [*formes de vie*] which we could define as lacking the poetic ear, characterised by what presents itself as a weak factor of transformability, by the lack of subjective observation and point of view, by histories at a low narrative and figurative level.
> (Smadja 2014a, p. 1504)

Smadja sees mental representation as a complex structure organised like an edifice integrating both past and present realities. What Marty termed *l'épaisseur du préconscient* – the depth of preconscious layers – are the dimensions of subjectivity that resonate in psychoanalysis. This, Smadja points out, is a relative wealth that can find itself retrograded to levels of impoverishment and destitution, in conjuncture with important developments in a patient's life. Under threat from inner disintegration, the life of affects faces strong currents of obliteration. If this is so, it will be the task of the psychoanalytic encounter to enable a re-liaisoning with desire, a process in which the psychoanalyst's own ability to form associations will have to act as a catalyst and introduce, once a foundation has been laid, elements that address the patient's situation but come to him/her as a surprise.

One difficulty that will come up is that, for the psychoanalyst, the functioning of the patient is deeply anti-analytic. The silence of the unconscious in the encounter constitutes a traumatic shock for the analyst that can only be overcome if the analyst takes an interest in the way the patient mentally functions. Smadja sees a reversal of roles at work in the encounter: it is the analyst in whom the situation of the helpless baby the patient once was is repeated, and it is the patient that has taken over the role of the smothering, death-bringing object.

It may be necessary to develop explorations of possible new mental space on separate rails from the patient's experience of the world of the *actuel* in a zone provisionally split off from this world of noise in a helpful way. In difference to the classical psychoanalytic attitude, the analyst, in exercise of a motherly function, will also make use of facial expression and bodily posture to accompany and re-animate a patient who behind his/her brittle *opératoire* facade has to make do with an extremely precarious and unstable mental economy. This 'economic' understanding of the patient's situation has to take into account three different territories: mental space, outside reality and the body, all of which impact the individual in his/her capacity for mental transformation.

The psychoanalyst faced with the autonomous logic of the body

Although the disorganisation of a patient's psyche will have consequences on the body, these processes, beyond a certain point, will follow their own autonomous logic in the physiopathology that has by then set in. In many cases the psychoanalyst will feel a deep disquiet and worry, difficult to pin down, about the somatic well-being of a patient who does not seem to be particularly discomfited. Sometimes the mental functioning of the patient will vary, depending on the stimuli provided by the tangible presence of the psychoanalyst. Smadja recommends making use of the nascent dramatic potential of the psychoanalytic encounter, suggesting in an accessible way implications of what is happening as the meeting unfolds. This can contribute to weaning the preconscious off its saturation with the yields of perception. The external frame of the sessions should be given careful consideration: it should be in a separate location, clearly demarcated from where the patient normally receives medical care. An arrangement in sitting may be preferable. If psychoanalysis were to be undertaken with a somatic patient, the unconscious of the patient (in the sense of Freud's First Topography) would have to have found a solid enough basis. On the basis of preliminary work it will depend whether this will be a psychoanalysis with or without a beginning.

The structuring role of intergenerational processes

As we have seen, the space in which early fantasies are developed (or pre-empted, as the case may be), receive particular attention in Braunschweig and Fain's thinking. In their contribution to a manual on Child and Youth Psychiatry, Michel Ody and Claude Smadja (2004) put the position of the mother into perspective, by including the role of the father in the development of mental functioning. The authors acknowledge the contributions of Lacan in underlining the huge symbolic importance of the father, but concede that his overwhelming structural importance in Lacanian theory pushes the real person of the father and the role his own desires play, into the background. They take a somewhat different path by including in their survey investigations into how fantasies among the parents interact with the child and his/her own image of the father:

> From before his/her birth, the child expected (or non expected) mobilises the fantasies of the parents in the way they mentally represent it (or refuse to represent it). The real, gendered child, at his/her birth is going to change these representation with limits that vary for each of the parents.
> In this triangular situation that is established, the quality of the well-being (or ill-being) of each of the partners depends as much on the investment towards the two others as on that between them.
> (Ody and Smadja 2004, p. 2610f.)

The mother, the authors point out, not only carries within herself representations of the father of her child, but also of her own father reverberating in her own history as a child. Children suffer the effects of conflicts previous generations were not able to resolve. The role a father can play for a child can sensibly be changed if there is no place for him in the mental world of the mother and the equilibria between her femininity and her maternal role are out of balance. Social processes, present from the beginning, also play a role in the way adolescents are able to achieve increased distance from their parents in a process of de-idealisation. Though constellations have been identified that arguably do not bode well for the future of the child, it also has to be admitted that a plurality of factors of considerable variety enter into the eventual outcome.

The psychoanalyst faced with the autonomous logic of the environment

Since any ideal type has to be confronted with multiple realities on the ground, it is only proper that the question has been raised whether the *opératoire* exists in only one major key or can be observed in a minor key in different configurations. Claire Rueff-Escoubes has pointed to the inter-relationship between the requisites of contemporary social life and modes of mental functioning and envisaged a situation in which the organisation of personal space in an increasingly *opératoire* society might marginalise those whom psychoanalysts have hitherto regarded as well mentalised subjects with individualised, subjective inner space: anti-psychoanalytic functioning on the part of individuals might be well-adapted to their particular environment.

Denys Ribas, more recently, has conceded that metapsychology sometimes seems to be ill equipped to lay account of environments that bring about psychic death by inducing the subject to withdraw investment in his/her own self: organised indifference deprives the subject of the opportunity of vital exchange, which it needs in order to thrive. If the world we move in is radically different from our patient's, Gottlieb's observation 'that which we can know is bounded by the circumstances of our own psychological development' (Gottlieb 2010, p. 369) must of needs receive a particular, unconscious, cultural slant.

One day, Marilia Aisenstein recounts, around 1979 or 1980, Pierre Marty, when she arrived at his office, took her out into the pouring rain to show her something, or rather someone:

> a carcass of a car, four sheets spread on the ground, an engine completely taken apart with the pieces thrown on the sheets, so that they would not be in direct contact with the mud. An Asian man crouched there, occupied, very calmly, with very meticulously putting together his car again, which he had completely taken apart the day before. Pierre Marty asked me, 'So, what do you see there?' I answer him, 'I see a Chinese who is completely mad'. He tells me that this is not at all the case, that I had not got it at all, had nothing understood, although I had been at the hospital for more than a year! 'This is a moment of *opératoire* life *in vivo*'. I was not very convinced and I told him that I found that very, very mad. He tells me, 'No, madam, for if this Asian were deranged by any fantasy life, he could not take apart a car screw by screw and calmly put it together again like that. And anyone among us, deranged as we are by our unconscious, could not do this kind of work'.
>
> (Aisenstein 1998, p. 18f.)

As Marty pointed out, looking at the foreigner confronted them with their own mode of mental functioning. In retrospect, Aisenstein thinks there is something akin to a cold form of psychosis at work in such starkly *opératoire* behaviour. Since the man, for reasons of his own, was clearly more interested in his car than in the diagnosis conferred on him by a group of uninvited bystanders to his persistent, determined work, this is a point that has to remain moot. What it also shows is that any psychoanalytic perspective that does not include the world view of the person glanced at from outside must remain severely handicapped.

The psychoanalyst faced with cultures alien to him/herself

In a contribution from the 1980s, Smadja observes the particular difficulties faced by a psychoanalyst in his work with a family with whose cultural moorings he is not familiar.

> The *psychosomaticiens* are wont to say that the analyst must often lend his/her preconscious to his/her patient. Can we do this, ourselves, to these families? For it is here that the rub really lies: we lack the representations, with cultural facts in our view working like latent thoughts, [insight into which] we fall short. [...] We progressively feel that our capacity to associate diminishes. In the worst case, we can no longer function in front of these patients: boredom, irritation, aggressivity and depression are the reflections of this mental dysfunctioning of the analyst.
> (Smadja 1985, p. 101)

It only requires a clash of cultures, it seems, for the analyst to come close to *opératoire* functioning himself. It is a strong reminder that any clinical assessment will have to be highly sensitive to the particular circumstances in a given person's life.

A situationalist dimension of the *opératoire*

With Smadja's remarks that the *opératoire* might at times be a transitory element, and his willingness to take cultural factors into account, it is easier to arrive at a reading that makes sense of a person's remedial measures at a certain moment of time. In this light we can also understand better the seemingly mad actions of people who are not necessarily mad but entangled in something that takes their all, which sometimes bypasses their minds.

As was raised in response to Smadja's presentation at the 1998 congress, we should take into consideration different levels of the *opératoire*, employed in different contexts and charged to get certain things done within an economy of inner ways and means, in which elements of the proto-imaginary are at times difficult to discern.

The interlocutor pushed against his/her ignorance

Marty in 1952, as we have seen, made the narcissistic difficulties of the observer confronted with functions invisible to him/her the linchpin of his inquiry. It is instructive to link this to Bion's words

> In short, there is an inexhaustible fund of ignorance to draw upon: it is about all we have to draw upon.
> (Bion 1978[1976], p. 317)

Balsamo and Mauger – taken up by Smadja as we have seen above – refer to the *oculus* that is not available to the psychoanalyst, creating a special condition which constitutes both a boon and a bane. The problem is aggravated if we deal with suffering at the workplace, which affects the subject in ways which he/she may find difficult to understand, feel or put into words. Our ignorance of this, it seems, is both structural and situational. Part of it might as well be due to a resistance to knowledge available, but not absorbed, because it has been cut out of the loop. In the following two chapters we will probe into how French psychiatry discovered the rhythms of the workplace, forgot most about them, and rediscovered them from a new psychoanalytic perspective.

Sources

Aisenstein, M. (1998), 'Pensée opératoire et traitement de la réalité', in: Duparc, F. ed., *L'art du psychanalyste: autour de l'oeuvre de Michel de M'Uzan*, Lausanne: Delachaux et Niestlé, pp. 15–25.

Aisenstein, M. (2014), Brève discussion du texte: "Le modèle pulsionnel de la psychosomatique" par Claude Smadja', *Revue Française de Psychosomatique* 45, pp. 30–40.

Aisenstein, M. (2020), 'La "pensée opératoire", de Pierre Marty et Michel de M'Uzan', *Revue Française de Psychanalyse* 84(5), pp. 1263–1278.

Aisenstein, M. and Smadja, C. (2001), 'De la psychosomatique comme courant essentiel de la psychanalyse contemporain', in: Green, A. ed., *Courants de la psychanalyse contemporaine*, Paris: Presses Universitaires de France, pp. 343–353.

Aisenstein, M. and Smadja, C. (2010a), 'Introduction to the paper by Pierre Marty: The narcissistic difficulties presented to the observer by the psychosomatic problem', *International Journal of Psychoanalysis* 91(2), pp. 343–346.

Aisenstein, M. and Smadja, C. (2010b), 'Conceptual framework from the Paris Psychosomatic School: A clinical psychoanalytic approach to oncology', *International Journal of Psychoanalysis* 91(3), pp. 621–640.

Aisenstein, M. and Smadja, C. (2017), 'Destins d'une rencontre', *Revue Française de Psychosomatique* 52, pp. 5–28.

Ameisen J.-C. (2007), 'La mort au cœur du vivant', *Revue française de psychosomatique* 32, pp. 11–44.

Balsamo, M. (2014), 'La rencontre avec l'*oculus*', *Revue Française de Psychanalyse* 78(5), pp. 1493–1498.

Bion, W.R. (1978[1976]), 'Evidence', in: Bion, F. ed. (1994), *Clinical seminars and other work*, London: Karnac Books, pp. 312–320.

Bouchet-Kervella, D. (2001), 'L'évolution des courants de pensée au sein de l'École de psychosomatique de Parsi à travers la "Revue française de psychosomatique"', in: Green, A. ed., *Courants de la psychanalyse contemporaine*, Paris: Presses Universitaires de France, pp. 442–444.

de M'Uzan, M. (2011), 'Réponse à Claude Smadja', in: Baruch, C. ed., *Nouveaux développements en psychanalyse. Autour de la pensée de Michel de M'Uzan*, Sévres: Éditions EDK, pp. 83–87.

Delourmel, C. (2010), '"Les modèles psychnalytiques de la psychosomatique" de Claude Smadja', *Revue Française de Psychanalyse* 74(3), pp. 825–836.

Edwards, C.L. (2013), 'Psychosomatic illness, history and sociology of', in: Scull, A. ed., *Cultural sociology of mental illness: An A-to-Z guide*, Thousand Oaks, California: SAGE Publications, pp. 726–729.

Fine, A. (2001), '"La vie opératoire. Études psychnalytiques, de Claude Smadja"', *Revue Française de Psychosomatique* 20, pp. 171–187.

Fine, A. (2002), 'La vie opératoire [Operative life]: Claude Smadja', *International Journal of Psychoanalysis* 83(5), pp. 1217–1220.

Geyen, D. (2013), 'Psychosomatic Illness, cultural comparisons of', in: Scull, A. ed., *Cultural sociology of mental illness: An A-to-Z guide*, Thousand Oaks, CA: SAGE Publications, pp. 725–726.

Gottlieb, R.M. (2010), 'Commentary on Pierre Marty's "The narcissistic difficulties presented to the observer by the psychosomatic problem"', *International Journal of Psychoanalysis* 91, pp. 365–370.

Green, A. (2001), 'Reculer pour mieux sauter', *Revue Française de Psychanalyse* 65(4), pp. 1303–1314.

Guillaumin, J. (1998), 'L'opérativité et le corps dans le "monisme" freudien', *Revue Française de Psychanalyse* 62(5), pp. 1477–1482.

Hale, N.G. (1995), *The rise and crisis of psychoanalysis in the United States. Freud and the Americans 1917–1985*, Oxford: Oxford University Press.

Kaswin-Bonnefond, D. (2004b), '"La vie opératoire: études psychanalytiques" de Claude Smadja', *Revue Française de Psychanalyse* 68(4), pp. 1327–1336.

Lipsitt, D.R. (2000), 'Psyche and soma: struggles to close the gap', in: Menninger, R.W. and Nemiah, J.C. eds, *American psychiatry after World War II*, Washington, D.C.: American Psychiatric Press, pp. 152–186.

Mauger, J. (2014), 'Le futur actuel', *Revue Française de Psychanalyse* 78(5), pp. 1499–1502.

Marty, P. (1952), 'Les difficultés narcissiques de l'observateur devant le problème psychosomatique', *Revue Française de Psychanalyse* 16, pp. 339–362

Ody, M. and Smadja, C. (2004), 'Carence paternelle. Importance du père et de la fonction paternelle dans le développement du fonctionnement mental', in: Lebovici, S., Diatkine, R. and Soulé M. eds, *Nouveau traité de psychiatrie de l'enfant et de l'adolescent*, volume 4, 2nd edition, Paris: Presses Universitaires de France, pp. 2603–2620.

Papageorgiou, M. (2009), '"Les modèles psychanalytiques de la psychosomatique" de Claude Smadja', *Revue Française de Psychosomatique* 36, pp. 181–187.

Porte, J.-M. (1998), 'La pensée opératoire peut-elle se décliner au pluriel?', *Revue Française de Psychanalyse* 62(5), *Revue Française de Psychanalyse* 62(5), pp. 1519–1526.

Press, J. (2010), 'A propos du livre de Claude Smadja', *Actualités Psychosomatiques* 13, pp. 183–187.

Ribas, D. (2014), 'La contrainte au désinvestissement de soi', *Revue Française de Psychanalyse* 78(5), pp. 1531–1537.

Roussillon, R. (2005), 'Affect inconscient, affect-passion et affect-signal', in: Bouhsira, J. and Parat, H. eds, *L'affect*, Paris: Presses Universitaires de France, pp. 117–135.

Roussillon, R. (2006), 'Neutralisation énergétique et affects extrêmes', *Actualités Psychosomatiques* 9, pp. 55–65.

Roussillon, R. (2008), *Le je et l'entre-je(u)*, Paris: Presses Universitaires de France.

Rueff-Escoubès, C. (1995), 'Allons-nous vers une societé "normalement opératoire"?', *Revue Française de Psychosomatique* 8, pp. 193–207.

Rueff-Escoubès, C. (2001), '"Dire non"', *Revue Française de Psychosomatique* 19, pp. 173–180.

Rueff-Escoubès, C. (2003), ' "On nous demande de ne pas penser": fatigues et conditions de travail, le point de vue sociopsychanalytique', *Revue Française de Psychosomatique* 24, pp. 157–169.

Rueff-Escoubès, C. (2004), 'Fatigues et valeurs sociales', in: *Vivre fatigué*, numéro spécial de la *Revue Française de Psychosomatique*, pp. 37–39.

Smadja, C. (1985), 'Les attitudes psychiques d'un thérapeute face à une famille de migrants', *Textes du Centre Alfred Binet* 7, pp. 93–104.

Smadja, C. (1990), 'La notion de mentalisation et l'opposition névroses actuelles/névroses de défense', *Revue Française de Psychanalyse* 54(3), pp. 787–796.

Smadja, C. (1991), 'Le concept de pulsion: essai d'étude comparative chez Freud et P. Marty', *Revue Française de Psychosomatique* 1, pp. 149–168.

Smadja, C. (1993), 'A propos des procédés autocalmants du Moi', *Revue Française de Psychosomatique* 4, pp. 9–26, reprinted in: Smadja 2001a, pp. 219–240.

Smadja, C. (1994a), 'Préliminaires techniques à l'analysabilité de patients atteints d'affections somatiques', *Revue Française de Psychanalyse* 58(4), pp. 1059–1076.

Smadja, C. (1994b), 'Pierre Marty, une brève histoire de son oeuvre', *Revue Française de Psychosomatique* 6, pp. 29–37.

Smadja, C. (1995a), 'Les autocalmants ou le destin inachevé du sadomasochisme', *Revue Française de Psychosomatique* 8, pp. 57–68, reprinted in: Smadja 2001a, pp. 241–254.

Smadja, C. (1995b), 'Le modèle psychosomatique de Pierre Marty', *Revue Française de Psychosomatique* 7, pp. 7–25.

Smadja, C. (1995c), 'A propos des procédés autocalmants du moi', in: Nicolaïdis, N. and Press, J. eds, *La psychosomatique hier et aujourd'hui*, Lausanne: Delachaux et Niestlé, pp. 231–258 (a reprint of Smadja 1993a).

Smadja, C. (1996a), 'Destins de la sensorialité et des affects dans la reconstruction du temps vécu', *Revue Française de Psychanalyse* 60(4), pp. 1073–1081, reprinted in: Smadja 2001a, pp. 255–266.

Smadja, C. (1996b), 'Le processus de dédifférenciation du Moi: hypothèse à propos du fonctionnement des états opératoires', *Revue Française de Psychosomatique* 10, pp. 39–46.

Smadja, C. (1997a), 'Angoisse et psychosomatique', in: Amar, N., Le Guen, A. and Oppenheimer, A., *Angoisses: pluralité d'approches*, Paris: Presses Universitaires de France, pp. 91–104.

Smadja, C. (1997b), 'Impensable douleur', in: Cournut, J., Israël, P., Jeanneau, A. and Schaeffer, J. eds, *Le mal-être (angoisse et violence). Débats de psychanalyse*, Paris: Presses Universitaires de France, pp. 181–187.

Smadja, C. (1998a), 'Le fonctionnement opératoire dans la pratique psychosomatique', *Revue Française de Psychanalyse* 62(5), pp. 1367–1440.

Smadja, C. (1998b), 'Après coup', *Revue Française de Psychanalyse* 62(5), pp. 1441–1450.

Smadja, C. (1998c), 'Logique freudienne, logique martyenne', in: Fine, A. and Schaeffer, J. eds, *Interrogations psychosomatiques*, Paris: Presses Universitaires de France, pp. 55–69.

Smadja, C. (1999a), 'L'énigme de la douleur dans la dépression essentielle', *Revue Française de Psychosomatique* 15, pp. 25–37.

Smadja, C. (1999b), 'Les galériens volontaires de Gérard Szwec', *Revue Française de Psychosomatique* 16, pp. 211–218.

Smadja, C. (2000a), 'Le déni de l'inachèvement pulsionnel: quelques remarques au sujet de l'observation de Jean-Paul Obadia', *Revue Française de Psychosomatique* 17, pp. 85–90.

Smadja, C. (2000b), 'Discussion des observations de Jean-Paul Obadia', *Revue Française de Psychosomatique* 18, pp. 79–86.

Smadja, C. (2001a), *La vie opératoire. Études psychanalytiques*, Paris: Presses Universitaires de France.

Smadja, C. (2001b), 'Clinique d'un état de démentalisation', *Revue Française de Psychosomatique* 19, pp. 11–27.

Smadja, C. (2001c), 'L'évolution de la pratique psychanalytique avec les patients somatiques', in: de Mijolla, A. ed., *Evolution de la clinique psychanalytique*, Bordeaux: L'Esprit du Temps, pp. 167–182.

Smadja, C. (2002a), 'La perte de l'espoir', *Actualités Psychosomatiques* 5, pp. 29–40.

Smadja, C. (2002b), 'Cadre actuel, cadre névrotique', in: Botella, C. ed., *Penser les limites. Écrits en l'honneur d'André Green*, Paris: Delachaux et Niestlé, pp. 362–365.

Smadja, C. (2002c), 'Une histoire critique du symbolisme organique', *Revue Française de Psychosomatique* 21, pp. 7–25.

Smadja, C. (2003a), 'La fatigue: symptôme et signe de la négativité psychique', *Revue Française de Psychosomatique* 24, pp. 33–36.

Smadja, C. (2003b), 'Quelques remarques préliminaires à l'étude psychosomatique des maladies auto-immunes', *Revue Française de Psychosomatique* 23, pp. 11–24.

Smadja, C. (2004a), 'La dépression inachevée', *Revue Française de Psychanalyse* 68(4), pp. 1239–1252.

Smadja, C. (2004b), 'Introduction à une clinique du silence', *Actualités Psychosomatiques* 7, pp. 23–34.

Smadja, C. (2004c), 'La fatigue: symptôme de l'économie psychosomatique', in: *Vivre fatigué*, numéro spécial de la *Revue Française de Psychosomatique*, pp. 15–22.

Smadja, C. (2005a), 'Transformations contemporaines de la méthode et du cadre analytiques', in: Richard F. and Urribarri, F. eds, *Autour de l'oeuvre d'André Green*, Paris: Presses Universitaires de France, pp. 67–77.

Smadja, C. (2005b), 'La place de l'affect dans l'économie psychosomatique', Bouhsira, J. and Parat, H. eds, *L'affect. Monographies de psychanalyse de la revue Française de Psychanalyse*, Paris: Presses Universitaires de France, pp. 163–179.

Smadja, C. (2006a), 'Les deux vies de l'opératoire', *Actualités Psychosomatiques* 9, pp. 67–79.

Smadja, C. (2006b), 'La solution somatique', in: Green, A. ed., *Les voies nouvelles de la thérapeutique psychanalytique*, Paris: Presses Universitaires de France, pp. 629–650.

Smadja, C. (2006c), 'Le travail du psychanalyste avec les malades somatiques', in: Perron, R. ed., *Psychanalystes, qui êtes-vous?* Paris: Dunod, pp. 115–119.

Smadja, C. (2007a), 'L'impératif de retour au calme', *Revue Française de Psychosomatique* 32, pp. 71–79.

Smadja, C. (2007b), 'La maladie avant la maladie', *Revue Française de Psychosomatique* 31, pp. 29–40.

Smadja, C. (2008a), *Les modèles psychanalytiques de la psychosomatique*, Paris: Presses Universitaires de France.

Smadja, C. (2008b), 'Construction et déconstruction de l'image du père', in: Cupa, D. ed., *Image du père dans la culture contemporaine. Hommages à André Green*, Paris: Presses Universitaires de France, pp. 356–359.

Smadja, C. (2008c), 'La dépression essentielle, trace négative de la mémoire psychosomatique', in: Chouvier B. and Roussillon, R. eds, *Corps, acte et symbolisation. Psychanalyse aux frontières*, Louvain-la-Neuve: De Boeck, pp. 73–78.

Smadja, C. (2009), 'La maladie somatique, une dimension de la santé psychique', *Revue Française de Psychosomatique* 36, pp. 9–26.

Smadja, C. (2010a), 'Introduction au concept d'économie psychosomatique', *Revue Française de Psychosomatique* 37, pp. 9–15.

Smadja, C. (2010b), 'The place of affect in the psychosomatic economy', in: Aisenstein, M. and Rappoport de Aisemberg, E. eds, *Psychosomatics today. A psychoanalytic perspective*, London: Karnac, pp. 145–161.

Smadja, C. (2011a), 'Des avatars de la séduction aux figures de l'opératoire', in: Baruch, C. ed., *Nouveaux développements en psychanalyse. Autour de la pensée de Michel de M'Uzan*, Sèvres: Éditions EDK, pp. 77–82.

Smadja, C. (2011b), 'Psychoanalytic psychosomatics', *International Journal of Psychoanalysis* 92, pp. 221–230.

Smadja, C. (2011c), 'Le travail de psychisation du corps', *Revue Française de Psychosomatique* 39, pp. 147–161.

Smadja, C. (2012a), 'Winnicott face aux psychosomaticiens de l'école de Paris', in: Braconnier, A. and Golse, B. eds, *Winnicott et la création humaine*, Toulouse: Érès, pp. 233–239.

Smadja, C. (2012b), 'Ferenczi, un précurseur de la psychosomatique contemporaine', *Revue Française de Psychosomatique* 42, pp. 23–34.

Smadja, C. (2012c), 'L'usage de l'expression dramatique dans l'interprétation', in: Chervet, B. ed., *L'interprétation*, Paris: Presses Universitaires de France, pp. 43–51.

Smadja, C. (2012d), 'Introduction à une clinique du silence', in: Cabrol G., Durieux, M. and Parat, H., *La dépression: Éclipse d'Éros ou triomphe de Thanatos?* Paris: Presses Universitaires de France, pp. 169–183.

Smadja, C. (2012e), 'Préface', in: Donabédian, D., *L'adolescent et son corps*, Paris: Presses Universitaires de France, pp. 1–6.

Smadja, C. (2012f), 'Introduction à la psychosomatique', in: Kapsambelis, V. ed., (2012), *Manuel de psychiatrie clinique et psychopathologique de l'adulte*, Paris: Presses Universitaires de France, pp. 197–212.

Smadja, C. (2013a), 'Deuil, mélancolie et somatisation', *Revue Française de Psychosomatique* 44, pp. 7–24.

Smadja, C. (2013b), 'Un préconscient saturé', *Revue Française de Psychosomatique* 43, pp. 165–171.

Smadja, C. (2014a), 'Le psychanalyste face à la menace de l'actuel', *Revue Française de Psychanalyse* 78(5), pp. 1503–1506.

Smadja, C. (2014b), 'Le modèle pulsionnel de la psychosomatique', *Revue Française de Psychosomatique* 45, pp. 11–30.

Smadja, C. (2015a), 'Introduction à la notion de régression intra-narcissique', *Revue Française de Psychosomatique* 47, pp. 141–149.

Smadja, C. (2015b), 'De la mort et des pulsions', in: Chervet, B. ed., *Le meurtre fondateur. L'acte psychique par excellence*, Paris: Presses Universitaires de France, pp. 67–74.

Smadja, C. (2016a), 'Principe de plaisir et mentalisation', in: Angelergues, J. and Cointot, F. eds, *Le principe de plaisir*, Paris: Presses Universitaires de France, pp. 83–94.

Smadja, C. (2016b), 'Le surmoi-corps', *Revue Française de Psychanalyse* 80(5), pp. 1521–1525.

Smadja, C. (2016c), 'Une découverte de la psychanalyse: la psychosomatique', *Revue Française de Psychosomatique* 49, pp. 11–17.

Smadja, C. (2017), 'Le travail de somatisation', in: Nayrou, F. and Szwec, G. eds, *La psychosomatique*, Paris: Presses Universitaires de France, pp. 47–68.
Smadja, C. (2018), 'Corps malade et surmoi', *Revue Française de Psychosomatique* 53, pp. 167–179.
Smadja, C. (2019), 'Le temps calme', *Revue Française de Psychosomatique* 55, pp. 5–18.
Smadja, C. (2020), 'Inconscient psychanalytique, inconscient cognitif', *Revue Française de Psychanalyse* 84(3), pp. 739–749.
Smadja, C. and Szwec, G. (1993), 'A propos du questionnaire "médecine et psychosomatique"', *Revue Française de Psychosomatique* 4, pp. 211–214.
Smadja, C. and Szwec, G. (2003), 'Michel Hautecouverture. Interview', *Revue Française de Psychosomatique* 23, pp. 163–176.
Smadja, C. and Szwec, G. (2015), 'Hommage à Catherine Parat', *Revue Française de Psychosomatique* 48, pp. 5–6.
Speth-Lepetitcolin, O. (2010), 'Les modèles psychanalytiques de la psychosomatique de Claude Smadja', *Actualités Psychosomatiques* 13, pp. 177–183.
Szajnberg, N. (2010), 'On: The possibly narcissistic difficulties among scientific cultures: A response to Marty's 1952 key paper', *International Journal of Psychoanalysis* 91(6), pp. 1523–1524.
Wilson, E. (2012), '"Revue Française de Psychanalyse" [review of volume 62(5) 1998: "Psychosomatics and instinctual drives"], *The Psychoanalytic Quarterly* 81, pp. 505–526.
Zwettler-Otte, S. (2011), *Ebbe und Flut – Gezeiten des Eros. Psychoanalytische Gedanken und Fallstudien über die Liebe*, Stuttgart: W. Kohlhammer.

11

ENTANGLEMENTS

The forgotten pre-history of the *opératoire*

The antecedents: patients' work in psychiatry – a means to energise or to subdue?

As Claude Smadja pointed out, *opératoire* is a qualification that should be regarded as highly context-sensitive. New as the word was when applied to clinical matters, some of the terrain it was used on was not. Thinking about *opératoire* behaviour had, in fact, existed in France before the term was coined. In its previous iteration it focused on what work did – or failed to do – to people who were in a difficult situation to start with. Before we look at Christophe Dejours' contribution in the following chapter, we need to take a brief look back to see what had been too optimistically discarded in the intervening period. To understand this, the effects of World War II on France have to be considered.

At a time when French psychoanalysis had to reconstruct under changed circumstances the underpinnings of its renewed existence from scratch, institutionalised psychiatry in the land was confronted by formidable challenges on its part. With neuroleptica not yet available, every effort had to be made to use prudently, under constrained conditions, what was at hand. One way to make professional manpower go a long way was to put a premium on any action that strove to mobilise a collective, as Bion and Rickman had done in their own way in the Northfield Experiment. In France, psychodrama, soon to be given a psychoanalytic penchant, was adopted to suit the needs of the times.

Another possibility, in continuation of a long tradition, established in France at least since Philippe Pinel (1745–1826), was to put patients to work. This, in the past, had had a number of less desirable collateral effects. In the 19th century, mental asylums, charged by the law of 1838 to open their gates to the mentally disturbed regardless of their pecuniary situation, increasingly became financially dependent on the labour of their patients, who were made to work up to ten hours a day to sustain the required output. In the famous legal provisions of 1857, work continued to be regarded as both a means of treatment and a source of distraction well suited to its inmates. It was, at any rate, seen as the method of choice to keep the ward calm by producing through its strict application submission, self-denial and self-forgetfulness in a workforce rendered both docile and listless – something that would well fit later descriptions of the *opératoire*. Not until 1938 did the *asiles d'aliénés* shed their former designation to become psychiatric hospitals at least in name, places in which one psychiatrist was responsible for up to six hundred patients and the 'guardians' involved in day-to-day handling of the patient population had received no regular training.

Whatever precarious balances may have been reached by this system, they were shaken up dramatically during the war years, in which an estimated one quarter to one third of their patient population perished in desolate conditions, from malnutrition and lack of heating, even in regions where more actively murderous German methods did not apply. On occasion, however, the breakdown of the system of traditional care showed unexpected effects as well. In June 1940, La Charité-sur-Loire, under imminent danger of bombardment, released some of its patients to their families, while others simply fled. After some time it was found that the ex-patients had adapted rather well and were contributing to the communities that had accepted them. In 1943, Paul Sivadon, previously responsible for a place lodging patients in family settlements, and now charged to run the former asylum Ville-Évrard at Neuilly-sur-Marne, decided to open up the place to the surrounding rural environment and was able to see some spectacular transformations in his patients.

Lessons drawn: increased attention to rhythm, suitability and context

The post-war years found Paul Sivadon centre stage in many of the reform debates within French psychiatry and, as medical adviser for the national health insurance introduced in 1945, with a wide-ranging network of professional contacts both within and outside the medical profession, in a position to influence the shape of necessary reforms. From his observations of patients at work he seemed to have developed a lively interest in ways to understand what sort of job would best stimulate a given patient: various parameters like rhythm, space, material and social context had to be considered to find the right kind of fit. Engagement with a task, he concluded, could only be sustained if it offered a manageable challenge to the subject performing it, kept alive the dimension of the as yet unknown and offered a tension that invited resolution. If this *écart*, and the tension created by it, disappeared, there would be either a drifting into mechanical behaviour under the sway of all-enveloping boredom or an onset of more pronounced aggression leading to a turning away from the job at hand, both of which moves would again bring pathological behaviour to the fore. Just as too much homogeneity in the surroundings would result in indifferentiation, too much heterogeneity would produce listless co-existence or outright rejection. In a theoretical move apparently both inspired by the philosophy of Vitalism and the psychology of Piaget, Sivadon posited it would be best for the individual if the personal environment were not only to sustain and to enable, but by some admixture of aversive qualities also manage to propel and incite the subject to transcend its constraints:

> Personality is nourished by its surrounding field [*milieu*] and structures itself by putting itself in opposition to it. Its development is only possible if the nutritive factor and the resistance by the environment correspond to the capacities of assimilation and independence the subject has.
> (Sivadon 1952, p. 457 quoted in Torrente 2004, p. 60)

Hospitals would be wrong to impose conditions that might cripple their patients' sociability and drive them into sterile exasperation of their aggressivity. Regression towards secure modes and progression towards accepting risks had to be able to alternate and should be brought into balance to assure personal equilibrium, a goal which would more readily be achieved if there was enough intermediary space provided. Not only should there be a certain range of tasks requiring different amounts of efforts: to grow, the individual should be exposed to different environments to stimulate its capacity of development.

From the observation of patients at work to the investigation of the world of work extra muros

From observing what work did to the patient to taking interest in his work place integration after release from hospital seemed but a small step to be taken in stride. In order to be successful, the rehabilitation process had to accomplish the re-insertion of the ex-patient in a work place, something Sivadon tried to achieve by every means at his disposal. In 1948, together with Suzanne Baumé, he founded the association *l'Élan Retrouvé* (Zest Regained), the programme of which was announced in its very name. It offered to former patients a place of sociability and welcome in form of a club, where they would also receive help by social workers to cope with administrative, professional and material problems. After an agreement with the national health insurance, this was extended into a *foyer de post-cure* [a post-treatment centre] in 1956, offering further help to ex-patients to come to terms with renewed social independence and to find appropriate work after release from hospital. In spite of all his efforts, at the beginning of the 1950s, structured offers with a similar goal were relatively scarce. It was against this background that Sivadon first introduced the term *psychopathologie du travail* to a wider professional public. Sivadon, in his presentation, approached his topic from three angles of investigation – the adaptation of the mental sufferer to his work; pathogenic work; therapeutic work – three areas of study that have since moved apart but which he tied together by focusing on the position of the mental patient in need of rehabilitation.

Casualties of the work place

It did not escape his and his co-workers' attention that the world of work in France at the time was undergoing massive transformations, putting new demands on the workforce, which was increasingly confronted with new modes of organisation and accelerated rhythms. All this put the meaningful social integration of ex-patients at risk by creating a gap between the new demands and their individual possibilities that could no longer be bridged. What if the resources of renewable psychic energy within the immediate environment were found to be lacking? Even if they managed to adapt, the adaptation demanded of them might well be alienating and malign, unknowingly side-tracking young, vulnerable people into a diminished life. Once caught up in the impasse, they would be at a loss to know how to transform situations by dreaming of them and enveloping them with an imaginary halo. They would lack sufficient resources provided by what he called interiorisation: reality, Sivadon believed, only jumped at one's throat if one did not dispose of an intermediary cushion formed by a network of symbolic connections which also provided the means to conceive possible futures. A future disenchanted, its back turned to desire, would turn the flow of time into something void and bloodless: for individuals with extinguished lives (*individus eteints*) time neither pulled nor beckoned. To them, and many others, help should have arrived earlier.

According to international studies at the time, there existed an elevated percentage of mental pathological disorders impacting on 'ordinary work'. In his 1952 article he referred to studies that put the percentage of those affected amounted to around 30 to 40 percent. It would, hence, he suggested, be important to ask oneself a number of questions:

> To what extent does the professional activity reverberate on the psyche and favour one psychopathological manifestation over another? To which measure, on the contrary, does a given mental structure steer the subject towards a certain mode of activity, while at the same time constituting favourable territory for the emergence of a given category of mental troubles?
> (Sivadon 1952, p. 469, quoted in Torrente 2004, p. 66)

Work might impact the individual in quite different ways, then: what was highly unlikely, however, was that it would not leave any mental impact on – or resonance with – the subject and his/her life. Though work may put florid pathological manifestations to some rest, Sivadon suggested it should not be used to put the whole person into a permanently reduced state. Compensation, even if it occurred, certainly did not equal healing and should not be confused with it.

Towards rallying the public: the work of the Mental Health League

If the thin red line of French reform psychiatry was to rise to the challenges posed by the transformations of post-war society, they had to educate the professional public. Only if awareness was sufficiently raised and training offered would the importance of preventive measures to promote mental health at the work place be more properly understood and the sensibility towards precursors of mental troubles be more widely spread. This was even more important under the conditions prevalent in France, where the exercise of the medical specialisations of psychiatry and work medicine were at the time stipulated to be mutually exclusive and doctors of work received no formal training as yet. It was an already existing platform, the *Ligue d'hygiène mentale*, that – apart from encounters gravitating around the *Élan Retrouvé* – was to constitute one of the focal points of endeavours in extended psychiatry and inter-professional dialogue. In the 1950s and early 1960s, under the guiding influence of Paul Sivadon, it increasingly became a centrepiece of national strategies for the prevention of mental disease with connections on an international scale. By dint of considerable effort, France was moving into somewhat closer affinity with American developments, which had seen concerns of national health move to the centre stage in public awareness.

In 1952, together with Claude Veil, Paul Sivadon founded a section within the *Ligue* specially dedicated to mental hygiene at work. In this field of specialisation there was an approach shared with contemporary British and Dutch studies, in a view which tended to lodge the source of disturbances in the personality structure of the worker, reflecting only on second thought on the type of work suitable for an already frail individual. This perspective at times entailed a call for tutelary care with strong paternalistic features: those who could not cope with the contemporary rhythms of daily life had to be provided with guidance and direction how to adapt, if necessary, by strongly pushing them to take the necessary steps or organising their environment. Seen from the workers' perspective, attempts by work medicine to encourage mental hygiene could seem like another attempt by state and employers to meddle with whatever compartments of precarious autonomy were left to them. From a perspective of professional strategy, on the other hand, psychiatry, at a time when clinical psychology was positioning itself as a possible competitor, was moving into territory left largely unoccupied.

Dissenting voices: Louis Le Guillant

While Paul Sivadon, in his understanding of the development of society, showed strong echoes of the sociologist Georges Friedmann, founder of a modern sociology of work in France, one of his fellow psychiatrists, Louis Le Guillant, equally engaged in studying the psychopathology of work, was moving into more markedly Marxist directions of a pro-Soviet flavour. He actively fought for an extended psychiatry engaging in preventive measures beyond the existing hospital structures. In 1948 he founded within the hospital in Villejuif, Paris, the association *Entr'Aide et Amitié*, which tried to involve local enterprises with the work of patients in protected workshops. The campaign of the *PCF* against 'reactionary psychoanalysis' in 1949 created internal rifts within the reform camp, to which Le Guillant responded by creating with Henri Wallon, who for a long time, in tension to Piaget, had emphasised cultural and social factors in the development of the infant, *La Raison*, a magazine which provided a platform of argument in favour of dialectical materialism.

His trade union contacts raised his interest in conditions of work in various professions and their consequences on mental dispositions. He notably pioneered, with Jean Begoin, work on the neurosis of telephonists and typists and initiated investigations into the conditions of housemaids. In his studies he insisted on the social habitat as a place that created tensions to which people adapted to the best of their abilities: it is the constant nervousness of telephonists acquired at the workplace that rendered them able to execute their task. When the noxiousness of a situation leant on individual histories, a pathogenic effect was very likely to take shape. At the *Centre de Traitement et de Réadaptation Sociale* of the Villejuif psychiatric hospital, Le Guillant was intrigued by the considerable number of Breton women taken care of in this service. Frequently working as domestic servants, uprooted from their provincial background, and living in comparative isolation, they had to face comparable problems. His reasoning is well presented in the following lines about Madame L., a patient working as a maid, in which he tries to assemble elements of a drama that escapes the patient:

> To a certain extent she has lost contact with the social reality that is hers.[…] she has alienated herself profoundly from the surroundings where she should live in […] Her lived experience, which is of such eloquent tragedy, speaks a language which she does not understand.
>
> (Le Guillant 2006, p. 185f)

Depending on the situation, your job might cut you off from a sense of belonging, imprison you in identifications contracted in your family of origin and effectively stall all meaningful desire, rendering you 'dispossessed of yourself'. Although different individuals might respond differently to finding themselves in an impasse, this condition is always the source of a considerable amount of mental tribulation. Le Guillant, in contrast to Paul Sivadon, as we can see, introduced something his colleagues were not developing in the same way: a clinic of subjective situations under the impact of social conditions.

A different emphasis: François Tosquelles

If work is to have a chance to be recuperative it has to involve the individual in all his/her subjectivity. Among his generation it was perhaps François Tosquelles, with his Spanish Civil War experience in the Catalan non-Stalinist Left, who argued most insistently the necessity to understand what kind of relationships set in a larger social world an activity opened up to. Transitional and, in particular, trans-actional objects were needed to enable exchanges with others that allied aggressive impulses to libidinal ones and were apt to enrich secondary narcissism. There was an evocative material dimension involved in the dynamics of exchange. How people handled themselves and presented themselves (*se portent*) was connected to the exchanges they were embedded in. Even before people began to reflect upon things, there had to be an implicit groundwork of rules – functioning as external attractors – that enabled the exchange. What was needed was an activity deeply rooted in the subjectivity of the individual that was participating in the construction of a social world: the very opposite of a dead-end assignment that, though known to be meaningless, had to be tackled endlessly, with at least a show of dogged persistence. Ergotherapy at an institution, if it was to have success, he argued, should not be like a new organ added to the body of the hospital but work like the hormonal system, furthering the growth and metabolism of the body.

If jobs did not perform this re-connecting and re-vitalising function, one of the consequences that seemed to resist the effects of short time rest was pervasive fatigue, a mental and bodily state that had risen in prominence in contemporary discourse but, irritatingly, bedevilled theoretical understanding. For the psychophysiology of work, it was difficult to pin down because it defied objective measurement in its development and impact on the individual. With many subjective, non-quantifiable factors evidently involved, the manifold manifestations of fatigue lacked a framework for proper analysis. What made matters worse was that attrition (*usure*) at work was regarded as external to their own fields of investigation by a plurality of disciplines, thus falling into a cranny beyond what each of them regarded as their methodologically properly constituted remit.

It might have helped if the lessons of Ignace Meyerson, founder of a historically grounded psychology, mindful of the socio-cultural context of human activity, had still widely been heeded, but he himself had been straddling the established boundaries of disciplines to an extent that made it impossible for him institutionally to establish his own school of thought. Beyond the epistemological difficulties resulting in an effective scotomisation of the subjective dimensions of fatigue within the academically constituted disciplines, there was also the problem that the sciences that dealt with labour problems did so on widely held utilitarian assumptions slanted towards solving the problems of the big players in the market and not ideally suited to an understanding of the problems of the individual worker. For psychiatrists, sudden fatigue remained a possible precursor of further trouble to come: but how exactly did this come about? Integration in a group and status at work seemed to protect against fatigue. Yet, Le Guillant's approach, which had yielded tangible results when focusing on house maids, ran into considerable difficulties when he investigated the complaints of French train drivers: he conceded that something was clearly amiss at their workplace but could not pin down and conceptually isolate the harmful factors involved.

Claude Veil's third way

Claude Veil, a generation younger than Sivadon and Le Guillant, and more markedly grounded in psychoanalysis and phenomenology than either of them, introduced new nuances in what amounted to the articulation of a third way: what rendered a situation pathological was the mounting saturation of a person's defences caused by work norms, the imperfections of which psychiatry throws some light upon. Understanding personal thresholds of tolerance is as important as extensive epidemiological research work. Disadaptation to the work he/she has been doing can happen to an individual for very tangled reasons at any given moment in time. Unless an exhaustion is correctly diagnosed and situated, the treatment of the resulting anxiety may reach an unsatisfactory stalemate. People can reach a point where they are so drenched in tiredness that, submerged in it, they have fallen prey to a measure of intoxication. If, as is common, the propensity to chronicity is thought to be lodged in the individual and not in his/her links to the environment, people who are considered as invalids will be pushed into social exclusion. We must therefore understand and take into account processes of *déliaison* to which the subject may find himself/herself exposed, as well as any available hinterland of counter-balancing measures. As Guillaume Le Blanc, reflecting as a philosopher on the work of Sivadon, Le Guillant and Veil, points out, there is always an inherent fragility in the creativity that an individual is able to muster when confronted with a situation which seriously throws into doubt the possibility of making one's activities fit into one's projects of identity. In continuation of previous leads by Sivadon, Veil keeps an eye on the economic balance of psychic investments of the subject while his phenomenological interests at the same time render him acutely aware of ways of being and feeling oneself in the world – something that draws him close to the ethnopsychoanalytic stance of Georges Devereux and, in particular, the interdependent entanglement between the inner and the outer proposed by the latter.

The waning of the movement

Although the movement in favour of the recognition of a psychopathology of work had consolidated its positions and had attained considerable sophistication – to which Veil's interdisciplinary research activities and positions within the *École Pratique des Hautes Études* and later the *École des Hautes Études en Sciences Sociales* greatly contributed – it petered out towards the end of the 1960s. Veil himself speaks of the following years as a trek through the wilderness (*la traversée du désert*). The reasons for this seem to be complex. On the basis of two government decrees (in 1960 and in 1970), French psychiatry was organised in a way that de-emphasised the importance of the psychiatric hospital. The territory of the nation was divided into sectors of around 70,000 inhabitants, which were served by smaller structures and interdisciplinary teams of mental health care, a measure usually referred to as *la sectorisation*. One of the examples of this new approach, much vaunted as a sign of progress in health policies in the Fifth Republic under de Gaulle, was the *ASM 13*, at which psychoanalysts from among the ranks of the *SPP*, were taking the lead. Seen from the perspective of 'the sector', the work place was extra-territorial to it and not the focus of their efforts. As Veil points out:

> For the activist fervently in favour of the *sectorisation* of psychiatric services, who had opted for the distribution of responsibility within mental health care according to the principle of residence, any move to take into account the workplace only threatened to upset things: anyone bold enough to suggest such a thing would qualify as an objective enemy.
>
> (Veil 1996, p. 334)

Concomitantly, the growth of the psychoanalytic movement in France was introducing a new emphasis: for many psychoanalysts, Veil observed, the worries of the psychiatrists of work were reeking of a futile interest in mere 'actual neurosis'. Within the Left, positions like that of Le Guillant were relegated to the margins by the new Structuralist interpretation of Marxism offered by Althusser. As Lacanism took off on its meteoric rise, interest in the activity of the subject at work, who might well be at a loss for words, was put on the back burner at the time. Within French psychoanalysis, concepts like psychic investment, affects and Freud's 'economic' angle on mental life became the concern of a rather cornered minority, and were by many regarded as less important than the key role of signifiers proposed by Lacan. Friedmann, who had pioneered the sociology of work and had influenced Sivadon, gradually turned from his former focus and took more of an interest in the media, communication and mass phenomena. When the students were on the march in May 1968, graffiti proclaiming *sous les pavés la plage* (beneath the pavement lies the beach) appeared all over Paris, a slogan as anti-*opératoire* as could conceivably be proposed. To do away with fatigue and suffering at work, not to study it, was for many the goal envisaged.

It was a decade which was to push work psychiatry – in the eyes of rebellious students peopled at best by geezers who had adjusted their sights for far too long to the pavement – into well-nigh oblivion. Seemingly the representatives of a dated approach, challenged in their conceptualisation by the new dominant ideologies, their previous chains of transmission unsettled, they faded into the background. What was left joined forces with Ergonomics or constituted research nuclei within higher studies. More recent digests of work accomplished in France show the abiding relevance of the problem but sometimes little awareness of earlier efforts to tackle it.

Towards new foundations

It took more than ten years for a new, second foundation of a psychopathology of work to take place. As Yves Clot points out about a different but related context: once the storm has blown over the social and institutional landscape is no longer the same. The first, post-war, generation had encountered considerable difficulties in trying to theorise the fruits of their experience. What had proved elusive for any psychiatric approach was the relationship of the subject to his/her own activity and the links this activity established to others. There was also some recognition that there was a considerable cultural distance between the psychiatrist and the worker.

By the late 1970s, the Structuralist ascendancy in social studies was waning and the concepts of subject, experience and agency were again becoming legitimate concerns in French academia. In 1980 Dejours presented his study *Travail: usure mentale* and initiated a new stage of inquiry by putting the focus on the inter-subjective processes mobilised by situations of work, a field of investigation he termed psychodynamics of work to encompass zones of experience that go beyond suffering. His psychoanalytic approach, centred on the clinic of the subject and its defence strategies, has since been challenged in critical dialogue by Clot, who has been proposing a 'clinic of activity' and a psychology of work environments.

For our purposes, it is essential to note that it was between 1960 and 1970 that psychoanalysts rediscovered a type of patient that had very much been in the focus of the school described, now virtually on the verge of demise. The name they gave to this phenomenon was strangely reminiscent of the world of work and its operating procedures that had been pushed to the margins. Half forgotten, the difficulties it had described in detail did not disappear. This is how Isabelle Billiard explains why the work psychiatrists of the 50s had a very difficult time understanding their patients:

Work is the object of 'doing' of 'giving a hand', of tacit consent among workers: the employed do their work more than they talk

of it […] if for no other reason, because their expression is put to defeat by the opacity and the 'inavowable character' of suffering.
(Billiard 2001a, p. 255)

On numerous occasions we encounter metaphors of energy and economy employed to discuss people whose dreams and daily lives are no longer on speaking terms but whose persistent malaise nonetheless defies any psychiatric understanding groping for factors of revitalisation. If the similarity is one in surface detail, it is yet close enough for it to be shrugged off as mere co-incidence. Edward Shorter, from his own perspective as a historian, has discussed the spread of fatigue as a mass phenomenon in the second half of the twentieth century and offered observations, presumably understood to be non-exhaustive, on particular medical subcultures centred on it. In a recent detailed and extensive study on the history of *la fatigue*, Georges Vigarello (2020) persuasively shows that much can be gained by delving more closely into the context in which the phenomenon appears.

Among the factors shaping experience, what happens at the job is certainly important. If work turns out to be an impasse, it is an impasse of considerable significance; if, on the other hand, a core team finds means to exercise creative agency in the midst of apparent disorganisation, it becomes a source of vital flux and steady revitalisation against all the odds.

Not surprisingly, it is the baffling multitude of social and personal contexts in which fatigue turns into incapacitating suffering that defined the field at which the new Psychopathology of Work in France cut its teeth. Psychoanalysts by the 1970s had inherited a phenomenon – at its most disquieting both chronic and endemic – that was not part of the core of their own clinical legacy. In trying to rise to the challenge they were, *grosso modo*, about to countenance, in the arena of their own clinical tradition, some of the theoretical moves the generation before them had been forced through in the course of their prolonged encounters with the terrain. As the Chinese strategist Sun Tzu reflected,

He who is ignorant of mountain and forest, defile and marsh, cannot lead an army. He who does not employ a guide, cannot gain advantage from the ground.
(Sun-tzu, translated in Ferguson 1908, p. 41f.)

We shall see in the next chapter on Dejours what psychoanalysts were beginning to make of this ground others had already fought battles on.

Sources

Billiard, I. (2001a), *Santé mentale et travail. L'émergence de la psychopathologie du travail*, Paris: La Dispute/SNÉDIT.

Billiard, I. (2001b), 'Claude Veil, un pionnier de la psychopathologie du travail', *Travailler* 5, pp. 175–188.

Billiard, I. (2002a), 'Les pères fondateurs de la psychopathologie du travail en butte à l'énigme du travail', *Cliniques Méditerranéennes* 66, pp. 11–29.

Billiard, I. (2002b), 'Lettre à la rédaction: réponse à l'article de S.Buisson "Les origines de la psychopathologie du travail: mythe ou légende?"', *Travailler* 8, pp. 211–214.

Buisson, S. (2002), 'Les origines de la psychopathologie du travail: mythe fondateur ou légende?' *Travailler* 8, pp. 199–210.

Callède, J.-P. (2021), '"Georges Vigarello, Histoire de la fatigue du Moyen Âge à nos jours"', *Revue européenne des sciences sociales*, online at: http://journals.openedition.org/ress/7240

Clot, Y. (1995), *Le travail sans l'homme? Pour une psychologie des milieux de travail et de vie*, Paris: La Découverte.

Clot, Y. (2006a), 'Aprés Le Guillant: quelle clinique du travail?', *Le drame humain du travail. Essais de psychopathologie du travail*, Toulouse: Érès, pp. 7–36.

Clot, Y. (2006b), 'Clinique du travail et clinique de l'activité', *Nouvelle Revue de Psychosociologie* 1, pp. 165–177.

Clot, Y. (2009), 'Postface. L'apport de François Tosquelles à la clinique du travail', in: Tosquelles, F. (1967), *Le travail thérapeutique à l'hôpital psychiatrique*, 2nd edition, Toulouse: Érès, pp. 143–162.

Clot, Y. (2010/2015), *Le travail à coeur. Pour en finir avec les risques psychosociaux*, new edition 2015, Paris: La Découverte.

Clot, Y. (2015), 'Postface à l'edition de 2015', in: Clot, Y., *Le travail à coeur. Pour en finir avec les risques psychosociaux*, Paris: La Découverte, pp. 189–196.

Cottereau, A. (1983), 'L'usure au travail: interrogations et refoulements', *Le Mouvement Social* 124, pp. 3–9.

Davoine, L. and Méda, D. (2008), 'Place et sens du travail en Europe. Une singularité française?'. *Document de Travail pour le Centre d'Étude de l'Emploi* 96(1).

Delion, P. (2009), 'Préface', in: Tosquelles, F. (1967/1972), *Le travail thérapeutique à l'hôpital psychiatrique*, new edition, Toulouse: Érès, pp. 7–15.

Delion, P. (2014), 'Préface', in: Tosquelles, F., *L'enseignement de la folie*, 2nd edition, Paris: Dunod, pp. vii–xvii.

Devereux, G. (1966), 'Dedans et dehors: la nature du stress', *Revue de Medecine Psychosomatique* 8, pp. 103–113.

Ferguson, E., transl., (1908), *Sun-tzu, the book of war: The military classic of the Far East*, London: J. Murray.

Ganem, V., Gernet, I. and Dejours, C. (2008), 'Le travail: que signifie ce terme en clinique et psychopathologie du travail?', *L'Information Psychiatrique* 84, pp. 801–807.

García Siso, A. (1993) 'El Dr. Francesc Tosquelles i Llauradó: Posición del autor dentro de la Psiquiatría catalana anterior a la Guerra Civil y la proyección de esta posición en su obra posterior' *Revista de la Asociación Española de Neuropsiquiatría* 13(46), 195–202.

Gourevitch, M. (2012), 'La législation sur les aliénés en France de la Révolution à la Monarchie de Juillet', in: Postel, J. and Quétel, C. eds, *Nouvelle histoire de la psychiatrie*, 2nd edition, pp. 172–179.

Hayat, M. (2008), 'Le psychodrame analytique, ses origines, son évolution, son aire d'application', in: Calevoi N., Darge, G., Gossart, R., Hayat, M., Kockelmeyer, S., Scandariato, R. and Sferrazza, R., *Le psychodrame psychanalytique métathérapeutique: Supervison, relance et dégagment*, Paris: De Boeck Supérieur, pp. 23–36.

Henckes, N. (2009a), 'Un tournant dans les régulations de l'institution psychiatrique: la trajectoire de la réforme des hôpitaux aux psychiatriques en France de l'avant-guerre aux années 1950', *Genèses* 76, pp. 76–98.

Henckes, N. (2009b), 'Les psychiatres et le handicap psychique. De l'après guerre aux années 1980', *Revue française des affaires sociales*, pp. 25–40.

Le Blanc, G. (2007), *Les maladies de l'homme normal*, Paris: Vrin.

Le Guillant, L. (1956), 'La névrose des téléphonistes', in: Le Guillant, L. (2006), *Le drame humain du travail. Essais de psychopathologie du travail*, Clot, Y. ed., Toulouse: Érès, pp. 131–148.

Le Guillant, L. (1957), 'Histoire de Madame L.', *La Raison* 18, pp. 82–94, also available in: Le Guillant, L. (2006), *Le drame humain du travail. Essais de psychopathologie du travail*, Clot, Y. ed., Toulouse: Érès, pp. 173–195.

Le Guillant, L. (1963), 'Incidences psychopathologiques de la condition de "bonne à tout faire"', in: Le Guillant, L. (2006), *Le drame humain du travail. Essais de psychopathologie du travail*, Clot, Y. ed., Toulouse: Érès, pp. 37–90.

Le Guillant, L. (1966), 'Réflexions sur une condition de travail particulièrement pénible: la VACMA', in: Le Guillant, L. (2006), *Le drame humain du travail. Essais de psychopathologie du travail*, Clot, Y. ed., Toulouse: Érès, pp. 149–171.

Le Guillant, L. (2006), *Le drame humain du travail. Essais de psychopathologie du travail*, Clot, Y. ed., Toulouse: Érès

Lhuilier, D. (2010), 'Les "risques psychosociaux": entre rémanence et méconnaissance', *Nouvelle Revue de Psychosociologie* 10, pp. 11–28.

Lhuilier, D. (2012), 'Introduction à l'œuvre de Claude Veil', in: Veil, C., *Naissance et actualité de la psychopathologie du travail*, Lhuilier, D. ed., Toulouse: Érès, pp. 9–51.

Molinier, P. and Flottes, A. (2012), 'Travail et santé mentale: approches cliniques', *Travail et emploi* 129, pp. 51–66.

Moreau Ricaud, M. (2004), 'Une "utopie" à la croisée de la psychiatrie et de la psychanalyse: la psychothérapie institutionelle', *Topique* 88, pp. 95–108.

Oury, J. and Gabarron-Garcia, F. (2010), 'Psychothérapie institutionelle et Guerre d'Espagne', *Chimères* 72, pp. 11–20.

Picard, D. (2006), 'Difficultes de la prévention des pathologies psychosociales liées au travail', *Management & Avenir* 8, pp. 199–217.

Pichot, P. (1996), *Un siècle de psychiatrie*, Paris: Collection Synthélabo.

Quétel, C. (2012a), 'Le vote de la loi de 1838', in: Postel, J. and Quétel, C. eds, *Nouvelle histoire de la psychiatrie*, 2nd edition, Paris: Dunod, pp. 180–186.

Quétel, C. (2012b), 'La vie quotidienne d'un asile d'aliénés à la fin du XIX siècle', Postel, J. and Quétel, C. eds, *Nouvelle histoire de la psychiatrie*, 2nd edition, Paris: Dunod, pp. 327–333.

Santiago-Delefosse, M. (2002), 'Notes de lecture: "Isabelle Billiard, Santé mentale et travail. L'émergence de la psychopathologie du travail, La Dispute, 2001, 283p."', *Travailler* 7, pp. 205–207.

Shorter, E. (1992), *From paralysis to fatigue. A history of psychosomatic illness in the modern era*, New York: The Free Press.

Sivadon, P. (1952), 'Psychopathologie du travail', *Évolution Psychiatrique* 1952(3), pp. 441–474.

Sivadon, P. (1977), 'La reeducation des fonctions mentales', in: Sivadon, P. and Gantheret, F. (1977), *La réeducation corporelle des fonctions mentales*, Paris: Les Éditions ESF, pp. 25–46.

Sivadon, P. and Amiel, R. (1969), *Psychopathologie du travail*, Paris: Les editions sociales françaises.

Sivadon, P. and Duron, J. (1979), *La santé mentale. La recherche de l'équilibre personnel et social dans la vie quotidienne*, Toulouse: Editeur Privat.

Sivadon, P. and Fernandez-Zoila, A. (1983), *Temps de travail, temps de vivre*, Brussels: Pierre Mardaga éditeur.

Torrente, J. (2004), *Le psychiatre et le travailleur. Cheminement de la psychopathologie du travail d'hier à demain*, Paris: Doin éditeurs.

Tosquelles, F. (1967/1972), *Le travail thérapeutique à l'hôpital psychiatrique*, new edition, Toulouse: Érès.

Tosquelles, F. (2003), 'Du group aux sources de la personne', in: Tosquelles, F., *De la personne au groupe. À propos des équipes soignantes*, Toulouse: Érès, pp. 91–147.

Trillat, É. (2012), 'Une histoire de la psychiatrie au Xxe siècle', in: Postel, J. and Quétel, C. eds, *Nouvelle histoire de la psychiatrie*, 2nd edition, Paris: Dunod, pp. 339–367.

Veil, C. (1957a), 'Phénoménologie du travail', in: Veil, C. (2012), *Naissance et actualité de la psychopathologie du travail*, Lhuilier, D. ed., Toulouse: Érès, pp. 53–85.

Veil, C. (1957b), 'Aspects médico-psychologiques de l'industrialisation moderne', in: Veil, C. (2012), *Naissance et actualité de la psychopathologie du travail*, Lhuilier, D. ed., Toulouse: Érès, pp. 87–114.

Veil, C. (1959), 'Les états d'épuisement', in: Veil, C. (2012), *Naissance et actualité de la psychopathologie du travail*, Lhuilier, D. ed., Toulouse: Érès, pp. 175–186.

Veil, C. (1964), 'Le législateur peut-il prévenir la chronicité?', in: Aboulker, P., Chertok, L and Sapir, M., *Psychosomatique et chronicité*, Paris: Librairie Maloine, pp. 335–337.

Veil, C. (1972), 'Fatigue et monotonie', in: Veil, C. (2012), *Naissance et actualité de la psychopathologie du travail*, Lhuilier, D. ed., Toulouse: Érès, pp. 235–286.

Veil, C. (1973), 'Epidémiologie des troubles névrotiques psychosomatiques et comportementaux', in: Sivadon, P., *Traité de psychologie médicale. Volume 3: La pathologie émotionnelle*, Paris: Presses Universitaires de France, pp. 71–84.

Veil, C. (1985), Où en est la psychopathologie du travail?', in: Veil, C. (2012), *Naissance et actualité de la psychopathologie du travail*, Lhuilier, D. ed., Toulouse: Érès, pp. 287–294.

Veil, C. (1994), 'L'imaginaire au travail', in: Veil, C. (2012), *Naissance et actualité de la psychopathologie du travail*, Lhuilier, D. ed., Toulouse: Érès, pp. 295–318.

Veil, C. (1996), 'Entretien avec Claude Veil', in: Veil, C. (2012), *Naissance et actualité de la psychopathologie du travail*, Lhuilier, D. ed., Toulouse: Érès, pp. 331–346.

Veil, C. (2012), *Naissance et actualité de la psychopathologie du travail*, Lhuilier, D. ed., Toulouse: Érès.

Vigarello, G. (2020), *Histoire de la fatigue. Du Moyen Âge à nos jours*, Paris: Éditions du Seuil.

von Bueltzingsloewen, I. (2002), 'Les "aliénés" morts de faim dans le hopitaux psychiatriques français sur l'Occupation', *Vingtième Siècle. Revue d'Histoire* 76, pp. 99–115.

von Bueltzingsloewen, I. (2007), *L'hécatombe des fous. La famine dans les hôpitaux psychiatriques français sous l'Occupation*, Paris: Flammarion.

von Bueltzingsloewen, I. (2008), 'Une étape dans la mise en question du modèle asilaire? La famine dans les hôpitaux psychiatriques français sour l'occupation', *Les Cahiers du Centre Georges Canguilhem* 2, pp. 47–61.

von Bueltzingsloewen, I. (2009), 'Histoire/Mémoire et transmision. Retour sur une enquête polémique: la famine dans les hôpitaux psychiatriques français sour l'occupation', in: Sassolas, M. ed., *Transmission et soins psychiques*, Toulouse: Érès.

von Bueltzingsloewen, I. (2010), 'Le militantisme en psychiatrie, de la libération à nos jours. Quelle histoire?!' *Sud/Nord* 25, pp. 13–26.

12

INDISPENSABLE EXTENSIONS
Christophe Dejours

Early descriptions of *opératoire* patients see them as adrift in the unstructured actual. This was at first believed to go with certain predominant personality traits. From the early 1980s, one line of reflection began to show a more pronounced interest in the arrangements a person entered into, both at the workplace and at home.

Obviously, nefarious adaptations to the dynamic resulting from this would have an impact on mental life. In this chapter I shall focus on the thought of Christophe Dejours, in whose work this approach has been developed most extensively. Member of the *Institut de Psychosomatique de Paris* (*IPSO*; since 1983), member of the *Association Psychanalytique de France*, and professor for Psychoanalysis, Health and Work at the *Conservatoire National des Arts et Métiers* (*CNAM*). He is president of the scientific council of the *Fondation Jean Laplanche*. For many years, Dejours has in creative ways been moving back and forth from studying the *mode opératoire* to investigating the *usure mentale*, the brutal mental attrition often encountered at work. At some distance from Pierre Marty's conceptual edifice, it shows that the consideration of *opératoire* modes of functioning went well with a move of psychoanalysis into new fields of application to which it had previously been extraneous.

While still a medical student, Dejours' interest was drawn to the abominable living conditions among immigrant workers. He has since conducted investigations in different professional environments, including the car industry, the building industry, cement works, the chemical industry, the nuclear industry and the police. At first, he encountered some animosity not only on the part of the management, but also from the unions, who did not take kindly to psychological explorations into the lives of their membership. When a wave of suicides struck the car industry and, more recently, *France Télécom*, he was very much in demand as a professional authority to elucidate the backgrounds of the events. The increased public attention also resulted in an investigation published by *CDFT France Télécom-Orange* on suffering at the work place, in which the professional help of Dejours was enlisted. A study of the relationship between psychiatry and the labourer credits his work with the revival of public interest in the psychopathology of work, which as a discipline had seemed in terminal decline by the end of the 1960s. To emphasise new considerations within a larger perspective, Dejours proposed to call the new discipline *psychodynamique du travail* rather than *psychopathologie du travail* from the early 1990s. He received the *Prix Maurice Bouvet* in 2001 for the sum of his contributions.

Dejours' work bears the signs of a long discussion process, in which arguments and counter-arguments have repeatedly been sifted to absorb new experiences and data, to revise positions and to present them in coherent form and clear language. It seems that his readership comprises two different groups, whose interests may touch but do not converge: his pychosomatic contributions are of clear interest to a psychoanalytic audience, while his ideas about the psychodynamics of work are more frequently discussed by a professional public focusing on social realities. Since I believe the two branches of his work form a whole, and as such are relevant to psychoanalysis, I will draw on both of them to describe his theoretical approach, which is in some continuation of Michel Fain's work, while at the same time influenced in important ways by Jean Laplanche.

Two threads of development: attachment versus libidinal subversion

In Dejours' approach it is not secure attachment that puts the body at ease but early contact with the fantasies of the environment. Desire has to be given the opportunity to work its wiles on the body if the subject is to keep in reasonably good shape. Dejours believes there exist two kinds of corporeal destinies intertwined in intricate ways. He focuses his investigations on what he terms the second body, which emerges in childhood in a process unlikely to be ever successfully completed from a first body of genetic endowment, physiological function and instinctual appetite. For all the usefulness of studies on this field of expertise, he believes, there is a hiatus with the prime preoccupations of psychoanalysis focusing on dream, fantasy and desire, subjective experiences that convey meaning and give direction to corporeal existence.

This surplus dimension, in Dejours' view, is contingent on a process he terms libidinal subversion, a development in which forbidden fantasies induced by the parents' sexuality inject covert layers of meaning into the adult–child relationship which then denaturalise the body, turning it away from its instinctual moorings and the dull weight of physiological factors. The emerging erotic body responds in novel ways, not hardwired into it at birth, to the stimuli of the world. As the child constructs his/her own sexuality by deciphering and subjectively translating the enigmatic messages directed to him/her, contaminated by adult sexuality in unconscious ways, he/she moves away from the sphere of biologically grounded instinct into the sphere of *pulsion*. Dejours stresses that Laplanche's work implies a theory of creative thinking: children have to strain to 'translate' the flood of enigmatic messages addressed to them into something coherent and comprehensible, which is never a predictable reproduction.

The carrier wave for adult messages, directed towards the child but inevitably affected and compromised by their own sexuality, is formed by the innate behavioural patterns that produce attachment. Caught in this tension, childcare induces a flowering of infantile sexuality in response to unacknowledged meaning hidden in the behaviour and speech of adults. The personal unconscious of the child is formed by residues of the infantile interpretation process that cannot further be broken down into a conscious translation of the messages. Liberties taken or restrictions imposed on body-to-body interaction leave their imprint on the nascent map of the erotic body in a series of sedimentations and, as a further consequence, define the extent and limits of unconscious fantasy.

Since the sensibility of the body is used to tentatively probe the world, not surprisingly, much of this affects the sensorium of the body's surface. Dejours sees natural conjunctions with Anzieu's theory of a skin-ego. It is this erotic body, and the demands it poses on the subject, which characterise the emerging mental life and conveys to it qualities that go beyond the merely intellectual: all communication, whether in words or in silence, will be accentuated by (inward and outward) movements of the body.

The mill by the waters: irrigation won from the torrents of the wilds

For any of this to happen, however, energy provided by the urges of nature has to be side-tracked off its course to gain shape in infantile sexuality so that the register of desire will be able to gain the upper hand on the register of need. Dejours uses the metaphor of the mill making use of water diverted from its natural riverbed to produce effects which potentially transform a whole landscape: *étayage* would correspond to the turning wheel which levies energy off the forces of instinct, sidetracking some of it, that is then put to use as libidinal *pulsion*. Not only will the riverbed be relieved of the potential overflow of turbulent excitement, it will also adapt to the new economy of forces as it turns into something that is no longer raw nature.

In Dejours' picture, the turns of the wheel produce a new rhythm of movement, regulating the respective plenitude and scarcity of water in canals down mill in new ways not pre-patterned in the given extraneous currents of the river: side channelling the brute forces of energy will also relieve the riverbed of pressure. If, and only if, this scheme of things is operating, will it be possible to apply Freud's dynamic viewpoint to drives, instead of the economic viewpoint more adapted to the understanding of comparatively inchoate, unchanneled forces. *Pulsion*, in order to come into its own, needs the other. Like Marty, Dejours is inclined to see Freud's First and Second Topography not as mere stages in Freud's thinking but as successive stages in any successful developmental process. Once the basic structures, contingent on successful *étayage*, are in place, energy is syphoned off auto-conservation to generate desire directed towards erotic goals that put self-conservation at risk.

Dejours underlines the paradoxical continuity between Freud's earlier theory of drives and his last theory of drives, which, in effect, means that the forces of auto-conservation seeking homeostasis finish up on the side of the death drive. Although attachment, as we have seen, serves as the carrier medium of libidinal subversion, it also produces residual zones untouched by libido as bastions of future psychic muteness, potential inroads to decompensation under the sway of the *pulsion de mort*. Erotic passion, like a biphasic wave, regularly introduces shocking, unsettling disturbance to pre-existant stabilities in its systole, which then in its diastole have to be reworked and integrated in dreamlife. In other words: Eros as a binding force and the sexual in its quest for excitement contradictorily work both with and against each other. Failure to achieve an equilibrium in this throws the subject back on the unhinging potential of ancient mutenesses to undo what has been developed so far.

Towards a situated history of selective numbness: zones gone cold

As we have seen, in Dejours' view, the spark kindled in the child's psyche originates from contact with worlds of adult fantasy. While the encounter between the adult and the child stimulates desire, it also produces zones practically impervious to it. When the adult takes care of the child, his/her unconscious is solicited in the close contact between bodies and nascent infantile sexuality reactivates conflicts in the carer stemming from his/her own childhood. Bodily registers that are excluded from play with the child are bound to leave their negative imprints on the emerging geography of the erogenous body of the child. Reasons for these parentally imposed dull blanks may vary: with the parents themselves these zones may have been left cold and unresponsive or, on the contrary, too frighteningly excitable. Certain affects may appear to be altogether inaccessible to the parents.

These areas will be excluded from the registers of interpersonal expression and, given the somatic disposition, will be the zones of choice for future disease to strike if the subject is exposed to a crisis which his/her mental system cannot perlaborate. Not that the symptom as such is *bête* (dumb) – as de M'Uzan famously postulated for psychosomatic disease – but the zone at which it strikes has been numbed out on the inner maps resulting from the bodily exchanges between adult and infant. Bodily zones that fell prey to proscription have been radically banished from emerging mental maps. This is particularly pronounced if the adult feels acutely threatened by scenarios initiated by the child he/she cannot handle and which have to be excluded by all possible means. If the child invites play on this territory, there will be a violent backlash on the part of the parents. In these regions, the protective shield of the libidinal body will not assume its full function, leaving the dead weight of physiology, mentally inadequately integrated, in its wake. Complex disablement results from early interactions that by their very nature are difficult to bring into narrative form.

Some families, at a very basic level, have fundamental problems with being made up of three and not just two, making it difficult for the mother to oscillate between being a mother and being a mistress to the father of the child. Personal structure builds on intersubjective processes as they unfold in their different temporal layers: the body of a person bears the mark of the erotic history of his/her parents and of what they loathed. The infant learns early on that it has to play its part in reassuring the parents to prevent a surge of excitement, which, were it to occur, would establish a connection to a traumatic primal scene inaccessible to thinking. Patients who turn to somatic malady as a remedy in crisis often come from a family background in which a violent parental attack directed against the child's capacity for reverie and fantasy is a distinct possibility. As a result, the child becomes an early expert in laying hold of perceptions which calm down his/her parents, distracting them from possible fantasmatic entanglements, stressing elements of control and having a grip on things. When the infant encounters a reality which the mother herself is not able to symbolise, it identifies, as Fain and Braunschweig have suggested, with the mother, joining her attitude of denial to protect her from threatening break down.

Another solution to the dilemma is to provoke the parent so that the unbearable tension is channelled into a violent beating of the child, and, as a consequence, evacuated so that calm is re-established. In contrast to the psychotic person, in whom thinking is warped, a limitation of mental territory and a restriction on the libidinal use of the body is more often the dominant problem for people with marked psychosomatic vulnerabilities. Deficiencies in the make-up of the 'second body' will lead to a lack of intuition and inventive ingenuity. For Dejours, it is the body, or rather the second body that pre-shapes thinking as it follows affect. If, as André Green (1973, p. 221) has suggested, affect is the '*regard sur le corps ému*', there are children for whom neither the regard on, nor the unrestricted movement of, the body can feel safe. Since this state of affairs has been prevented from forming any link to thought, it cannot be repressed in the classical sense.

People suffering from these restrictions, in order to keep stable, try to neutralise within themselves any proprioceptive sensation that might, if followed in surging excitement, lead down a slippery slope. The problem what to do with 'impossible' excitement is exacerbated if socio-cognitive resources are scarce because early learning processes were hampered; lack of education, as such, does not preclude a rich fantasy life.

The subject pushed against its own unresponsiveness

If in adult life a person is in a situation calling for the activation of functions laid waste to from childhood, he/she is helplessly pushed against an inexplicable, selective impotence. Coming up against it feels like staring death into the face. The subject finds no way to give psychic form to the tension he/she is under and, primarily, tries to safeguard him/herself against the emptiness in him/herself where the unavailable function should have sprung into being. The first impulse would be to annihilate the source of trouble: the object necessitating a response not forthcoming from within.

There is a dangerous crisis if the subject finds himself/herself totally incapable of putting the inner drama into scenes but at the same time finds no means of projecting it on an inter-subjective stage. If there were traces of expressive behaviour, this could, in advance of understanding, prepare the way for it. Since there are not, this means that there will be no possibility to observe the response of others. *Pulsion* – always addressed to the other – has been eclipsed and the subject is at the mercy of his/her rather confused residual instincts. While some patients try to find recognition at the job, as an attempt at sublimation, this will only work if there are exchanges with a sufficiently supple preconscious. A violent first response inhibited, a somatic affection in the body part interdicted to 'speak' could be the means of last resort. Dejours uses the concept of *l'agir expressif* – a use of the body in symbolic interaction – that is crucial to further development. If barred, a pathogenic development can easily set in.

Dejours (2001a), in his vignette of Madame B., describes the case of a sixty-year-old lady working as a high-ranking civil servant working in the administration of museums. Of Jewish origin, she had fled to France towards the end of World War II, where she learned the language, and despite a difficult start, had a brilliant career. Her overarching goal, taking precedence over relationships, is to be able to lay the foundations of a museum which she has been planning. Whenever her husband is slighted or experiences a setback at work, this reverberates sharply with her. She feels incapable of expressing hostile sentiments in situations that hurt her, if only in defence. The lung cancer with which she has been diagnosed could well be a consequence of her strong habit of smoking. But there is also a fracture in her life she herself is aware of. It occurred two years before the tumour was discovered: her daughter, Jewish without knowing it, married a handsome aristocrat, whose father is an active, militant member of a right-wing extremist party, leading members of which are frequently present at family gatherings of the in-laws. Antisemitism has invaded her family space and all ways to address this seem barred because there is no possible register of expression available to her.

This is a problem she is familiar with: both her parents were quite incapable of showing anger. The unbearable situation charges her with a tension that cannot be laid to rest because it is kept from social exchange. Since no dramaturgy of wrath is conceivable, the depths of pain are driven underground and become invisible. Whenever tension mounts, she effaces it by lighting another cigarette, a habit which exposes her to considerable risk since there is a high incidence of cancer running in her family. If the subject disposes of no mental resources to grant a stage to what hits him/her, one of his/her last resources is to meddle with the ability to receive unbearable stimuli, excluding them from sinking into the preconscious. They are being put down before they can get saturated with meaning capable of repression, resulting in the much more radical means of suppression. In this it is related to inhibition, but works at a more basic level, closer to the body. As one of the last resorts against reality for the psychotically untalented, suppression provides an alternative to suicidal acts by re-routing tension in ways that in the end present the bill to the body.

Putting fantasy at bay for the sake of the job

Dejours provides an example of how this works from an area of experience in which it has been studied more fully as a regular feature of social life: highly mechanised industrial piece-work, where the worker has to regiment his mental life in order to keep up with the necessities of the stereotyped, repetitive, machine-geared processes. In jobs like this, a paralysis of all fantasy is actively sought for, so as to be able to accomplish the work at hand. Dejours concedes that the amount of mental elaboration of being swallowed up by the machinery of work seems to vary. He refers to Miklós Haraszti's *Le salaire aux pieces* and Charly Boyadjian's *Le nuit de machines* as witnesses in written form of lives on the short leash of piece work. For some people at least, as Haraszti shows, the imperative of keeping themselves fully functional cannot be conciliated with even momentary flights of fantasy. One instructive way for workers to handle this is to throw themselves head over heels (*à corps perdu*, one might be tempted to say) into the work rhythm to suppress any mental activity to become nothing but the act. They turn insensitive by means of senso-motoric hyperactivity, a mode of auto-acceleration that deliberately steps up the pace so as to channel into motricity what cannot be disposed of in any other way.

> For, if one were to take too much pleasure in thinking freely and in meeting up with oneself again, one had to, after returning to the conveyor belt line, to start afresh the whole infernal cycle of auto-acceleration necessary to reach the stage of adaptive mindless brutishness. Much better to keep up the defences outside work and to avoid letting go the reins on the harnessing collar put on free imagination. Leisure time, if there is, is used to engage in exhausting activities so as to leave place, if one finds calm eventually, to nothing else but the wish for sleep,
> (Dejours 2009c 2: p. 59)

To sync into the rush of sense impressions so as to stay adapted, especially if attention has to remain relentlessly transfixed, may actually be experienced as helpful by the person. At one factory, workers protested against noise reduction measures taken at their workplace because the ceaseless background din helped them to keep up their vigilance directed towards a screen. The vanishing of customary ambient noise levels was experienced not as an improvement but as an additional source of stress. In fact, the way in which the economy of sense perception and motricity is being managed may be an important tool in constructively acquitting oneself of the job at hand. To keep at bay a possible invasion of thinking, for some people, is one step towards staying on top of things. Perception is being glued to the meaningless so as to side-line representation, which could leave its traces on inner maps in ways too painful to be countenanced. Aggression, sometimes artificially induced by the company's management to enhance output, has to be marshalled and channelled into movement and speed. Interruptions, if they occur, call to mind the precarious nature of established equilibria. This is one reason why times of rest prescribed by a doctor are often seen as a threat to the status quo and the ability to bear the depersonalisation required at work. Far from being a phenomenon restricted to a relatively small number of pathological cases, Dejours believes that what psychosomatics calls *pensée opératoire* concerns potentially most of the workers he encounters. The difference to the cases studies by Szwec, Dejours argues, is that in Szwec's view a disposition is needed that turns people into 'voluntary galley slaves'. In those investigated and documented by Dejours, *pensée opératoire* is something that is related to the workplace and which disappears once the situation there changes.

The costs of maintaining defensive shields

The functional shield kept up at work will also have to be negotiated when a parent returns to a home with small children. On such occasions, a potential zone of play, desire and curiosity is brought into contact with zones of self-effacement and inhibited aggression. The way this is being handled will have long term consequences. Sometimes, traditional ways of doing things are called into question and have to be abandoned. Dejours (2010a) recounts the case of Mr. A., an Algerian man in his forties, who had been working in the building industry for about fifteen years. He was earning about 1,000 Euro per month, left home at 5:45 and came back at 20:15. When he came to France, he had to leave his wife, with whom he had six children, behind. The marriage was one of mutual choice, not arranged in traditional manner by the parents. He talks of his wife and children with great tenderness. For many years he had been saving to make it possible for his wife and children to move to France. When he finally managed to accomplish the transfer of his family, they had another child. Then he fell sick.

Various possibilities of inter-psychic and interpersonal conflicts were explored but did not yield promising material. What finally emerged was that the amount of feeling he had for his newly arrived family had caused a lack of adaptation to the harsh requirements of his workplace and the type of person he needed to be there. He found that he could no longer keep up his defensive shield and at the same time permit himself to be tender at home. Mr. A. managed to change his place of work from the building site to a place of small commerce. He regained his health and evidently thrived. The balances in his life had become manageable again, the reverse outcome of the alternate possibility in which the job is kept but the affective register at home severely curtailed. In such a case, children may learn quickly to give the parent the wide berth he/she so patently requires – defensive strategies thus have a pernicious tendency to be exported.

Although not every patient has a work-related symptomatology, it is instructive to understand the manoeuvres of self-effacement radiating from the job. They appear to be the defensive measure of choice in other cases as well, when analysts see patients seemingly incapable of grasping the transformational potential of the encounter. At times, the patient only shows a vivid response to something that interferes with the frame of the encounters, an incident often involuntary on the part of the analyst. In such a situation the analyst can adapt as best as he/she can, modify the *cadre* or confront the violence contained in the attempt to turn him/her into something inanimate. For this he needs an approximative assessment of the forces at work in the patient.

Dejours, in a recent contribution, points out that it took many years before a public debate between perspectives focusing on the clinic of work and those focusing on psychoanalytic psychosomatics was able to be held, on the topic of fatigue, in 2004. There, one of the points of divergence was a difference in the assessment of where to locate the root of the trouble: would one rather see hyper-activism as a personal problem or rather as something emanating from the workplace people need to adapt to? Based on his clinical experience with a patient whose illness was the result of improper treatment to which he was enticed by a criminal medical network, and whose mental situation was much improved by treatment, Dejours raises the question whether reduced mental functioning might not be the consequence, rather than the cause, of somatic illness.

Splitting as core of a Third Topography

Dejours observes that there are neurotic patients who regularly make use of non-neurotic defence mechanisms. If suppression were to be regularly pointing towards a non-neurotic character structure, this should not occur. Discerning in a patient excitement not tied to meaning, one might be tempted to give interventions that provide a protective shield against it. The goal then would be to avoid a crisis that might draw the rug under a patient suspected of dangerously lacking in structural robustness. This, Dejours points out, is not the only way to view things. Dejours believes that Freud's concept of a split in the Me – according to which a patient might function in two different modes mutually out of touch with each other – has not received attention enough in psychosomatic theory. Yet, it is a challenge to bring splits in the subject into relation with the topographical maps sketched out by Freud. How can one conceive of two different modes of mental functioning within the same subject?

The amental unconscious

In his Third Topography, Dejours works with the assumption that there are two different sectors of the unconscious. In one sector neurotic repression has worked and material of a sexual nature keeps pressing into the preconscious. The other sector is the product of violence on the part of the parent(s) exercised against the thinking capacity of the infant. It corresponds to mute zones of the body excluded from the infantile erogenous body. Since its development took place outside thinking, Dejours terms it *l'inconscient amental*. It does not produce mental activity. When activated by events, it spawns disintegration of the Me and goads the subject to compulsive behaviour. Whether this activation takes place depends on the quality of compensating arrangements taken by patients in their lives. Quite possibly, for prolonged periods of their lives, their amental unconscious will rest mute.

What is bolstering the dyke put up to provide a barrier against the amental unconscious is an implementation of *opératoire* thought. In a 'normally' functioning individual the dyke put up against the amental holds and the subject appears to be reasonably well adapted. The question of the relative size of these 'territories', situated on either side of the split, is of considerable consequence. Although there are zones of the amental in everyone, the question is how extensive they are in comparison to the remaining part of the personality, in which ordinary repression keeps up a reasonably functioning dynamic. Is there enough of an erotic body left to hold out against the mute traces of violence if life takes a difficult turn?

There is a zone of heightened sensibility of the unconscious, as suggested by Fain (1981a), which is a psychic territory in which the two compartments of the unconscious converge in contact with outside reality. It is not possible to experience the territory beyond the dyke directly, but it may become accessible in an encounter with reality. Potentially traumatic stimuli arriving there impact on layers of the preconscious doing its best to ring-fence the amental: its only strong bulwark is denial. If this line of defence does not hold, decompensation threatens. The psychotic will hallucinate, while those for whom their character forms a rigid fortress, will channel it, bypassing the mental apparatus, into action. In cases where the breach is not too massive, and containable, the perception of it may be processed after the event.

> In a way, one could say that reality has provided an 'interpretation' from outside of a particular state of excitement in the body after the lifting of denial in the encounter with reality. This 'interpretation', which works directly on a perceptive level and involves the sense organs, is different from the analytic interpretation.
> (Dejours 2001a, p. 95)

At the end of this process, the repressed unconscious has absorbed new material. Further encounters with reality will be able to draw on already established memory traces. Finding yourself doing something you would not have done in your dreams will provide food for thoughts. Little by little territory may be won from the amental by displacing the dyke so as to increase the zone of the neurotic unconscious.

If this encounter is too unsettling, but can neither be repressed nor rejected, the response will have to be forged in the register of violence. This may range from strategic aggression against unbearable parts of reality to violent, uncontrollable fits. In other cases in which all resistance to reality is deemed to be futile, a vehement suppression of all motions of violence takes place, leading sometimes to moments of stupor or more long-term channels of somatisation. If excitation remains unbridled, it will trigger mental confusion throwing into disarray the psychic apparatus. There may also be sexual co-excitation, with the erotic element a passenger on a ride offered by violence: interpreting only the erotic element will not be effective.

Dejours avails himself of the explanatory potential of his Third Topography to differentiate between phenomena that bear a certain resemblance to each other but present with significant elements of divergence. Thus, the discourse of a socially well-embedded paranoid person may bear a surface similarity to the *opératoire* one. What distinguishes them is the amount of passion involved in paranoid reasoning, reaching peaks of exasperation it does not have in the *opératoire*, for whom the ultimate defence is in his character. Paranoiacs make use of hypertonic operational thinking, while the classical mode of *pensee opératoire* is hypotonic. In the latter, there is less agitated pressure from the amental. In case of crisis, pressure is directed towards the body so that the split can be maintained: the pathological character at the height of the crisis can appear not only quite normal but calm, gentle and settled. Behind this camouflage, the violence at the root of the decompensation stays hidden. Once it is routed into corporeal responses, it will shape the future handling of crises. What was originally a breach has turned a safety valve. There is the likelihood it will be used again.

We should, Dejours insists, bear in mind that defensive strategies always form a whole: although one particular mode may predominate, others can be used as accessories in a complementary fashion. He very much doubts that defences can be classified according to personality types, and *contra* Marty, maintains that marked neurotic and psychotic structures do not necessarily protect from somatisation and from resorting to acts that bypass the preconscious – which constitute a defence open to all. Defensive strategies will be embedded in the social and built on what was acquired in early childhood. This will play out differently depending on job choices: fighter pilots have better chances than labourers in the construction industry to tap into childhood fantasies. The social stage at which inner resonances can be sought and found takes different shapes depending on the structure of the work field, or constraints of gender roles in a particular environment. Sublimation or suppression of desires are choices intimately linked to the nature of the job and the space for self-realisation it permits.

The amental – a reservation of the *pulsion de mort*?

There are close connections between the amental and the *pulsion de mort*. The amental forms a reservoir of lethal potential: it is closely associated with the compulsion to repetition; violent in nature, it attacks all binding capacity. This push towards deadly dissolution bypasses elaborative channels of the preconscious along lines untouched by desire. External violence is resorted to so as to counteract the looming disorganisation of thought.

Alternatively, relief may be sought by resorting to the exercise of sense perception in compulsive ways, a recourse unpropitious to sublimation. Since the amental cannot be fed into thought, the subject is driven to find in the outside world a situation that somehow offers a form – unattainable inwardly – to the motion he/she is currently experiencing. This does not create anything new, a result which is hardly noticed because there is little lasting memory of these acts. Satisfaction by perception does not destabilise the splits under the shadow of which it blossoms, and usually receives the benedictions of society, which does not feel threatened by it: it is also an innocuous activity for children whose parents would respond aversely to unbridled fantasy.

There are other ways in which society lends support to the inner balances of the person who cannot respond more personally to the challenges posed by the moment: it provides thoughts ready-to-use, loaned from the social imaginary of the times (*pensée d'emprunt*), which fit in well enough to patch up the gaping absence of a response that would mobilise the subject more fully. Once the link between the amental and the trappings of the social imaginary has been formed, the relative gain has to be propped up by an arrangement continuously bypassing thought. The subjective is put into abeyance, in a move that, for Dejours, does not partake of passion but owes everything to compulsion. If the split holds, a certain measure of normality can be maintained.

Dejours takes care to differentiate this from Laplanche's *pulsion sexuelle de mort*. He defines *sexuel* as any activity actively engaged in or passively submitted to that aims to increase within the body sensual effects of excitement. To this he contrasts cases where death is wrought by a compulsion lashing out against a body deserted of the power to experience itself: a reaction *in extremis* against the terror to watch on as subjectivity slips away and what is left is hurled into an abysmal fall down into a body *sans pulsion*. There is a third possibility: somewhere along this tumble into nothingness, sexual co-excitation may kick in, which will turn the free fall into something capable of ascension. In spite of this possible liaison, Dejours insists on the fundamental difference between *pulsion* and *compulsion*, maintaining that the latter always takes its force from the cold, the empty, the devitalised, which nestles in flawed erotic maps of the body.

The gendered distribution of suffering

Domestic life, as we have seen, plays an important part in a person's overall balances. The way erotic love tends to more permanent arrangements has important consequences for identity, narcissism and sexuality and will entail a distribution of roles in looking after shared affairs. Since these roles will not be identical for the two partners, the relationship will take place within a force field of inequalities aggravated by corresponding problems in socially established gender roles. Love hearkens back to childhood, in which care, attention and attachment in asymmetrical relationships of authority were closely linked. This will bring into play questions of domination versus submission. The one who submits will accept the lion's share of the domestic workload and this, in a heterosexual couple, will normally be the woman.

Paradoxically, the sensuously erotic also activates zones of alienation that are difficult to grasp for sociological theory. They are recalcitrant to the work of thought even in psychoanalysis. Increased self-love founded on the ability of the body to experience pleasure and give pleasure with a concomitant heightened sense of autonomy in the erotic register perplexingly reawakens questions of dependence on the other and his/her gaze. With the *pulsion* to get a grip on things/the other entering into play, some actively seek out a partner whom they can manipulate or make the object of their cruelty, giving rise to a tyrannical relationship. To make the other subservient to one's need is also a means to keep the upper hand vis-à-vis one's own amental. The split they keep in place prevents them from feeling any culpability about this; the stability of the arrangement depends on the capacity not to think conveyed by it. Alliances may be formed which grant both partners the feasibility to bolster up their splits, resulting in uneasy equilibria between need and desire.

Although, in principle, the positions may be reversed between the partners, this is not likely to happen: relationships tend to stabilise into inequality. Being exploited at the work place for a woman thus may be exacerbated by being subjected to the domination of her spouse in a relationship which, though it may have originated in an erotic encounter, has settled down into the dreary humdrum of self-demeaning dependency. This state of affairs is more often denied by the man, whilst acknowledged by the woman. Since denial is frequently an integral part of the collective defensive strategies of men at work, this is complemented by a similar denial of any dependence vis-à-vis the spouse. This denial protects the husband from a potential, painful loss of composure. Suffering is always sexed both in the family and at work.

Dejours builds on the difference between sex and gender acknowledged in the work of Laplanche. If gender is a social construction, it still becomes part of the *vie d'âme* in a process of creative self-appropriation. Assignation, as widely discussed in feminist literature, in Dejours' view, is the sum total of all messages transmitted to the infant on the matter of gender identity. An essential conduit to the child is formed by mothering, something into which a considerable amount of work is invested by the mother, understood as maternal work by Jane Messer. Messer (2013), taken up by Dejours, emphasises the discrepancies between what a mother would like to feel, what she ought to feel and what she tries to feel, and the burdens this places on her. Dejours thinks that the psychoanalytic take on the sexual is considerably enriched by the concept of assignation, which provides an angle that might turn out to be more Freudian than Freud's own social theory.

As Dejours observes, at the workplace the social should not and cannot be reduced to the sexual. If a young woman wishes, as in a case he presents (2010b), to have a differentiated relationship to men in her personal life but does not want to be dominated by men in her social life, it would be a mistake for the psychoanalyst to interpret this as simply a phallic demand. Not yet twenty, Mlle Mulvir refuses to give up her passion for electronics but, in order to do so, has to adopt strategies to blend in at her workplace dominated by men. Certainly, the psychosexual conflict needs to be addressed. But the analyst also has to learn to understand when developments in sexual identity are threatened by the psychodynamics of the workplace.

Work as the second arena central to self-fulfilment

Since identity has two mainstays of self-fulfilment in love and in work, inquiries into one cannot be separated from those into the other. Dejours traces Freud's thinking on work: If one defines work as an activity of either production or in services there is little to go on. Yet, work can never be a factor neutral to a person's self esteem and mental balances. It puts a person into contact with a reality independent of his/her wishes that resists attempts at mastery. It is from the clash of confronting a subject with concrete material at hand that new shape arises. This is an intermediary stage Freud leaves out of consideration. There are two stages: one of experiencing a setback in the struggle with the task; and one of rising up to the challenge in finding new ways of dealing with it in making use of one's body. Interposed between the two, dreamlife is the subjective zone in which the relationship of the body to the world is being reworked.

In most cases, work will require a cooperation with others, the results of which cannot be easily predicted. Work, Dejours suggests, provides people who look back on a chequered history of erotic encounters with a second chance to find out what they are, can become and can reach out for. Failure to be recognised on this important social field, where one's mettle is tested, is bound to be a source of destabilisation and will put an additional strain on the domestic arrangements of the individual. There is the continuing paradox of a double centrality of work and love in the unfolding of a person's life.

If things go wrong, both the legacies of childhood and the hazards of life at work contribute to the *mêlée*. It stands to reason that the individual will go to any lengths not to be pushed against his/her own limitations. A split in the personality, as we have seen, is maintained for protection. To choose a socially recognised occupation grants social legitimacy to partitioned off impulses.

Mental erosion as a cumulative factor in nefarious arrangements

Dejours emphasises that the real world is a permanent challenge to the individual: it consistently resists comprehensive description and is recalcitrant to being mentally provided with a handle. Tradition provides various resources that bring perception and symbolisation to bear on the task. From this repository of techniques, various defensive strategies to deal with the exigencies of work place are collectively cultivated. To be socially accepted at the job, one has to be seen to be a co-player in the performance of their implementation. They might range from enforced superficial conviviality to pouring manly derision on the physical risks at the work site. While these are ploys to maintain a cheerful front, they also perpetuate situations that produce the very tensions they are charged with ritually to keep in check. Tributes to a mandatory can-do mentality, they work like an anaesthetic that permits the subject to keep opaque to him/herself the causes for his/her suffering and to reject out-of-hand any need for change.

To make things worse, social zones of relatively relaxed informal exchange between employees are increasingly regulated away and pushed off the premises. It is the resulting compartmentalisation of suffering, shut off from finding ways into expression, that is apparently among the causes for an increasing number of work-related suicides in France. This includes suicide by highly motivated and qualified members of staff driven to despair by the cynical power play at work, acts of desperation that do not fit easily into socially acceptable narratives. The subject that does away with himself/herself may well want to preserve subjectivity in one final expression, while the person who delivers what is required, in order to do accomplish this, may have to do away with his/her own affectivity in a prescribed *mode opératoire* that leaves little emotional resonance with one's own sources of pleasure: suffering, without resonance, becomes inaudible and invisible, even to oneself if deprived of any conceivable audience as a court of appeal. In this perspective, normality becomes an enigma: how do people at work manage to resist its constraints and ward off decompensation and lunacy?

Dejours is able to show that superficial epithets like professional hyperactivity may hide more than they reveal if not backed up by careful investigation of the particular circumstances encountered by the patient concerned. In a quite similar manner, one must suppose, the *mode opératoire* has to be carefully placed into the context of the total situation of the person numbed by it. This may be of particular importance because there are indications that work places select people whose foibles and weaknesses pre-dispose them for the defensive strategies required there. The biographically grounded personal *opératoire* and the socially functional *opératoire*, one has to conclude, must liaise to maximise the effect of defensive mindlessness. On the whole, Dejours seems to be interested in forms of suffering which, at first glance, do not strike us as conspicuous but constantly trickle into increasingly strained containers, wearing down long-accustomed resistance, incrementally reaching ever higher levels of the as yet just but hardly bearable.

Akrasia facilitated by a split

For all of this, the maintenance of a fundamental split in the subject is indispensable:

This split which traverses the whole of the psyche [*l'appareil psychique*], including the unconscious, installs in the functioning of the soul [*dans le fonctionnement psychique (ou "animique")*] the fundamental possibility of a duplicity which is perhaps the fundamental problem left behind by this trajectory between sexuality and work. The human being is double. In the name of work, of productivity and of rentability, people can be led to provide support to acts which they morally disapprove of. And they do not always enter into crisis, in spite of the flagrant contradictions.

(Dejours 2009c 1: p. 186)

The weakness of will – *akrasia*, according to the ancients – shown in the lack of action taken is accompanied by intellectual sloth making use of slogans to hide behind, which again serve as a collective screen of defence: 'things are like that', 'it has always been like this', 'there is no choice'. This simple device permits to maintain the split without too much effort and to live both as a moral being as an opportunist, and – thanks to this – in 'good health'. Apparently, for the subject thus stabilised, it would not do at all to get unduly curious about things: what exactly would be the use of that? In Dejours' assessment, the *opératoire* becomes a superb tool of staying on course without being too much bothered about how one manages to achieve this and warding off any need for change.

Métis: applied social intelligence as an act of covert infiltration

While various exertions like hyper-virility, submission, and even feminine competence as such, or self-irony, grant only limited protection. In the long run, there is a manoeuvre, which, given minimal opportunity, manages to infiltrate social intelligence into sometimes oppressive external conditions. Dejours reminds his readers of the ancient Greek word *métis*: the cunning which dares to trust one's implicit experience to deal with emergent situations for which official regulations provide no guidance at best, asking for the total suffocation of common sense, at worst. It is an intelligence

> constantly in breach with norms and reglementations, it is an intelligence fundamentally transgressive. It is at the heart of what one calls *métier*: this is *métis* or 'cunning intelligence' ['*intelligence rusée*']

> [...] it subverts [official reglementation] for the purpose of work and in order to attain objectives by using more efficient procedures than the strict implementation of prescribed modes *opératoires.*
> (Dejours and Abdoucheli 1990, p. 90f.)

This very much seems to bear a family resemblance to a *subversion libidinale* adapted under the conditions of the work-place. Engaging in it is a way not to avoid going *opératoire* in a psychoanalytic sense. Ambiguous signals of the hierarchy about what really counts are creatively decoded so as to unlock new territories of movement which enable experience that can *post festum* be re-introjected to increase subjectivity. This requires spaces that can be opened up, if needs be covertly, and made 're-permeable' for subjective agency to introject – one might say with Ferenczi – and not just to incorporate. If this can be fed into social communication, work, though linked to suffering, will be instrumental to the expanding of subjectivity. Where this is not possible, suffering is increased. The psychodynamics of work, as a discipline, attempts to throw light on actions that help to transform suffering by reintroducing creativity into social space.

As we have seen, Dejours puts what has been discussed as *opératoire* into a larger context. There is a story to be heard about mental erosion, though the subject may be at a loss to know how to tell it. In the next chapter we shall see Jacques Press focusing on the destruction of frameworks needed for the individual to make sense of his/her own experience and how psychoanalysis may help or hinder this process.

Sources

Alderson, M. (2004), 'La psychodynamique du travail: object, considérations épistémologiques, concepts et prémisses théoriques', *Santé Mentale au Québec* 29(1), pp. 243–260.

Angella, M. (2016), 'Work, recognition and subjectivity: Relocating the connection between work and social pathologies', *European Journal of Social Theory* 19(3), pp. 340–354.

Berthou, B. and Guislain, G. (2005), *Les grands auteurs contemporains*, Paris: Jeunes Éditions.

Boyadjian, C. (1978), *La nuit des machines*, Paris: Gallimard.

CDFT France Télécom-Orange and Dejours, C. (2012), *Souffrance au travail. Regards croisés sur des cas concrets. Comprendre, prévenir, agir*, Lyon: Chronique Sociale.

Couvreur, C. (1990), 'Notes de lecture: "Le corps entre biologie et psychanalyse" de Christophe Dejours', *Revue Française de Psychanalyse* 54(3), pp. 875–882.

Dashtipour, P. and Vidaillet, B. (2017), 'Work as affective experience: The contribution of Christophe Dejours "psychodynamics of work"', *Organization* 24(1), pp. 18–35.

De Bandt, J., Dejours, C. and Dubar, C. (1995), *La France malade du travail*, Paris: Bayard Éditions.

Debray, R., Dejours, C. and Fédida, P. (2005), *Psychopathologie de l'expérience du corps*, Paris: Dunod.

Deiahaye, B. (1987), 'Notes de lecture: Christophe Dejours "Le corps entre biologie et psychanalyse. Essai d'interprétation comparée", Paris, Payot 1986', *Revue Belge de Psychanalyse* 10, pp. 97–99.

Dejours, C. (1980), *Travail, usure mentale. Essai de psychopathologie du travail*, Paris: Bayard Éditions.

Dejours, C. (1984a), 'Le corps de la psychosomatique: A propos de "Corps malade et corps érotique" sous la direction de M. Fain, Éditions Masson', *Revue Française de Psychanalyse* 48(5), pp. 1289–1295.

Dejours, C. (1984b), 'Avant-propos', in: Fain, M. and Dejours, C. eds, *Corps malade et corps érotique*, Paris: Masson, pp. vii–xiv.

Dejours, C. (1987a), 'La théorie psychanalytique du sujet face au développement scientifique (sciences biologiques et sciences sociales), in: Dejours, C. (2016a), *Situations du travail*, Paris: Presses Universitaires de France, pp. 51–70. Originally published as Dejours, C. (1987), 'La théorie psychanalytique du sujet face à l'interdisciplinarité', *Cahiers de l'Institut de Psychopathologie Clinique* 7, pp. 67–84.

Dejours, C. (1987b), 'Economie de la perception et processus de somatisation', *Psychanalyse à l'Université* 12 (47), pp. 417–435.

Dejours, C. (1988a), 'Commentaire' [on the report by Hirata, H. and Kergoat, D. summing up the discussion], in: Dejours, C. ed., *Plaisir et souffrance dans le travail*, volume 2, Paris: Laboratoire de psychologie du travail et de l'action, CNAM, pp. 165–176.

Dejours, C. (1988b[1986]), 'Souffrance et plaisir au travail: l'approche par la psychopathologie du travail', in: Dejours C. ed., *Souffrance et plaisir dans le travail. Séminaire interdisciplinaire de psychopathologie du travail*, volume 1: Orsay: AOCIP, pp. 15–24.,

Dejours, C. (1988c[1986]), 'Note de travail sur la notion de souffrance', in: Dejours C. ed., *Souffrance et plaisir dans le travail. Séminaire interdisciplinaire de psychopathologie du travail*, volume 1: Orsay: AOCIP, pp. 115–124.

Dejours, C. (1989), *Recherches psychanalytiques sur le corps*, Paris: Payot; new augmented edition published under a new title as: Dejours, C. (2009a), *Les dissidences du corps. Répression et subversion en psychosomatique*, Paris: Payot.

Dejours, C. (1992), 'Pathologie de la communication. Situation de travail et espace public: le cas du nucléaire', *Raisons Pratiques* 3, pp. 177–201.

Dejours, C. (1993a), 'Pour une clinique de la médiation entre psychanalyse et politique: la psychodynamique du travail', *Revue TRANS*, pp. 131–156.

Dejours, C. (1993b), 'Intelligence pratique et sagesse pratique: deux dimensions méconnues du travail réel', *Éducation permanente* 116, pp. 47–70.

Dejours, C. (1993c), 'Le corps dans l'interprétation', *Revue Française de Psychosomatique* 3, pp. 109–119.

Dejours, C. (1994), 'La corporéité entre psychosomatique et sciences du vivant', in: Billard, I. ed., *Somatisation, psychanalyse et sciences du vivant*, Paris: Editions Eshel, pp. 93–122.

Dejours, C. (1995a), 'Doctrine et théorie en psychosomatique', *Revue Française de Psychosomatique* 7, pp. 59–80.

Dejours, C. (1995b), 'Comment formuler une problématique de la santé en ergonomie et en médecine du travail, in: Dejours, C. (2016a), *Situations du travail*, Paris: Presses Universitaires de France, pp. 195–217.

Dejours, C. (1996), 'Sens et destructivité dans la névrose de comportement', *Revue Française de Psychosomatique* 10, pp. 17–27.

Dejours, C. (1997), 'Causalité psychique et psychosomatique: de la clinique à la théorie', in: Le Goues, G. and Pragier, G. eds, *Cliniques psychosomatiques*, Paris: Presses Universitaires de France, pp. .47–65.

Dejours, C. (1998a), *Souffrance en France. La banalisation de l'injustice sociale*, 2nd edition 2009, Paris: Éditions du Seuil.

Dejours, C. (1998b), 'Travailler n'est pas déroger', *Travailler* 1, pp. 5–12.

Dejours, C. (1999a), 'Violence ou domination?', *Travailler* 3, pp. 11–29.

Dejours, C. (1999b), 'Neues Leiden an der Arbeit'. Interview with Pasche, C and Streckeisen, P. in: WoZ-Online, 11.3.1999.

Dejours, C. (2000a), 'Choix de l'organe et indication "thérapeutique"', *Revue Française de Psychosomatique* 17, pp. 15–24.

Dejours, C. (2000b), 'Travail, modernité et psychanalyse', in: Boukobza, C. ed., *Où en est la psychanalyse? Psychanalyse et figures de la modernité*, Toulouse: Érès, pp. 32–40.

Dejours, C. (2001a), *Le corps, d'abord. Corps biologique corps érotique et sens moral*, Paris: Payot.

Dejours, C. (2001b), 'Le travail entre banalisation du mal et émancipation', in: Bass, H.-P., Dimon, M.-L. and Ferrières-Pestureau, S. eds, *D'un siècle* à l'autre, la violence en héritage: Perspectives psychanalytiques et anthropologiques, Paris: In Press Editions, pp. 19–34.

Dejours, C. (2002a), 'Technique psychanalytique et référence au corps érogène en psychosomatique, *Revue Française de Psychosomatique* 21, pp. 119–131.

Dejours, C. (2002b), 'Les rapports domestiques entre amour et domination', *Travailler* 8(2), pp. 27–43.

Dejours, C. (2002c), 'Le corps, comme "exigence de travail" pour la pensée', in: Debray, R., Dejours, C. and Fédida, P., *Psychopathologie de l'expérience du corps*, Paris: Dunod, pp. 63–10.

Dejours, C. (2003), 'Réhabiliter la normalité?', *Le Passant ordinaire*, pp. 56–59.

Dejours, C. (2004a), 'Il corpo tra seduzione e scissione', *Rivista di Psicolanalisi* 50(3), pp. 773–798.

Dejours, C. (2004b), 'Activisme professionnel: masochisme, compulsivité ou aliénation?' *Travailler* 11, pp. 25–40.

Dejours, C. (2004c), 'La fatigue d'être soi: revers de l'émancipation ou signe d'aliénation?', in: *Vivre fatigué*, numéro spécial de la *Revue Française de Psychosomatique*, pp. 27–36.

Dejours, C. (2004d), 'Le corps entre séduction et clivage', in: Aïn, J. ed., *Résonances*, Toulouse: Érès, pp. 59–83.

Dejours, C. (2005a), 'Le corps, comme "exigence de travail" pour la pensée', in: Debray, R., Dejours, C. and Fédida, P. (2005), *Psychopathologie de l'expérience du corps*, Paris: Dunod.

Dejours, C. (2005b), 'Corps érotique et sens du symptôme en psychosomatique', *Actualités Psychosomatiques* 8, pp. 13–28.

Dejours, C. (2006a), 'Entre désir de travailler et psychopathologie du travail: le piège de l'évaluation', in: Boukobza, C. ed., *La psychanalyse encore*, Toulouse: Érès, pp. 193–204.

Dejours, C. (2006b), 'Entretien', temporel. revue littéraire & artistique, available at: http://temporel.fr/Christophe-Dejours-Entretien.

Dejours, C. (2006c), 'Évaluation et institution en psychanalyse. Revendications d'autonomie et critique de l'institution', *Revue Française de Psychanalyse* 70(4), pp. 947–959.

Dejours, C. (2006d), 'Travail du rêve et enrichissement de la mémoire', in: Chouvier, B. and Roussillon, R. eds, *La temporalité psychique*, Paris: Dunod, pp. 41–59.

Dejours, C. ed. (2007a), *Conjurer la violence. Travail, violence et santé*. Paris: Payot.

Dejours, C. (2007b), 'Le travail entre corps et âme', *Libres Cahiers Pour La Psychanalyse* 15, pp. 115–127.

Dejours, C. (2007c), 'Vulnérabilité psychopathologique et nouvelles formes d'organisation du travail: approche étiologique', *L'Information Psychiatrique* 83(4), pp. 269–275.

Dejours, C. (2008a), *Travail, usure mentale. Essai de psychopathologie du travail*, 4th edition, Paris: Bayard Éditions.

Dejours, C. (2008b), 'Psychosomatique et troisième topique', *Le Carnet PSY* 126, pp. 38–40.

Dejours, C. (2008c), 'Suizid am Arbeitsplatz'. Zur Psychopathologie der modernen Arbeitswelt, Polar. *Zeitschrift für politische Philosophie und Kultur* 4, pp. 51–54.

Dejours, C. (2008d), 'Clinique du travail et psychiatrie: itinéraire interdisciplinaire', *Travailler* 20, pp. 9–17.

Dejours, C. (2009a), *Les dissidences du corps. Répression et subversion en psychosomatique*, Paris: Payot; new augmented edition of Dejours, C. (1989), *Recherches psychanalytiques sur le corps*, Paris: Payot.

Dejours, C. (2009b), *Souffrance en France. La banalisation de l'injustice sociale*, 2nd edition, Paris: Éditions du Seuil.

Dejours, C. (2009c), *Travail vivant*, volume 1: *Sexualité et travail*, volume 2: *Travail et émancipation*, Paris: Éditions Payot & Rivages.

Dejours, C. (2009d), 'Corps et psychanalyse', *L'Information Psychiatrique* 85, pp. 227–234.

Dejours, C. (2009e), 'La résistance', in: Dejours, C. (2016a), *Situations du travail*, Paris: Presses Universitaires de France, pp. 287–300.

Dejours, C. (2009f), 'Propos sur la santé: entretien de Christophe Dejours par Jean-Jacques Pailler', *Revue Française de Psychosomatique* 36, pp. 39–53.

Dejours, C. (2010a), 'Folie et travail: de l'analyse étiologique aux contradictions théoriques', in: Dejours, C. ed., *Observations cliniques en psychopathologie du travail*, Paris: Presses Universitaires de France, pp. 17–45.

Dejours, C. (2010b), '"Centralité du travail" et théorie de la sexualité', in: Dejours, C. ed., *Observations cliniques en psychopathologie du travail*, Paris: Presses Universitaires de France, pp. 73–108.

Dejours, C. (2010c), 'Nouvelles formes de servitude et suicide', in: Dejours, C. ed., *Observations cliniques en psychopathologie du travail*, Paris: Presses Universitaires de France, pp. 131–162.

Dejours, C. (2010d), *Le facteur humain*, 5th edition, Paris: Presses Universitaires de France.

Dejours, C. (2010e), 'Corps et sexualité', *Bulletin de la Fédération Européenne de Psychanalyse* 64, pp. 201–212.

Dejours, C. (2011a), 'Le corps entre "courant tendre" et "courant sensuel"', *Revue Française de Psychosomatique* 40, pp. 21–42.
Dejours, C. (2011b), 'Sortir de la souffrance au travail', *Le Monde*, 21st February 2011.
Dejours, C. (2012a), *La panne. Repenser le travail et changer la vie. Entretien avec Béatrice Bouniol*, Montrouge: Bayard.
Dejours, C. (2012b), 'Préface. La théorie sociale de Freud', in: Freud, S., *Psychologie des foules et analyse du moi*, Paris: Éditions Payot & Rivages, pp. 7–15.
Dejours, C. (2012c[1993]), 'From the psychopathology to the psychodynamics of work', in: Smith, N.H. and Deranty, J.-P. eds, *New philosophies of labour – Work and the social bond*, Leiden: Brill, pp. 209–250.
Dejours, C. (2013a), 'L'inné et l'acquis. La cohabitation entre l'infantile (pulsionnel) et le pubertaire (instinctuel)', *Le Carnet PSY* 173, pp. 37–41.
Dejours, C. (2013b), 'Effets de la désorganisation des collectifs sur le lien à la tâche et à l'organisation', *Revue de psychothérapie psychanalytique de groupe* 61, pp. 11–18.
Dejours, C. (2014), 'La sublimation: entre clinique du travail et psychanalyse', *Revue Française de Psychosomatique* 46, pp. 21–37.
Dejours, C. (2015a), 'Genre et théorie de la sexualité', in: *Association Psychanalytique de France: Annuel 2015: La conviction*, Paris: Presses Universitaires de France, pp. 159–170.
Dejours, C. (2015b), *Le Choix. Souffrir au travail n'est pas une fatalité*, Montrouge: Bayard Éditions.
Dejours, C. (2015c), 'Freud et le travail', in: Perron, R. and Missonier, S. eds, *Sigmund Freud*, Paris: Éditions de L'Herne, pp. 277–285.
Dejours, C. (2015d), 'Pour une clinique de la souffrance au travail. Entretien avec Benoît Schneider', *Bulletin de Psychologie* 538, pp. 285–291.
Dejours, C. (2016a), *Situations du travail*, Paris: Presses Universitaires de France.
Dejours, C. (2016b), 'Corps, narcissisme et travail', in: Joly, F. ed., *Corps et narcissisme*, Paris: Éditions in Press.
Dejours, C. (2016c), 'Bisexualité, genre et corps érogène?', *Le Carnet PSY* 197, pp. 20–25.
Dejours, C. (2017a), 'Clinique du travail et psychosomatique', in: Nayrou, F. and Szwec, G. eds, *La psychosomatique*, Paris: Presses Universitaires de France, pp. 175–192.
Dejours, C. (2017b), 'Troisième topique et analyse de la destructivité', *Le Carnet PSY* 206, pp. 42–49.
Dejours, C. (2018), 'Entre séduction et aide à la traduction: le mytho-symbolique, l'imaginaire social et la question de la liaison', in: Dejours, C.

and Tessier, H. eds, *Laplanche et la traduction: une théorie inachevée. Le mytho-symbolique: aide ou obstacle à la traduction?* Paris: Presses Universitaires de France, pp. 263–278.

Dejours, C. and Abdoucheli, E. (1990), 'Itinéraire théorique en psychopathologie du travail', *Prévenir* 20, pp. 127–149.

Dejours, C. and Abdoucheli, E. (1992), 'Biologie et psychanalyse: les enjeux', in: Gros, F. and Huber, G. eds, *Vers un anti-destin? Patrimoine génétique et droits de l'humanité*, Pais: Odile Jacob, pp. 267–276.

Dejours, C. and Bègue, F. (2009), *Suicide et travail: Que faire?* Paris: Presses Universitaires de France.

Dejours, C. and Deranty, J-P. (2010), 'The centrality of work', *Critical Horizons* 11(2), pp. 167–180.

Dejours, C. and Duarte, A. (2018), 'La souffrance au travail: révélateur des transformations de la société française', *Modern & Contemporary France*, pp. 1–12.

Dejours, C. and Gernet, I. (2016), *Psychopathologie du travail*, 2nd edition, Issy-les-Moulineaux: Elsevier Masson SAS.

Dejours, C. and Tessier, H. eds (2018), *Laplanche et la traduction: une théorie inachevée. Le mytho-symbolique: aide ou obstacle à la traduction?* Paris: Presses Universitaires de France.

Delaunoy, J. (2005), 'D'un siècle è l'autre: la violence en héritage. Editions In Press', *Revue Belge de Psychanalyse* 47, pp. 100–104.

Demaegdt, C. and Dejours, C. (2016), 'La souffrance éthique', in: Danon-Boileau, L. and Tamet, J-Y. eds, *Des psychanalystes en séance. Glossaire clinique de psychanalyse contemporaine*, Paris: Gallimard, pp. 511–514.

Fain, M. (1981a), 'Vers une conception psychosomatique de l'inconscient', *Revue Française de Psychanalyse* 45(2), pp. 281–292.

Ganem, V., Gernet, I. and Dejours, C. (2008), 'Le travail: que signifie ce terme en clinique et psychopathologie du travail?', *L'Information Psychiatrique* 84, pp. 801–807.

Gernet, I. and Dejours, C. (2009), 'Evaluation du travail et reconnaissance', *Nouvelle revue de psychosociologie* 8, pp. 27–36.

Gernet, I. and Dejours, C. (2016), 'L'inconscient amential', in: Danon-Boileau, L. and Tamet, J-Y. eds, *Des psychanalystes en séance. Glossaire clinique de psychanalyse contemporaine*, Paris: Gallimard, pp. 365–368.

Green, A. (1973), *Le discours vivant. La conception psychanalytique de l'affect*, Paris: Presses Universitaires de France.

Haraszti, M. (1976), *Salaire aux pièces: ouvrier dans un pays de l'Est*, Paris: Seuil.

Hirata, H. and Kergoat, D. (1988), 'Rapports sociaux de sexe et psychopathologie du travail, in: Dejours, C. ed., (1988), *Plaisir et souffrance dans le travail*, volume 2, Paris: Laboratoire de psychologie du travail et de l'action, CNAM, pp. 131–163.

Jung-Rozenfarb, M. (2003), '"Le corps d'abord" de Christophe Dejours', *Revue Française de Psychanalyse* 67(2), pp. 703–707.

Messer, J. (2010), 'Churned and spurned in the flexible world of work. A corporative narrative', *Cultural Studies Review* 16(2), pp. 75–101.

Messer, J. (2013), 'Reconceptualizing maternal work: Dejours, Ruddick and Lionel Shriver's We Need to Talk About Kevin', *Women's Studies International Forum* 38, pp. 11–20.

Obadia, J.-P. (1986), 'Le corps entre biologie et psychanalyse de Christophe Dejours', *Revue Française de Psychanalyse* 50(5), pp. 1509–1514.

Oksenberg Rorty, A. (1986/1980), 'Self-deception, akrasia and irrationality', in: Elster, J. ed., *The multiple self*, Cambridge/New York: Cambridge University Press, pp. 115–131.

O'Neill, B. (2011), 'Response to Christophe Dejours "Body and sexuality"', *EPF Bulletin* 64, pp. 204–210.

Rau, A. (2009), 'Suizid und neue Leiden am Arbeitsplatz', *Widerspruch. Beiträge zu sozialistischer Politik* 56, pp. 67–77.

Rivals Fotaki, G. (2011), 'Les dissidences du corps de Christophe Dejours', *Revue Française de Psychosomatique* 39, pp. 173–179.

Rolo, D. and Dejours, C. (2015), 'Travail et usage de substances psychoactives: évolution de la clinique', *Psychologie Clinique et Projective* 21, pp. 243–256.

Sievers, B. (1995), 'Characters in search of a theatre', *Free Associations* 5(2), pp. 196–220.

Steinberg, T.I. (2002), 'Leid ohne Gegenwehr. Einige Erklärungsansätze', available at: www.steinbergrecherche.com/asleid.htm

Tessier, H. (2003), 'Le Corps, d'abord', *Canadian Journal of Psychoanalysis* 11(1), pp. 217–222.

Tweedie, D. (2011), 'A critical assessment of orthodox economic conceptions of work', in: Deranty, J.-P. and Smith, N. eds, *New philosophies of labour. Work and the social bond*, Leiden: Brill, pp. 327–346.

Van Belleghem, L., de Gasparo, S. and Gaillard, I. (2014), 'The development of the psychosocial dimension of work', in: Falzon, P. ed., *Constructive ergonomics*, New York: Taylor and Francis, pp. 33–47.

Willsher, K., 'Heading for a breakdown', *The Guardian*, March 10, 2007, available at: www.guardian.co.uk/money/2007/mar/10/careers.workplacestress

––––––––––– 13 –––––––––––

BRIDGES

Jacques Press

Jacques Press, in different ways to Dejours, builds on the state of the debate to give it a new twist. We shall follow the various strands of his contribution by starting with an important event.

When presenting one of the two key reports at the 68th *Congrès des Psychanalystes de Langue Française* in Geneva in 2008, Press, gave to his paper the title *Constructions with and Constructions without End*, a contribution that was ultimately to form the nucleus of his 2010 study. One of the vignettes he used by way of illustrative sketches was the case of a young woman, who, towards the beginning of her analysis, reported a dream. She was in a holiday home together with her lover. He announced to her that there was another woman in his life. She took revenge by grabbing a hose to douse him with water.

At first glance, the motif of oedipal rivalry and a phallic element were imposing themselves. Following up on the patient's associations, however, Press noticed that things took a different turn. After the vacation the young woman was planning to change her professional orientation. She had been to her new place of work, which had reminded her of a Third World hospital, sending a ripple of echoes through her mind. She herself came from a family of Maghrebinian immigrants, was born in the Third World, and had had to be taken to hospital when her parents had confided her to the care of her grandmother. The memory of the distress she had experienced then was still very much with her. Every time she was reminded of it, she was close to tears. Interpreting the sexual content of the dream, Press reflected, would have obscured the memory of being abandoned, which had made use of hallucinatory wish fulfilment to mask the underlying traumatic trace.

Marty revisited

This way of looking at things, while it does not flatly contradict it, diverges from the way of clinical assessment systematically laid out by Pierre Marty. Taking our cues from that blueprint, we would have expected to see some careful probing into the patient's degrees of *mentalisation* so as to understand whether the patient could safely be treated in psychoanalysis. Over decades of practice, Jaques Press, however, not without struggle, has arrived at a different path of interpreting his theoretical heritage, by paying close heed to the variation introduced by Fain and Braunschweig, digging into the lasting legacy of the Freud-Ferenczi debate and articulating his findings in a sensibility honed by his reflections on Winnicott – just to mention three main lines of the trajectory documented in the considerable creative wealth of his output.

Ferenczi: the Me assailed by early trauma

For the sake of presentation these threads have to be somewhat artificially disentangled. With the above vignette in mind, it is easy to see that Ferenczi might provide food for thought. Press points out that Ferenczi leads us to think that every inscription in the psyche could have two faces: one turned towards figurability, the other turned towards trauma and immediate discharge. For adaption to reality to take place, stretches of the Me have to be ceded and parts of a hostile, alien world have to be introjected. This leaves memory traces that bear the scars of these early processes, but which the forces of Eros strive to employ for their own ends: partial self-destruction gives rise to a more robust mode of being. Press draws our attention to the fact that in delineating the infant's interactions with its early objects in this way, Ferenczi provides a more generalised form of what, a few years later, he was to isolate as pathological identification with the aggressor.

Ferenczi, as Press reminds us, recognises three factors that dramatically overburden the capacities of the child: in addition to abusive sexual seduction he mentions passionate, punitive sanctions, often meted out by an adult foaming with rage and the terrorism of suffering, in which the child is engulfed in the drama of a close relative. To protect itself against conditions to which it cannot as yet respond alloplastically, by changing its surroundings, the main line of defence has to be autoplastic action. Rather than giving up all links to the object, the personality relinquishes its cohesion and splits into a 'wise baby', shielded in early maturity against adult passion, and another, traumatised part, which keeps its proximity to it in raw form.

In Press's view, it is in this rift that an identification with the aggressor installs itself, stitching together disparate parts of the personality, and permitting anaesthesia of affects. Reinforced by the reign of silence imposed by adults, the child unconsciously takes upon itself the unacknowledged guilt of the aggressor. Without the sustained inner relationship to the mad object, Press concludes, the patient fears losing all his/her bearings and sinking into an abyss of unspeakable distress. The traumatic becomes the measure of all real passion, sometimes leading to a veritable addiction to it. A harsh superego is set up against this, which, on closer inspection, seems to be borrowed from the aggressor. Steps taken that threaten its severity are not experienced as welcome relief but rather perceived as a collapse threatening the Me. In the rift between *the wise baby* and the traumatised part, repressive mechanisms borrowed from the environment take hold. Membership of the social group is maintained by a shared identification in denial that ensures the unspoken rule of silence. In this situation, the analyst has to be particularly attentive to who is doing the talking: is it the patient himself/herself or is it an implant, which functions like a core of the actual (in the Freudian sense) around which the personality has constructed itself, a grain of sand both traumatic and indispensable?

As is well known, Freud strongly took exception to Ferenczi's 1932 paper. Jacques Press traces the subterranean effects of Ferenczi's thinking on Freud's later work. He follows Ilse Grubrich-Simitis (1991/1994) in regarding Freud's *Moses and Monotheism* as the central piece of Freud's continuing auto-analysis in his later life, at a time at which the spread of vitriolic antisemitic hatred in German-speaking culture, his illness and his aging, pushed him to revisit inner places of early trauma. As Press points out, Freud hardly published anything between May 1933, the death of Ferenczi, and January 1936, although his letters to Arnold Zweig, in this respect almost a second Fliess, reflect his intense inner interrogations at the time. Beginning with his work on *Moses and Monotheism*, to which his letters to Zweig contain early references – indicative of both the turmoils and the deep personal significance of its production – there is a new version of Freud's approach to trauma. Running like a strong thread through Freud's later thought, it shows several points of engagement with Ferenczi's work, as if Freud was continuing the discussion with his deceased friend and pupil.

The obliteration of shared memory as a point of reference

In trying to come to terms with the lasting legacy of Moses, Freud also grapples with how to arrive at a sufficiently truthful construction of what has left an impact but has to remain beyond the grasp of individual memory. Press finds the approach of the German Egyptologist, Jan Assmann, highly conducive to a contemporary understanding of the problem: What are the traumatic events that have led to the cultural memory focused on Moses? With Assmann, Press finds them in the suppression of polytheism by Akhenaten, whose memory in turn was obliterated after his death. What remains of these traumatic upheavals has crystallised around the figure of Moses. Whereas Moses is a figure of cultural memory but not of tangible history, Akhenaten is a figure of tangible history, but not of cultural memory. In understanding Moses as an Egyptian, Freud shows that a price had to be paid for establishing a culturally formative distinction. Press writes,

> To link the Egyptian origin of Moses to the sources of anti-semitism, as Freud does, constitutes therefore a terrible affirmation: not only is there the Other (the Egyptian) in the Me (the Jew), but that which founds the Jewish identity and which conveys to it its unique and specific character is the very quiddity of the stranger.
>
> (Press 2007b, p. 792)

Assman's thesis on the 'Mosaic distinction', separating the true God from the idols, and his followers from the gentiles, has raised an animated controversy. Though constituting echoes from intellectual battle grounds somewhat removed from the psychoanalytic session, these debates furnish an apt reminder that we are often dealing with nuances: 'division' and 'separation' are expressions a thesaurus of synonyms might yield – together with 'damage' – under the entry 'split'. Consulting, in a slight change of emphasis, on the other hand, the entry 'distinction' might direct the reader to 'difference', 'judgment', 'perception', 'separation', 'discernment' and 'discretion', concepts not intrinsically alien to 'individuation'. Ferenczi, in a fragment, indeed postulates that intellect only emerges from suffering of a traumatic nature, linked, he seems to suggest, to a memory that springs from psychic scar tissue.

Assmann, Press contends, throws an important light on a psychoanalytic understanding of trauma when he underlines that an event only becomes experienceable, communicable, and memorable by frames of experience based on everyday culture and in a dialectical relationship with the social imagination and the practice of memory enshrined in it. When Akhenaten did away with traditional religion, the symbolic universe in which the average Egyptian found his/her moorings was shattered. Since Akhenaten's successors proscribed his memory, paths towards a reconstructive imagination were obstructed: 'only the imprint of the shock remained' (Assmann 1997, p. 28) Press is particularly intrigued by a passage in the French edition, which is missing from the English edition:

> Hence, traumatic experiences are characterised by the incapacity of the framework of pre-established cultural meaning to grasp them.
> (Assmann 2001, p. 56)

Understanding the traumatic legacy of the Amarna period, Assmann, while taking a fresh turn, integrates, as he points out, contributions by Benedict Anderson on 'imagined communities', by Maurice Halbwachs on 'collective memory' and 'affective communities', by Ernst Cassirer on 'symbolic forms', and by Aby Warburg on culture as a phenomenon of memory. Press, receptive to Aby Warburg's thought, is most concerned with the effect on the individual. If, as in Egypt, a plague strikes at a time when the cultural frames of reference have just been shattered, the conjuncture will be traumatic. The traumatic character of the event is reinforced by the systematic suppression of all visible traces until, in the end, there is not even a reminder of its suppression: only the shock wave, bereft of a frame, subsists, witness to the 'economic' dimension of trauma. A veritable attack on linking, in Bion's sense of the term, has occurred, initiated not by the individual but by forces beyond his/her control. As for the child, it is easy to see that trauma touches it preverbally at a narcissistic and bodily level, before the sexual comes into play. Press, as we have seen, takes particular interest in cases in which a non-event did not leave an 'inscription' in the psyche. In its wake there remains a gap, a trace of a non-trace, which leads Press to think of Winnicott's (1974) reflections on the non-integration of an experience of break-down.

Vicissitudes of defence and self-preservation in a deficient environment: waste-disposal at risk

Both Ferenczi's and Winnicott's work, Press points out, provide elaborations of what Freud had recognised as worthy of investigation in *The Introductory Lectures* but did not pursue in any systematic fashion either then or after the major turn of 1920, when in *Beyond the Pleasure Principle* he introduced the *Todestrieb* (in French: *le pulsion de mort*): the destiny of the *Selbsterhaltungstriebe* (in French: *pulsions du Moi*, in Strachey's translation: self-preservative instinct). These proved to be both more fragile than Freud had initially envisaged and, to an important extent, dependent in their development on the qualities of the environment. Is it safe enough for the child so that it will not strive for early autarchy at all costs?

While Freud in 1913 assumed that in normal development libidinal impulses were in advance of the impulses of the Me, his take on things in 1924 postulated a prior sway of the Todestrieb, which in many respects had taken over some of the conceptual territory once held by ego impulses. Implicitly, the ego impulses now appear in two guises: on the one side we find the *Todestrieb* expressing a tendency of the Me to refuse radically everything that is 'not-Me'; on the other side we find ego impulses tied to the workings of the libido engaged in sustaining life. Winnicott, as is known, had little regard for the concept of the death drive. This dissent in principle notwithstanding, we can observe that he arrives at an analogous result by a different path: it is the incapacity of the environment that produces the kiss of death to the potential of the individual. As with Ferenczi, the deficient object for Winnicott is not necessarily absent. What fails to happen in the early relationships may be as important as any actual event. Press evokes Winnicott's (1965[1962]) suggestion of a difference between unintegration and disintegration. Haunted by what did not arrive at its own good time, leaving in its wake unintegration, the subject tries to protect itself against distress by actively pursuing the path of disintegration. Since the way to regression under the circumstances is fraught with dangers, withdrawal, in place of regression, becomes the default fall-back position. If a meaningful passivity is to be reached it has to be painstakingly made possible and put within reach through treatment first.

Coming to Winnicott from a long-standing engagement with the thought of *IPSO/EPP* analysts, Press is struck by how much the work of Fain and Winnicott on the dawn of the psyche is in resonance with each other and mutually enriching for the reader. While Fain focuses on formative experience in absence of the object, Winnicott's emphasis is on indispensable experience in presence of the object, both perspectives arguably complementing each other. It was when re-reading Fain's *Prélude à la vie fantasmatique* that he more fully began to realise, as he says, the importance of Winnicott's 'Fear of breakdown'. What Fain conceives of as a distortion in the Me appears with Winnicott as a false self, built in defence against a deficient environment, congealed in a response pattern likely to reappear in treatment. If as, Fain once remarked in one of his seminars, the *opératoire* patient is the equivalent of the zero level of countertransference, Press finds clues in Winnicott to understand more fully how this could be seen as a re-enactment of an early environment in urgent demand of a better solution.

With Winnicott, Press believes that the subject has to develop the capacity to make use of an object. For this to happen the subject has to experience that it is safe to expose the object to an attempt of destruction. Press turns to reflections of Winnicott's, published posthumously (1989[1968]), to understand possible obstacles: when is the non-use of an object an act of hatred and when is it an automatic attempt to protect the object? There are cases when an imputation of hatred would not only be far off the mark but could be seen as an act of retaliation on the part of an object feeling threatened. In one of his last papers, 'The use of an object in the context of Moses and Monotheism', Winnicott situates the rise of offensive impulse at a primordial stage, earlier than frustration, the reality and the pleasure principle. Permitting this to develop into a workable liaison, Press points out, requires of the analyst not to take this move as destructivity. 'Let me learn how to say no so that I can say yes', may well be a spark of hope buried in the cinders of negativity: aversion has to be discovered as a possibility before desire can be given a chance. Following Winnicott, Press suggests repetition compulsion should be seen in conjunction with a failure in the proper constitution of external reality in the aftermath of the survival of the object. In this case waste-disposal – as Winnicott terms it – is obstructed, something Press links with Freud's reflections on the protozoa that can rid themselves only insufficiently of the products of their own metabolism and in the end die from the mounting accumulation of them.

The analyst put on the spot: the need to discern what is missing and to hear what cannot be said

Press had established himself as a doctor of internal medicine, before, in his forties, he effected a complete turn of professional orientation, trained as a psychoanalyst and set out on a second career. It comes as no surprise, therefore, that he takes special interest in Ferenczi as a somatising patient. Looking at what we know about Ferenczi's life, the correspondence between Freud and Ferenczi and that between Ferenczi and Groddeck, Press sees evidence of a somatisation process of increasing severity under the weight of Ferenczi's own trauma and of the perturbations in his relationship with Freud. Where Freud emphasised rivalry, discounting love, Ferenczi emphasised love, discounting rivalry. In absence of the possibility of working this through with Freud, the unattainability of love and mutual understanding remained like an open wound. In this crisis, Ferenczi's latent homosexual position, which had served as a protection against the traumatic early object, no longer worked as a protective shield, a development that was unsettling for his inner economic equilibria and exposed him to grave somatic dangers, which in the end, Press is inclined to think, cost him his life. It was an impossible choice: he could follow Freud and thereby give up things he could not afford to lose, or follow the rebellious and unanalysed, yet creative part in himself and thereby forego all anti-traumatic protection provided by Freud. Faced with this stark a dilemma, Ferenczi may quite possibly have lost hold on the wish to exist altogether in his desire to preserve what seemed essential to him. Perhaps, Press argues, Marty's take on what happens when vital structure disintegrates, should be complemented: there are instances when a subject gives up on life in order to conserve something essential, something dyed into the very fibres of his/her individuality. At times 'one can die from a desperate effort to stay oneself' (Press 2012, p. 48).

What is to be done in difficult cases like this? Press picks up Fain's remarks about the importance of *femmelité*, a life-preserving quality, which, according to Fain, precedes even the mythical rule of the tyrant of the horde. An interpretation given from this position works, Fain argues, not because it transmits knowledge, but because the patient comes under the spell of the illusion of which it is but a token. In this promise a secret message, emanating from the patient, has been received and translated – a sign that the analyst has succeeded where the builders of the Tower of Babel have failed. If such an interpretation followed the lost language only a mother would comprehend, could this not go some way towards repairing what was missing in early interactions, exchanges that forced a brittle maturity on an infantile self for which it was as yet woefully ill prepared?

Press follows cues of Fain's: what is the echo in psychoanalysis of an event that did not take place? Press argues that to be receptive for this requires modifications in the way the analyst is listening: free-floating attention may not be enough. Since the analyst is used to working with fantasies, he/she will be looking for what is latent. It is more difficult to be receptive to what is manifest without meaning, as a nucleus of the actual. Offering silence as a response does not work well, because it can too easily be taken for indifference. What is required is a quality of presence tangible to the patient – a 'body to body' of the psyche into which enter not only the tonality of the language but also every physical particularity of the analyst's presence in the session. It is not just the preconscious of the patient that might be said to have a certain depth, we also have to look at the quality and range of the zone in treatment that permits echoes and grants access to sensations as yet undigested by thought. To the extent that this develops, the cure of words can gain a foothold. If, as Fain once said, there are patients to whom it is important to show how little things that are self-evident to them should really be taken for granted but, rather, are making one wonder, there are moments, Press suggests, at which cures have to proceed per *via di porre*, adding to what has already taken shape in the patient.

Sometimes things have to happen in external reality first so that the patient can make important steps in coming to terms with the traumatic. By not insisting on differentiating himself/herself from the patient, but becoming the medium against which an image can gradually gain shape, the analyst underwrites a bill of rights for the patient to exist. It is of particular importance to be highly attentive at moments when the patient inwardly takes leave of the analyst and waxes numb and dumb; on the other hand is has to be investigated which interventions bring him/her back to life. Presence and absence of the analyst need to be brought into a dialectical relationship, just as the enabling ground of receptive passivity needs to be complemented with an *élan* reaching out towards the patient, which is yet secure in its own framework. Press is aware that discontinuities within the flux of stimuli are necessary for the good functioning of the psyche. It is such discontinuity that protects, together with the tough skin provided by deadened outward layers of the psyche, the mental apparatus. Periodically the unconscious

> stretches out feelers, through the medium of the system Pcpt.–Cs., towards the external world and hastily withdraws them as soon as they have sampled the excitations coming from it.
> (Freud 1925[1924], p. 8; translation: Standard Edition)

For some patients an analyst insisting too narrowly on the rules of the trade seems to offer a blank relationship in *opératoire* functioning, which does not address the patient's basic needs in treatment. Fain believed there was the danger a person whose mental structure had not evolved might feel mortified by the encounter with the analyst. Press turns this around: should it not rather be the analyst who feels this mortification in being insufficiently equipped to help?

Psychoanalytic psychosomatics: towards finding a frame for the encounter

In keeping with his general thrust, Press is sceptical of Marty's push to establish psychoanalytic psychosomatics as a medical discipline geared towards an objectifying approach and intent on garnering a sufficiently robust mass of hard data. Although Marty's clinical practice centred on the importance of finding the patient wherever he/she was to be found, the classification he promoted as his scientific legacy carries the considerable risk of lodging the deficit too one-sidedly in the patient, reifying his/her supposed structure and thus keeping him/her at a supposedly safe distance. There is the constant danger of finding too much comfort in classificatory elements or time-hallowed conceptual formulas, *prêt-à-penser*. 'Have you ever', Press repeats de M'Uzan's metaphor with some relish, 'tried to put a cat [alive] into a [stationary] shoebox?' (Press 2004c, p. 47; echoing de M'Uzan 2004, p. 61).

Not only is the diagnostic attribution of structural deficit fraught with danger, the imputation of defensiveness in a patient's behaviour is as likely to miss its target if done without paying proper attention to the context of the situation. Sometimes the experience against which the patient is supposed to be mounting a defence has had no previous chance to constitute itself, and is thus without reach. In the worst possible case the analyst's classificatory push becomes the instrument by which *une pure culture d'instinct de mort* is installed in the sessions: as with a mother ill-adjusted to the potential of the child, everything still on its way towards becoming significant is being put on mental tranquiliser in an act of non-receipt.

Working with theory: a paradigm or a model?

Press is intrigued by Michael Parsons' (1992) reflections on re-finding psychoanalytic theory in day-to-day work with patients in a process of discovery for which the cognitive grasp on a certain set of propositions is only the starting point. Work on theories implies work on the difficulties in everyday practice, a process that requires coming to terms with the countertransference when our expectations are being confounded. What he commends in a case presentation by Marta Calatroni is evidently the triple objective he is used to setting himself: establishing contact with the patient, gauging his/her psychosomatic status and at the same time engaging in the first opening moves of an approach that keeps close to the actual needs of the patient in his/her state of disorgansation.

In his own personal take on theory, Press differentiates a paradigm from a model. While a paradigm gives voice to a new intuition, a hunch of how things could be connected, it organises thought but does not turn it into a fully-fledged system. A model tries to go further, striving to dot the i's and to cross the t's, so as to offer comprehensive cohesion. Marty's new paradigm established a correlation between the effacement of mental functioning in a *vie opératoire* and the onset of somatisation: not anxiety as such would lead to somatisation, reduced mental space, however, would. Therefore the better one mentalised, the less one would be liable to somatise. To spell this out, Marty proposed a model that was hierarchical, suffused with Vitalism and Monism, and which in its linear take on evolutionary processes, its third conceptual pillar, looks, as Press points out, rather dated today. Lines of development that look clear-cut in a model may not be so at all in clinical reality. We may, indeed, at times encounter cases in which the model proves deficient but the paradigm continues to be useful. To prove its central thesis in the world of hard data, Press argues, double blind research would have to be conducted on large, representative samples constituted without any bias of selection, observed on a long-term scale, while at the same time taking appropriate measures to exclude the distorting work of factors not under investigation – a gargantuan task, certainly beyond the reach of present-day psychoanalytic psychosomatics.

Press learned from Marty that trauma might lead to the effacement of a given psychic function rather than to traumatic neurosis resulting in a psychic economy that does not follow the blueprint of neurosis but does not fit easily into the register of borderline disturbances either. In dealing with this, it is important what kind of regard is accorded to what appears not to be there. We have to be particularly attentive to factors we would expect to be in evidence, but which are not, without losing sight of our possible relationship to this condition. This may determine whether any openings to future developments can be found. What resists treatment the most, Press suggests, is also a potential source of creativity: where there is a grain of sand there may, ultimately, be a pearl that will surround it. Press draws on the work of the British social anthropologist Jack Goody to point out that our bewilderment may be a useful beginning: it shows that a difference has not found a frame useful enough to give rise to a productive potential.

Influenced by his own patients, his understanding of the *opératoire* has changed over the years. In 1995, when he discussed the concept of suppression, he started with Marty's finding of 'secondary gaps in the preconscious' and in his case vignette in the same year considered this a precursor of a *vie opératoire*. In later work he was much more cautious and discernibly shied from making too sweeping statements: in using the term *vie opératoire*, he conceded, there was a risk that it could be used to lift from the analyst the burden of difficulties he was encountering in his/her countertranference. With Winnicott it was not too difficult to see another dimension to this: in his take on 'fear of breakdown' this state is bereft of any psychic representation and is not analysable as such. As long as this flight continues, precocious splits in the self are perpetuated. Ancient internal borders, set up to hem in breaches of containment, may have provided temporary fixes, but also reduce the space within which the Me can move freely. It is in better understanding the economic plight of a split Me that Press would now expect to see clues emerge on the impasse of *opératoire* functioning. That is why zones of potential mental collapse specific to each analysand have to be carefully investigated.

Reflecting on Henry James' *The Beast in the Jungle*, Press points out that a subject exposed to the destructivity of others may respond with effacement.

> The incapacity of the partner to respond to this demand does not lead to a reaction of active destructivity in them, but rather to a silent extinction, a physical destruction, which constitutes the exact counterpart of the psychic destructivity at work with their vis-à-vis. There occurs a phenomenon of resonance between an enclave of non-psychisation in the subject to which corresponds in the interlocutor an enclave characterised by unbound destructivity.
> (Press 2000f, p. 92f.)

In the work with patients who learned not to trust their early environment it is important to be mindful of their need to keep an inner place of refuge that is, however, constantly exposed to the vicissitudes of the person's life. To constitute an inner zone of withdrawal can be vital to them. Treatment may easily be experienced as a threat to their core of identity. This puts them under pressure to act out, or if this way is blocked, tension will be channelled into the body. To deal with this, the analytic process has to put together a holding frame that can be trusted to uphold the pleasure principle so that experiences incongruous with it can be spotted and addressed. Only then, in patient work, can ancient distress be faced and find a chance to turn into something to which traits of the enigmatic can be restituted.

Press believes this way of looking at things is better suited to an understanding of what he had hitherto treated under the term suppression, which is always a response to a given situation. In recent work he deals with the resulting problem under the term 'impasse', which beyond a merely structural diagnosis, opens the perspective for the subjective trajectory of a person finding him/herself in dire straits with scant means at disposal and limited space for manoeuvre, in a situation in which words only seem to add insult. If there can be no words, the body is likely to bear the brunt.

In one of his contributions, Press focuses on a group of patients whose strong inner investment in their jobs masks an underlying frailty of their narcissistic economies. The elation they experience only if things go their way works for them like the ingestion of anti-depressants. The equilibrium thus achieved is utterly contingent on external factors, continued accommodation to which consumes all their strength. Yet, there is a knowledge that this state of relative success will not last – outspending their resources they are running on borrowed time, trying to put off a major crisis that sooner rather than later is bound to happen, but which so far has not found a framework to be safely addressed.

Social anthropology, again, provides useful insights to Press: Marshall Sahlins' concept of the structure of the conjuncture leads him to reflect on the situational attributes of an encounter in which mutual expectations are being frustrated, but from which a new structure might well emerge in a violent clash of perspectives, given the chance. The meeting between analyst and patient, to some extent, resembles that between cultures alien to each other. Its meaning, which emerges in the conjuncture, can create surprising effects. This encounter will reverberate in the countertransference of the analyst, shaking his/her sense of identity. Diffuse tension, where it occurs, first has to receive a frame suitable to transform it into pain with borders circumscribed enough to provide more discernible contours to what is narcissistic and what is object related, separating the two in the experience.

A complement to the First Topography: elements of a General Theory of Trauma

In accordance with strands of thought within the *EPP/IPSO*, the Second Topography is not regarded as simply having superseded the first but both topographies are seen as complementary. Press points out that the atemporality of the unconscious seems to be an achievement rather than a given. If the mental apparatus is not differentiated enough, the traces of trauma are apt to disturb profoundly the perception of temporality and libidinal rhythms articulated in the outstretched antennae of the unconscious tentatively venturing into degustation.

While Jean Laplanche, drawing on Freud and Ferenczi, proposes a Theory of General Seduction to account for the vicissitudes of *pulsion* and desire in the individual, Press leans towards the late Freud.

As he emphasises, we can assume that there exist inscriptions in the body that do not belong to the psyche but exert an influence on it. There is always a traumatic background against which early psychic development takes place: it needs an irritating grain of sand, Press points out, around which the pearl of conscience can grow. What if this grain of sand has not constituted itself? What is left in its place is a black hole that acts like an internal foreign body, which for all the constant irritation it inflicts, evades mental grasp and pushes the subject towards perception rather than representation.

If we follow Freud's line of thought on Moses in the light of Assmann's recent work, Press argues, there is an alien element, a stranger and quintessential other, both present and buried within the constitutive separation from the pots (and gods) of the country of slavery: an Egyptian to whom, paradoxically, the distinction from the world of Egyptians is owed. This finds some correspondence in psychoanalysis: only if the patient is able to face up to the stranger in him/herself, the implanted grain of sand, around which the personality went into construction to safeguard survival, can change take place.

The emergence of the intimate between the traumatic and the formless

In his preface to the Hebrew edition of *Totem und Tabu* Freud writes,

> If the question were put to him [the author]: 'Since you have abandoned all these common characteristics of your countrymen, what is there left to you that is Jewish?' he would reply: 'A very great deal, and probably its very essence.' He could not now express that essence clearly in words; but some day, no doubt, it will become accessible to the scientific mind.
>
> (Freud 1934, p. 569)

There is something just beyond the grasp that is, however, closely related to a person's deepest sense of self. Press evidently believes that Freud returns to this very essence in question for his construction work on the role of Moses both in his own life and the life of his people. It may be a 'historical novel', 'a great image on feet of clay' and yet contain a core of historical truth necessary to throw light on current experience. Not only can the archaic only be revisited in retrospect, it may well be that it never existed in archaic purity. If successful, construction has a counter-traumatic effect remedying to some extent what could not take place earlier.

Winnicott, Press observes, managed to express deep ideas in simple, everyday language. Press, recently, has followed the example, leaving behind the customary density of French argumentative and expository prose to render an account of his thinking in somewhat different terms, couched in language much closer to Christopher Bollas than to either Michel Fain or André Green. Although this may not be in contradiction to earlier work, it offers an appreciable amount of rephrasing, providing new echo zones to previous thought. A significant part of psychoanalytic work, he now says, is to bring the unknown, the intimate and the formless into play and mutual interaction. The intimate – the way a person has constructed his/her own identity and history – has two faces, he argues: one turned towards the traumatic, the other opening to formlessness. Formlessness, in his view, can be seen as another name for 'drive', a drive as yet in quest of a transformational object and of potential expression: chaos results from the failure of or defeats in transformation, in the absence of transitional form within reach.

Perhaps coincidental to this change of register, Press has in recent years used Walter Benjamin's reflections on the task of the interpreter to express his understanding of what is happening in psychoanalysis. The translator always works with what remains refractory, Press points out. In continuing to exist in the new form of the translation the original is being changed. This is why a translation of great works can never be definitive but has to be taken up afresh generation after generation, because it contains, as Press says in reference to Bion's thought, unsaturated elements.

Transmission is easier if a theory does not appear too saturated, a danger that has been a recurrent risk in Marty's classificatory scheme. It would be a great achievement, he says, if our theories indeed managed to be sufficiently incomplete. If they are not, institutions can be relied upon to inject a dose of entropy into any wish to break out of the mould, just as the bad mother, in Fain's reflections, would plant the kiss of mental death on her child by surreptitiously smothering it in forceful calm. He believes it is absolutely necessary to arrive at an inter-fertilisation of theories but also to permit the encounter with the patient from the patient outside our own culture of reference shake the foundations on which we enter into it.

Press is aware how much countertransference goes into making theories – he happily confesses himself the problem patient of the theories he is holding – but also has a sense how much a particular theory gives voice to the intellectual background noise of a period, in which it is rooted as if it were the navel of its dream.

Trauma: general or specific, visible or invisible?

It has been pointed out that Press joins Winnicott to build a general aetiology on the universal occurrence of primitive agony suffered in precocious trauma. And, indeed, there is that: in his thinking the inchoate seems to be ever present waiting to disturb what has been considered successfully shored up. Yet, Press also reminds us that Freud believed cases involving a traumatic core had better chances of treatment. This would show the continuing importance of having a specific theory of trauma for a more limited number of cases alongside a general theory of trauma, a question which Press, however, does not pursue. To some extent, Press approaches early trauma in the way desire is handled under the auspices of the First Topography, its existence assumed unless proven otherwise. Seen this way, the hypothesis of early trauma would be a paradoxical generator of hope where else there might be little or none.

There seems to be a catch, though: as Press himself concedes, there is no guarantee that early processes detrimental to the subject have left a residual awareness of what has been done to it:

> the psyche may have been undermined by something that touches it and alters it while it is not able to preserve the traces of this [intervention], not even in negative form. [...] These modifications are not inscribed in the *psychisme*, but will modify the way in which this will treat further experiences to which it will find itself exposed, to the extent it has undergone a deformation, not only in complete ignorance, but also any possibility of knowing.
>
> (Press 1997c, p. 62)

Apparently, there are some poisons that escape notice. What would the analyst find if he/she, as Press suggests, were to take upon himself/herself to be in the present the object in charge of accumulated deficiencies? To some extent the situation bears a resemblance to the dilemma facing political firebrands past and present: if agony is rife among the populace, and an ardent desire is spreading to break the yoke, then a decisive turn of events may still be possible. But what if things are grinding on in their own miserable way, unpromisingly but stably? When Fain metaphorically spoke of the dark fairy sitting at the head of the new-born child's cradle he did not necessarily imply that this would register as agony with the child. As fairy tales are apt to teach us, the complications following from such an untoward early presence will make themselves felt, though the visit as such may not. They are likely to entangle the subject in a string of strangely inexplicable repetitions of misfortune weaving a web of misery. People drawn into this will have difficulties to transform what is happening to them into stories that make sense, clinging to limited damage control in an attempt to pre-empt any need for more substantial transformation.

In the footsteps of Georges Canguilhem, the eminent French philosopher-physician, Michel de M'Uzan reminds us of an old medical treatise – Raymond (1816[1757]) – on illnesses that are dangerous to cure because a cure would fatally destabilise the patient. Press, when he takes a patient in treatment, is confident that old woes, left unwrapped in thought, can be brought to a salutary crisis within the framework of the sessions. While one of the goals of Marty's classification was to provide orientation on whom *not* to take into psychoanalytic treatment, lest this endanger the patient, Press's implicit general theory of trauma provides not a guide on counter-indications to psychoanalytic treatment, but daringly turns things on their head: it is not so much the structure of the patient that, for all the traps it offers, puts treatment at risk, but the mental and emotional unreadiness of the analyst exposed to it. There are certainly patients for whom analysis is counterindicated: in most cases they are those who do not ask for it. The problem is complex, emerging from the lay of the land, as it were, as we try to gauge it. Press, via Winnicott, arriving in territory more usually held by relational psychoanalysis, has to hold what happened in the past for all its severity as less decisive than what may yet happen in the psychoanalytic encounter. Since it is only by breaking that the hyacinth bulb sets free its fragrance, as he says, how can we, before the event, with any certainty 'smell' the outcome? If we cannot be completely sure what the result will be, it is certainly worth trying.

Press seems to be well aware of the magnitude of the challenge. In fact, he is one of the few practitioners who has gone on record with a pertinent question too often left unasked: discussing the problems of false positives and false negatives in the classification, he raises the possibility that *opératoire* patients seen in private practice, might present with different modes of mental functioning from those seen in an institutional context. This points to something essential: what exactly is the frame of an encounter that has given rise to the impression that the patient in question has but a shallow fantasy life?

Practically all the non-clinical literature which Press draws upon highlights the importance of social processes within a given cultural framework. If, as Press affirms, maternal care (with its discontinuities) ensures the subject can both create and express what already exists in him/her, it seems that social conditions very much shape the arena in which the child will find the expressive syntax for these ventures. It is likely that both push and pull factors will have to interact to make this happen. Desire and *Ananke* do not enjoy a level play field: subjective anticipation of what has to count as *Ananke*, in relation to assumptions shared with others, will determine the space left for desire. The way a patient can make use of his/her own culture to process the as yet formless, may deserve our interest as much as the more established attention to object usage – in particular, if the frames of reference have been mauled beyond recognition.

In this context, the case study Assmann presents is clearly of significance. As Press shows, a psychoanalytic session is a new encounter, for both parties, embedded in a reality insufficiently understood by both. Yet its presence offers an arena in which past impingement can be revisited in the light of a future that has to be seen with the eyes of the patient before it can be rebuilt. For this, the practitioner has to keep both mentally agile and emotionally present. In private practice, as Press implicitly shows, this may well mean shanghaiing every useful concept within reach into psychoanalytic service while permanently reworking the implications of the psychoanalytic tradition in its different manifestations.

Sources

Assmann, J. (1997), *Moses the Egyptian: The memory of Egypt in western monotheism*, Cambridge, MA: Harvard University Press.
Assmann, J. (2001), *Moïse L'Égyptien. Un essai d'histoire de la mémoire*, Paris: Aubier.

Bernstein, R.J. (1998), *Freud and the legacy of Moses*, Cambridge: Cambridge University Press.

Bronstein, C. (2016), 'Formlessness and countertransference: Discussion of J. Press, *Metapsychological and clinical issues in psychosomatics research*', *International Journal of Psychoanalysis* 97(1), pp. 115–122.

Charbonnier, G. (2008), 'Construire autour d'un grain de sable; intervention sur le rapport de Jacques Press', *Revue Française de Psychanalyse* 72(5), pp. 1351–1358.

Ciavaldini, A. (2007), 'L'hallucinatoire: de l'espoir à l'émerveillement. Discussion du texte de Jacques Press', *Actualités Psychosomatiques* 10, pp. 63–69.

de M'Uzan, M. (2004), 'Nosographie et auto-conservation', *Actualités Psychosomatiques* 7, pp. 61–70.

de M'Uzan, M. (2008), 'Réponse à Jacques Press', in: de M'Uzan, M. ed., *La chimère des inconscients*, Paris: Presses Universitaires de France, pp. 39–48.

Freud, S. (1925[1924]), 'Notiz über den Wunderblock', in: *Gesammelte Werke*, volume 14, London: Imago Publishing [1940–1952], pp. 3–8.

Freud, S. (1934), '"Vorrede" [zur hebräischen Ausgabe von "Totem und Tabu"', Jerusalem, Stybel Verlag], *Gesammelte Werke*, volume 14, p. 569.

Green, A. (1995), 'Commentaire de l'observation de Jacques Press', *Revue française de psychosomatique* 8, pp. 41–48.

Groarke, S. (2010), 'Unthinkable experience: Winnicott's ontology of disaster and hope', *American Imago* 67(3), pp. 399–429.

Grubrich-Simitis, I. (1991/1994), *Freuds Moses-Studie als Tagtraum*, 2nd edition, Frankfurt/Main: Fischer Verlag.

Mellier, D. (2014), 'The psychic envelopes in psychoanalytic theories of infancy', *Frontiers in Psychology* 5, article 734, pp. 1–9.

Nigolian, I. and Press, J. (2018), 'Préface', in: Press, J. and Nigolian, I. eds, *Enfances: mémoire sans temps, corps orphelin*, Paris: Éditions In Press, pp. 7–13.

Olick, J.K. (2008), 'The ciphered transits of collective memory: Neo-Freudian impressions', *Social Research*, pp. 1–22.

Parsons, M. (1992), 'The refinding of theory in clinical practice', *International Journal of Psychoanalysis* 73(1), pp. 103–115.

Press, J. (1995a), 'La répression, refoulement du pauvre?' *Revue Française de Psychosomatique* 7, pp. 121–139.

Press, J. (1995b), 'Une observation clinique', *Revue Française de Psychosomatique* 8, pp. 25–39.

Press, J. (1996), 'Discontinuité, rythme, temps, (a)temporalité: atemporalité de l'inconscient et perception du temps', *Revue Française de Psychosomatique* 10, pp. 139–155.

Press, J. (1997a), 'Culture, mesure et démesure', in: Schmid-Kitsikis, E. and Sanzana, A. eds, *Concepts limites en psychanalyse*, Lausanne: Delachaux et Niestlé, pp. 343–362.

Press, J. (1997b), 'Temps et pulsion', *Revue Française de Psychanalyse* 61(5), pp. 1707–1720.

Press, J. (1997c), 'Caractère(s), traumatisme(s), somatisation(s)', *Revue Française de Psychosomatique* 11, pp. 49–70.

Press, J. (1997d), 'A propos du livre de Nicos Nicolaïdis: La force perceptive de la représentation de la pulsion', *Revue Française de Psychosomatique* 11, pp. 211–217.

Press, J. (1997e), 'Note sur la manie essentielle', *Revue Française de Psychosomatique* 12, pp. 103–120.

Press, J. (1998a), 'Rencontres', *Revue Française de Psychanalyse* 62(1), pp. 121–134.

Press, J. (1998b), 'Le bruit de la rue: des mécanismes de maîtrise aux processus de somatisation', *Revue Française de Psychanalyse* 62(5), pp. 1591–1600.

Press, J. (1998c), 'Une observation clinique', in: Fine, A. and Schaeffer, J. eds, *Interrogations psychosomatiques*, Paris: Presses Universitaires de France, pp. 91–104 (largely identical to Press 1995b).

Press, J. (1998d), 'Introduction', *Actualités Psychosomatiques* 1, pp. 5–9.

Press, J. (1998e), 'Commentaire. Ecriture et inscription psychique, *Actualités Psychosomatiques* 1, pp. 79–89.

Press, J. (1998f), 'Valeur heuristique du modèle psychosomatique de Pierre Marty: quelques éléments de réflexion', *Actualités Psychosomatiques* 1, pp. 107–124.

Press, J. (1998g), 'Brèves remarques sur l'activité du facteur traumatique dans le système sommeil-rêve', *Revue Française de Psychosomatique* 14, pp. 113–126.

Press, J. (1999a), 'Le système sommeil-rêve et l'équilibre psychosomatique', in: Duparc, F. ed., *La censure de l'amante et autres préludes à l'oeuvre de Michel Fain*, Lausanne: Delachaux et Niestlé, pp. 35–49.

Press, J. (1999b), *La perle et le grain de sable. Traumatisme et fonctionnement mental. Essai psychanalytique*, Lausanne: Delachaux et Niestlé.

Press, J. (1999c), 'A propos de l'article d'Anna Potamianou' [Potamianou 1999a], *Revue Française de Psychosomatique* 15, pp. 65–77.

Press, J. (2000e), 'Traumatisme et mécanismes de défense', *Actualités Psychosomatiques* 3, pp. 17–30.

Press, J. (2000f), 'La bête dans la jungle: somatisation, contre-transfert et enclaves psychiques', *Revue Française de Psychosomatique* 17, pp. 91–105.

Press, J. (2001a), 'Mécanismes de répression, travail de contre-transfert et processus de somatisation', *Revue Française de Psychanalyse* 65(1) pp. 85–100.

Press, J. (2001b), 'Mouvements de mentalisation-démentalisation, présence de l'analyste et processus de somatisation', *Revue Française de Psychosomatique* 19, pp. 39–55.

Press, J. (2001c), 'Rêver, fantasmer, somatiser', *Actualités Psychosomatiques* 4, pp. 17–25.

Press, J. (2001d), 'A propos de l'article de Marta Calatroni', *Actualités Psychosomatiques* 4, pp. 137–42.

Press, J. (2002a), 'Entre l'espoir et la douleur', *Actualités Psychosomatiques* 5, pp. 55–69.

Press, J. (2002b), 'Le travail de membre: acte de candidature et/ou acte de passage?', *Bulletin de la Société Suisse de Psychanalyse* 54, pp. 12–16.

Press, J. (2003a), 'Fixations somatiques et fonctionnement mental', *Revue Française de Psychosomatique* 23, pp. 145–162.

Press, J. (2003b), 'De quelques sources du sentiment inconscient de culpabilité', *Revue Française de Psychanalyse* 67(5), pp. 1623–1632.

Press, J. (2004a), 'Narcissisme de l'analyste et fonction de la théorie dans le champ psychosomatique', *Revue Française de Psychosomatique* 25, pp. 155–164.

Press, J. (2004b), 'Modèles, sens et processus en psychosomatique', *Revue Française de Psychanalyse* 68(5), pp. 1681–1687.

Press, J. (2004c), 'La psychosomatique est-elle soluble dans la psychanalyse?' *Actualités Psychosomatiques* 7, pp. 45–60.

Press, J. (2005a), 'Acquisition du sens de la réalité, folie et somatisation: un regard psychosomatique sur l'oeuvre de Sandor Ferenczi', *Revue Française de Psychosomatique* 27, pp. 49–66.

Press, J. (2005b), 'Construction, interprétation et confusion de langues', *Bulletin de la Fédération Européenne de Psychanalyse* 59, pp. 55–63.

Press, J. (2005c), 'La construction du sens en psychosomatique', *Actualités Psychosomatiques* 8, pp. 59–75.

Press, J. (2005d), [contribution], in: 'Discussion sur les deux présentations, par Colette Combe, les orateurs et le public', in: Duparc, F. ed., *Winnicott en 4 squiggles*, Paris: In Press Éditions, p. 128f.

Press, J. (2006a), 'Constructing the truth: from "Confusion of tongues" to "Constructions in analysis"', *International Journal of Psycho-Analysis* 87(2), pp. 519–536.

Press, J. (2006b), 'Les sédiments de deuil: deuil, impasses psychiques et somatisations', *Revue Française de Psychosomatique* 30, pp. 9–25.

Press, J. (2006c), 'Des théories du déficit au déficit des theories ... et à leur nécessité', *Actualités Psychosomatiques* 9, pp. 81–91.
Press, J. (2007a), 'Entre le monde et le soma: le langage', *Revue Française de Psychanalyse* 71(5), pp. 1529–1535.
Press, J. (2007b), 'La construction de la vérité; de "Confusion de langue" à "Construction dans l'analyse"', *Revue Française de Psychanalyse* 71(3) pp. 783–802.
Press, J. (2007c), 'Somatiser, agir ... espérer peut-être', *Actualités Psychosomatiques* 10, pp. 45–62.
Press, J. (2008a), 'Avatars du spectre d'identité en psychosomatique', in: de M'Uzan, M. ed., *La chimère des inconscients*, Paris: Presses Universitaires de France, pp. 13–37.
Press, J. (2008b), 'Construction avec fin, sans fin', *Revue Française de Psychanalyse* 72(5), pp. 1269–1337.
Press, J. (2008c), 'La construction de la théorie en psychosomatique', *Revue Française de Psychosomatique* 34, pp. 151–168.
Press, J. (2009a), 'Investiguer "L'investigation psychosomatique": quelques pistes', *Revue Française de Psychosomatique* 35, pp. 143–153.
Press, J. (2009b), 'Inachèvement et après-coup dans le processus théorisant', *Revue Française de Psychanalyse* 73(5), pp. 1591–1598.
Press, J. (2010a), 'A propos du livre de Claude Smadja', *Actualités Psychosomatiques* 13, pp. 183–187.
Press, J. (2010b), *La construction du sens*, Paris: Presses Universitaires de France.
Press, J. (2010c), 'L'analyste femelle', *Revue Française de Psychanalyse* 74(1), pp. 165–180.
Press, J. (2010d), 'L'équilibre psychosomatique, une si fragile conquête', *Revue Française de Psychosomatique* 37, pp. 39–49.
Press, J. (2010e), 'Trauma et pulsion', *Libres Cahiers Pour La Psychanalyse* 21, pp. 35–51.
Press, J. (2010f), 'Être psychosomaticien aujourd'hui', *Actualités Psychosomatiques* 13, pp. 133–145.
Press, J. (2010g), 'Un mal nécessaire', *Bulletin de la Société Suisse de Psychanalyse* 70, pp. 43–45.
Press, J. (2011a), 'Angoisse et processus de somatisation', *Psychologie clinique et projective* 17, pp. 9–28.
Press, J. (2011b), 'Culpabilité primaire, défense maniaque de comportement et rêverie diurne', *Revue Française de Psychosomatique* 39, pp. 51–65.
Press, J. (2011c), 'L'inoubliable, limite de l'analysable', in: Manzano, J. and Abella, A. eds, *La construction en psychanalyse: Récupérer le passé ou le réinventer?* Paris: Presses Universitaires de France. pp. 171–193.

Press, J. (2011d), 'La projection inachevée', *Revue Française de Psychanalyse* 75(3), pp. 665–679.

Press, J. (2012a), 'Ferenczi, patient somatisant, homosexualité latente et équilibre psychosomatique', *Revue Française de Psychosomatique* 42, pp. 35–49.

Press, J. (2012b), 'La sexualité impure ou l'hystérie primaire à l'épreuve du contre-transfert', *Revue Française de Psychanalyse* 76(5), pp. 1471–1478.

Press, J. (2013a), 'Capacité de rêverie et fonction maternelle', in: Press, J. ed., *Rêver, transformer, somatiser,* Chêne-Bourg: Georg Editeur, pp. 33–43.

Press, J. (2013b), 'Régression et transformation', in: Press, J. ed., *Rêver, transformer, somatiser,* Chêne-Bourg: Georg Editeur, pp. 181–198.

Press, J. (2013c), 'L'informe, l'intime, l'inconnu, les processus de transformation et l'objet', *Bulletin de la Fédération Européenne de Psychanalyse* 67, pp. 32–41.

Press, J. (2013d), 'Nous et "les autres"', *Bulletin de la Société Suisse de Psychanalyse* 75, pp. 5–9.

Press, J. (2014a), 'Un contre-transfert bardé d'éclats: états traumatiques et travail de contre-transfert', in: Tovmassian, L.T. and Bentata, H. eds, *Quels traitements pour l'effraction traumatique? Apports de la clinique et de la pratique psychanalytiques,* Paris: In Press, pp. 83–93.

Press, J. (2014b), 'La psychosomatique, une invention occidentale? Travail clinique, processus théorisant et détour par l'autre', in: Press, J. ed., *Corps culturel, corps malade,* Chêne-Bourg: Georg Editeur, pp. 159–177.

Press, J. (2014c), 'La transmission de la théorie: transmission de vie, transmission de mort', *Revue française de psychanalyse* 78(2), pp. 453–464.

Press, J. (2015a), 'Lire Winnicott', *Revue Française de Psychosomatique* 47, pp. 65–78.

Press, J. (2015b), 'Le transfert du négatif. Histoire d'une possession blanche', *Revue Française de Psychanalyse* 79(4), pp. 1123–1135.

Press, J. (2015c), 'Masochisme et organisation de la sexualité infantile: une théorie à démanteler', *Revue Française de Psychanalyse* 79(5), pp. 1596–1601.

Press, J. (2016a), 'Metapsychological and clinical issues in psychosomatics research', *International Journal of Psychoanalysis* 97(1), pp. 89–113.

Press, J. (2016b), 'L'analyse, expérience corporelle, et l'informe. Réflexions libres sur le fonctionnement du couple analytique en séance', *Revue Française de Psychanalyse* 80(3), pp. 792–804.

Press, J. (2016c), 'Le psychosomatique et l'expérience de l'informe', in: Press, J. and Nigolian, I. eds, *Corps parlant, corps parlé, corps muet,* Paris: Éditions In Press, pp. 115–130.

Press, J. (2016d), 'La présence sensible de l'analyste', in: Danon-Boileau, L. and Tamet, J-Y. eds, *Des psychanalystes en séance. Glossaire clinique de psychanalyse contemporaine*, Paris: Gallimard, pp. 202–205.

Press, J. (2017a), 'Enjeux épistémologiques et cliniques de la recherche en psychosomatique', *Revue Française de Psychanalyse* 81(2), pp. 541–570 (= French version of Press 2016a).

Press, J. (2017b), 'L'écriture, l'analyse et la vie', *Bulletin de la Société Suisse de Psychanalyse* 83, pp. 15–19.

Press, J. (2018), 'Séances', *Revue Française de Psychanalyse* 82(1), pp. 76–88.

Press, J. (2019a), 'Au-delà de la mélancolie. Mélancolie et crainte de l'effondrement', *Revue Française de Psychanalyse* 83(2), pp. 527–540.

Press, J. (2019b), 'Le psychanalyste et le psychésoma. Transformer le destin en destinée, un enjeu psychosomatique', *Revue Française de Psychosomatique* 56, pp. 93 -103.

Press, J. and Nigolian, I. (2016), 'Préface', in: Press, J. and Nigolian, I. eds, *Corps parlant, corps parlé, corps muet*, Paris: Éditions In Press, pp. 7–10.

Raymond, D. (1816[1757]), *Traité des maladies qu'il est dangereux de guérir*, new edition, Paris: Brunot-Labbe

Ribas, D. (2008), 'Traumatisme précoce restreint ou généralisé? discussion du rapport de Jacques Press', *Revue Française de Psychanalyse* 72(5), pp. 1339–1349.

Winnicott, D.W. (1965[1962]), 'Ego integration in child development', in: Winnicott, D.W. (1965), *The maturational processes and the facilitating environment*, London: The Hogarth Press, pp. 56–63.

Winnicott, D.W. (1974), 'Fear of breakdown', *International Review of Psychoanalysis* 1, pp. 103–7.

Winnicott, D.W. (1989[1968]), 'The use of the word "use"', in: Winnicott, C., Shepherd, R. and Davis, M. eds, *Psychoanalytic explorations*, London: Karnac, pp. 233–235.

Winnicott, D.W. (1989[1969]), 'The use of an object in the context of Moses and Monotheism', in: Winnicott, C., Shepherd, R. and Davis, M. eds, *Psychoanalytic explorations*, London: Karnac, pp. 240–246.

CONCLUSION

As Edith Kurzweil pointed out, Pierre Marty's and Michel Fain's work was grounded in early object relations in a manner that made Anna Freudians feel uncomfortable about it. Their emphasis on elements outside language was nothing that Lacan at that stage, as we have seen, was inclined to look upon with sympathy. The way in which they made the emergence of fantasy contingent on early interactions was unlikely to gain traction with Kleinians of the times.

Although the reception of the group's work was therefore not facilitated abroad, it remained a significant contribution to psychoanalysis: it opened a way to suggest new ways of looking at baffling facts, turning them from vexing obstacles into enigmas worthy of resolution.

Constituting an impediment to a psychoanalytic approach, the *opératoire*, as it turned out, was a fertile concept, but similarly difficult to pin down in one, and only one, location as the psychoanalytic process by its very nature: as Michael Parsons (2014) pointed out, in agreement with Samuel Abrams (1987), there has been some variability in the understanding of what the term should be taken to refer to: was it something primarily happening within the patient; within the analyst; in both of them; between the patient and the analyst; or a combination of processes?

In *Das Unbehagen in der Kultur* Freud suggests that the person dissatisfied by reality tries to escape from it by fleeing into neurosis, or this failing, psychosis. The development of neurosis, in this passage, is predicated upon a wish to escape from reality. French psychoanalysts belonging to the *EPP* thought that this high road might not be the one taken by everyone. In the 1999 film fantasy *The Matrix* the protagonist was given a choice between two pills: take the blue pill and things continue more or less as they are; take the red pill and another reality will reveal itself.

Psychoanalytic reflections on the *opératoire* started with the clinical hunch that some patients had, as it were, taken a different pill from the neurotic, the psychotic or the perverse. They did not want to distance themselves from reality – they fled in the opposite direction, directly into it. Initially, it was thought that this was something enshrined in personality structure, which meant that once this path had been taken, it was difficult to opt out of it. Taking this path would predispose the subject to respond to tension by channelling it through the body and into activity.

Significantly, the emergence of the concept of the *opératoire* attached itself to two areas of life which Freud himself did not think were propitious to psychoanalytic thinking, but with which French psychoanalysis, in its march through the institutions, was increasingly confronted: affections of the body and conditions of work. In one of the early responses to the theses of the *EPP*, a Swiss psychiatrist reminded his readers of a passage in Marcel Proust:

> It is in moments of illness that we are compelled to recognise that we live not alone but chained to a creature of a different kingdom, whole worlds apart, who has no knowledge of us and by whom it is impossible to make ourself understood: our body. Say that we met a brigand by the way we might yet convince him by an appeal to his personal interest, if not to our own plight. But to ask pity of our body is like discoursing before an octopus, for which our words can have no more meaning than the sound of the tides, and with which we should be appalled to find ourself condemned to live.
> (Proust 1925, p. 408; see Schneider 1973, p. 46f.)

Patients seen by Marty for his investigations were at a low point. It remains uncertain to what extent the encounter with psychoanalysis on hospital grounds, in the presence of a group of assistants, shaped the manner of their self-presentation. At this stage there is little indication that their previous experience with medical institutions, the structure of interactions they had come to expect there, and the adaptation to this according to their own cultural codes, was sufficiently taken into account.

Conclusion

Yet, there was an element in the psychoanalysts' toolbox which permitted them to make allowances for the particular situation these patients found themselves in: considerations of the inner libidinal economy of a person. To put it bluntly: a person may have been born poor and remained impoverished or he/she may find him/herself momentarily out of pocket at a particular conjuncture. What we encounter in a person showing signs of limited leeway are exhausting effects, of whatever origin, on a given repertoire of ways and means.

As Ian Hacking pointed out, once you adopt a concept it gives new focus to your perceptions and shapes your experiences. In the case of France, as it happened, the adoption of the new construct led the debate to be pursued on a number of different work sites, separate, yet inter-related by a common reference to the concept of the *opératoire*. Let us, before we draw further conclusions, go over some major lines of development.

One line of development tried to re-imagine the world of the early infant: in the version proffered by Fain and Braunschweig, a good early environment was not so much predicated on the mother's abounding love as it was on the oscillation between this and a world full of passion hidden, yet easily intuited, beyond the mother's discontinuities in loving attention. Those times the mother's focus was on the infant, it was important what her inner eye saw and how much space this inner perspective left to the real living being on her knees. In a bold theoretical step, the *pulsion de mort* was now thought to emanate from the mother, in the manner a cold wet blanket might be applied to bring down heat, so as to reduce the boisterousness of the child when intolerable to the mother.

The time a child was weaned off the more continuous presence of the mother called for counterweights to be in place, making the transition feasible. Among them, speculated Nicos Nicolaïdis, were elements combinable in the manner of the letters of an alphabet, which would furnish building blocks for the child's imagination. While Marty was interested in the fluidity and depth of the preconscious, this approach added something new. It was now also looking for the range of permutations supported by the mother's culture, a potential that could only be accessed once a certain distance to the dyad could be established. Structure, in this view, does not self-replicate: what is handed down is the variability of expressive means that has to be made available to the subject as a kind of starter kit to deal with inner and outer worlds.

If the starter kit is of a more rudimentary kind, a more 'muscular' approach to meet the challenges of life will be required, studied in many varieties by Gérard Szwec: in the case of tension arising, the subject may wish to fight fire with fire and gear up for action in order to calm down, a preference that will not easily make him/her a likely patient on the couch. This may have deep roots in a person's experience: sometimes alimentary disturbances in an infant point to very early incompatibilities with the mother's inner worlds, in other cases it is very difficult for a child to develop a sufficiently solid aversion to the incongruities to which it is exposed.

Though this does not work in its favour, the child may be drawn into bonds of identification based on a shared denial of what is happening. Anna Potamianou conceives of ways of forgetfulness that bolster community life. In other parts of her work, she takes a deep look at how even hope can go rancid if it has been shorn of all transformative potential. Tenaciously clung to, hope has become a dead end and may have turned into a retreat offering a holdout against the need for change.

In Potamianou's interest for communal practice there is some point of contact with Jean Benjamin Stora's focus, pervasive in his work, on a cultural dimension in the shared imaginary that determines what a person can or cannot express within its terms. There are self-regulatory systems embedded in a social and cultural environment, which, if thrown off-kilter, send shock waves into the body.

So far, the picture emerging points towards the *opératoire* as a defensive mode against restricted options, a baseline of standard operating procedure resorted to when other, more fluid, means are found to be beyond reach and the Me's territory is under threat. From the outside, it may seem as if the zones of the psyche amenable to fantasy-based interaction and dream life have contracted and shrunk so that the inner echo room resonating with events has been diminished.

This can only constitute a major conceptual challenge if fantasy is regarded as a composite phenomenon and not considered to be rising organically and inevitably from the natural order of things, just like teething. In a major contribution, César and Sára Botella forcefully argue that the ability to give shape to mental life – figurability – is not a given. There is an important proviso: it is the integrity of the holding field that permits inevitable experiences of absence to perform a creative function. To be able to get to this will require access to the image of a 'double' in early life, a development, which if it was impeded early on, especially requires the 'work of the double' in psychoanalytic treatment. Nothing, they reflect, will be as terrifying as having an intense experience to which one cannot find any means to give form.

In this, context does matter: Smadja's emphasis on the economic aspect goes hand in hand with recognition of the situational context of the *opératoire*, in which, in some instances, the subject takes a nap from his/her subjectivity, withdrawing into a convalescence of being.

If this is so, earlier work by French psychiatrists after the war exploring the effects of the workplace on the psyche goes towards showing that convalescence is not always a process supported by the environment in its own demands on the functioning of the subject. Work is a place, Dejours points out, where the individual grapples with a reality that resists, though the subject will look for wily ways of adaptation that leave room for creative practice. It is also a part of life which, if radically split from other compartments of a person's life, is likely to fortify zones of the amental, the unthought, armoured in temporal layers. While there are sources of vitalisation to be had at the job, there are apparently also sources of devitalisation, a 'dementor's kiss' for those willing or frail enough to accept it. 'Dead on arrival' as a phenomenon may appear once it makes it to the consulting room; there will be a story to it, which the subject may not have found ways to access and process.

Having taken stock of some major lines of developments of the *opératoire*, it is time to face difficulties that have been lurking in the margins.

A similarity between the opératoire and responses to survivors' trauma

According to the way in which the person in *opératoire* mode is described, he/she might well be a deeply traumatised soldier escaped from a war we know nothing about, but which we suspect from where we stand is not only profoundly strange but also vaguely repulsive. Jonathan Shay describes the strange way Vietnam veterans whom he encountered conducted some of their conversations:

> Civilian friends and family members may be by turns bewildered, amazed, bored, and then annoyed by veterans' ability to talk with each other for hours on end about details of weapons that they used, of the contents and texture of different C rations.... The speech rhythms, the jargon, the technical minutiae are the only

doorway a veteran finds into the rooms that they carry: Farmer, the veteran of the brown water Navy we met above ... once spoke at length in group therapy about the 20mm cannon in the turret of his boat.... The language of weapons, of the military setting, was his doorway into the traumatic material of his friend's maiming.

(Shay 2002, p. 90f.)

One might say that in the example above endless repetition of trivia of material culture, shared in a community of remembrance, held deposits of raw experience, which, against all hope, were in quest of a possible transformation. Shay found access to this by reading Homer on the inner injuries left by war, a source that was not in the mind of his patients but which worked like a bridge to connect to what previously had seemed beyond comprehension. Alain Fine (1997) once pointedly asked whether the psychosomaticians were the facilitators of legends for the patient population, and perhaps there are cases in which it is imperative the psychoanalyst connect to a story line that can keep a balance between accessibility and required distance.

Marion Michel Oliner (1996) has pointed out a striking similarity between *opératoire* thinking and responses to trauma: the intermediary zone where external reality and unconscious fantasies are integrated has been impaired in its functioning. In contradistinction to Shay's Vietnam veterans, who talk about something that can be localised in history, we may be at odds to discern concrete traumatic events that have led to an *opératoire* state.

As with clinical work on the aftermath of trauma, it emerged that numbness, to some extent, was partial. Fain, followed most systematically by Dejours in this, has pointed out that there is a split inside the patient between the person who knows and the person who does not know. In a parallel development, Claude Barrois, having extensively worked with soldiers, has described three possible responses to mortal danger: severe depressive breakdown; alternating episodes of depression and the narcissistic illusion of control; and, finally, a split in the subject in combination with partial denial. The last solution shows some similarity to what the *EPP* has described as *opératoire* coping mode:

The subject accepts to have already died and becomes a dead man walking, reduced to bare automatisms of self-conservation, alimentation and [routine] everyday actions. In war, this is the combatant competent to a fault, [highly] professionalised, but whose every desire, every feeling have been expelled. This leads to a split [...] the future development of which is problematic: once the danger has passed, will the subject be able to retrieve his live double capable of desire? This split is in fact very different from psychotic and perverse splits.

(Barrois 1998/1988, p. 209f.)

Significantly, Barrois reserves prognosis: were it to be pronounced, it would be tied to a vector into highly unknown futures. What he does not have to be uncertain about, apparently, is the person's past. This is an advantage we do not always have. Sometimes we find it difficult to understand what happened to the person who has turned numb. Smadja sees the *opératoire* as a possible second stage after traumatic devastations, put into place for its analgesic function, so as to permit the individual to conserve his/her forces. If so, and it is indeed part of a combat mode, the narrative of the war in which it is being employed has often been effaced.

If this comparison is valid, and it very much seems it is, it underscores the view emerging from various strata of the discussion that *opératoire* modes do not need a particular personality structure to be put into effect. Press, among others, makes use of the word impasse, which is not necessarily tied to a particular way a person got into his/her present straits, but emphasises the limited options subjectively available in a given situation.

The *opératoire* as a response rooted in a sense of place

If *opératoire* behaviour is a stand on inauspicious territory meant to limit damage, its results are a reminder of the poignant warning, written in a different context, that 'containers will not fix your broken culture' (Kromhout 2018). Something about the place that *opératoire* patients live in, for all we know, does not lend itself easily to revitalisation and sufficiently comfortable containment. Christopher Bollas has argued that

> People who dislike the area where they live are in a sad state of disrepair, for they are denied the vital need for personal reverie. Each person needs to feed on evocative objects, so called 'food for

thought', which stimulate the self's psychic interests and elaborate the self's desire through engagement with the world of objects.

(Bollas 2009/2000, p. 63)

Those affected do not appear to have anything to lean back unto, once their personal resources are about to get exhausted. They seem intent on bootstrapping a sense of agency in ambient conditions that are failing them. In more extreme cases this verges on the attempt to pull oneself out of the mire by one's own hair for want of a better solution. As a defence, *opératoire* behaviour is a stop gap measure against an untoward turn of events. Yet, it may have built up over the years as an attempt at appeasement of a world that was not friendly to start with. Just as people sometimes find it difficult to sell stocks on which they have been massively losing money, the subject may be loath to leave behind the past – to destroy the past as Bollas (1995) put it – *especially* if it was suffused with memories of pain.

In a sense, the world in which *opératoire* behaviour is felt to be the only possible move has not been made safe enough for Winnicott's ideas, nor does it abound in accessible evocative objects, important to Bollas. In it, proto-psychoanalytic concepts that emerged in the Romantic movement and which, as Matt Ffytche (2012) argued, have continued to shape the implicit assumptions of major psychoanalytic thinkers on individuality, have to all intents and purposes failed to leave a major imprint. Perception is not linked to deep personal meaning steeped in culture, as it is in the contemplation of the cherry blossom in Japanese culture. There is a lack of psychic generativity with the subject largely unaware of what it is missing. It is, Alain Fine (1995) believes, the plight of the *opératoire* person that he/she suffers from a lack of the unreal which surrounds the perceived world as a halo of what is not there but enters as a play of the possible. In the mental ecology in evidence, there is some echo of the alimentary disturbances vividly described by Szwec: the 'food for thought' available to the psyche is not sufficient to provide adequate sustenance. It has yet to become clear what might and would.

For the individual not to reduce his/her impulses to naught, he/she requires living links to others that reverberate in fantasy, stimulated by a sustainable position that is centred and decentred by others at the same time. It seems that, to the *opératoire* patient, social life does not provide a ground fertile enough to develop expressive form capable of being integrated into viable projects. There is a mismatch between the potential space needed and the space on offer. Jean-Claude Ameisen provides a useful image of the complex exchanges needed to thrive. Cells that are bound into a living exchange with other cells are inhibited in their self-termination programme by virtue of the signals they receive in this exchange. The ongoing work of the negative, chipping away at the living being, paradoxically sustains form by keeping balances in motion: if not for the self-termination of cells, the human body could not gain or, having gained, retain functional shape. Cells that refuse to die off if no longer needed give rise to tumorous growth that brings death to the whole.

In the *opératoire*, balances have become skewed in ways that may be opaque to the person to whom it has happened. Following Fain, we might conjecture that the baby sent on its trajectory as a future person permanently gifted for *opératoire* options could, in its mother's mind, represent a recalcitrant cell that refuses to shut down, thus threatening her mental life with tumorous growth.

It might, on the other hand, be that the present, in turning poisonous to the psyche, retroactively declares the past to be a ground insufficient for a sustainable future. Jean-Luc Donnet has written about the effects of a changing social landscape on the work of the *Centre Jean Favreau* in Paris, at which the SPP is offering free consultations and psychoanalytic treatment to patients who otherwise would not be able to afford the cost. New forms of precarisation, he points out, had brought forth 'a form of *névrose de guerre économique*' (Donnet 2005/1995, p. 198), which psychoanalysts have to come to terms with in their offer of a treatment. Apparently, there are wastelands of daily life that do not easily lend themselves to narration and Dejours shows that work, and the way it is organised, plays an important part in this.

It has been pointed out that the present and the past continuously interact with each other. There is also the further crucial influence of the future, as imagined by the subject, on the individual perception of both the past and the present.

> Cut away the future, and the present collapses, emptied of its proper content. Immediate existence requires the insertion of the future in the crannies of the present.
> (Whitehead 1933, p. 191)

Gregorio Kohon, in recent work (2015), points to Agamben's reflections on the idea of a poverty of experience that appears in

Walter Benjamin's work. There are connections in this to Louise Berlant's analyses of 'impossible' subjective futures, hemmed in by forms of 'cruel optimism', in which the subject is in

> a relation of attachment to compromised conditions of possibility whose realization is discovered either to be impossible, sheer fantasy, or *too* possible, and toxic.
>
> (Berlant 2011, p. 24)

Some of them, she reflects

> move towards a normative form to get numb with the consensual promise, and to misrecognize that promise as an achievement.... In the middle of all that, we discover in the impasse a rhythm that people can enter into while they're dithering, tottering, bargaining, testing, or otherwise being worn out by the promises that they have attached to in this world.
>
> (Berlant 2011, p. 28)

This addresses the various, sometimes ambiguous, forms illusion may take, an inner perspective which inevitably gives hostages to fortune. While Freud uses 'illusion' as a term indicative of an erroneous assessment of reality, Winnicott's use of the word includes a mother's confidence in her child's future that goes beyond what can safely be ascertained at the moment. Not for every baby do a mother's fond hopes offer enough of a protective shield to make the child world's safe for the experience of aggression and desire. At a crossroads, one approach will gain the upper hand, shaping the horizons of the future. Public representations of pathways open to be chosen colour the perception of future generations. French psychoanalysis has shown a long-standing interest in inter- and transgenerational phenomena and there are some echoes of this in the reflections of the authors discussed. In cultures suffused with pain transitionality is endangered, benign forms of illusion are nipped in the bud, and there appears to be no meaningful crisis within reach, which, once weathered, might present the world in a new light. If this is so, the *opératoire* mode of behaviour is expressive of what Nineteenth Century German scholarship termed the *Sitz im Leben* [seat in life], the concrete multidimensional context from which form, or lack thereof, arises, and in which the life of the *pulsions* must find its setting.

Non psychic reality impacting on the patient

Since the *opératoire* reflects the impact on the psyche of a dynamic reality that is not adequately represented, the lay of the land creates difficulties for the psychoanalyst who has to discern what is not there, in which way and to what effect. This, it turns out, is delicate: what is the difference between links repressed, links effaced and links nonexistent? What the difference between denial and complex impairment of the psyche? How would the psychoanalyst know without having an accurate enough picture of the raw forces impacting on the patient? Oliner (2013b; 2012; 2008) has deplored a tendency towards too exclusive an emphasis on 'psychic reality' in many strands of contemporary psychoanalysis. Focusing mainly on what can be mentally digested and put into language would naturally tend to remove from the analyst's remit much of what happens in the body and at the workplace. Fernando Urribarri (1999, p. 374) regretted that psychoanalysis showed a 'systematic disregard for and exclusion of issues connected with the social-historical field'. If this is so, there will have to be extra care taken that the analyst does not fall prey to splits between hermetically sealed spheres that produce fertile ground, as Dejours shows, for the *opératoire* to flourish.

Fluidity, depth and reliable availability, three attributes that Marty thought were vital to the preconscious, are also important for the quality of intermediary space between psychoanalyst and patient. It is, as we have seen, not sensible to talk of an *opératoire* mode without giving heed to the context the patient is enmeshed in. Considered in this way, the *opératoire* addresses a further problem: it is not just within the patient that intermediary space might be lacking, it might as well be lacking between the patient and his/her analyst. What the *opératoire* individual therefore requires is the reconsideration of the analyst's procedures in the face of unaccountably subdued mental life. As Bion once wrote,

> I suggest that somebody here should, instead of writing a book called 'The Interpretation of Dreams', write a book called 'The Interpretation of Facts', translating them into dream language – not just a perverse exercise, but in order to get a two-way traffic.
> (Bion 1980[1977], p. 31)

Giving heed to what has been left unserviced by frames past and present

Related considerations have led Press to a radical shift in perspective: the standard operating procedure which robs the patient of a fuller potential is also a dangerous lure to the analyst who has to come to terms with the clash of realities between him/herself and the patient. The early 1970s, as we have seen, brought French psychoanalysts into contact with Winnicott's and Bion's thinking. Building on what has previously been established as a link, Press welds French thinking about the necessity of having a frame for thinking, feeling and imagining to Winnicott's reflections on the fear of a breakdown. In the resulting picture, it is the crisis that cannot take place for lack of a properly framed interpersonal space that has damaging future effects. Experience has gone missing because a crisis cannot be risked. Negativity under such conditions lacks a containing field. Approaching matters this way introduces a qualifier to the assumption that fantasy life is a given: rather than being omnipresent, it is contingent on a frame. Having to deal with the shattering of frames, French reflections on the effects of absence meet Winnicott's thinking on the qualities of presence.

This fits in with a strong influence of Ferenczi in various strands of French psychoanalysis, another latent point of contact with British Independent thinking: what has been done to a person in an asymmetric relationship is very important to the development of his/her inner life. There is traumatic potential submerged in the ordinary and in adaptation to its requirements, which leads to levels of exhaustion not owed to the repression of latent meaning.

If we follow Press (and the Botellas) on the necessity of a frame, this also means that the contrast to other schools of thought becomes more nuanced: fantasy and representation draw on proto-forms that, given the right frame, can eventually take shape more fully. Although interactions precede language in the infant, these are interactions with parents embedded in worlds of language and emotion preceding the child's birth.

With no wish or need to emulate Lacan, the French psychoanalysts studied in my book found it easier than Lacanians of the times to focus on the reverberations of action-based scenes on inner echo rooms. With undercurrents evasive of language, the individual may or may not be able to navigate this in sufficiently adequate ways.

The idea of the economic aspect, harking back to Freud, introduced an element that cast doubt on the supremacy of language and symbolic structure, but put the question of transformations firmly on the agenda.

An *opératoire* state, seen in this light, speaks of a crisis of a transformation much needed but stalled for lack of inner and outer means to weather it: as Antonio Gramsci once observed,

> The crisis consists precisely in the fact that the old is dying and the new cannot be born; in this interregnum a great variety of morbid symptoms appear.
> (Gramsci 1975[1930], p. 311)

Understanding the concrete conditions under which this strange interregnum operates will go some way towards getting beyond the desperate stalemate. If this is so, the concept of the *opératoire* also interrogates what the psychoanalyst understands about the different faces of the reality the patient has to live in. For all we know, Marty's quite un-Hegelian assumption of a negative unbound into any dialectical process, and of destruction without recompense, might well be part of a person's reality, as walls are closing in and vital forces are being drained away.

Finding new interfaces and receptive space

As Dejours' investigations into the world of work have amply shown, stronger connections to research on the social field might yield interesting results. Special care would have to be taken to differentiate situations in which a patient unfamiliar with psychoanalysis is seen in a hospital setting from those in which he/she has already made his/her way to a private practice. Surprisingly, there has not as yet been any major systematic reflection in print on a potential elephant in the room: presentational differences between patients encountered in dissimilar social frameworks. Szwec, in a recent contribution (2017b), has remarked upon a slow process of separation between the *EPP* and psychosomatic medicine. If this is so, repercussions on the prevalent use of concepts are to be expected, and may already have contributed to a shift of tone. Controversies into which framework psychoanalysis is to be inserted lie at the very roots of the splits in French psychoanalysis. Emerging from this, Marty tried to provide one possible answer. The new overall situation, very much changed since the 1950s and 1960s, has quite possibly shifted the discussion markedly towards those patients that are currently seen in private practice.

As previous moorings keep changing, new challenges are developing: thinking about experiences with past encounters that inexplicably fall flat is now acquiring new relevance in Western societies that increasingly have to deal with the aftermath of forced migrations, leading to encounters in which people may talk to each other without necessarily producing a meeting of minds in any deeper sense. When the need to get things done in the face of adverse reality is threatening to swallow up mental space, there is the need for a third who in spite of difficulties may yet be capable of accommodating what is mentally alien to him/her as a host. Marie R. Moro (2009) speaks of the ongoing need to decentre oneself by working with what one is not familiar with. The way we do this will connect to our own histories and how we interpret them. While Marty took an interest in West African children uprooted by their mothers' sudden migration from the traditions of a village to a big conurbation, the past decades have made it unnecessary for us to travel far to encounter a similar phenomenon. People travel to us, many die in the attempt, and survivors carry with them the memories of those who did not make it. As Virginia de Micco has graphically written,

> Survival is therefore, above all, a form of incompleteness which acquaints us with a logic that is not that of loss and mourning and the psychic operations connected to these, but that of disappearance and reappearance, deletion and re-emergence: a paradoxical dimension in which nothing stays dead forever and nothing ever really comes back to life.
>
> (de Micco 2018, p. 118)

Lacunae, which we might have preferred not to engage with, begin to claim our attention. Psychoanalysis, if it wants to stay relevant, is forced to work on a reality in which hope, at times, is a refugee without papers, hiding behind a false wall. To have a professional preconscious well-nourished enough to deal with situations seemingly closed in upon themselves, might be worth the occasional step out of theoretical certainties.

Conclusion

Reading the *opératoire* as a probe into the permanently difficult dented by the terrain it is employed on

As Fitzgerald and Ryan (2014) put it, in talking about attempts to work out solutions for Afghanistan, the landscape always finds a way to speak back. French psychoanalysts congregating around the *EPP*, in many ways were forced to revisit territory previously held by French reform psychiatrists striving for a better understanding of the work place after World War II. In doing so they also traversed old battlegrounds of the Freud–Janet controversy on repressed meaning versus traumatic lack and reached terrain in more recent time held by debates on how to understand resilience and its limits.

What I have shown in my study in some detail is that the concept of the *opératoire*, as it was appropriated by practitioners over decades, has, in the process, gained elasticity that adapts it to work in new contexts, with new angles protective of nuance. It has proven highly performative in throwing light on the various ways in which mental life is quietly put to death in adaptation to the dynamics of the early and the actual environment. In this development it also bears the marks of the idea of the other – a concept which widely gained traction with Lacan – as it meets the non-Lacanian *pulsion de mort*, understood not as sound and fury but as a silent wasting away. Shedding some of its initial focus on the patient's structural deficits, it has more recently been extended to address an analyst's difficulties to find shape in what has never been represented in those patients who fail to thrive. In this new functionality it has gained the potential to link to areas of experience in which social, cultural and work-related fields help little to absorb the shock of events. In its present form it offers a network of linked considerations that we may, with Dejours, understand as a form of professional *métis* [professionally sly moves] developed by a given group of psychoanalysts to tackle situations for which more traditional classifications have been of limited helpfulness.

Delineating what range of concerns a concept comes to address, I have found, helps to find paths through dense argumentative undergrowth of fine differences. From this perspective, although this is beyond the scope of my present work, it would also be easier to compare the *opératoire* with stratagems other strands of psychoanalytic traditions have developed to address analogous situations of conceptual kernel shock. This would shift the emphasis from the unique brilliance that a concept may deploy to the amount of stress it can take while accommodating a wide scale of differential factors in practice. As the French example shows, international psychoanalysis would deprive itself of important resources, if it were to insist on being conducted in linguistically demarcated parallel worlds.

Towards developing a sense of possible futures on which the past is mute

When a person makes use of things apparently devoid of significance as prosthesis to keep going, we will be groping for clues what this does to him/her in the inner economy of things. Like the poet's imaginary ear in William Blake's lines

> The caterpillar on the leaf
> Repeats to thee thy Mothers grief

we will not only attempt to listen to what we cannot hear, we will strive to listen to what could never have been turned into words because it was not available as an experience at a time when it could have made worlds of difference. It will share its lack of forceful push with the phenomenon of ignorance, which, as Bion well saw, does not push people afflicted with it to seek for change. If the mother was not able to grieve what the world leaves to be desired, the caterpillar will fall silent, stopped cold in its possible transformation into a butterfly: another mute fact in a world filled with facts to the brim.

Yet, its silence will conserve a past unable to unveil a future, in what the caterpillar does not say about a grief that did not take place to an ear that is not there. What can be made of this? If the patient does not know, there might be the need for an encounter with someone in whom a hunch is developing for what did not happen, where and why not.

Sources

Abrams, S. (1987) 'The psychoanalytic process: A schematic model', *International Journal of Psychoanalysis* 68, pp. 441–452.

Altounian, J. (1993), '"Transferts" déculturants et inconvenance culturelle', *Revue Française de Psychanalyse* 57(3), pp. 899–915.

Altounian, J. (2005), *L'intraduisible. Deuil, mémoire, transmission*, Paris: Dunod.
Ameisen, J.-C. (2003/1999), *La sculpture du vivant. Le suicide cellulaire ou la mort créatrice*, 2nd edition, Paris: Éditions du Seuil.
Ameisen J.-C. (2007), 'La mort au cœur du vivant', *Revue française de psychosomatique* 32, pp. 11–44.
Balint, E. (1993), 'One analyst's technique', in: Balint, E., *Before I was I. Psychoanalysis and the imagination*, ed. Mitchell J. and Parsons M., London: Free Association Books, pp. 120–129.
Barrois, C. (1993), *Psychanalyse du guerrier*, Paris: Hachette.
Barrois, C. (1998/1988), *Les névroses traumatiques. Le psychothérapeute face aux détresses des chocs psychiques*, 2nd edition, Paris: Dunod.
Becker, L.C. (1998), *A new Stoicism*, Princeton: Princeton University Press.
Berlant, L. (2011), *Cruel optimism*, Durham, N.C: Duke University Press.
Bion, W.R. (1977[1971]), 'The grid', in: Bion, W.R. (1989/1977), *Two papers: The grid and caesura*, London: Karnac Books, pp. 2–33.
Bion, W.R. (1980[1977]), 'New York', in: Bion, F. ed., *Bion in New York and Sao Paulo*, Perthshire: Clunie Press, pp. 9–74.
Bohleber, W., Jiménez, J.P., Scarfone, D., Varvin, S. and Zysman, S. (2015), 'Unconscious phantasy and its conceptualizations: An attempt at conceptual integration', *International Journal of Psychoanalysis* 96(3), pp. 705–730.
Bokanowski, T. (2014), 'Trauma et crise de la représentation', available at: www.spp.asso.fr/textes/textes-et-conferences/reflexions-de-psychanalystes-2/trauma-et-crise-de-la-representation/
Bollas, C. (1995), 'The functions of history', in: Bollas, C. (1995), *Cracking up. The work of unconscious experience*, London: Routledge, pp. 103–145.
Bollas, C. (2009/2000), 'Architecture and the unconscious', in: Bollas, C. (2009), *The evocative object world*, London: Routledge, pp. 47–77.
Borgogno, F. (2007), 'Ferenczi and Winnicott: Searching for a "missing link" (of the soul)', *The American Journal of Psychoanalysis* 67(3), pp. 221–234.
Boulanger, G. (2002b), 'Wounded by reality: The collapse of the self in adult onset trauma', *Contemporary Psychoanalysis* 38(1), pp. 45–76.
Bourke, J. (2014), *The story of pain. From prayer to painkillers*, Oxford: Oxford University Press.
Brackelaire, J-L. (2002), 'Pas l'un sans l'autre. Psychanalyste et ethnologue en terre d'exil', in: Florence J. ed., *La psychanalyse et l'université*, Académia Bruylant: Louvain-La-Neuve, pp. 155–159.
Busch, F. (2018), 'Searching for the analyst's reveries', *International Journal of Psychoanalysis* 99(3), pp. 569–589.

Cavell, M. (2006), *Becoming a subject. Reflections in philosophy and psychoanalysis*, Oxford: Oxford University Press.

Cohen, S. (2001), *States of denial. Knowing about atrocities and suffering*, Cambridge: Polity Press.

De Micco, V. (2014), 'Trapiantare/tramandare. Legami e identificazioni nei transiti migratori', in: De Micco V. and Grassi L. eds, *Soggetti in transito. Etnopsicoanalisi e migrazioni, Interazioni. Clinica e ricerca psicoanalitica su individuo-coppia-famiglia* 39, Milano: F. Angeli.

De Micco, V. (2016), 'La pelle che abito, il nome che porto: Fratture culturali e legami transgenerazionali nei bambini migranti', *Rivista di Psicoanalisi* 62(1), pp. 231–240.

De Micco, V. (2018), 'Migration: Surviving the inhumane', *The Italian Psychoanalytic Annual* 12, pp. 117–125.

Des Pres, T. (1976), *The survivor: An anatomy of life in the death camps*. New York: Oxford University Press.

Donnet, J.-L. (2005/1995), 'Sur l'évolution de la demande', in: Donnet, J.-L. (2005), *La situation analysante*, Paris: Presses Universitaires de France, pp. 195–206.

Dozio, E., Feldman, M., El Husseini, M. and Moro, M.R. (2015), 'L'approche transculturelle, une mère sans berceau culturel', in: Mellier, D., Delion, P. and Missonier, S. eds, *Le bébé dans sa famille. Nouvelles solitudes des parents, nouveaux soins*, Toulouse: Érès, pp. 219–233.

Dreher, A.U. (2000), *Foundations for conceptual research in psychoanalysis*, London: Karnac Books.

Duthoit, J.-P. (1999), *Essai sur les phénomènes transgénérationnels. Les dents de fils*, Paris: L'Harmattan.

Ehrenberg, A. (1998), *La fatigue d'être soi. Dépression et société*, Paris: Odile Jacob.

Ffytche, M. (2012), *The foundation of the unconscious. Schelling, Freud and the birth of the modern psyche*, Cambridge: Cambridge University Press.

Fernando, J. (2009), *The processes of defense. Trauma, drives, and reality – a new synthesis*, Lanham, MD: Jason Aronson.

Fine, A. (1995), 'L'opératoire comme négatif de la réalité psychique', *Revue Française de Psychanalyse* 59(1), pp. 173–186.

Fine, A. (1997), 'Le phénomène psychosomatique au regard de réalités supposées, *Revue Française de Psychosomatique* 12, pp. 121–142.

Fitzgerald, D. and Ryan, D. (2014), *Obama, US Foreign Policy and the Dilemmas of Intervention*, London: Palgrave Macmillan.

Fraser, N. (1997), 'Structuralism or pragmatics? On discourse theory and feminist politics', in: Fraser, N., *Justice interruptus. Critical reflections on the 'postsocialist' condition*, New York: Routledge, pp. 151–170.

Garland, C., Hume, F. and Majid, S. (2002), 'Remaking connections: Refugees and the development of "emotional capital" in therapy groups', *Psychoanalytic Psychotherapy. Applications, theory and research* 16(3), pp. 197–214.

Gottlieb, R.M. (2003), 'Psychosomatic medicine: The divergent legacies of Freud and Janet', *Journal of the American Psychoanalytic Association* 51(3), pp. 857–881.

Gramsci, A. (1975), *Quaderni del carcere, Edizione critica dell'Istituto Gramsci*, volume 1, ed. Gerratana, V., Torino: Einaudi.

Groarke, S. (2018), 'Making sense together. New directions in Independent clinical thinking', in: Kohon, G. ed., *British psychoanalysis. New perspectives in the Independent tradition*, Abingdon-on-Thames: Routledge, pp. 133–147.

Grubrich-Simitis, I. (1981), 'Extreme traumatization as cumulative trauma – psychoanalytic investigations of the effects of concentration camp experiences on survivors and their children', *Psychoanalytic Study of the Child* 36, pp. 415–450.

Hounkpatin, L., Wexler-Czitrom H., Perez, A. and Courbin, L. (2011), 'Vers un nouveau paradigme: la clinique de la multiplicité et la fabrique de "l'intime collectif"', in: Guerraoui, Z. and Pirlot, G. eds, *Comprendre et traiter les situations interculturelles. Approches psychodynamiques et psychanalytiques*, Brussels: Éditions De Boeck, pp. 55–107.

Kohon, G. (2015), *Reflections on the aesthetic experience. Psychoanalysis and the uncanny*, London: Routledge.

Kromhout, B. (2018), 'Containers will not fix your broken culture (and other hard truths)', *Communications of the ACM* 61 (4), pp. 40–43.

Kurzweil, E. (1989), *The Freudians. A comparative perspective*, New Haven: Yale University Press.

Lear, J. (2000), *Happiness, death, and the remainder of life*, Cambridge, MA: Harvard University Press.

Lear, J. (2017), *Wisdom from illness. Essays in philosophy and psychoanalysis*, Cambridge, MA: Harvard University Press.

Levine, H.B. (2008), 'The work of psychic figurability: Mental states without representation', *The Psychoanalytic Quarterly* 77(2), pp. 639–648.

Levine, H.B. (2010), 'Partners in thought: working with unformulated experience, dissociation, and enactment', *The Psychoanalytic Quarterly* 79(4), pp. 1166–1177.

Levine, H.B. (2012), 'The colourless canvas: Representation, therapeutic action and the creation of mind', *International Journal of Psychoanalysis* 93(3), pp. 607–629.

Levine, H.B. (2013), 'Comparing field theories', *Psychoanalytic Dialogues* 23(6), pp. 667–673.
McNay, L. (2000), 'Psyche and society: Castoriadis and the creativity of action', in: McNay, L., *Gender and agency. Reconfiguring the subject in feminist and social theory*, Cambridge: Polity Press, pp. 117–154.
Moro, M.R. (2002), *Enfants d'ici venus d'ailleurs. Naître et grandir en France*, Paris: La Découverte.
Moro, M.R. (2009), 'Les débats autour de la question culturelle en clinique', in: Baubet, T. and Moro, M.R., *Psychopathologie transculturelle*, 2nd edition 2013, Paris: Elsevier Masson, pp. 31–48.
Moro, M.R. (2015), *La violence envers les enfants, approche transculturelle*, Bruxelles: éditions Fabert.
Nettleton, S. (2017), *The metapsychology of Christopher Bollas. An introduction*, Abingdon, Oxon: Routledge.
Ogden, T.H. (1992a), 'The dialectically constituted/decentred subject of psychoanalysis I: The Freudian subject', *International Journal of Psychoanalysis* 73, pp. 517–526.
Ogden, T.H. (1992b), 'The dialectically constituted/decentred subject of psychoanalysis II: The contributions of Klein and Winnicott', *International Journal of Psychoanalysis* 73, pp. 613–626.
Oliner, M.M. (1988), *Cultivating Freud's garden in France*, Northvale, NJ: Jason Aronson.
Oliner, M.M. (1996), 'External Reality: The elusive dimension of psychoanalysis', *Psychoanalytic Quarterly* 65, pp. 267–300.
Oliner, M.M. (2008), 'Die Psychoanalyse: ein Zimmer ohne Aussicht?' *Psyche. Zeitschrift für Psychoanalyse und ihre Anwendungen* 62(11), pp. 1122–1147.
Oliner, M.M. (2012), 'The elusive dimension of external reality in psychoanalytic theory', in: Oliner, M.M., *Psychic reality in context. Perspectives on psychoanalysis, personal history, and trauma*, London: Karnac, pp. 39–51.
Oliner, M.M. (2013a), '"Non-represented" mental states', in: Levine, H.B, Reed, G.S and Scarfone, D. (2013), *Unrepresented states and the construction of meaning. Clinical and theoretical contributions*, London: Karnac Books, pp. 152–171.
Oliner, M.M. (2013b), 'An essay on Bion's beta function', *Psychoanalytic Review* 100(1), pp. 167–183.
Parsons, M. (2002), 'Le cadre. Utilisation et invention', in: André, J. and Thompson, C. eds, *Transfert et états limites*, Paris: Presses Universitaires de France, pp. 69–84.

Parsons, M. (2014), *Living Psychoanalysis. From theory to experience*, London: Routledge.
Pirlot, G. (2011), 'Psychopathologie et psychosomatique psychanalytiques et interculturelles', in: Guerraoui, Z. and Pirlot, G. (2011), *Comprendre et traiter les situations interculturelles. Approches psychodynamiques et psychanalytiques*, Brussels: Éditions De Boeck Université, pp. 145–192.
Proust, M. (1925), *The Guermantes way*, part 1: *Remembrance of things past*, translated by Scott-Moncrieff, C.K., New York: Random House.
Shay, J. (1994), *Achilles in Vietnam. Combat trauma and the undoing of character*, New York: Scribner.
Shay, J. (2002), *Odysseus in America. Combat trauma and the trials of homecoming*, New York: Scribner.
Sherman, N. (2005), *Stoic warriors. The ancient philosophy behind the military mind*, Oxford: Oxford University Press.
Schneider, P. (1973), 'Zum Verhältnis von Psychoanalyse und psychosomatischer Medizin', *Psyche. Zeitschrift für Psychoanalyse und ihre Anwendungen* 27(1), pp. 21–49.
Raphael-Leff, J. (2012), 'The intersubjective matrix: influences on the Independents' growth from "objects relations" to "subject relations"', in: Williams, P., Keene, J. and Dermen, S. (2012), *Independent psychoanalysis today*, London: Karnac, pp. 87–162.
Reed, G.S, Levine, H.B and Scarfone, D. (2013), 'Introduction: From a universe of presences to a universe of absences', in: Levine, H.B, Reed, G.S and Scarfone, D., *Unrepresented states and the construction of meaning. Clinical and theoretical contributions*, London: Karnac Books, pp. 3–17.
Snell, R. (2013), *Uncertainties, mysteries, doubts: Romanticism and the analytic attitude*, London: Routledge.
Stern, D.B. (2015b), 'Unrepresented states and the construction of meaning: Clinical and theoretical Contributions by Howard B. Levine, (2015)', *International Journal of Psychonalysis* 96(2), pp. 493–498.
Stern, D.B. (2018), 'Decentering relational psychotherapy', in: Aron, L., Grand, S. and Slochower, J.A. eds, *Decentering Relational Theory: A comparative critique*. Abingdon-onThames: Routledge, pp. 41–62.
Tal, K. (1999), *Worlds of hurt. Reading the literatures of trauma*, Cambridge: Cambridge University Press.
Tisseron, S. (2007), *La résilience*, Paris: Presses Universitaires de France.
Tummala-Narra, P. (2015), 'Cultural competence as a core emphasis of psychoanalytic psychotherapy', *Psychoanalytic Psychology* 32(2), pp. 275–292.

Urribarri, F. (1999), 'The psyche. Imagination and history. A general view of Cornelius Castoriadis's psychoanalytic ideas', *Free Associations* 7, pp. 374–396.

Verhaeghe, P. and Willemsen, J., (2015), 'Concurreren voor de waarheid: neoliberalisme en wetenschapsfraude', *Tijdschrift over Cultuur & Criminaliteit* 5(1), pp. 22–37.

Wurmser, L. (2014), 'Psychic reality in context', *International Journal of Psychoanalysis* 95(5), pp. 1025–1029.

Whitehead, A.N. (1933), *Adventures of ideas*, New York: The Free Press.

Index

ability to say no 96, 121–22, 268, see also aversion, lack of 196
Abraham, N. 113, 144
Abrams, S. 287
absence: mother inwardly absent 69; quality and duration of maternal absence 116–17; dialectical relationship with desire 94; of an inner response 248; formative experience of: 268; dialectical relationship with presence 9, 271, 298; creative potential of 101, 290; see also experience of discontinuity
actual neurosis 175, 198, 226
actual, the 11, 133, 234, 264, 270
Adorno, T. W. 35
aesthetics, psychoanalytic 103
Agamben, G. 295
Aisenstein, M. 15, 200, 206
akrasia 252–53
Alexander, F. 58, 192–93
Alexandridis, A. 146
alexithymia 18, 19, 20, 159
Ali, S. 122, 169
alimentary disturbances in early childhood 116, 117–18, 121–23, 290, 294
Althusser, L. 32, 226
Ameisen, J.-C. 200–01, 295
amental unconscious, the 8, 245–248, 249, 291
Anderson, B. 266
animistic thinking 71, 72, 74, 172, 175, 177
Anzieu, D. 22, 32, 33, 34, 157, 158, 236
APF (Association Psychanalytique de France) 32, 33, 234
apoptosis 135
Arendt, H. 123
ASMc 13 (Association de santé mentale du 13e arrondissement de Paris) 36, 44, 58, 114, 144, 191, 226
Assmann, J. 265–66, 276
asthma 43, 53, 119, 120
Aulagnier, P. 33, 97, 141, 142
auto-conservation 237, 292
auto-eroticism: facilitated by the mother's love life 69; impeded 73, 78, 119–20; and the animistic double 174–75; see also

infantile sexual theories; libidinal subversion; psycho-sexuality
automation 53, 54, 55
autonomous logic: of the body 204; of the environment 205–07
autopoiesis 134, 161
aversion, lack of 196, 268

Balsamo, M. 203, 208
Barrois, C. 292–93
behaviour: identically repeated 111–12, 114; as a form of defense 77, 161, 202, 294; narcissism invested in codes of 7, 197, 199; mechanical behaviour produced by boredom 218; unacknowledged meaning 236; compulsive 245; perverse sexual 53; neuroses of 54
Benjamin, W. 277, 296
Bergson, H. 47
Berlant, L. 296
Billiard, I. 227
Bion, W. R. 22, 28, 31, 74, 81, 82, 83, 84, 102, 103, 120, 155, 172, 179, 208, 216, 297, 298, 302
Bollas, C. 35, 277, 293–94
Bonaparte, M. 29, 45
Botella, C. and S. 7, 105, 135, 163, 166–184, 290, 298
Bouvet, M. 15, 22, 29, 32, 49, 181
Boyadjian, C. 241
Braunschweig, D. 6, 16, 17, 20, 68–84, 94, 121, 126, 191, 204, 239, 263, 289
Browning, R. 94, 100
Buchan, J. 9

Cannon, W. B. 192
capacity to defer action 45

Cassirer, E. 266
Castoriadis, C. 22, 100
censure de l'amante 69–70
character: 16, 50, 161, 244, 246, 247; formation 122; neuroses of 54, 60
Chasseguet-Smirgel, J. 139
child psychoanalysis 178
Clot, Y. 227
CNAM (*Conservatoire National des Arts et Métiers*) 234
collective defensive strategies 249–250, 253; exported from the workplace and made use of in family life 244
collective psychology 7, 76, 82, 196
community: of practice 2, 159; of remembrance 159, 292; of forgetfulness 6, 133, 290; of regression 177
concentration/extermination camp survivors 10, 16, 173, 199
countertransference 21, 268, 272, 275, 278

Damasio, A. 159
David, C. 1, 5, 33, 35, 37, 48, 50, 51
de Ajuriagurra, J. 33, 43, 46, 58, 60
de M'Uzan, M. 1, 5, 33, 35, 37, 48, 50, 51, 238, 271, 279
De Micco, V. 11, 300
de Mijolla, A. 2, 29, 32, 139
Dejours, C. 8, 14, 15, 17, 19, 22, 216, 227, 229, 234–254, 262, 291, 292, 295, 297, 299, 301
denial: distinct from non-perception 81; distinct from non-representation 172, 182; distinct from complex

impairment 297; as a bulwark of the amental 246; part of collective defensive strategies 249; a protection against a loss of composure 250; *partial denial see also*: *identification dans une communauté de déni*
dépression essentielle (essential depression): 11, 16, 36, 51–52, 54, 77, 141
desaparecido 9
Devereux, G. 225
Devoto, T. 180
Di Benedetto, A. 103
Diatkine, R. 44, 46, 144
differentiation: lack of 35; in response to parental reality 71; insufficient 95; arrested 102; and Stranger Anxiety 119; personal myth as an aid in 142; crises wasted leading to lack of 145; dis- 101; non- 104, 134, 218, 275
disengagement 75–76, 156
disorganisation 95, 101, 141, 204, 228, 248; progressive disorganisation 36, 52–53, 56, 57
distance management: muscular armour as a tool in 44–46; varieties of object distance 49, 126; in objectifying oneself 202; towards the patient 271, 292
distinct from latent: 159, 182; working with 160; cultural frame required: 183–84
distortion in the Me 74, 268
distress: distinct from fright 113; from anxiety 117, 119, 126; non-integrated ancient distress 124; 127; not enveloped in masochism 126; and cultural responses 182; disintegration as protection against 267–68
Dolgopolski, S. 2
Donnet, J.-L. 29
double 7, 163, 174–75, 179, 180, 181, 182, 290, 293
Dunbar, H. F. 193
Duparc, F. 68

economy (mental): consideration of, a factor in psychoanalysis 78, 144–45, 163, 181, 289, 302; role of the other in 84; limited defensive depth granted by 79; comportment as an indicator of 194; narcissistic subsistence economy 134, 140, 197–98, 200, 203–04; showing little evidence of elements of the proto-imaginary 208; in association with metaphors of energy 228; of sense perceptions at the workplace 242; not following the blueprint of neurosis 273
envelope(s): maternal investment: 70; psychic 157–58; of pain 137; provided by an institution 156; *EPP* (*École Psychosomatique de Paris*), 5, 7, 14, 15, 19, 33, 35, 48, 58, 166, 184, 193, 194, 268, 275, 287, 288, 299, 301
Erikson, E. 182
ethnopsychoanalysis 7, 58, 146, 155, 225
exhaustion: hiding behind functioning facades 60; cycles from tension to exhaustion 136; safeguards against 140; necessity to understand in

context 224–25; unconnected to repression of latent meaning 298; self- 6, 111, 114, 121
experience of discontinuity: importance for fantasy life 69, 70, 73, 84, 116; 171; protective function of: 271
Ey, H. 17, 30, 31, 33, 52, 53, 95, 102

Fain, M. 5, 6, 9, 14, 15, 17, 33, 43, 44, 45, 46, 47, 51, 52, 55, 58, 61, 68–84, 94, 102, 116, 126, 137, 166, 191, 193, 197, 199, 239, 245, 263, 268, 270, 271, 277, 279, 289, 292, 295
fantasmatic: interaction(s) 115, 127; object relations 121; potential 126; worlds 127; entanglements 239
fatigue 201, 223, 224, 226, 228, 244
fear of breakdown 268, 273
Federn, P. 78
Ferenczi, S. 8, 163, 254, 263–64, 266, 267, 269, 275, 298
Ffytche, M. 294
figurability 166–67
Fine, A. 292, 294
First Topography 22, 53, 55, 57, 72, 76, 168, 172, 204, 275, 278
flexible building blocks of form 100, 104, 111, 289
Fonagy, P. 18
foreclusion 74, 99, 136, 172
Forster, E. M. 101
French, T. M. 45
Freud, A. 29, 144, 146
Freud, S. 2, 3, 20, 28, 31, 58, 68, 81, 82, 96, 102, 122, 123, 132, 136, 167, 168, 172, 174, 177, 178, 179, 183, 196, 198, 199, 201, 245, 251, 263, 264–65, 267, 269, 271, 275–76, 278, 287, 288, 296, 299, 301

Garma, A. 192
gendered distribution of suffering 249–250
Goody, J. 273
Gottlieb, R. M. 20–21, 206
Grady, S. 145
Gramsci, A. 299
Green, A. 16, 20, 29, 31, 32, 56, 69, 100, 101, 139, 153, 159, 179, 182, 191, 194, 195, 197, 239, 277
Groddeck, G. 192
group membership: defines reality 72, 76; shared style and ideals of masculinity 77–78, 84, 112; providing a mental cover 80; in non-Western societies 155; modes of conformity with 197; integration in a work group possibly protective against fatigue 224
Grubrich-Simitis, I. 264
Guillaumin, J. 202

Hacking, I. 4, 125, 289
Halbwachs, M. 266
hallucinatory processes/solutions impediments to hallucination 119, 166–180; *passim*, 196, 263
Haraszti, M 241
headache(s) 45, 49, 82, 193
heart transplant patients 159
Heenen-Wolff, S. 180
Hegel, G. W. F. 168–69, 182

Index

holding: frame in the analytic process 274; field required for figurability 290; structure required for the development of fantasy 46; deficient frame as evidenced in a *pure culture d'instinct de mort* 74, 82; provided by hypochondria 118; holding fast to traumatic traces as defense against disobjectalisation 280

hope: deposited in repetition/automation 54, 135; turning stagnant 6, 139–140, 290; connections to the *idéal du Moi* 139; loss of hope and destructive energy 199; conserved in negativity 268; and the hypothesis of early trauma 278; deposited in the rehearsal of trivia 292; psychoanalysis faced with hope stowed away 300

Hôpital Sainte-Anne 30, 31, 58

Horkheimer, M. 35

hospital culture 55, 156, 194, 202

hyperactivity 73, 115, 120–22, 242, 252

idéal du Moi 45, 139

identification dans une communauté de déni 6, 76–77, 79, 239, 264, 290

identification(s): primary narcissistic identification 45; in a dialogue body to body 46; against the reality of the parents' relationship 69, 71, 116; bound to the mimetic 120; with impersonal tradition and the consensus 123, 197; identification sickness 6, 138, 146; alienating identification 7, 223; with the aggressor 263–64, see also *identification dans une communauté de déni*

identity: confusion 79; masculine: 112; collective 143; projects of 225; assignation of gender identity 250; mainstays in love and in work 250; treatment as a threat to core identity 274; the intimate as expression of 277

illusion: capacity for impaired 115; conducive to the inception of meaning and form 7, 98, 162, 270; different meaning in Freud and Winnicott 163, 296; of control 292

imageless states of terror 173–74

impairment 144, 292, 297

impasse 22, 220, 228, 274, 296

impingement 126, 145, 280; self-impingement 126 *see also* impairment

indifference 80–81, 170, 175, 206, 270; indifference as mental absence 175

infantile sexual theories 171, 172

insomnia 51, 73, 120

instinct de mort: as silent disintegration 52, 81; by proxy 81; *see also pure culture d'instinct de mort*

inter-fertilisation of theories 32–33, 178–79, 183–84, 268, 277

internal foreign body 276

IPSO (Institut de Psychosomatique) 5, 7, 44, 114, 153, 161, 166, 191, 193, 194, 234, 268, 275

James, H. 274

Janet, P. 22, 95, 102, 301

Jung, C. 28

Index

Kabat-Zinn, J. 154–55
Kernberg, O. 20
Khan, M. 32
Klein, M. 16, 20, 21, 29, 81, 82, 83, 99, 103, 105, 118
Kleinian 16, 78, 98, 101, 103, 287
Koestler, A. 173
Kohon, G. 295
Kreisler, L. 73, 126
Krystal, H. 16

l'agir expressif 240
L'investigation psychosomatique 1, 35, 43, 48, 50, 181, 193, 195
Lacan, J. 2, 10, 14, 20, 28, 29, 30, 31, 32, 33, 34, 43, 46, 58, 73, 74, 75, 98, 99, 100, 105, 142, 204–05, 226, 287, 298
Laforgue, R. 30
Lagache, D. 29, 31, 32, 58
Laplanche, J. 20, 32, 33, 126, 235, 236, 248, 250, 275, 301
latency 68, 72, 78, 81, 161, 178
Le Guen, C. 119
Le Guillant, L. 221–24, 225, 226
Lebovici, S. 14, 44, 73, 127, 144
Lechat, F. 47
Levine, H. 20, 145
libidinal subversion 126, 235–37, 254
Ligue d'hygiène mentale 220–21
Loewald, H. W. 103
loss of representation 170
lullaby 70

Marcuse, H. 35
Marty, P. 1, 5, 10, 15, 18, 19, 20, 32, 33, 35, 37, 42–61, 68, 77, 81, 83, 94, 96, 119, 123, 126, 132, 141, 153, 159, 160, 161, 162, 174, 181, 193, 194, 195, 202, 203, 206, 208, 237, 247, 263, 272, 273, 288, 289, 297, 299, 300
masochism: calm a substitute for 114; constructive build-up impaired 121, 126; distinct registers of trauma and masochism 81, 126; masochistic core 71, 156; as a guardian of life 137, 199
mastery 74, 112, 135, 250
maturation 46, 53
Mauger, J. 202, 208
Mauss, M. 159
McDougall, J. 15, 18, 34
memory: 94; 126; 161; memory traces 71, 104, 246, 263; body memory 171; gap or dent in place of 7, 8, 117, 134, 142, 169, 173–74, 176, 177, 178, 180, 199, 278; fleeting memory 248; collective memory 9–10; obliteration of shared memory 8–9, 265–66
mental erosion/attrition 224, 227, 234, 251–252, 254
mentalisation (as a concept of Marty's) 18, 36, 55–56, 60, 263
mentalisation (British concept) 18, 20
Messer, J. 250
Meyerson, I. 224
Mill, J. S. 103–04
Milton, J. 180
Moi idéal 55
Moore, Y. 180
Moro, M. R. 300
mosaïque première 53, 96
mothering function 54–55

Index

motor skills 45 *see also* motricity
motricity 105, 116, 133, 242
Munchausen syndrome by proxy 118
Murakami, H. 124
muscular: armour 44, 46, 49; masculinity 77
Music, Z. 173
music: mood music 70, 180
myth 72, 95, 133, 139, 143, 144; family myth 104; as a force of irrigation:141–42; historically contingent 98–99

Nacht, S. 15, 29, 31, 33, 43, 46, 57, 58
narcissism: not born with but born into 84; 'his majesty the baby' 70; pain ringfenced by 137; lack of, leading to low levels of aversion 196; invested in codes of behaviour 7, 197; last line of defense 198; transactional objects conducive to secondary narcissism 223; frailty of narcissistic economies 275
narcissistic depletion 7, 195–96, 200, 201
narcissistic: identification 45; investment 70, 137, 198; cover 71; deficiencies/fragility 77, 195, 275; capital/resources 102, 194, 200; wounds 140, 177; core 141; regression 172; cohesion 172; satisfaction 174; double 175; difficulties of the analyst 181, 193, 208; subsistence economy 197; depletion 7, 201; illusion of invulnerability/control 115, 292

Nathan, T. 58, 155
negation 75–76, 83
negativity (unbound) 56, 169, 181–82, 299
néo-besoin(s) 77–78
Neyraut, M. 21, 137
Nicolaïdis, N. 6, 32, 84, 94–105, 111, 182, 289
Nietzsche, F. 182
nightmare(s) 11, 115, 118, 170, 173, 175–76
non-cuddly children 114–15, 121
non-event 76, 117, 176, 183, 267, 270, 277, 302; *see also* absence(s)
non-perception 81, 170
non-representation 134, 135, 171–72, 175, 182
normopathy (normotic behaviour) 35
numbness, selective 238–40

object capture 47
oculus, lacking in psychoanalysis 202–03
Oliner, M. M. 10, 16, 20, 292, 297

Pagès, C. 181–82
pain: perception of a substitute for the object 112; preferable to formlessness 113; prolonged pain with babies 115; made use of against what cannot be processed 117; sense of self coalescing around 122; as an envelope 137; ringfenced by narcissism 137; another person needed to process pain 11, 143–44; composure in the face of 161; becoming invisible 241; tension lacking a frame to turn into pain 275;

315

transitionality endangered in the face of 294, 296
Panseppj. 162
paradigm, as opposed to model 272–73
paranoid-schizoid position 71
Parat, C. 122
Parsons, M. 272, 287
Pasche, F. 170
passivity 74, 114, 116, 121, 156, 175, 197, 248, 268, 271
pathogenic workplace conditions 222, 224
perception 6, 11, 71 (of lack), 95–97, 100, 112 (of pain), 113, 135 (gap between perception and representation), 142, 158 (culturally mediated), 171–77, 196, 199, 201, 204, 242, 246, 248, 251, 266, 275, 276, 294, 295, 296
Philoctetes 137, 143
Pontalis, J.-B. 32, 33
Potamianou, A. 6, 127, 132–146, 290
potential form: difficulties to grasp 35; theory as an aid in gauging 145; dispersed, diluted 177; undeveloped 195; resistance to treatment a potential source of creativity 273; in formlessness 277
potential to maintain links 52
Pouchelle, M.-C. 156
Pragier, G. and S. 134
preconscious: pivotal in Marty's conceptual approach 5, 53, 203; deficiencies in 36, 57; and mentalisaton 55; in conceptual conflict with "ego" autonomy 83; enriched by elements culturally provided 72, 98–99, 104, 160; regressing to memory traces 104; modelled in accordance with an image of the object 138; losing functionality in emergencies 202; aided or impeded by the quality of the analytic setting 204, 270; and sublimation 240; acts bypassing the 247; and intermediary space 297; professional 207, 300
prematurity 74, 81, 83, 116, 122
prenatal disbalances 119
prequel to fantasy life 32, 68–73, 268
Press, J. 8, 17, 143, 144, 254, 262–280, 293, 298
programmation 53, 55, *see also* differentiation
projective identification 179
projective reduplication 50, 123, 181
protective: mother periodically withdrawing protective cover: 70; shield systematically deployed by families 75; cover provided by routine behaviour and social location 77, 123; layers comparable to outer peel of the vesicle 111; integrity of the body shape of the child a protective shield for the mother 118; inadequate shield provided by the mother 121; anti-traumatic shock absorption: 137; puncturing of the protective shield 137, 140; institution as protective shield 156; mental organisation a protective

Index

shield for the body 198; shield provided by the libidinal body 238; protective defense strategy breaking down 269; quality of shield offered by the mother 296

Proust, M. 288.

psycho-sexuality 16, 96, 100, 116, 137, 198, 250

psychoanalytic encounter: shock in 1, 21, 35, 275; and a confusion of tongues 8; and intercultural factors 19; and conceptualisation 21; mental space in not to be taken for granted 160, 183; lacking an oculus 202; reversal of roles in 203; dramatic potential of 204; mortifications in and inadequacies of the psychoanalyst 181, 271–72; mutual expectations frustrated 275; unpredictable results: 279–80; in a hospital setting 59; 288

pulmonary tuberculosis 44–45, 57

pulsion de mort: not considered to surge by the individual's own workings 101; and decompensation 101, 237; used to run down tension 126; permitting libidinal disentanglement when needed 136; and the amental 247; considered to emanate from a non-responsive mother 6, 81, 126, 289; emanating from the mother's superego 120–21; and the position of the other 301

pure culture d'instinct de mort 74, 80–81, 198, 272

Quatrième Groupe 34

reality (external): different from 'the real' 72; periodically turning one's back on 75–76; as an organiser 134; stolidity derived from preoccupation with 158; self-cradling in 196; threat emerging from 75, 180, 202; constraints and effects emerging from 80, 204, 270; and intermediary cushions present or lacking 56, 97, 136, 220; alienation from social reality 222; not adequately coped with by the mother 239; two compartments of the unconscious converging in contact with 245–46; responses to in the register of violence or disarray 246; resistance offered by reality towards attempts of mastery 250, 291; partial self-destruction in adaptation to 263; and inner waste disposal 269; insufficiently understood by both patient and analyst 280; tackling of by throwing oneself into 288; wily moves to come to terms with 253–54, 291; dangers of a too one-sided focus on psychic reality 297; a challenge to the understanding of the psychoanalyst 34, 202, 299, 300

référent 97, 101, 102

regredience 177

regression: self-exhaustion replacing 6; different from disorganisation 52–53; stifled by a *Moi idéal* 55; periodically required to counter

exhaustion 75–76; and fantasy space not imposed on the child 121; and sleep 172; to perception traces 174; facilitated by the presence of a double 174, 177–180; facilitated or impeded by a given culture 55, 84, 182, 198; somatic 120, 193; facilitated by a medical institution 156, 197–98; put at risk by circumstance 268
Reich, W. 46
renouncement 135; as *kenosis* (self-emptying) 133
repetition compulsion 81, 132, 137, 146, 247, 268–69
repetition: preservative/obliterative impact 6; of intergenerational patterns 36, 50, 204; to induce exhaustion 114; as a servant to the status quo 133; as a deposit of relationship 133; as a residual shock absorption system 135, 137; conserving a precarious potential 135, 138; *see also* repetition compulsion
resources, cultural: 103–04, 157, 251; social: 79, 201
Ribas, D. 206
Rimbaud, A. 138
Rose, J. 180
Rosenberg, B. 137
Roussillon, R. 200, 201
Rueff-Escoubes, C. 205
Ruelle, D. 162

safety principly 144
Sahlins, M. 275
Sainte-Anne, see Hôpital Sainte-Anne

Sandler, J. 4, 144
scotomisation 224, 299
Second Topography 7, 53, 191, 194, 202, 237, 275; suggesting an axis object-reality-denial 168
sectorisation 7, 44, 225–26
security 44, 144, 145, 158, 162
self-calming 6, 124, 198, 199, 201, 242, 290
self-cradling 120, 121, 196
self-denial 217
self-effacement at the workplace 242–44
self-regulation: unmanageable burden of 6; at risk 134; benefit of selective regulatory brakes 140; auto-regulatory oscillations 161–62; and the paradox effect of aiming for homeostasis 237
Selye, H. 162, 192
shared imaginary: necessary for treatment 6, 146, 155, 160, 162–63, 207, 290; lack of 153; facilitating inner leeway 158; a barrier against disintegration 162; *see also* community
Shay, J. 291–92
Shorter, E. 81, 228
shrinking of the Me: under the impact of trauma 78; in re-enforcement of links to a social environment 132–33, 135; under emergency conditions 140–141, 146; in partial self-destruction to accommodate the environment 263; and keeping an inner place of refuge 274; *see also* narcissistic depletion
Sivadon, P. 217–26
Smadja, C. 7, 191–208, 216, 293

sobbing spasms 73, 121
socio-cultural domain 59, 100, 123–124, 143, 207
Soulé, M. 73
Spitz, R. 117, 119
split (in the subject): not originating in the subject 78; and denial 81, 200; performative 124, 203; and the Third Topology 244–45; pressure routed towards the body to maintain the split 247; used to maintain normalcy 248, 251, 252–53; to ward off culpability 249; bolstered in alliances, split into a wise baby and a traumatised sector 264; weakening the mental economy 273–274; bolstering an amental sector 8, 291–92; and partial denial 292; caused by trauma and different from psychotic or perverse split 293
SPP (*Societé Psychanalytique de Paris*) 2, 28–30, 33, 43, 58, 226, 295
Stern, D. B., 179
Stoic thinking 158–59
Stora, J. B. 6, 7, 146, 153–163, 166, 290
stranger anxiety, absence of 117, 119
Structuralism 100, 179, 226, 227
sublimation 102–03, 240, 247, 248
subversive cunning at the workplace (*métis*) 253–54
superego: 197, 202, 264; of the mother 121
suppression: used by the 'wise child' 122; compared to repression 122; as an alternative to suicide 241; used irrespective of character structure 244; of motions of violence, leading to stupor 246; required at work if sublimation is not possible 247; of memory 265–66; producing secondary gaps in the preconscious 273; a response to a given situation 274

terrain 9, 167, 216, 228, 301
Third Topography 244–47
Thom, R. 134, 162, 171
tonus 46, 51, 52, 117, 141, 195
Torok, M. 113, 144
Tosquelles, F. 223
transformation: put on hold 9, 141; extinction replacing transformation 74; under the impact of artificially engineered new needs 77–78; conceptualised as algorithm 100; as autopoiesis 161; problems of a central concern of psychoanalysis 172; requiring a double 180; questions of, not central to considerations in American psychosomatic theory in the 1950s 192–93; mental space, outside reality and the body factors in a given potential of 204; negatively affected by the absence of transitional form 277; limited damage control as an alternative to 279; quest for, deposited in trivia of material culture 292; crisis of 299; impeded 202–03, 302
transition: from one culture to another 55, 123; transitional objects provided by the parents 75; transitionality impeded

77–78; crisis of 99, 102; and hope 132; requiring a multilayered psychic skin 157–58; function of hallucinatory stages in 171; building of transitional space for survivors 180; transitional and transactional objects needed in social life 223; absence of transitional form 277; building blocks for, required 289; transitionality endangered in cultures suffused with pain 296

trauma: psychoanalysts confronted with 10–11; early trauma not necessarily due to flaws in the mother 73; small quantities of trauma 76; shrinking the borders of the Me 78; imposed by a relationship 121; environments marked by 125; separate registers of trauma and masochism: 126; a vein that runs through all psychic territory 136; sexual co-excitation caused by 137; as unbound negative 169; and non-representation 171–72; and emptiness in the regard of the object 175; in a negative key, due to what did not happen 176, 183; as yet shapeless 177; requiring a double to be processed 182; weakening the mental economy 198; turned away from figurability 263; revisited under the pressure of politics of murderous hatred and systematic exclusion 264–65; and the effacement of shared memory 266–67; and the effacement of psychic function 273, 292; and psychoanalytic theory 275–76, 278–79; intermediary zones between reality and fantasy impaired 292

traumatophilia 112–13, 114, 120
trivia as a shared bond 159, 291–92

Urribarri, F. 297

Valabrega, J.-P. 192
Valdre, R. 102–03
Veil, C. 221, 224–26
visitors in the Me 138
Vitalism 5, 10, 61, 218, 272
Voltaire 167–68
von Uexküll, T. 161

war veterans 291–93
Warburg, A. 266
West Africa, Marty in, 55, 123, 300
Winnicott, D. 32, 75, 96, 97, 100, 103, 105, 126, 139, 163, 176, 179, 180, 263, 267, 268, 269, 273, 277, 278, 279, 294, 296, 298
Winterson, J. 101
wise child 122, 264
Wordsworth, W. 104
work-related suicides 235, 252

Zweig, A. 264